The Smouldering Flax

THE INCOMPARABLE COMFORT OF ISAIAH

AMBASSADOR

BELFAST, NORTHERN IRELAND
GREENVILLE, USA

The Smouldering Flax

THE INCOMPARABLE COMFORT OF ISAIAH

A Daily Devotional

DERICK BINGHAM

AMBASSADOR

BELFAST, NORTHERN IRELAND
GREENVILLE, USA

THE SMOULDERING FLAX
© Copyright 2002 Derick Bingham

Colin Woodward, Photographic Artist
www.colinwoodward.com

The Photographer wishes to thank Eugene McConville, Michael Lyttle on behalf of Herdmans Irish Linen Spinners, and all at the Irish Linen Centre and Lisburn Museum.

We acknowledge the following:-
McConville's Flax - January
Herdmans, The Irish Linen Spinners - April - July
Irish Linen Centre and Lisburn Museum Collection - August - December

ISBN 1 84030 124 4

Ambassador Publications
A division of
Ambassador Productions Ltd.
Providence House
Ardenlee Street
Belfast
BT6 8QJ
Northern Ireland
www.ambassador-productions.com

Emerald House
427 Wade Hampton Blvd.
Greenville
SC 29609, USA
www.emeraldhouse.com

Foreword

This Daily Devotional officially began its life on the morning of September 11th 2001. My publisher and I had spent part of the morning quietly discussing a book on the subject of Comfort from The Book of Isaiah, to be published, God willing, the following year in the United States. After our discussion and some lunch, we got into our cars and switched on the radios, to discover the news of the outrage in New York and Washington.

Over the past year, I have been privileged to write on the chosen subject almost every day. The more I studied Isaiah's prophecy, the more I discovered how relevant it was to the huge questions now facing the world. Here is a vision of the future, as well as practical help for the present. In chapter 42 of his prophecy, Isaiah writes about the characteristics of the coming Messiah, and states, the smoking, or smouldering flax, 'He will not quench.' Flax, when ignited, smoulders. Sparks follow one another slowly along its fibres. So it is, that love for God does the same. It can be a very fitful, irregular thing. Yet the intermittent love of a believing heart is not despised by God but cherished, so that it can be brought to a flame by His power.

Here, then, is a study of Isaiah chapters 40-66. Please note that throughout this book, the term 'Israel' is used to refer to the descendants of Jacob/Israel. It is to be remembered that, after the death of Solomon, Israel in the national, political sense, only survived in the separate kingdoms of Israel and Judah. During the Babylonian captivity, Israel in the national, political sense had ceased to exist altogether. As we follow Isaiah's writing, we shall find that his images are vivid, lively, and even staggering, and are written in a style filled with incredible variety. His writing comforts, refreshes, and even sustains the weary, the exhausted, the frustrated, and the despairing. In our world, these terms describe most of us at some time or other. Here is pity that is unrivalled, and comfort that is divine. So, let me enter your life for a year, and we will share that pity and comfort together.

Derick Bingham
Belfast
September 2002.

This book is dedicated to

Samuel Harold Swan Love, M.D., F.F.A.R.C.S.

*This good doctor was once the Dean of the Faculty of Anaesthetists,
Royal College of Surgeons in Ireland,
and President of the Association of Paediatric Anaesthetists of Great Britain and
Ireland.*

*Nevertheless, I have found that he has a deep affection
for the unanaesthetised truth!*

January

The flax plant, whose botanical name is linaceae, is affectionately known as 'the wee blue blossom.' The growing of flax for fibre from which linen cloth is woven has been a characteristic of subsistence agriculture in many parts of the world, and particularly flourishes in river valleys. We are told that Pharaoh clothed Joseph in 'garments of fine linen.'

"Comfort, yes comfort My people!" says your God. Isaiah 40:1.

In life, to find that trouble comes looking for you is painful enough; but to know that, at times, you have brought that trouble on your own head, is a bitter experience. The people of God thought God had forgotten them because of their sins, that He had cancelled His Covenant with them. Their sins had been graphically exposed: heavy consumption of alcohol was 'cool,' and men were proud and arrogant (5:11-15). Women put huge emphasis on how they looked, paying disproportionate attention to their anklets, bracelets, veils, headbands, perfumes and rings, and walked with outstretched necks and wanton eyes (3:16-23).

In their land there was oppression instead of justice, evil was called good and good evil, darkness was put in place of light, false gods were worshipped. They brought the judgment of God on their heads, and His chastisement was severe. But then came the comfort of God! The word 'comfort' literally means 'to cause to breathe again.'

All believers know about the chastisement of God (Hebrews 12:5-13). But when it has passed, the relief of His comfort is awesome. In childhood, after punishment, who has not known the enfolding embrace of a mother? Who has not welcomed the comfort of a friend, even when we were wrong and knew it? Ah, the gentle Email, the timely call, the comforting touch on the shoulder, the look of kindness in a caring eye!

It is an immeasurably greater experience, though, when God calls, touches, or looks in comfort. To the erring Moses by a burning bush, to the deceiving Abraham at Bethel, to the cowering Jacob at Penuel, to the unbelieving Joshua at Ai, to the gift-wasting Samson at Gaza, to the disgraced and disgusting David at Jerusalem, comfort came – certainly, proportionately and divinely.

And what about you? Yes, there is comfort promised. And not only once, but it is repeated! It is an urgent promise, for God knows you need it now.

"Comfort, yes comfort My people!" says your God. Isaiah 40:1.

In your life, have you known deep sorrow? Has tragedy overwhelmed you, and lead-in-your-heart-days been your companion? Others soar to success, as deemed by the world; but your circumstances have been narrow, and opportunities to widen your horizons, few.

When sorrow comes, what is chic with the world does not comfort: position, wealth and affluence are poor comforters. Academic knowledge does not dry your tears. When your heart is breaking through a divorce or a failed relationship, even the stars, which certainly look romantic, do not comfort. When your business is failing, the beauty of nature does not take away the ache of sorrow, or the gnawing worry of unrelenting trouble.

F. B. Meyer tells the story of a kind-hearted man who found a schoolboy crying because he did not have money to pay his fare home. Suddenly the man remembered that years before he had been in the same plight, but had been helped by an unknown friend, who then urged him to pass the kindness on. Now that moment had come, so he approached the weeping boy, told him the story, paid his fare, and asked that he in turn would pass the kindness on. As the train moved from the station the lad shouted cheerfully "I will pass it on, Sir." That initial act of comfort and kindness is still rippling on, encircling the earth.

The moral of this little story is very relevant to you in your sorrow. You will be comforted by God, so that you may be able to comfort those who are in trouble 'with the comfort with which you yourself have been comforted' (see 2 Corinthians 1:4). So, make a mental note of how God comforts you in your sorrow; and then, when the opportunity arises, pass it on. This will be your ministry, which the world could never match.

January 3ʳᵈ

"Speak ye comfortably to Jerusalem ..." Isaiah 40:2 (AV)

The city stands for the people; and the Lord not only wants to comfort them, but to win their hearts. 'Comfortably' means in Hebrew, 'to speak to the heart of.' It is the same word used of a man, seeking to win the heart of the woman he loves. His words are soft, gentle, reassuring, protective and encouraging.

In the story of Ruth, when the godly Boaz fell in love with her, despite the deep poverty of her situation, and he moved to protect her from men who would have harmed her, she said " . . . you have comforted me, and have spoken kindly to your maidservant, though I am not like one of your maidservants" (Ruth 2:13). And so God speaks to His people.

I remember very well, staying in a hotel in a little town in Northern Ireland. I was suddenly awakened in the wee hours by a woman's voice from the street below. It was a raging voice, edged with fierce hardness; and wave upon wave of words of accusation poured out. It was soon obvious that her boyfriend had shown deference to another woman, and this behaviour was now his bitter reward. She did not care who heard her, she was beside herself with jealous rage.

The people of Israel had provoked the Lord to jealousy. They deserved His anger and accusations. But His words are gentle, loving and kind. Have you provoked your Lord to jealousy by flirting with other gods? Do you feel far from Him in your spirit? Do you feel He will never speak to your heart in gentle, reassuring tones again? You are wrong! He still loves you, though He may have been hurt by your behaviour, and chastised you for holding Him in contempt. But the chastisement will pass. He comes to you in love, to remind you that you are His own.

'Why do You stand afar off, O Lord? Why do You hide in times of trouble? How long, O Lord, will You forget me forever? How long will You hide Your face from me?' said the erring David in Psalm 13. 'But,' he added, 'I have trusted in Your mercy; my heart shall rejoice in Your salvation. I will sing to the Lord, because He has dealt bountifully with me.'

" . . . cry out to her, that her warfare is ended." Isaiah 40:2.

Israel's exile was to end! ". . . her warfare is ended," says God. 'Warfare' means 'hard service.' This term primarily denoted a conscript in military service, then it was used of feudal service. In the Hebrew language, it came to be used to describe any miserable state. The deportation to Babylon took place in stages between 605 and 587 BC. This prophecy must have seemed beyond belief. As it always does, the sin of God's people had brought its wages. Sin costs us more than we want to pay, and keeps us longer than we want to stay. It brings hard misery, for 'the way of the transgressors is hard' (Proverbs 13:15). But now their misery was to cease.

As you read this paragraph, do you wonder if what you are enduring will ever end? Like Israel, your sin has brought dire wages. Job's words could be yours, "Is there not a time of hard service for man on the earth? . . . When I lie down, I say, 'When shall I arise and the night be ended?' For I have had my fill of tossing till dawn . . . so that my soul chooses strangling and death rather than my body. I loathe my life . . ." (Job 7:1-4,16).

But, as He did to Israel, God says to you, "cry out to her, that her warfare is ended." God has used your foes to teach you lessons; but now the time of hard service is over. Enough is enough! God will not chastise you forever. You will be leaner, fitter, wiser, and more even-tempered. You will remember your days of hard service under sin's wages, and learn to live your days under the fellowship of His 'easy yoke' (see Matthew 11:28-30).

Later in Isaiah's prophecy, we will learn of that Liberator whose 'yoke is easy and whose burden is light.' To follow the Lord Jesus means wearing a yoke. I cannot do as I like, think as I like, chase what I like, and say what I like. I have not been set free to do as I want, but as He wants. But His yoke is easy! As His disciple, I carry a burden that I never carried before. But His burden is light! Wouldn't you rather be yoked to Him than to the pleasures of sin, any day of the week?

" . . . cry to her . . . that her iniquity is pardoned." Isaiah 40:2.

If I thought that the face of God was against me forever, and, like Robert Burns, I would have to constantly 'forward cast my eye and fear,' life's joys would be clouded, and dread would dog my footsteps. But to be pardoned – this means freedom, and the incredible erasing of a sad record! 'Speak comfort to Jerusalem; and cry out to her, that her iniquity is pardoned,' says God to His prophet. The message is addressed particularly to Jerusalem, for the city is in ruins and its people in exile. 'For Jerusalem stumbled, and Judah is fallen: because their tongue and their doings are against the Lord, to provoke the eyes of His glory. The look on their countenance witnesses against them, and they declare their sin as Sodom: they do not hide it. Woe to their soul! For they have brought evil upon themselves' (Isaiah 3:8-9).

Now these people are to be pardoned! The verb means 'to receive satisfaction by the payment of a debt.' The basis for the pardon is that God's justice has been met. Without justice, real comfort is impossible. Shades of Isaiah 53 are reaching back to Isaiah 40. They are soon to learn that, by His own blood, their coming Messiah will lay down the basis of their pardon.

How can God both judge and pardon our sins at the same time? How could Christ say to the woman taken in adultery, "Neither do I condemn you; go and sin no more" (John 8:11), if His law says she should be executed? It was because, within weeks, He who wrote that law would climb the hill of Calvary, and by being executed in her place He would bear the full penalty of that law. On her repentance toward God and faith in Jesus Christ, her sins were pardoned.

'Your sins and your iniquities I will remember no more,' says the Scripture, (Hebrews 8:12). This does not mean that God the Father looks upon the nail prints in His Son's hands, and says 'I just cannot remember why those nail prints are there!' No! God remembers very well that it was my sins that put them there. As a king's remembrancer would remind him of events that had occurred in his kingdom (see Esther 6:1), no remembrancer will ever remind God of my sins to condemn me. My sins will never be raised against me, 'they will be remembered no more.'

Pardoned! Paid in full! Forgiven! There is no comfort like it!

JANUARY 6TH

"For she has received from the Lord's hand double for all her sins." Isaiah 40:2.

I have a friend called Billy Jay, a Welshman of note. As he passes through life, he has a favourite expression: "It is the Hand of God!", he will say. It is a very Biblical expression. To receive from the Lord's hand payment for all your sins, though, is something very special. In today's text, what is the meaning of the expression, 'double'?

There is the helpful picture of a tradesman, pinning a folded account, once it has been paid, to the door of his customer. 'Double' also has the meaning of something being two-sided, as in a coin. On the spiritual level there are two sides to the Cross of Christ, where our debt was paid. On one side are our sins – our iniquities and our transgressions – for which Christ was wounded and bruised. There is also God's side. Isaiah 53 says 'It pleased the Lord to bruise Him, He has put Him to grief.' Staggering though it is, the Father made the soul of His Son 'an offering for sin.' It is awesome to think about the God-ward side of the cross. There is a mystery in it that is beyond our explanation.

It would appear that in the context of this passage, 'double' means 'punishment meted out in full measure.' As something is folded over, and each half corresponds exactly with the other half, so our text tells us that the punishment was 'for all' the sins of His people. Nothing is left requiring punishment. 'The blood of Jesus Christ His Son cleanses us from all sin' (1 John 1:7).

I can see her yet, waiting to talk to me. She was an older Christian woman, but when she poured out to me what she had done, it beggared belief. She was beside herself with sorrow and grief. Her repentance was obvious, but she had been deeply marred by her sin. I tried to counsel her with the truth of the forgiveness of God in Christ. When I think that the words 'double for all,' applied even to her case, I am aware that forgiveness and cleansing follow in their wake. Meditate on them today: 'Double for all.' 'Double for all.'

January 7th

The voice of one crying, in the wilderness: "Prepare the way of the Lord; make straight in the desert a highway for our God. Every valley shall be exalted, and every mountain and hill brought low; the crooked places shall be made straight, and the rough places smooth." Isaiah 40:3, 4.

There are four voices speaking in Isaiah chapter 40. They are all voices of God, each one with a different accent. As we saw yesterday, the first is a voice of forgiveness. The second is a voice of deliverance.

When a United States President comes to a modern city, traffic is diverted, roads are cleared, and buildings are made secure. We have had a United States President in our city three times in recent years, so I know that, for weeks beforehand, Secret Service agents are in the city preparing the way. In the ancient world, when an Eastern monarch travelled, courtiers went ahead. Towns through which he or she would pass were required to repair roads and highways. This also applied to the preparation of processional routes along which images of the gods were carried at times of festival.

It is important to understand that this way that is being prepared, is for the Lord to come to the aid of His people. No barrier is too high, too low, too crooked, or too rough for Him to reach them. Valleys will be filled in, mountains and hills will be levelled, the crooked will be straightened, and the rough will be smoothed. Even before we call, He will answer (Isaiah 65:24). No obstacle can thwart Him. He will deliver us.

Do all kinds of barriers seem to stand between you and the Lord's deliverance? Failure, self-doubt, disappointment, fear, confusion, loss, threats, and oppression. The Devil's power seems to be overwhelming. But the message is that nothing – yes, nothing! – can stop the Lord reaching you exactly where you are. He reached Israel, despite her captivity in a city with double defensive walls, and set her free. He will deliver you, too. Let your expectation be from Him; for the Lord, in the fullness of His presence, will be revealed in your circumstances. You will sing again. It's a guaranteed promise. How do I know? "The mouth of the Lord has spoken it" (40:5).

January 8th

The voice said, "Cry out!" And he said, "What shall I cry?" "All flesh is grass, and its loveliness is like the flower of the field. The grass withers, the flower fades, because the breath of the Lord blows upon it; surely the people are grass. The grass withers, the flower fades, but the word of our God stands forever." Isaiah 40:6-8.

The third voice in Isaiah 40 has two accents. The first is the absolute transience of the earthly, and the second is the absolute permanence of the divine. As the seasons change, the beautiful wild flowers that grow across the countryside – Tufted Vetch, Hedge Woundwort, Ragged Robin, Yellow Flag Iris, Dog Rose, Bugle, Meadow Buttercup, Sweet Violet, Primroses and Marsh Marigold – are all touched by decay, and with a blast of the East wind they are gone.

So, too, are we. One day, the velvet skin of the new born baby will wrinkle; the vigorous step of the young man will slacken; and the clear look of the young woman will grow misty. The earthly passes. Even the best party you ever went to, you knew it would soon be over. 'Why does time pass so quickly when you are enjoying yourself?' you ask. The familiar, gentle hand of an encourager now lies in death; the voice that thrilled you is now silent. The frightful, horrific transience of human existence is endemic.

Over all this transience, a Voice calls with a second accent, stating that something stands forever. It is the Word of our God. No decay touches its freshness; no catastrophe kills it. It is never 'here today and gone tomorrow.' It delivers on every promise it makes. Lean on it. Obey it. Rest your soul, your very eternity, upon its directions. The heavens as you now know them, and the earth beneath your feet, will pass; but God's Word will not (Matthew 24:35). 'Those who honour me, I will honour' (1 Samuel 2:30): so honour Him! 'Seek my kingdom first' (Matthew 6:33), and it promises your earthly needs will be supplied: so put His kingdom first! 'Love your wife, as Christ loved the church,' (Ephesians 5:25): so, loving is not divorcing – is it? Loving your wife means loving her to the cost of giving your life for her, if necessary. Listen to God's word at every level, for it stands forever!

9ᵀᴴ January

O Zion, you who bring good tidings, get up into the high mountain; O Jerusalem, you who bring good tidings, lift up your voice with strength, lift it up, be not afraid; say to the cities of Judah "Behold your God!" Behold the Lord God shall come with a strong hand, and His arm shall rule for Him: behold His reward is with Him, and His work before Him. He will feed His flock like a shepherd: He will gather the lambs with His arm, and carry them in His bosom, and gently lead those who are with young. Isaiah 40:9-11.

The fourth voice now bids the people to have a look at their God. The mighty One approaches, whom no obstacle can obstruct, to bring retribution on His enemies, and blessing to the faithful. The voice is clear and strong; there is no hesitation in it. It speaks of the God who is coming to Israel's aid. He has a strong hand and a ruling arm. 'See! See! See!' says the voice. All eyes look: what is their God going to look like?

It is a good question! Myriads of gods are worshipped on earth. Recently I have been to a country where there are 30 million of them. Their temples are ornate and colourful, and the gods multi-variant, including crows and ancestors. What, then, will the Living God look like? Da Vinci's *Creator*, as depicted in the Sistine Chapel? William Blake's long-bearded old man? Superman, hurtling through space?

Mark well the description: here is a Shepherd feeding His flock. He cares about what they eat, for He makes sure they are led to higher ground – the table-land, where rich, luxuriant food is available, and poisonous weeds are avoided. Here is a little, weak lamb that He gathers with His arm, and puts in His bosom. Here is a ewe, heavy with young, being gently led by the Shepherd's staff across rough terrain. There is no overdrive here; He goes before His sheep, and does not hesitate when a wolf comes to take them, but faces and slays it. Who is he? He is the Lord God.

Just today I received an Email from a Christian woman who had been expecting a baby. Last Sunday she went for a walk with her husband, and suddenly she realised that she hadn't felt any movement from the baby for a few hours. They went to the hospital, only to be told that their precious little one had died. She writes, "I never had a more terrible week . . . but in the midst of it all, we have found a faith that we didn't know we had. There is an awful, aching void in our hearts and in our home; but we have decided that where we don't know, we will trust, and we believe that God in His wisdom knew best." The insertion she and her husband put into the newspaper read, 'The Lord gave and the Lord has taken away, blessed be the name of the Lord' (Job 1:21). Faith in such a Shepherd is never misplaced, even in the darkest of days.

JANUARY 10ᵀᴴ

Who has measured the waters in the hollow of His hand, measured heaven with a span and calculated the dust of the earth in a measure, weighed the mountains in scales and the hills in a balance? Isaiah 40:12.

We now move into the anthropomorphic language of Scripture. "The what?" I hear you ask! The Bible is full of them. Anthropomorphisms are descriptions of God in language drawn from the life of human beings. We know that God is a spirit; but anthropomorphisms help us to understand what He is like. We read of God hearing and seeing, of His arm, eye, and finger, His tenderness and His laughter. We even read of God whistling (Isaiah 7:18)! We are made in the image of God, so when God pictures Himself in human terms we find this more illuminating than if He used other terms of reference.

In our text, Isaiah speaks of God's hand. In its hollow, He has measured the waters. A litre of sea water weighs about 1,030 grams. The oceans and the seas cover approximately 70% of the earth's surface. Some oceans plunge to a huge depth: the Marianas trench in the Northwest Pacific Ocean, at 11,034 meters, is the deepest-known point on earth. God is separate from, and above His creation, but He is vastly greater. If, as Jesus said, no one can pluck the believer from His Father's hand, then we are safe. They are very big, and very strong hands!

God has also measured the heavens between His thumb and His little finger. Think of the galaxies, which are made up of millions upon millions of stars. The largest stars occupy several million times as much space as the sun does, and each galaxy may be as much as 60,000 light years across! A light year is the distance that light travels in a year – which is about 9 million kilometres. If you were to have a litre bottle full of material from, say, a neutron star, it would weigh ten thousand-million tons! And God measures all this between His finger and His thumb! It is breathtaking.

And what about the mountains and hills of the world: Chimborazo in Ecuador, Kilimanjaro in Kenya, the Matterhorn in Switzerland, and Everest in Nepal? The highest mountain ranges run in two great lines, the one encircling the Pacific Ocean, and the other stretching from Spain to the East Indies. God has weighed all these mountains in His scales, and the hills in His balance. We measure small, light things in our scales and balances; but God measures the heaviest. Don't you think that we have too small a view of God? Why not stop whatever you are doing just now, and worship Him.

JANUARY 11TH

Who has directed the Spirit of the Lord, or as His counsellor has taught him? With whom did He take counsel, and who instructed Him, and showed Him, and taught Him in the path of justice? Who taught Him knowledge, and showed Him the way of understanding?
Isaiah 40:13-14.

We all have had our mentors and teachers. In the world of sport or business, art and literature, architecture and construction, in the field of politics and government, most successful people would say that they have simply stood on the shoulders of giants. They will readily yield up names of mentors, teachers, and advisers who have deeply inspired and helped them.

When it comes to God, though, who gave Him a standard by which to act? To which expert did He go for advice? Which counsellor did He consult? Which teacher enlightened Him? Who illuminated God as to how things work? No one! God is the source of all knowledge, wisdom and understanding. No one was before Him.

So, what is the practical lesson for us in God's omniscience? If He is the source of all knowledge and understanding, then would it not be wise to talk to Him before we launch out on any new project, marry that man or woman, give up that position, buy that house or apartment, choose that University, or apply for that job? The Bible promises, 'In all your ways acknowledge Him, and He shall direct your paths' (Proverbs 3:6). God teaches us – no one teaches Him. His Word is full of His teaching. David writes 'You, through your commandments, make me wiser than my enemies . . . I have more understanding than all my teachers, for your testimonies are my meditation; I understand more than all the ancients' (Psalm 119:98, 99).

Should you 'surf the Net,' and download all the received wisdom of the ages, it would not give you the insight that comes from reading the Scriptures, and having God lead you into His truth through His Spirit. Should you attend the most prestigious University or College in the world, even with the best teachers available they could not instruct you like the living Word of God. Receive it! Believe it! Stand fast in it!

> O Word of God Incarnate,
> O Wisdom from on high,
> O Truth unchanged, unchanging,
> O Light of our dark sky,

We praise You for the radiance
That from the hallowed page,
A lantern to our footsteps,
Shines on from age to age.
                (W. W. Howe, 1823-97)

JANUARY 12ᵀᴴ

Behold, the nations are as a drop in a bucket, and are counted as the small dust on the scales: Look, He lifts up the isles as a very little thing. And Lebanon is not sufficient to burn, nor its beasts sufficient for a burnt offering. All nations before Him are as nothing; and they are counted by Him less than nothing, and worthless. Isaiah 40:15-17.

This text is worth a long ponder! Nations of the world can be extremely frightening. To Israel, the Babylonians looked invincible; but, as we shall see, they crumbled. Tutored by the Greek philosopher Aristotle, Alexander the Great became king of Macedon before he was twenty; and in twelve years he conquered great kingdoms, without ever losing a battle. Once he faced an army of more than a million men under the Persian King, Darius, and defeated it. But when he died at thirty-three years of age, his empire split up.

The Romans ruled their empire with an iron fist: from Britain in the North, to the desert sands of Africa in the South; and from the Atlantic Ocean in the West, to the borders of Mesopotamia in the East. Their magnificent theatres, houses, and market places dignified their towns; and their villas, the countryside. Their great roads ran from one end of the country to the other. Where is it all now? Most of it is rubble!

In modern times, we think of Nazi power, which at one time stretched from Paris to Stalingrad. Was there any end to their vicious advance? Yes, it too collapsed! As his empire fell apart, their leader committed suicide in a Berlin bunker.

In 1989, who would have thought that the Communist flag would come down from over the Kremlin? Lenin would not have credited it, or Stalin either. Gorbachev started something that eventually overwhelmed him.

What shall I say of the New World Order that unravels before our very eyes? Nations are uniting, under the threat of the terror that brought down the twin towers of the World Trade Centre in New York, and part of the Pentagon in Washington. Regimes come with their terror and threats; and they disappear almost as quickly as they came. From His standpoint, how does God describe them? 'Like a drop of water hanging on a bucket, as a speck of dust or sand on a scale. The land masses (the isles) of the world, as fine dust that is lifted up by a puff of wind.'

The living God is so great that, if all the wood in Lebanon were used to provide wood for an offering, and all of its animals used in sacrifice, it would not make Him indebted to us. Before Him, the nations are as nothing; and compared to Him in stature, less than nothing and worthless. But does this mean that they do not matter to Him? Of course not! One might be tempted to say, with Thomas Middleton, 'It's a mad world, my masters.' But there is a purpose to the history of the world's nations and peoples: God is working out His purposes (see Ephesians 1:10). The message of this text is that, no matter how powerful a nation or an empire might be, in comparison to God it does not feature. So don't be frightened; or ever think that, because of them, all that God has promised for you and your soul will not be fulfilled.

JANUARY 13TH

To whom then will you liken God? Or what likeness will you compare to Him? The workman moulds an image, the goldsmith overspreads it with gold, and the silversmith casts silver chains. Whoever is too impoverished for such a contribution chooses a tree that will not rot; he seeks for himself a skilful workman to prepare a carved image that will not totter. Isaiah 40:18-20.

Human craftsmanship can be awesome, but in comparison to the limitlessness of God it is severely limited. A rich man may hire a craftsman to make a mould of his idol, a goldsmith to fill that mould with gold, and a silversmith to attach silver chains to it. A poor man may choose a sturdy tree, and hire a craftsman to prepare his idol of wood. The images may be very beautiful, but they are just images, and no more. They are powerless. It is laughable to think that a crafted image could be God! It deserves the same sarcasm as Elijah expressed on Mount Carmel to the worshippers of Baal: "Cry aloud, for if he is a god, either he is meditating, or he is busy, or he is on a journey, or perhaps he is sleeping and must be awakened" (1 Kings 18:27).

We should be careful how we treat art. We must not worship it. Once when I was preaching at a great University City in England I visited one of its famous cathedrals. A religious painting by a world-renowned artist was displayed there. It was exquisite! As we entered the building, a Christian who accompanied me said she felt that the emphasis often seemed to be on the holiness of beauty, rather than on the actual beauty of holiness.

Nothing that we create, in sculpture, painting, writing, or building, should be worshipped. Admired and appreciated, certainly; but never, ever, worshipped. No image could ever compare with God. He is incomparable. In childlike wonder, let us realise our limitations and worship the Incomparable.

Let's not be like the little boy, who joined in the kindergarten exercise of drawing what was important to them. After everyone was finished, he was still labouring at his drawing. "What are you drawing, Johnny?" asked the teacher. "God," replied Johnny. "But no one knows what God looks like," said the teacher. "They will, when I'm through!" he responded.

JANUARY 14TH

Have you not known? Have you not heard? Has it not been told you from the beginning? Have you not understood from the foundations of the earth? It is He who sits above the circle of the earth . . . Isaiah 40:21-22a.

Like those Children of Israel in Babylon, do you sit today in a very difficult situation? Like them, are you thoroughly discouraged and humiliated? Maybe your head is bowed in deep sorrow, and nobody seems to understand the pain you are experiencing. Depression has come in, like fog off the bay. Everything is grey. Colour, life, spontaneity, hope, even humour, are gone. You simply cannot get your spirits lifted.

A few days ago I was in Switzerland, at a very beautiful place called Villars, in the French-speaking part of that amazing country. The magnificent mountains were like an encircling womb around me, and I just fell in love with the place. We went high into the mountains on a little train, and walked back to the village through the breathtaking scenery. Somehow, up there any problems seemed different. I was reminded of the astronaut who was asked how it felt inside his space capsule. "It really makes you think," he replied, "when everything is done according to the lowest bidder."

Today's verse is asking us to go much higher than any Swiss mountain. It is challenging us to lift our perspective way above the circle of our blue planet. There we will find God. Rather impatiently, He asks us four questions, as He asked Israel. We try His patience with our horizontal, rather than vertical, view of things, so He wants us to recall something. In all of our lives, have we not known, have we not heard, has it not been told us from the beginning, have we not understood from the very foundations of all things, that He sits above the circle of the earth?

He is telling us to remember that we do not see things as He does. Let God be the standpoint of our vision. If we could see as God can see, our problems would look very different. The important thing is not that we get out of the problem; but what we get out of the problem! God is teaching you something, so listen and learn. Your problems will be a highway for God to show His power. You'll see.

JANUARY 15TH

. . . and its inhabitants are like grasshoppers, who stretches out the heavens like a curtain, and spreads them out like a tent to dwell in. He brings the princes to nothing; He makes the judges of the earth useless. Isaiah 40:22b-23.

Here is a great cure to the problem of the fear of evil, intimidating people. Notice how God asks us to think about such people. He begins by asking us to realise that the blue skies of the earth are stretched out like a curtain. The word means a thin, transparent fabric, as in gauze. He spreads it out like a tent for a traveller to rest in. If the blue heaven above us is God's tent – what do these people look like in comparison? They are like grasshoppers. They are also like vegetation, because their reign is limited; they become as the stubble blown away by the whirlwind.

It may be a Herod or a Pol Pot, a Darius or a Stalin, a Sennacharib or a Hitler; but God assures His people that it is He who determines when these tyrants will die. Their reign is limited. The breath of God will consume them. By contrast, believers will find their souls will be safe, and their work will have eternal repercussions. Take as an example the great 'morning star' of the Reformation, John Wycliffe. He was the moving-force behind the first

English translation of the Bible. His foes were formidable, and I stand in awe of his courage. Condemned as a heretic, after his death the Council of Constance ordered that his bones be exhumed and removed from consecrated ground. So, Wycliffe's remains were disinterred and burned on a little arched bridge that spanned the River Swift, a tributary of the Avon; and his calcined dust cast into the stream. A prophecy arose from the dastardly action:

> The Avon to the Severn runs,
> The Severn to the Sea;
> And Wycliffe's dust shall spread abroad,
> Wide as the waters be.

The prophecy came true, and the historian, Macaulay, wrote of Wycliffe's translation work: 'If everything else in our language should perish, it alone would suffice to show the extent of its beauty and power.'

Fear not, Christian, the work you do for the Lord Jesus will carry on, long after the fearsome powers that oppose you have perished; so keep spreading the good news!

JANUARY 16TH

"To whom then will you liken Me, or to whom shall I be equal?" says the Holy One. Lift up your eyes on high, and see who has created these things, who brings out their host by number; He calls them all by name, by the greatness of His might and the strength of His power; not one is missing. Isaiah 40:25-26.

I love the hymns of Timothy Dudley-Smith! In one of them he tries to describe what, in his subjective experience, the Lord is like: 'As water to the thirsty, as beauty to the eyes . . . Like calm in place of clamour, like peace that follows pain, like meeting after parting, like sunshine after rain.' My favourite line is, 'As sleep that follows fever, as gold instead of grey.' Having watched my children go through all kinds of fevers and then go peacefully to sleep, I know what he is writing about. Bishop Dudley-Smith is following in a long tradition of what millions of believers do – they try to express what they think God is like.

In today's text God asks, "to whom will you liken Me?" We could all give our personal response to that amazing question. He then gives one of the most exquisite descriptions of His nature and character in all of Scripture. He describes Himself (as F. B. Meyer put it) as 'the Shepherd of the stars.' He leads them through Space, He calls them all by name. There are trillions upon trillions of stars, and all are accounted for by the might and power of this Shepherd. Not one is missing.

What are the implications of all this? If God can do this for the stars, He can do it for you, His child! If He maintains these stars in a perfect system that stretches the minds of the greatest astro-physicists, He can maintain His purposes of love for you! Go out and have a look at the stars tonight. Watch the Heavenly Shepherd at work, and remember that He is ordering your steps and planning your future, as He did your past. It will be deeply reassuring.

In the Mediterranean, Napoleon Bonaparte was on deck, walking past a group of officers, when he heard them mocking the idea of a Supreme Being: "A God of Creation, what a joke!" He stopped, stared at them, and sweeping his hands towards the stars of the sky he said, "Gentlemen, you must get rid of these first!"

JANUARY 17ᵀᴴ

Why do you say, O Jacob, and speak, O Israel, "My way is hidden from the Lord, and my just claim is passed over by my God"? Have you not known? Have you not heard? The Everlasting God, the Lord, the Creator of the ends of the earth, neither faints nor is weary. His understanding is unsearchable. Isaiah 40:27-28.

If God orders the Milky Way, we might understandably feel that our way is hidden from Him. Why would God, who runs heaven and earth, move heaven and earth to help us? It can often seem as if He has forgotten us. In their immediate situation, the Children of Israel felt that the Babylonians had taken their rights away from them. For seventy years they had suffered in, what seemed to them, a God-forsaken place, where they felt there was no justice for them. Maybe you feel the same today? Perhaps you are sometimes tempted to be like those famous Deists, David Hume and Voltaire, who believed that God had created the world, but then abandoned it to its own devices, like a Divine Clockmaker. According to them, God no longer intervenes in history; and they have influenced a lot of people's thinking ever since.

God may seem to have forgotten us, because of some trial into which we have been plunged; but this is simply not true. He never tires, He never flags, His strength is not fitful or intermittent. No matter what barriers we may erect, He is not exhausted by the fickleness of those in whom He 'has begun a good work' (see Philippians 1:6). His understanding is unsearchable. Did God abandon David when he sinned? Did God move Joshua from his position of leadership when he lay down in despair at Ai? Jacob, the deceiver, became Israel – a prince with God. Peter, the denier, became Peter, the affirmer. In His 'school of holiness' in the Upper Room, when Christ washed His disciples' feet, they did not appear to be a group of men who would change history. Yet the work which Christ had begun in them, He completed.

He has taken you on, too. Because God is awesome, that does not mean that you and your problems are irrelevant to Him. He understands you inside-out; but you have been spoiled for the world. He will never weary in the work of conforming you to the image of His Son, and present you faultless before His throne. He is everlasting, so He sees the end as well as the beginning. The ends of the earth are His habitation, so there is no place on this planet that He cannot reach. He will never lose track of you; He cares about what happens to you.

In light of these things, why do you say that your way is hidden from the Lord? You always need to adjust emotional thinking into line with Biblical thinking!

This year in Japan, at the Osaka Keswick Convention, four and a half thousand people came for several days of Bible teaching. I was waiting to speak in the Osaka Town Hall, towered over by a giant and beautiful flower arrangement, when the thought occurred to me, 'How on earth did the Lord ever get me here!' It is not impossible for the Lord to get you and me to the ends of the earth – is it?

JANUARY 18TH

He gives power to the weak, and to those who have no might He increases strength.
Isaiah 40:29.

I derive no enjoyment from the television quiz show, 'The Weakest Link.' Contestants vote off other contestants, and the show's host, Anne Robinson, dismisses them with her famous catch phrase, "You are the weakest link. Goodbye!" Failing contestants have to take the 'Walk of Shame.' Identifying and then ridiculing the weakest link is not my idea of entertainment or fun. I get no joy from seeing people being insulted for their ignorance. As my mother used to say, "It's not a shame to be ignorant; but it is a shame to remain so."

Of course, the Scriptures show a different perspective: 'God gives power to the weak, and to those who have no might He increases strength.' 'But God,' says Paul, 'has chosen the foolish things of the world to put to shame the wise, and God has chosen the weak things of the world to put to shame the things which are mighty; and the base things of the world, and the things that are despised, God has chosen; and things which are not, to bring to nothing things that are; so that no flesh should glory in His presence.' Even Paul could say, 'When I am weak, then am I strong' (2 Corinthians 12:10).

In the Scriptures we are constantly told of weak people whom God used mightily. They include Joseph, who went from being thrown into a dark pit in the hills Dothan, to the Premiership of Egypt. We read of Moses, the crying baby that moved the heart of Pharaoh's daughter, who brought salvation to the Hebrew people. And what about David, the shepherd-boy, facing the giant, Goliath; and Ruth, in her poverty, gleaning corn in Bethlehem; and the little servant maid in Naaman's house? God has enabled the weakest of links to become some of the strongest in the chain of history.

And what shall we say of Him, who seemed to be the weakest link of all – who walked the most harrowing 'walk of shame' along the Via Dolorosa? But He was bearing shame that was not His own. It was the path to the greatest victory ever known; and by it Christ has led millions of people to incalculable blessing.

The invitation to His kingdom still says, 'Weak link? Welcome!'

JANUARY 19TH

Even the youths shall faint and be weary, and the young men shall utterly fall. But those who wait on the Lord shall renew their strength; they shall mount up with wings like eagles, they shall run and not be weary, they shall walk and not faint. Isaiah 40:30.

We live in a day when sporting prowess has a higher a profile than ever it did. Sporting heroes are icons. They earn amounts of cash that look like telephone numbers! Their lifestyles are envied, and shape the dreams of a younger generation for their own lives. Yet, even at the very height of their careers, the best sportspeople can get sick and experience their strength ebbing away. There is no guarantee that a young sportsperson's strength will hold out. After a time, even the fittest can become exhausted.

Of course, young people are filled with an admirable quality: great enthusiasm for whatever truly engages their hearts. Yet even youthful enthusiasm can wane and fall away, because of the 'school of hard knocks.' There is an old saying: 'When you are up to your eyes in alligators, it is hard to remember that your original idea was to drain the swamp!'

There is a source of strength, though, that will never be exhausted, and which cannot be threatened by life's tough ways. It can be constantly renewed, like the eagle's. An eagle moults one feather at a time, which means that it is being constantly renewed as it continues flying. People who wait on the Lord will find that their strength will be constantly renewed; they will be enabled to keep going on in their faith, day-in and day-out, year after year.

I have a friend in Christ, who is a very distinguished person. He was the Lord Advocate of Scotland, and eventually became the Lord Chancellor of Great Britain. When I have seen my friend in action, even on national television, I have always noticed his remarkable calm. In dealing with very controversial issues, and people ranged on either side of him stoutly disagreeing, I have marked the indefinable look of gentle assurance on his face. Intrigued with this, I once asked him how he remained so calm. He said, "I read a verse in the Bible: 'Thy shoes shall be iron and brass; and as thy days, so shall thy strength be'" (Deuteronomy 33:25, AV).

Here is a living example of what today's text is saying. Notice that the progression seems strange. Normally, the order would be from walking to running, and then to flying; but in the text it is reversed. Why? Well, often when we start out on something we go at full speed, but few of us have great staying power. In pursuing the path the Lord has laid out for your life, you have a guarantee. If you are patient in waiting for Him, then, if you must mount up, you will – like an eagle; if you must run, you will run – and not be weary; if you have to walk, you will walk – and not faint. And as a bonus, your shoes will be iron and brass! If you doubt me, ask Lord MacKay of Clashfern!

JANUARY 20TH

"Keep silence before Me, O coastlands, and let the people renew their strength! Let them come near, then let them speak; let us come near together for judgement. Who raised up one from the east? Who in righteousness called him to His feet? Who gave the nations before him, and made him rule over kings? . . ." Isaiah 41:1-2.

This is a very dramatic scene! The peoples of the land masses of the world are summoned before God, to make a decision. The Judge of all the earth wants them to decide who shapes history. It is a very important question. The British Prime Minister, Harold McMillan, used to speak of one huge 'shaper' of politics. He said, famously, "Events, dear boy, events". But who is behind those events? Is history all meaningless, or is it moving towards a purpose?

I am moved by the statement of a very important figure in the history of the United States, the 2nd President, John Adams. At a very difficult time, Adams worked tirelessly as a diplomat in Europe to get recognition and money for the newly-formed nation. He led it through those early days, fraught with dissention and party politics. To George Washington, he expressed much of his philosophy in three sentences: "My administration will certainly not be easy to myself. It will be happy, however, if it is honourable. The prosperity of it to the country will depend upon Heaven, and very little on anything in my power." He was right!

In today's text, Isaiah prophesies of God raising up a king from the East. This was King Cyrus. God stirred him up, as one called from sleep. He gave him his victories swiftly, one after another. He was not a believer; but God used him for the righteous purpose of rescuing His people.

Notice that seven times in these short verses God asks the question, "Who?" The answer is unquestionably given: 'I, the Lord, am the first; and with the last I am He' (v.4). Here is the Lord of history. There is immense comfort in this unassailable truth. It implies that, from the beginning to the very end of history – from first to last – God's presiding presence has been above, beyond, and within world events. And within your personal history, too, through events and people outside of your control, the Lord is initiating and achieving His will in your life. So be calm and trusting, even though a storm may rage around you!

JANUARY 21ˢᵀ

The coastlands saw it and feared, the ends of the earth were afraid; they drew near and came. Everyone helped his neighbour, and said to his brother, "Be of good courage!" So the craftsman encouraged the goldsmith; he who smoothes with the hammer inspired him who strikes the anvil, saying, "It is ready for the soldering"; then he fastened it with pegs, that it might not totter. Isaiah 41:5-7.

The challenge God gives to the nations creates a lot of activity. The idol worshippers got very busy, and they all helped each other. They were afraid of what God was saying, so they furbished dilapidated idols, and made new ones. The carpenter and goldsmith applied their skills. They soldered their idols to make sure they were intact, and drove in pegs to make sure they would stand.

But did their activity meet God's challenge? Far from it! God was challenging them with His power to prophesy. Through Isaiah He was foretelling the rise of King Cyrus and his subsequent victories, leading to the repatriation of the Hebrew people in Babylon. His prophecy would be fulfilled to the letter. Could the idols of earth make such a prediction? No, they are silent, and they cannot deliver. Why? Because they are man-made, and consequently man-centred.

On one occasion the head of the Philistine god, Dagon, fell off (see 1 Samuel 5:3). What on earth can you do with a god whose head falls off? The only answer is that you have to stick his head on again! The god is limited by man's strength, because its source is man.

By contrast, the living God makes many predictions. Out of 23,210 verses in the Old Testament, 6,641 contain predictions: 28.5% of the Old Testament is prophecy. Out of 7,914 verses in the New Testament, 1,711 contain predictions: 27% of the whole Bible is prophecy. God can predict the future with 100% accuracy, 100% of the time.

In our modern day, millions read their 'stars' in the newspapers, turn to Nostradamus, or psychic phone lines, longing to know the future. For the sake of your very life, stay away from them! Man-centred sources ultimately fail; but that which is sourced in God is completely trustworthy.

No matter how well soldered or pegged down the countless idols of earth may appear to be, they cannot deliver on accurately predicting the future. Only God can! 'He is the first; and with the last.' Not one of the Bible's prophecies will fail. Be assured that the greatest, and most inspiring of all its prophecies will be fulfilled: Jesus will come back soon!

JANUARY 22ND

"But you, Israel, are my servant, Jacob whom I have chosen . . ." Isaiah 41:8a.

Just this morning, on the day of writing this piece, I was in one of Northern Ireland's most beautiful counties. I had breakfast with a man of God. He is shy by nature, and yet God has hugely used him in recent days. I saw his eyes fill with tears, as he told me stories of lives which had been ruined by abuse of one kind and another, who had then found the Saviour. He has risen in his community as a real Christian statesman. God has given him the ear of the people, and he is winning souls for Christ. Yet it has all come upon him as a surprise. He doesn't see himself as a natural leader; but here he is, leading! And he finds it daunting.

I spent some time with him, hoping to encourage him in his noble work. As this great passage in Isaiah does, I tried to emphasise that God raises up people for specific tasks. I told him of a glassblower I had watched in Ambleside in Cumbria, who took his molten material, and put it in and took it out of the heated furnace. He rolled it, cooled it, stretched it, hammered it, and eventually produced something very different to what I thought he was making. But what did it matter what I thought? All that mattered was what the creator had in mind, as he was making the finished article!

I reminded my friend that God had made this ministry for him, and had moulded his life to suit that ministry. Therefore, 'as his days, so would his strength be.' We prayed together, and returned to our different ministries, refreshed and inspired.

After Israel's long years in exile, imagine how comforting God's words must have been. Think of the self-doubt these people must have endured. And now to be called 'God's servant,' emphasised their role as His people in His plan.

'Servant' is a key word in the subsequent chapters of Isaiah. It will be attributed to King Cyrus, and to the Messiah. In every case it means that they performed God's bidding and glorified His name. In the New Testament, it is a term constantly applied to Christians. Being a servant of God is a high privilege. So, whether you are shy or extrovert, rich or poor, sharply intellectual or starkly straightforward and practical, young or old – of whatever race, and in whatever place, Christian, you can serve God today as His servant!

"... the descendants of Abraham my friend." Isaiah 41:8b.

Christian, where are your roots? People will say 'I'm a Methodist;' or, 'I'm a Baptist;' or, 'I'm an Anglican;' or whatever. For Christians of whatever denomination, the question must be asked: Where are your true roots? Are you rooted in Calvin, or Luther, or the Puritans, or even the Apostles? The Bible takes Christian roots back much further than that. As Israel did, Christians, too, have roots in Abraham.

God showed Abraham the stars, and told him that his children would be just as numerous; and 'Abraham believed God, and it was counted unto him for righteousness' (Romans 4:3). All who exercise faith in God's Word have their roots in that act of Abraham. He was sure of God, and convinced that, 'God ... is the rewarder of those who diligently seek him' (Hebrews 11:6). Despite failure and faltering, God honoured Abraham's faith. Jesus taught that, to be a true child of Abraham, you must live by faith (John chapter 8); and Paul said 'Abraham is the father of us all' (Romans 4:16).

Of all the characters in the Bible, only Abraham is called the friend of God. God has friends in all ages; but only Abraham has this description in Scripture. We read of it three times: here in Isaiah, in 2 Chronicles 20:7, where Jehoshaphat calls Abraham 'God's friend forever;' and once in James 2:23, where he is called 'the Friend of God.' The word 'friend' means 'my loving one,' or 'the one who loved me' – one who is both beloved and loving. God is telling His people what they owe to their ancestor, Abraham.

Even in the twenty-first century, He is reminding us of what we owe him too. As we go about our busy lives, would it not be a great thing if we were marked by these two great qualities: faith in, and friendship with, God? Any Christian – whether a child, teenager, young adult, or older person – has the potential to live such a life. Think about your roots!

JANUARY 24TH

"You whom I have taken from the ends of the earth, and called from its farthest regions ..." Isaiah 41:9.

In the days when this text was written, from Isaiah's point of view, Ur of the Chaldees was so remote that it could have been called 'the ends of the earth.' It was in such a spot that God called Abraham, and founded the Hebrew people through him.

But it was no insignificant place. Situated in Southern Mesopotamia, in the near vicinity of the Persian Gulf, ships came into Ur, bringing alabaster for making statues, copper-ore, ivory, gold, and hard woods. The great ziggurat to the moon god, Nanna, was found at Ur. Education was well developed. In fact, archaeological excavation has revealed that Ur of the Chaldees had a very high standard of material and intellectual civilization. Recently the remains of a house were unearthed, and an unfinished clay tablet discovered. Whoever had been using that tablet, was working out a problem that was still being investigated in the universities of Oxford and Cambridge in the twentieth century!

Abraham was called to leave it all behind, in order to become a blessing to the whole world. It must have seemed absurd to many around him. God told him to leave such a situation and 'go out to the place which he would receive for an inheritance.' So he went out, 'not knowing where he was going . . . for he looked for the city which has foundations, whose builder and maker is God' (Hebrews 11:10).

Has God called you out of your situation to do a work for him, and people who worship the idols of earth think you are mistaken? God has 'taken hold of you,' and called you. His voice is unmistakable: when God speaks, you know He has spoken, for there cannot be a call without a caller. Then, do not look back. Do not hesitate to follow His call.

I well remember sweltering in the heat of an airport in the Persian Gulf, and I suddenly realised that I was not far from Ur of the Chaldees. It occurred to me that the thing we most remember about it was the fact that Abraham left it – and millions have been blessed as a result!

JANUARY 25TH

" . . . You are My servant, I have chosen you and have not cast you away." Isaiah 41:9.

Do you feel that you have failed God? Have you wandered from the path of commitment to the Lord? Is your heart sad and your spirit depressed, when you think of what might have been? Other things, even trifling things, have cluttered your imagination and thinking. Precious years have been frittered away. Opportunities came your way, but you were so busy with the trivial, you missed the serious. Now, like Elijah, you are cowering in the back of some 'cave,' somewhere; and the Lord is saying to you, 'What are you doing here?' You could have been a significant blessing in your community, even helping to lead it, but you pulled back.

Tell me, did Israel transgress? Of course they did! Read the opening chapter of Isaiah's prophecy, and you will see just how seriously they had transgressed. The result was exile in Babylon. They could have done so well, been a light to the nations; but the rot had set in. The Lord was not being recognised as King, false gods were being worshipped. They were a poor, broken, needy, backslidden, powerless people! But God comforted and forgave them, and drew them back to Himself.

In fact, out of them He made a name for Himself, and brought praise to His glory. To these weak, spiritually famished, tempted, and wandering people, God sent blessing. He chose them. He did not despise them, or cast them away.

Christian, do not despair! God will not cast you aside. You are still God's servant, and there is more work for you to do. Your weakness is an opportunity for His strength. You can be too big for God to use; but you can never be too little!

JANUARY 26TH

"Fear not, for I am with you . . . " Isaiah 41:10a.

You know how it is! You are shy, or anxious, or have deep insecurity about going into a certain situation. Lots of people will be there; or maybe there will be just one person who intimidates you. You feel very vulnerable! So, what do you do? You take a friend with you. That friend might be right out of the circle you are entering, but that makes no difference. His or her empathy protects you. They travel with you in the car, talk with you in the crowd, sit with you in the room; and somehow your fear is eased, or even transformed. A fellow-feeling in a hostile environment is deeply comforting. Today's text promises that, whatever fearful situation you might find yourself in, God's presence will be with you. In fact, 'He will never leave you, nor forsake you' (Hebrews 13:5).

I have always loved the statement of the great Irish missionary to India, Amy Carmichael. She pointed out that, even if the Lord is the only person you know in a strange land, 'He is enough.'

After the debacle with the golden calf, God said to Moses, "Depart and go up from here, you and the people . . . and I will send my angel before you. Go up to a land flowing with milk and honey . . ." (Exodus 33:1-3). Moses gave a very interesting reply: "You have not let me know whom You will send with me, yet You have said, 'I know you by name, and you have also found grace in my sight.'" What does Moses mean? He is implying that God's sending someone else before him, is not enough; God's saying that He knows him by name, and that he has found grace in His sight, is not enough. Moses adds "If I have found grace in Your sight, show me now Your way, that I may know You." God's answer came immediately: "My presence will go with you, and I will give you rest" (v.14).

This was how Moses was going to get to know God and His ways. His response is one of the most beautiful statements of faith in Scripture: 'If Your presence does not go with us, do not bring us up from here;' even a land flowing with milk and honey is not enough to meet our deepest need. In fact, being in a wilderness with God is better than being in affluence without Him. His Presence is the complement to our every need!

JANUARY 27TH

" . . . Be not dismayed, for I am your God." Isaiah 41:10b.

This promise has to do with a relationship. God is saying that He is committed to you in a personal way. Once again, the promise is to counteract any fear you might have. Are you filled with alarm, apprehension, consternation, or trepidation? Have you been taken aback, are you unnerved, or frightened? Do you look this way, and that, unsure of which direction to take? Has some incident dealt you a body-blow, and you are filled with dismay? The place where you now find yourself, was never expected to play any part in the script of your life. It has been said that if you want to make God smile, at the end of this year tell Him how you felt the year was going to be!

This promise, though, is more than just a promise. It is a command: "Be not dismayed," says God. If you only pay attention to your external conditions, you will often be dismayed. If you think of the One who is your God, your dismay will turn to trust.

But who is our God? "I am," says Jehovah. He is the One who turned the pressures of Esther's predicament into national blessing. He is the One who turned the bleakness of Ruth's bereavements into the coming of the Saviour of the world. The One who turned the loneliness of Elijah's life at the dried-up brook into Zarephath, with its unfailing supply of flour and oil. He is the One who turned the weariness of Job's woes into certainty in his Redeemer – and gave us one of the most contemporary books on suffering in our modern world. He is the One who turned Lydia's heart into the highway for His gospel through the continent of Europe.

Be not dismayed, Christian: your God is the Lord (Psalm 144:15)! That is the best antidote to fear on the face of the earth. He will make a way for you.

JANUARY 28TH

". . . I will strengthen you . . ." Isaiah 41:10c.

With the advantage of the teaching of the New Testament, let us apply this verse to our lives. In Ephesians 3:14-21, we read a prayer of Paul: 'I bow my knees to the Father of our Lord Jesus Christ . . . that He would grant you, according to the riches of His glory, to be strengthened with might through His Spirit in the inner man . . .'

Obviously, Christians do not need to pray for the Holy Spirit to come, in the way that He has already come at Pentecost. The promise, given long ago by the Prophets, has been fulfilled. Yet there is a sense in which Christians do need to pray for the Holy Spirit to come! Like Paul, we need to pray that He would come in strengthening power to our inner person. If we ask for this power, we will get it.

Do you face some service for God for which you feel inadequate? Is there some responsibility in your life which you find daunting? "I will strengthen you," says God. Ask for 'the strengthening with might through the Holy Spirit,' and it will make a distinctive difference in whatever you do. All of us need this renewing – this special spiritual energy. We all need that fresh touch from the Holy Spirit.

The Old Covenant was a two-way thing. If Israel kept her part, God kept His. If Israel did not keep her part, God could walk away. But the New Covenant is very different! If I am faithless, God remains faithful. The Holy Spirit came upon people in Old Covenant days; the Holy Spirit now, and forever, indwells every believer. This indwelling does not mean, though, that I am not to ask for that special strengthening. It's like charisma: it's hard to define, but you certainly know when it isn't there!

JANUARY 29TH

". . . Yes, I will help you, I will uphold you with my righteous right hand." Isaiah 41:10d.

"Yes!" says God. The word gathers up all that precedes it, and adds assurance to all that follows. At times our Living God does say 'No'; and there is no thwarting Him when He says it. But when He says 'Yes,' there is no thwarting Him either. "Yes, I will help you," He says.

Do you need guidance? He will help you! Do you need protection? He will help you! Do you need comfort? He will help, as no other can! I would rather have the whole world against me, and God for me; than God against me, and the whole world for me. If you have the Lord's help in what you are doing, then you need have no fear of those who say and do things that are of no help.

What kind of help is it that God gives? One of the best examples is shown at the occasion when Israel fought with Amalek. Moses decided to stand on the top of a hill during the battle, with the rod of God in His hand. 'And so it was, when Moses held up his hand, that Israel prevailed; and when he let down his hand, Amalek prevailed. But Moses' hands became heavy; so they took a stone and put it under him, and he sat on it. And Aaron and Hur supported his hands, one on one side, and the other on the other side; and his hands were steady until the going down of the sun' (Exodus 17:11-12).

This is a helpful picture of what God does for us. The mighty hand that measures the heavens and the oceans, will support you. His powerful hand will hold up your weak hand. And it is a righteous hand – that is, it is not a deceptive one that withdraws support on a whim – it delivers on all its promises. It is a faithful hand.

So, put your hand in His hand today, and watch divine help transform the nitty-gritty of your life!

JANUARY 30ᵀᴴ

"Behold, all those who were incensed against you shall be ashamed and disgraced; they shall be as nothing, and those who strive with you shall perish. You shall seek them and not find them – those who contended with you. Those who war against you shall be as nothing, as a non-existent thing." Isaiah 41:11-12.

Do you have enemies? Particularly because you are a follower of Christ, are there those who seem to be in overwhelming opposition to what you seek to do for the Lord? Meditate on these two verses. There are four expressions used to describe the attitude of Israel's enemy. 1. They are 'incensed' against God's people: they are raging against them. The red-hot heat of antagonism is real. 2. They 'strive' with them: they are in conflict with them. 3. They 'contend' with them: they feud with them. 4. They 'war' against them: they are in open warfare with them. God promises that all the opposition which Israel faces will come to nothing: 'those who war against you shall be as nothing, as a non-existent thing.' Reflect long on that phrase!

In today's reading, there is a telling image used to describe the demise of Israel's opposition. It says that Israel will go looking for her adversaries, and simply will not find them! And it will be so for you, too. Why should you stop your good work because of opposition that ultimately will be brought to nothing? 'Will it really?', I can almost hear you say! The forces of opposition have taunted you, slandered you, deprived you, even hurt you. They are everywhere. Every move you make for God, they counter it. But the promise from God for you today is that, one day, you will go looking for them and you won't find them!

I sometimes think about a lady I know, who was the Superintendent of a Sunday School in Scotland with 800 members. On Prize Day, some nasty individual in her church decided to mix up her 800 prizes, which she had set out in perfect order. Wanting to embarrass and frustrate her, he wrecked the day. What did she do: cause a rumpus, and storm away from Christianity?

She told me what she said to her sister in reaction to the debacle: "'tis a lang time afore next Sabbath, and we will move mountains afore then!"

JANUARY 31ST

"For I, the Lord your God, will hold your right hand, saying to you, 'Fear not, I will help you.'" Isaiah 41:13.

The irreplaceable F. W. Boreham, one of the most gifted Christian essayists of the 20th century, told a beautiful story concerning his mother. One evening she was asked by one of her boys to tell them a story about the time when she was young. So she told them a very memorable one. She had arranged to visit Canterbury Cathedral with a cousin, who was then unable to keep the appointment. As she walked up and down, a gentleman noticed her dilemma, and asked if she would kindly allow him to show her around the Cathedral. "I am deeply attached to the place, and happen to know something of its story," he said. His manner won her confidence, and she accepted his invitation. And what an experience it was! The gentleman seemed to know every nook and cranny of the place. From Augustine, to the Danes, to Thomas á Beckett, to the Great Fire of 1667, to the time of the Huguenots, he held her spellbound with his silver tongue. For more than an hour he gave her the history of the place.

As she was leaving, he gave her his card. She took it without glancing at it, merely thanking him very sincerely for his courtesy and attention, and turned on her homeward way. When she settled herself in the train, she took out the card and examined it. His name? Charles Dickens!

"And that's one reason," said Mrs. Boreham to her spellbound boys, "why I'm so fond of reading to you stories about Paul Dombey, Little Nell, Tom Pinch, Pip, Oliver Twist, and all the rest of them. Don't you understand now?" Yes, they understood!

It is not the great Charles Dickens who wants to lead you and help you. This person knows more history than the historians, for He orchestrates it. He does not even leave a calling card; He will stay with you right through your life's journey! He will hold your right hand – the symbol of your activities. "Fear not, I will help you," He says. His name? God!

Don't you understand now why I tell you stories of His exploits, and write of His comforting heart? I pray that you do!

February

The flax crop is harvested just before the seed is fully ripe in order to preserve its suppleness of fibre. It is not cut but is pulled by hand to maintain its maximum length of fibre. There were hangings of 'fine woven linen' in the court of the Old Testament Tabernacle and God commanded that the High Priest's tunic was to be skilfully woven 'of fine linen thread.'

"Fear not, you worm, Jacob, you men of Israel! I will help you," says the Lord, and your Redeemer, the Holy One of Israel. Isaiah 41:14.

T his is a further meditation on how small and weak God's people looked and felt when facing huge obstacles. A worm is a prostrate creature of the dust, and suggests a helpless, struggling condition. It is an object of contempt and disgust, something negligible. It is certainly an apt picture of how God's people were treated as exiles in Babylon. They had been relegated to the lowest strata of Babylonian society. Because they worshipped Jehovah, they were disenfranchised, despised, and treated with contempt. They were an insignificant people. The Hebrew language suggests that we could translate "you men of Israel," as 'O, little Israel.' It means, 'few in number.'

It is comforting to realise that Israel's significance was not found in themselves. Their power had nothing to do with their circumstances. They faced a great and evil power, but they did not face it or fight it on their own. The Holy One of Israel would help them, because He was their Redeemer. In Israel, it was a legal obligation for the next-of-kin to bail out his relation who was in trouble; that is what the word 'Redeemer' means. God is His people's Kinsman-Redeemer. He has put Himself under obligation to help His people in their troubles.

The wider implications of this truth are comfort indeed. The extent to which God is prepared to go to identify Himself with us in our lowly condition was seen at Calvary, where the Messiah died. Meditate on the words of David's Messianic Psalm 22. In verse 6 we read that the Lord Jesus actually said, "But I am a worm and no man, a reproach of men and despised by the people". He, who did no sin, became sin for us, that we might know the righteousness of God. Knowing such a Redeemer counteracts all fear.

"Behold, I will make you into a new threshing sledge with sharp teeth; you shall thresh the mountains and beat them small, and make the hills like chaff." Isaiah 41:15.

W as there ever anyone who wrote of contrasts, like Isaiah? On the one hand, the people of God are likened to a helpless, lowly worm; and now, they are likened to a new threshing sledge with sharp teeth! A threshing sledge was an instrument for separating the corn from the chaff, a heavy wooden platform with sharp cutting edges fitted underneath. The Lord was going to transform Israel into a threshing sledge to thresh mountains. He was speaking metaphorically, but what did it mean?

It meant that they were going to be able to do impossible things by the power of God. They would also be used in the process of the judgment of God upon nations, because nations would be judged by how they treated the people of God (Genesis 12:3). Threshing is a metaphor for judgment. In God's hands, His people would affect the whole world.

When we come to the New Testament, God's people are also depicted as being little in the context of the society in which they live and work. Yet, in such society, Jesus said that His followers would be as salt and light. At school I used to love to buy my potato crisps with the blue bag of salt inside the bigger packet. It wasn't very big, but it made all the difference to how those crisps tasted! "Have salt in yourselves," said the Lord Jesus (Mark 9:50). This means that Christian character and discipleship have a great impact upon society, a society that is often vastly different to Christian standards.

As with salt, so it is with light. When things are in darkness, a little candle or torch can make a difference that is out of all proportion to their size. When Christian character is lived out in true words, backed by deeds, the darkness can often be dispelled.

The Lord can transform you into 'salt' and 'light' in your community. Yet let us never forget that salt is useless if it is contaminated by impurities, and light is also absolutely useless if it is concealed.

FEBRUARY 3RD

"You shall winnow them, the wind shall carry them away, and the whirlwind shall scatter them; you shall rejoice in the Lord, and glory in the Holy One of Israel." Isaiah 41:16.

This week I sat on board the missionary ship, Logos II, listening as Peter Conlan spoke. Operated as an outreach by Operation Mobilisation, it visits dozens of countries around the world, including China and Vietnam. Peter just stood there glorying in what the Lord had done. Millions of people visit the OM ships, Logos II and Doulos II, buying Christian literature and hearing the Christian message. The results are phenomenal. Peter has been working for three decades in this ministry, and his face glowed as he spoke of what God had done. He described the criticism they had received when they started, and the odds they faced; especially when their leader, George Verwer, sent him to Athens to see the shipping magnate Aristotle Onassis. "But I don't know anything about ships!" Peter protested. "Here's a book about ships to read on the aeroplane!" said George. The rest is evangelical history!

You may not be helping to organise a missionary ship; but be assured that whatever you are doing for the Lord today, He will make you into the instrument in His hands that He requires. And our text says "you shall winnow." This metaphor obviously had a particular emphasis for Israel; but there is a practical application of this truth for all Christians. It refers to fanning or tossing grain, to free it of chaff. What a ministry for any believer! The truth you teach and live out will determine what can go into the granary, and what is to be burned. All around you, there is so much that is not worth holding on to; and people are selling their very souls for it. You can be used by God to show them what is worth putting into the granary of their lives, and how to 'lay up treasure in Heaven.'

Notice that the Lord will come to your aid. His irresistible whirlwind will remove the obstacles that stand in your way. He did it for Israel again and again, and He will do it for you. When He does it, don't forget to give Him the glory – just like Peter Conlan.

"The poor and needy seek water, but there is none, their tongues fail for thirst. I, the Lord, will hear them; I, the God of Israel, will not forsake them. I will open rivers in desolate heights, and fountains in the midst of valleys; I will make the wilderness a pool of water, and the dry land springs of water." Isaiah 41:17-18.

Provision! God reminds His people that He can sustain them, even in a wilderness. He did it for forty years, when He redeemed them from Egypt; and now He is promising to do it again, from Babylon. In fact, He can provide for His people in any place or circumstance, at any time in history. He will 'open rivers in desolate heights': no height, however bare, is impossible for this thirst-quencher. He will create 'fountains in the midst of valleys': no depth, however profound, is beyond His refreshing touch. He will make 'the wilderness a pool of water': no barren, resourceless landscapes are beyond His resources, or His power of transformation. He will make 'the dry land springs of water': no ground is so parched and arid that He cannot create springs to bubble up through its drought.

Spiritually this truth is applied by Paul: 'All drank the same spiritual drink. For they drank of that spiritual Rock that followed them, and that Rock was Christ' (1 Corinthians 10:4). And John writes in his Gospel: 'On the last day, that great day of the feast, Jesus stood and cried out, saying, "If anyone thirsts, let him come to Me and drink. He who believes in me, as the Scripture has said, out of his heart will flow rivers of living water." But this He spoke concerning the Spirit, whom those believing in Him would receive; for the Holy Spirit was not yet given, because Jesus was not yet glorified' (John 7:37-38).

I care not how dry, barren, or desolate your circumstances may be, the Lord can make your life a blessing. Out of your heart can flow rivers of living water – those conversations in the local supermarket, at the school gates, on the aircraft, by the bedside, in the local café, at the sales conference, on that farm, at the factory, in that office, by those Emails – through the Holy Spirit, you can be a spiritual thirst-quencher. Today.

"I will plant in the wilderness the cedar and the acacia tree, the myrtle and the oil tree; I will set in the desert the cypress tree and the pine and the box tree together." Isaiah 41:19.

Shade! On the wilderness journey, the relentless sun saps the strength of the fittest and bravest traveller. God offers shade, refreshment, and comfort on that journey, by saying that He will plant seven trees in the wilderness. There is the brown-seeded cedar, or juniper, of the mountains. There is the acacia tree, from which the Ark of the Covenant was made. There is the myrtle – a large evergreen shrub, with fragrant flowers and spicy, sweet scented, leaves: all parts of the plant are perfumed, and out of its twigs, wreaths were made for acclaim. There is the oil tree, sometimes called 'Jerusalem willow,' that produces a fruit from which medicinal oil can be pressed. There is the cypress tree, with its hard, durable, reddish-hued wood, from which authorities believe Noah's Ark was constructed. There is the pine tree, tall and easy to cut and tool. There is the box tree, a hardy evergreen, whose wood can be used to provide inlays for cabinetwork.

The most interesting word in today's text is the word 'together.' God says that He will plant all seven trees 'together.' God is no killjoy. In our journey through life, even in the most desolate and barren locations, He provides a communion with Himself that is not only fragrant, but also permanent. The Spirit of God will see to it. A weary traveller would bless God for the shade and fragrance of these seven trees, growing together in locations across the desert. So, as we face life's difficulties, we would bless Him for Spirit-given communion, whose shade and fragrance is so refreshing. We are not alone. We are not without inspiration. We are not comfortless.

FEBRUARY 6TH

"That they may see and know, and consider and understand together, that the hand of the Lord has done this, and the Holy One of Israel has created it." Isaiah 41:20.

"Do you believe in cause and effect?" I asked an astrophysicist. "I do" she replied. "We can prove that butterflies moving their wings in India can affect the weather in North America!"

Isaiah is also into cause and effect. He is saying that the provision of transformed circumstances and redeemed lives amongst God's people proves that His hand is behind it. There is a fourfold realisation of the activity of the hand of God, and the evidence of a Divine agent being involved: they will 'see,' 'know,' 'consider,' and 'understand.'

See: they will see the evidence. Their God is a God who does things. God's people are not without evidence, even regarding the Messiah. He did turn water into wine. He did feed thousands from five barley loaves and two small fish. He did heal the blind, and raise Lazarus from the dead. Our faith in God is not a leap in the dark. And these people would see repatriation, back to Jerusalem. Know: they would know the facts. It would not merely be a dream. Consider: they would consider the implications. If God was able to do this, then He was worth trusting. Understand: they would all perceive the meaning of what they had been through. And they would all See, Know, Consider, and Understand it, together. This was not to be an isolated experience of any individual person.

Paul's prayer in the New Testament was that the Ephesian Christians would be 'able to comprehend with all the saints what is the width and length and depth and height, and to know the love of Christ which passes knowledge' (Ephesians 3:18,19). His desire for them was that, whatever their circumstances, the extravagant dimensions of Christ's love would be a shared experience. Here was no denominational exclusivity. All true believers were to take in and know all the far reaches of Christ's love, together. Let's keep that in mind wherever we find ourselves across the world.

FEBRUARY 7TH

"Present your case," says the Lord. *"Bring forth your strong reasons,"* says the King of Jacob. *"Let them bring forth and show us what will happen; let them show the former*

things, what they were, that we may consider them, and know the latter end of them; or declare to us things to come. Show the things that are to come hereafter, that we may know that you are gods; yes, do good or do evil, that we may be dismayed and see it together." Isaiah 41:21-23.

The cosmic Court sits after a recess! In the first session, the Lord reminded Israel of His call to them, as His servant among the nations of the world; and backed up that ancient and ever-present call by the comforting promises of His word. He had also called the nations of the landmasses of the world to consider who really rules the world. Now God summons the Court, and this time He asks that the idols themselves, whom the nations worship, be carried into the Court. The idols are to be challenged, not the idolaters! It is the King of Jacob versus the gods of earth. The point at issue: who is truly divine? The gods are asked to produce their evidence, and to prove their deity. Was there ever a courtroom more fascinating?

God asks the nations of the world to explain the flow of history. In the light of what has happened in the past, He asks them to deduce what the future will be. Are they omnipotent? Could they ever foretell the immediate future?

God pushes the idols of earth in His challenge. "Yes," He says, "Do good or do evil, that we may be dismayed and see it together." He is asking them to express themselves one way or another, to show some sign of life. Indeed, to show any sign of life, that 'we may be dismayed.' That is, that one side might look the other in the face, and measure how each is doing in the contest!

As we sit in this courtroom, watching all that is going on, it is worthwhile asking ourselves the question, 'Does the God whom I worship *do* anything?' Does He? The answer is that He is 'the same yesterday today and forever' (Hebrews 13:8). The Christ, who stilled the storm on Galilee, continues to still storms. He, who gave sight to the blind, still dispels darkness. He, who blessed little children, still blesses little children. He, who set captives free of the Devil's power, still sets captives free. He is an active God, not a passive God. When Adam sinned, He went after him. He still goes after sinners and draws them to Himself. Speak to God, and He will fulfil His promises to you: 'Has He said, and will He not do? Or has He spoken and will He not make it good?' (Numbers 23:19).

FEBRUARY 8TH

"Indeed you are nothing, and your work is nothing; he who chooses you is an abomination." Isaiah 41:24.

Imagine the silence of the court! The idols sit mute. 'Look,' God is saying, 'there is not a word out of you.' Imagine idols from every Continent on earth, sitting row upon row. Not only is there no explanation from them about the flow and meaning of history, there is a deafening silence. They do not, and cannot, speak. Despite all the pleadings of the millions who have prayed to them through centuries of time, and the regard in which they are held, there is not an ounce of life in them. They are fake-gods, and fool-making gods.

The Judge of all the earth now addresses the silent ranks. (My imagination could run wild at this point, couldn't yours?) The withering scorn! The derision! The disdain! The disregard! Here is no omnipotence. 'Here,' says God, 'is nothing.' They say nothing, because they are nothing. Their work has no substance whatsoever.

It is so easy to make gods out of all kinds of things, even worldly and material success. Speaking of their drive to gain worldly achievement, many admit that they are deeply disappointed by what they discover. After satiation with material things, did not Marie Antoinette say, "Nothing tastes"? The gods of earth are truly useless in terms of lasting value. Do people choose them? They certainly do! The warning is given in today's text, as to what the Lord thinks of all those who worship sham gods. They are abhorrent to the Lord. Standing recently in a Japanese temple, watching people throw money to a god who was one of their ancestors, I was reminded how perilously close I have come in my heart to worshipping even Christian leaders, rather than the Lord who gifted and used them. He will not give His glory to another.

Meditate on these words from Psalm 115:1-8:

'Not to us, O Lord, not unto us, but to Your name give glory, because of Your mercy, because of Your truth. Why should the Gentiles say, "So where is their God?" But our God is in heaven; He does whatever He pleases. Their idols are silver and gold, the work of men's hands. They have mouths, but they do not speak; eyes they have, but they do not see; they have ears, but they do not hear; noses they have, but they do not smell; they have hands, but they do not handle; feet they have, but they do not walk; nor do they mutter through their throat. Those who make them are like them; so is everyone who trusts in them.'

The message is clear. You become like what you worship! The people who worship the gods of earth simply do not have the hope that burns in the heart of all those whose God is the Lord. They do not have the true promises of God for their life and future, reaching out into the vast eternity. They do not have the peace that knowing Him brings. If you become like what you worship, then be like your living Lord this day, wherever you go, whatever you are doing.

FEBRUARY 9TH

"I have raised up one from the north, and he shall come; from the rising of the sun he shall call on My name; and he shall come against princes as though mortar, as the potter treads clay." Isaiah 41:25.

God now turns from the silence of the gods of earth, and makes His case. The challenge of the Court was that the gods of earth were to predict what would happen in the future. But they made no case whatsoever, said nothing whatsoever. Through Isaiah, the Lord again meticulously predicts what is going to happen to Israel. King Cyrus was eventually named as the one He is going to raise up (see Isaiah 44:24–45:7).

Earlier we read of Cyrus being raised from the east (Isaiah 41:2). Now we are told that he will be 'raised up from the north . . . from the rising of the sun he shall call on My name.' What does this mean? It means that he originated in the east, and came and besieged Babylon from the north. He actually entered the city on October 29th 539 BC. With the rise of Cyrus, began the renowned Persian Empire that was to continue until the coming of Alexander the Great. Cyrus's actions would fulfil the Lord's prediction; so that His name would be honoured, and He would be praised as the only God.

The princes of earth would be as mortar (a mixture of lime, sand, and water) before this coming conqueror; and he would be as a potter treading (or kneading) clay. The Lord would be the instigator and originator of all that would happen.

Again, we draw deep comfort from this courtroom. It is saying that no prince of earth, no 'corridor of power,' no 'school of thought,' no 'coalition of nations,' nor any individual, is all-powerful. Despite evil in our world, the Lord knows what He is doing as He works out His purposes. Sit in this courtroom for a little while today, and meditate on the way God can use individuals, as a builder uses mortar, or as a potter kneads clay. With the eyes of faith, recognise that there is a loving purpose running through your circumstances, even the painful ones; and anticipate the fact that, one day, you will see what the Lord has foreseen all the time. He is working towards it day and night. As Augustine said, "Nothing, therefore, happens unless the Omnipotent wills it to happen; He either permits it to happen, or brings it about Himself." The will of God may be a sigh for you at the moment, but one day it will be a song. Be patient!

February 10th

"Who has declared from the beginning, that we may know? And former times, that we may say, 'He is righteous'? Surely there is no one who shows, surely there is no one who declares, surely there is no one who hears your words." Isaiah 41:26.

Through all times and seasons, God has been proved right. The older I grow, the more I see it. Don't you? No prophecy made by God has ever been proved inaccurate. No principle taught in His Word has ever been proved unworkable, or false. No one has ever been able to do this but God. Human prophecies, and even views of history and its ultimate goal, have crumbled.

Take, for example, the Communist theory. It says that, as governments change, they go from feudalism to capitalism to socialism to communism; the inevitable laws of change in history will bring this about. So, people in developing countries are urged to fight for communism, because the very laws of history are on their side. Helped by the Communist Party, change will bring in a great millennium. Sadly, people are called to sacrifice their lives for a millennium that they will never see. They believe that when life is done, it is done forever; and millions are influenced by this false teaching. They think it will bring in a great age of peace, but they are wrong. The closing decade of the 20th century has surely proved that conclusively!

In the book of Daniel, we read that God 'changes the times and the seasons; He removes kings and raises up kings; He gives wisdom to the wise and knowledge to those who have understanding. He reveals deep and secret things; He knows what is in the darkness, and light dwells with Him' (Daniel 2:21-22). He tells of a vision he had, in which he saw 'One like the Son of man, coming with the clouds of heaven! He came to the Ancient of Days, and they brought Him near before Him. Then to Him was given dominion and glory and a kingdom, that all peoples, nations, and languages should serve Him. His dominion is an everlasting dominion, which shall not pass away, and His kingdom the one which shall not be destroyed' (Daniel 7:13-14).

To suppose that there are some absolute laws in history, that lead to a blissful, man-made millennium, is a form of idolatry. As today's text indicates, idolatry brings no understanding or declaration of true prophecy. But Gods' Word does, constantly, unerringly, and truthfully. God will always be proved right. Trust Him!

FEBRUARY 11TH

"The first time I said to Zion, 'Look, there they are!' And I will give to Jerusalem one who brings good tidings. For I looked, and there was no man; I looked among them, but there was no counsellor, who, when I asked of them, could answer a word. Indeed they are all worthless; their works are nothing; their moulded images are wind and confusion." Isaiah 41:27-29.

Now we have the verdict of this awesome Court. The summing-up is not full of phrases that say, 'We are all worshipping the same God,' or, 'There is more that unites us than divides us,' or, 'Let them have their view, and you yours, and we will all get along fine.' But here is no syncretism; in totally unflattering terms, the Lord God sums up the idols, and the people who worship them.

His verdict? The idols are worthless, i.e., false and fraudulent, there is no value to be found in them. The moulded images are empty of thought or purpose. They are as wind. There is nothing but confusion. Too right! In a temple that was part of a tourist route through Tokyo, I watched an American couple pick out a piece of paper with a so-called prophecy on it. It was a 'bad' prophecy. (The guide had warned that 30% of all prophecies in the temple were bad.) I will long remember the confusion on that young woman's face. Was there a counsellor to sit down with her to eradicate her pain? No, there was none. She would be haunted by that prophecy, and she left that temple sadder than when she entered it.

Don't think that this text is only related to Israel at the time of Isaiah. It could not be more relevant for today. God gave good news through His prophet, Isaiah, for the time when Israel would be surrounded by false gods. The good counsel of God's Word sustained a weary, embattled, downtrodden, depressed people. God's Word still speaks, and the gods of earth are still silent and useless. The Word of God is still a revelation of God to us, and has inherent qualities and health-giving results.

'The law of the Lord is perfect, converting the soul; the testimony of the Lord is sure, making wise the simple; the statutes of the Lord are right, rejoicing the heart; the commandment of the Lord is pure, enlightening the eyes; the fear of the Lord is clean, enduring forever; the judgements of the Lord are true and righteous altogether. More to be desired are they than gold, yea than much fine gold; sweeter also than honey and the honeycomb. Moreover by them Your servant is warned, and in keeping them there is great reward' (Psalm 19:7-11).

So the great Court closes. The gods of earth have not delivered. The living God, who has called and redeemed His people, is proved to be the Lord of History; and His promises undergird all who trust Him, forever. It's the best Court I've ever attended!

FEBRUARY 12TH

"Behold! My servant . . ." Isaiah 42:1.

'Behold' is a word frequently used by Isaiah. Every time he uses it, he is introducing a new theme, or a distinction to a theme he has introduced earlier. Here the prophet is given a new insight to a theme he has dealt with before. Israel has been called God's servant-nation (41:8-9); and Nebuchadnezzar and Cyrus have been called servants, too. This Servant, though, is different from all the others. He is different from people like Abraham, Jacob, Joseph, Moses, and David. This Servant is the Messiah, our Lord Jesus Christ. Matthew's Gospel directly refers this passage of Scripture to Him (see Matthew 12:18). Isaiah does not identify Him immediately. He shows Him to be a sinless redeemer, the great sin-bearer, and God's perfect (not idealised) Servant. There are four majestic servant-songs in Isaiah; this is the first. (See also Isaiah 42:1-9; 49:1-7; 50:4-9 and 52:13–53:12). 'Here is my servant,' says God – 'Look at Him!'

Is it not a relief to turn away from dumb, worthless, speechless, effervescent idols of earth, to the Lord Jesus? Here is a Counsellor beyond all counsellors. Here is the Prophet, Priest and King, who is simply incomparable. An anonymous writer wrote, 'All the armies that ever marched, and all the navies that ever were built; all the parliaments that ever sat, and all the kings that ever reigned; have not affected the life of humankind on this earth as powerfully as that one solitary life.' That one life was to be given as a substitution for sinners; and to all who believe in Him, a full salvation is available.

> He, who for men their surety stood
> And poured on earth His precious blood,
> Pursues in heaven His mighty plan,
> The Saviour and the Friend of man.

'Look at My Servant!' says God, through Isaiah, to His servant, Israel, in their weakness and failure. A look at Him would show them that, where they were weak, He was strong; where they had failed, He would not, nor could not, fail. 'Look at my servant!' says God, through Isaiah, to you and me. Here is the source of our inspiration, our hope, our joy, our wisdom, our salvation, our righteousness, and our eternal security. Wherever you are today, Christian, whatever you face, steal a look at Jesus! It will lift the dullest day and cheer the saddest heart. And what a day, when the Father will say to us in Heaven 'Look at my servant!' With our own eyes, for the first time, we shall see our Saviour in reality. Perhaps it will happen even before this day is through. Ah, bliss!

42

"Behold! My servant whom I uphold, My Elect One in whom My soul delights!"
Isaiah 42:1a.

This is a very tender, even awesome, text. We are about to be called by God to consider the rare qualities of the Lord Jesus as a servant. As we are filled with the Holy Spirit, and held by the hand of God, we can repeat these qualities in our service for Him. In this text, though, we learn primarily of the relationship between God and the Lord Jesus, and its dynamics. Here is one of the most mysterious, yet beautiful, relationships in the Universe – perfect in every way.

The nature of the relationship is intimate and personal. God, the Father, says that the Lord Jesus is 'My servant.' This Servant is 'upheld' by the Father. In Hebrew, this literally means He is 'gripped fast.' He is the Father's elect One; meaning that He was chosen in the eternal counsels of God in the past for the ministry of servanthood, to bring about results that would change the course of history, and the eternal destiny of souls. This Servant would fulfil that ministry to the letter. Indeed, the New Testament teaches that, when those untold multitudes will sit down to eat in His kingdom, He will serve them at the table! This chosen Servant would be in contrast with the frequently disobedient Israel. He would be obedient in every detail. He was, and is, the Servant King.

Our text tells us that the Lord Jesus is the One in whom the Father's soul delights. '"Soul" here represents personal commitment,' writes Alec Motyer, 'as we might say "delight with all my heart". Someone can be chosen for a task without being necessarily approved of, or even liked – as every employer knows! Not so here! He is not only the Lord's man for the job (like David, 1 Samuel 13:14; Acts 13:22) but the Lord's man for the Lord Himself.'

What Christian reader does not find that the Lord Jesus is their soul's delight? I have known Christ since boyhood, and the older I grow, and the more evil I find in the world, the more I delight in the sinless perfection, beauty and loveliness of the Lord Jesus. There is no flaw in Him. 'There is no marble without its flaw. There is no flower without its freckle. There is no fruit without its blight. There is no face without its blemish. There is no joy without its taint of regret. There is no heart without its sin,' wrote F. B Meyer. Yet, to know God through Jesus Christ is to come into contact with absolute purity. It is to be introduced to a fellowship that is like drinking from a fountain of unfailing freshness and delight. The illusions of money, fame and fortune on earth lead to disappointment. Following the Lord Jesus is not an illusion: it is an endless adventure of eternal delight. Enjoy!

"I have put my Spirit upon Him; He will bring forth justice to the Gentiles."
Isaiah 42:1b.

God the Father showed His delight in the Lord Jesus in a very special way. He demonstrated it in the coming of the Holy Spirit upon Him. In Isaiah, there are three great prophecies connecting the Holy Spirit with Christ. In 11:2, we read the prophecy of His birth, and how 'the Spirit of the Lord shall rest upon Him, The Spirit of wisdom and understanding, The Spirit of counsel and might, The Spirit of knowledge and of the fear of the Lord.' In today's text, it is a prophecy pointing to the baptism of Christ. And in 61:1-2, we read the prophecy of how the Holy Spirit would be upon Him during His public ministry, as He 'preached good tidings to the poor, healed the broken-hearted, and proclaimed liberty to the captives.' This is the prophecy which Christ read in the synagogue in Nazareth, and said that it was being fulfilled in their ears that day!

John the Baptist had been told that the one on whom he would see the Spirit descend would be the Messiah. When his cousin came to him for baptism, John had no idea that He was the chosen Messiah. So, when he had baptised Jesus, we can only imagine John's feelings, when he saw the Holy Spirit descend from Heaven in a visible shape – as a dove might, with gentle, fluttering motion – and alight on his relative! Imagine further, his feelings, when a voice came from Heaven, saying, "This is My beloved Son, in whom I am well pleased" (Mathew 3:17). Here was the fulfilment of Isaiah 42:1!

The prophecy says that Christ, endued with the Holy Spirit, 'will bring forth justice to the Gentiles.' What a clear message of comfort there is in this beautiful phrase!

FEBRUARY 15TH

"He will not cry out, nor raise His voice, nor cause His voice to be heard in the street." Isaiah 42:2.

I saiah now begins to describe the character of God's perfect Servant, the Lord Jesus. Here are some of His rare qualities. In this verse, he speaks of His modesty: this Servant does not call attention to what He does. He is not aggressive: He does not use His voice to establish His authority. His authority lies in His character, not in His ability to advertise Himself. He does a lot of things, quietly. He creates the dew, His power raises the sun in the morning, and organises its setting in the evening. He directs the planets, He plots the course of billions upon billions of stars, each one larger than the earth. And does He make a sound? He does it all so quietly and unobtrusively, that some say He isn't there at all!

Compare His character with what goes on in our world. We get the weather forecast, sponsored by some famous Company or other, until almost subliminally we think they produced the weather! Companies spend billions to brand their name. Few sporting geniuses take part in any public event without some Company's brand name on their clothing. Often, commercial radio virtually shrieks its advertising. In the world of politics, politicians seek to grab headlines, and governments 'spin' their own agendas. In everyday life, aggressive, bullying individuals try to push and shove their way to the top. Any day of the week, just drive your car anywhere, and you will soon see how aggressive people are. Road rage is a common disease! Once in Hong Kong, I watched a taxi driver kick in the door of a colleague's taxi, because he had 'bumped' him. Life in the fast lane is very loud and aggressive. In the world of fashion, being brash and bold often gets the Fashion Houses the attention they seek.

Mark well the words of F. B. Meyer: 'The only work that God approves, that is permanent and fruitful, that partakes of the nature of Christ, is that which neither seeks nor needs advertisement. The bird is content to sing; the flower to be beautiful; the child to unfold its nature to the eye of love; and the true worker to do the will of God.'

Consider God's perfect Servant. He constantly told the people whom He had healed not to make Him known. The paralytic amongst the crowds at Bethesda's pool did not even know who had healed him! When His disciples argued as to who was the greatest, He took a little child and set him before them, and told them they must become like a child – one of the most dependent beings on earth. Christ did what His Father told Him, and that was all that mattered.

A word to your heart, Christian: let the Lord lift your work and bless it! He can lift a Joseph's work in a prison, and, without him raising his voice, make him Prime Minister. He can lift a quiet, spiritual woman, like Mary from Nazareth, and make her into one of the most blessed women in history. "My soul magnifies the Lord, and my spirit has rejoiced in God my Saviour," sang Mary. "For He has regarded the lowly state of His maidservant . . . for He who is mighty has done great things for me . . . He has put down the mighty from their thrones, and exalted the lowly . . . He has filled the hungry with good things, and the rich He has sent away empty." Selah.

FEBRUARY 16TH

"A bruised reed He will not break, and smoking flax He will not quench: He will bring forth justice for truth." Isaiah 42:3.

These beautiful words contain promises. They speak of the way in which Christ will bring the revelation of God to earth. Imagine a reed by a river somewhere, that some passing animal or person has trampled on and bruised. Of what use is it? Would some expert flower arranger make a journey to collect it, and put it in a display to set off flowers in a palace or home? Most people would treat it as useless. See, then, how God takes the image of the bruised reed, to show how His perfect Servant behaves towards lives that are bruised. Lives get bruised by all kinds of things: failure, stress, abuse, selfishness, jealousy, envy, bullying, and unkind words. Every day, people's hearts and lives are bruised. Some people get so bruised they retreat into themselves, and others treat them as useless. Christ, by His power and truth, can lift such bruised lives and mend them. He does not break the bruised and cast it aside. It is an inspiration to take a quiet meditation through the Scriptures, on a host of people whose bruised lives were mended. Remember, it's a promise: 'A bruised reed He will not break.'

Imagine someone in an ancient day, in need of a torch. He or she pulls some flax, winds it into a torch-like shape, and sets it alight. It burns, but only dimly. It is fitful and irregular. It smoulders, but it does not burst into a flame. So is my love for God: it is often a very intermittent thing. God uses the image of the smouldering flax to show how His perfect Servant behaves towards those in whose hearts love for God burns dimly. 'The smoking flax He will not quench,' God promises. I am so glad of that! Despite the fact that my love for God is often dim, He knows that it is there; He does not put it out, but graciously works to bring it to a flame.

As Peter warmed himself by the fire in the courtyard of the High Priest, his love for Christ burned so low that, had you not known the whole story, you would have been sure that there was no love at all. But on the Day of Pentecost it was a very different Peter who declared: "Let all the house of Israel know assuredly that God has made this Jesus, whom you crucified, both Lord and Christ" (Acts 2:36), and three thousand people were converted in one day! So, bruised and smouldering one, the Lord will use you again, perhaps even more effectively than before. He will renew and restore you.

FEBRUARY 17TH
"A bruised reed He will not break, and smoking flax He will not quench: He will bring forth justice for truth." Isaiah 42:3.

Let me stay another day with this richly endowed text of Scripture, and apply it to Christian service. If God's perfect Servant does not break bruised reeds or quench smoking flax, how about us? It is very easy to think that the better form of Christian service is to influence the influential, the strong, the intelligent, the literate, and the leaders, for God. It is so easy to forget how it has often been proved, 'God has chosen the poor of this world to be rich in faith and heirs of the kingdom which He promised to those who love Him' (James 2:5). Paul wrote to the Corinthians, '. . . not many mighty, not many noble, are called . . . the things which are despised God has chosen, and the things which are not, to bring to nothing the things that are, that no flesh should glory in His presence' (1 Corinthians 1:26, 28-29).

May I be used of God today, to inspire you to reach out to someone within your orbit, who is not counted of much worth by the world around you? Ask God to lead you to some 'bruised reed' or 'smoking flax'. Be kind, speak gently to them, and encourage them to higher things. Don't wait for the great occasion: make every occasion great.

Imagine a small, poverty-stricken house in London. In that house lived a woman who had to work extremely hard to keep body and soul together. Her back was bent because of years at the washtub; taking in washing was her only source of income. Despite the pressures of her life, she prayed constantly for her son who had been press-ganged into Navy service, and had ended up in Africa as a slave of the wife of a slave-owner. If ever there was a bruised reed, her son John was that reed. She died before her prayers were answered. Answered? Yes, John was converted, and wrote the hymn 'Amazing Grace,' that is still sung around the world. He was used to bring a sceptic called Thomas Scott to Christ, who in turn was used to bring William Cowper to Christ, one of the greatest Christian poets in history. Newton was also used to influence William Wilberforce for Christ, who in turn helped to abolish the slave trade. And it can all be traced to the prayers of a woman, bent over a washtub in a poverty-stricken house in London, all those years ago! Prayer for a 'bruised reed' can achieve more than this world could ever dream of.

FEBRUARY 18TH

"He will not fail nor be discouraged, till He has established justice in the earth; and the coastlands shall wait for His law." Isaiah 42:4.

'The coastlands,' or, the Gentiles, would wait in terror for the coming of Cyrus and his army. According to Isaiah, however, Gentiles shall wait in hope for the coming Messiah, and His establishment of justice in the earth. In accomplishing this, Christ would not fail nor be discouraged. Here is the truth of Divine perseverance. Linked with the images already given, it is also a promise. To be discouraged, is to be bruised or broken; Christ would not, and never will, be discouraged. As displayed in the image of the smouldering flax, the failure to burn brightly was not, nor ever will be, Christ's experience. Christ is neither a bruised reed nor smouldering flax, though He is deeply involved with those who are!

There is nothing that Christ has set His hand to that He has not completed. He is not motivated by whim or impulse; He is not deflected by scorn or pitiless criticism. No difficulty at any time will stay His hand in accomplishing what He has set out to do. All the powers of Satan and his angels cannot stop Him. He is never thwarted by discouragement. He came to earth and was laid in a borrowed manger. During His earthly ministry He had to borrow a coin, and a boat, and an upper room. His cross was meant for a robber. He was laid in a borrowed tomb. He was not discouraged when the mighty and powerful despised Him, so He talked with Moses and Elijah on the Mount of Transfiguration about 'His death which He was about to accomplish at Jerusalem' (Luke 9:31). There was never any thought of it not being accomplished.

And does He get discouraged about His work in our lives? Never! 'Being confident of this very thing,' writes Paul, 'that He who has begun a good work in you will complete it until the day of Jesus Christ' (Philippians 1:6). The day you were converted, Christ began a good work in you. He is the author of that work, and He will be the finisher of it. One day there will be a new earth, under a new heaven, and you will dwell with Christ forever. You will enjoy final emancipation and complete redemption. Christ started this work, He is going on with it, and He will complete it. We constantly fail; He will not fail. We get deeply discouraged; He never gets discouraged. Our constant 'bruising' and 'smouldering' do not deflect from His character and work. My, this fellow Isaiah is a comforting writer, is he not?

FEBRUARY 19TH

Thus says God the Lord, who created the heavens and stretched them out, who spread forth the earth and that which comes from it, who gives breath to the people on it, and spirit to those who walk on it. Isaiah 42:5.

Here is the Lord of all creation, and He is about to promise something. First of all Isaiah tells us about Him, and what he tells us will be the basis of our believing His promise. Once He spoke to nothing, and it became something: that something was the heavens and the earth. That's what a word from God can do! Scripture teaches, 'the worlds were framed by the word of God' (Hebrews 11:2). He created the heavens – that means the untold galaxies. He 'stretched them out.' How far did He stretch them? Where do the stars stop? I do not know, but the question fascinates me! God 'spread forth the earth.' It was originally 'without form,' then came light and darkness and the first day. Every day since, God has maintained that which He created, and 'that which comes from it.'

Don't you find that creation is such an incredible source of wonder to your mind and spirit? Take the humble oyster. Did you know that it lays 60 million eggs a year? If all the descendants of one oyster survived until it was a great-grandmother, their shells would make a mound eight times the size of the earth! Take a common mushroom, three inches in diameter. It drops 40 million spores an hour, and goes on until it has dropped 16,000,000,000 of them! Take even the lowly limpet. When it puts its foot down, a force of 60 pounds per square inch is required to pull it off a rock! If it were dissected, you would find a file about two inches long that works like a handsaw. Limpets cut out a hollow in the rock with their file, and however far they wander in search of food they always return to rest in their own hollow! From galaxies to limpets, creation is awesome. The God who created it all is about to promise something. It must be worth listening to!

He who spread forth the earth, 'gives breath to people on it, and spirit to those who walk on it.' Of course, there are those who maintain that humankind is nothing but a gene machine, blindly programmed to preserve its selfish gene. This is the theory of reductionism. If you look at a road-sign, saying 'No Entry,' you could say that it nothing but enamel or metal. But it is much more! And it is false to suggest that humankind is nothing but a carrier of selfish genes. By doing so, you invalidate other levels of human significance. It is a disgrace to science! True science does not claim to answer our quest for meaning. Science deals with what it can quantify. The Scriptures, however, are into pre-history. They tell us who we are, what we are here for, and where we are going. They tell us that it was God who gave us life and spirit, and His promises are worth trusting.

FEBRUARY 20TH

'. . . and spirit to those who walk on it.' Isaiah 42: 5.

I believe that there is no such thing as an 'ordinary' person. Every individual has a uniqueness that makes him or her different. When God creates a person, He gives that person 'spirit'. The spirit of a person is a very difficult thing to define; but we do speak of people being 'spirited'. By that, we mean they are brave, or gallant, or bold, or firm and resolute, or intrepid. We speak of the essence of a person's character: temperament, manner, capability, or mood. As an adjective it means, 'that which is derived from within': that which is subjective, intrinsic, instinctive, indigenous, 'in the grain,' 'in the blood,' 'at the core.'

Our very idea of style has to do with the 'spirit' of a person. We speak of people being natural, homespun, blunt, straightforward or flamboyant, cerebral, or practical. The 'spirit' of a person is even defined by his or her activity. We say a person is vivacious or lethargic; patient or restless; thoughtful or interfering – a busybody, and a meddler. We speak of people plodding on, persevering, taking pains. 'That person does not let the grass grow under his feet,' we say. 'He puts his best foot forward,' we comment; or, 'she sticks at nothing.' While some are described as those who 'make things hum,' others are described as 'dull.'

With all my heart, I believe that a person is not defined by what he or she 'does,' but by what they are. If my mind is fed and dominated by the world, the flesh, and the devil, then it will show in my spirit. I will be intolerant, restless, irritable, skittish, reckless, selfish and unhappy. If, on the other hand, I am feeding my mind on the things of God, it will show in my spirit. There will be love, joy, peace, longsuffering, goodness, gentleness and meekness. In truth, what I feed my mind on will show in a thousand ways. It will even show by the look in my eye and the tone of my voice. Sow to the Spirit, and reap the Spirit; sow to the flesh, and reap the flesh. Keep on making the right decisions, and the blessings from your life will be incalculable.

Recently in Belfast, where I live, I was privileged to attend a Christmas Carol Service for the Royal National Institute for the Deaf. I was so moved as I watched hands signing out the language of those brave-spirited people. It was truly the most meaningful Christmas Carol Service I have ever attended. Those deaf people were so joyous and animated. They proved to me that one does not need to speak words in order to praise God, or to communicate spirited greetings and a sense of community. One of them even portrayed a book with her hands and, with a beam on her face, pointed at me. It sent me back to my writing with an inch to my step, and encouraged me to dip my pen even deeper into the ink for the Lord. Thank God for such an encouraging spirit. May you and I be such today.

FEBRUARY 21ST

"I, the Lord, have called You in righteousness, and will hold Your hand; I will keep You and give You as a covenant to the people, as a light to the Gentiles." Isaiah 42:6.

What, then, is the promise made by the great Creator? It is that He has got a very special work for the Lord Jesus, His perfect Servant. Israel, the imperfect servant, broke the covenant God gave to her; but this perfect Servant will bring in a new and better Covenant, that will bring light to the Gentiles. Through His life, and His once-and-for-all sacrifice, the Saviour introduced the New Covenant, and opened up a new and living way to the very heart of God: '. . . we have been sanctified through the offering of the body of Jesus Christ once for all' (Hebrews 10:10).

There are many differences between the Old and New Covenants. The Old Covenant was a two-party covenant: its blessings depended on what you did. If you obeyed God, then your children were healthy, your crops flourished, etc. If not, you suffered; and God could walk away (see Hebrews 8:8-9). The New Covenant does not depend on what we do, but on what God does. God will fulfil all His promised terms, as He said He would. The New Covenant is not written on stone, but on people's hearts and minds. By the new birth He gives us new hearts and minds. Now we want to do God's will and obey His laws, not just out of a sense of duty but willingly, from the very heart of our new nature. By the New Covenant, we will come to know God directly and personally, not just know about Him. We do not have to qualify for this knowledge, but the New Covenant is promised to us as a free gift through the Holy Spirit (see Galatians 4:6).

To know a Covenant-keeping God, is a truly wonderful experience; but what about the final clause to this New Covenant? It is nothing less than the total and full forgiveness of sins: 'For I will be merciful to their unrighteousness, and their sins and their iniquities will I remember no more' (Hebrews 8:12 AV). Does this set us free to do as we like? No! It sets us free to do as God likes. Recognised in this covenant is our capacity for failure, even when God's law is written on our hearts and minds. Yet, even when we fail, God will not walk away, as He was entitled to do under the Old Covenant. He assures us that, if we have trusted Christ as Saviour, we are completely forgiven. In that knowledge, then, let us go on in our Christian lives to become more holy and Christ-like. And who promises all this? "I, the Lord," says today's text. Onward, Christian, onward!

FEBRUARY 22ND

"To open blind eyes, to bring out prisoners from the prison, those who sit in darkness from the prison house." Isaiah 42:7.

L et us think about an amazing day right at the beginning of Christ's public ministry. 'He came to Nazareth, where He had been brought up. And as His custom was, He went into the synagogue on the Sabbath day, and stood up to read. And He was handed the book of the prophet Isaiah' (Luke 4:16,17). He immediately turned to the passage you and I are studying. He read it, sat down, and declared, "Today this Scripture is fulfilled in your hearing." He was, in fact, declaring that He was the Messiah. So audacious was that claim to these people, that they '. . . were filled with wrath, and rose up and thrust Him out of the city; and they led Him to the brow of the hill on which their city was built, that they might throw Him down over the cliff. Then passing through the midst of them, He went His way' (Luke 4:29, 30).

Obviously Christ believed that, amongst other things, His awesome mission was 'to open blind eyes, to bring out prisoners from the prison, those who sit in darkness from the prison house.' But this means a lot more than mere physical sight, which Christ did give; or the release of all prisoners from the prisons in the world. It sums up the beautiful message of the gospel. Listen to Paul, brought before King Agrippa, speaking of his mission in life. He told him how Christ had met him on the Damascus road, and told him, 'I will deliver you from the Jewish people, as well as from the Gentiles, to whom I now send you, to open their eyes, in order to turn them from darkness to light, and from the power of Satan to God that they may receive forgiveness of sins and an inheritance among those who are sanctified by faith in Me' (Acts 26:17-18).

So the gospel brings people out from spiritual darkness into spiritual light. The gospel also releases people who are captives to lust, to love of money, to pride, envy, and jealousy, to bigotry, and the kinds of sin triggered and dominated by Satan and his power. It brings forgiveness of sins and a discharge from every penalty.

The primary application of the promise in today's text, then, is in regard to our Lord Jesus. The second application is to all who serve the Lord Jesus. By Christ's power, we can bring spiritual light to those who are in spiritual darkness around us; and we can certainly bring liberty to those who are captives to sin and Satan. So, Christian, let the gospel loose through your lips today. Light and liberty will change lives, like you could never dream of.

FEBRUARY 23RD

"I am the Lord, that is My name; and My glory I will not give to another, nor My praise to carved images." Isaiah 42: 8.

There was a writer, whose Saturday column in *The Times* of London, I used to follow with deep interest. His name was John Diamond. Under huge stress, having crippling cancer, he continued to write fascinating prose. John was a Jew, but confessed that he had a problem with God. He felt it was egotistical of God to want everyone to worship Him. I asked my daughter, Kerrie, what she thought about John's problem, and she quietly answered that she felt John was looking at it from an earthly standpoint. She was right!

God spoke to Moses from a heavenly standpoint. In Egypt, Israel had got far removed from God, and many Israelites were worshipping other gods. In fact, they had got so far away from God, they no longer knew His name! Moses asked the Lord a penetrating question. 'Then Moses said to God, "Indeed, when I come to the children of Israel and say to them, 'The God of your fathers has sent me to you,' and they say to me, 'What is His name?' what shall I say to them?" (Exodus 3:13). Imagine a people being so far away from the God of their fathers! 'And God said to Moses . . . "Thus you shall say to the children of Israel 'I AM has sent me to you'" (v.14).

This means, of course, that God never had a beginning. He is self-existent. Try to work it out from an earthly standpoint, and your mind will reel! "This is My name forever," God told Moses (v.15). God is immutable: He does not get weaker or stronger; He does not grow older; He never loses any power He once had; He does not mature. God is eternally changeless: 'with whom there is no variation or shadow due to change' (James 1:17). His views do not change; His words stand forever; He never amends anything He says. When the great 'I AM' puts His name to a promise, all will be well – this is the guarantee of all guarantees! And it is the same with His Son: 'Jesus Christ is the same, yesterday, today and forever' (Hebrews 13:8).

Did not David, the shepherd, write of the Lord, his Shepherd, as One who made him to lie down in green pastures, who led him beside the still waters, who restored his soul, and led him in the paths of righteousness? Why? For His name's sake! In other words, if the Lord does not make His sheep to lie down in green pastures, lead them beside still waters, restore their souls and lead them in the paths of righteousness, then His good name will be undermined, and its guarantee exposed as a fake. All the gods of earth are fakes! The great 'I AM' will not share His glory with another, for any other would sully it. His glory is incommunicable.

"Behold, the former things have come to pass, and new things I declare; before they spring forth I tell you of them." Isaiah 42:9.

Has God ever predicted something that did not come to pass? Has God ever promised something on which He did not deliver? Ever? As you face your future, take huge comfort from today's text, because God's Word is dependable at all times. The prophet looks back, and traces the predictions of God as they actually unfold. Then he predicts the coming Messiah, God's perfect Servant and His work, as new things that would 'spring forth.'

Here we have the beautiful topic of the Timing of God. Do not underestimate it! Few in Nazareth would have seen the hand of God at work, as Mary and Joseph headed out of that obscure place to take part in a census at Bethlehem, ordered by the Roman Emperor, Augustus. Apart from a few shepherds, some wise men from the East, and those they shared it with, few knew of the birth of Jesus Christ. As a spring leads to a river, that leads to the ocean, the living God of history brought that Child to birth, which led to His public ministry, which led to the crucifixion and resurrection, which led to the forming of the church, which now awaits the Second Coming, which will eventually lead to an unimaginable future. Incredible? Isaiah writes of it: "For behold, I create new heavens and a new earth; And the former shall not be remembered or come to mind. But be glad and rejoice forever in what I create" (Isaiah 65:17).

God's timing brought Haman to the court of King Ahasuerus, at the very moment the king discovered that Mordecai had done him great service. Haman was coming to suggest to the King that Mordecai be hung. In fact, Haman had already raised a gallows, fifty cubits high; but Mordecai, God's man, was promoted to great eminence, and Haman ended up on the gallows.

God's timing brought Philip the evangelist from Samaria to a desert place where, riding in his chariot, an outstanding Ethiopian was reading from Isaiah. 'Then the Spirit said to Philip, "Go near and overtake this chariot"' (Acts 8:29). So Philip ran; but remember if he hadn't run, he would have arrived at the wrong verse!

God's timing brought Jesus to the tree in which Zacchaeus sat; to the woman at the well; and to the grave of Lazarus. Lazarus' sisters thought that His timing was wrong, but Mary and Martha found that not only had Christ power over disease, but that He had power over death. God's delays always have a reason. Twice, God said 'No' to Paul. He wanted to preach the gospel, first in Asia, and then in Bithynia; but God wanted him to bring the gospel to the Continent of Europe (see Acts 16:6-10). Imagine, God actually stopped a man preaching the gospel in one place, so that he could preach it in another!

Are you restless? Are you frustrated? Is there no sign of God in your circumstances? Does His timing not suit yours? "What's wrong?" a friend asked Philip Brookes, when he found him pacing up and down. "I'm in a hurry, but God isn't!" he replied. Be glad that God's ways are not our ways, His thoughts are not our thoughts; and His perfect timing is not our constantly-bungled timing.

Sing to the Lord a new song, and His praise from the ends of the earth, you who go down to the sea, and all that is in it, you coastlands and you inhabitants of them! Let the wilderness and its cities lift up their voice, the villages that Kedar inhabits. Let the inhabitants of Sela sing, let them shout from the top of the mountains. Let them give glory to the Lord, and declare His praise in the coastlands. Isaiah 42:10-12.

With the declaration of such stupendous truths, Isaiah can't help singing! With such a God doing such wonderful things, his heart and soul burst into praise. This is a new song, responding to the new things God has announced He will do. The whole earth is invited to join in the song. Here sailors join with nomads; villagers with city dwellers. From the coastlands at sea level, to the mountain tops, from the islands of the sea to the deserts of Arabia and Moab, praise is called forth for the announcement of the Messiah.

This song has a very different tone to the songs sung to the gods of earth. In Romans 8:21 we read that in a coming day 'the creation itself also will be delivered from the bondage of corruption into the glorious liberty of the children of God.' This passage of Scripture is certainly pointing to the future day; but the fact of the coming of the Lord Jesus and all He has accomplished, is already a cause for singing.

However, I am reminded of the church at Ephesus: "I have this against you," the Lord said, "that you have left your first love" (Revelation 2:4). What was wrong? Dr G. C. Morgan once commented that the Lord no longer heard the song of the Ephesian Christians, 'at the unusual hour.' The church gathers to sing God's praise together. This is what is expected, it is usual. They always do it at a given hour. But for the Lord to hear a song of praise to His name at an unusual hour, now there is something very special!

As you iron those clothes, dig in the garden, drive your car, lie on your bed, walk in the forest, rock that baby to sleep, gather in the harvest, ride the escalator, you can hum that chorus of praise, or raise that hymn of thanksgiving. It's when you 'leave your first love,' that the Lord no longer hears you praise Him at the unusual hour. He misses it! It is an indicator that your love has cooled, that your fire is burning low. Get back to your first love this very day. Don't be icily regular, but glow once more at the unusual hour.

The Lord shall go forth like a mighty man: He shall stir up His zeal like a man of war. He shall cry out, yes, shout aloud; He shall prevail against His enemies. Isaiah 42:13.

This verse appears to be a contradiction to what Isaiah said earlier (42:2), where he stated that the Messiah 'will not cry out, nor raise His voice, nor cause His voice to be heard in the street.' W. E. Vine points out, 'the verbs rendered, "cry," are different. The first has to do with His people, the second with His enemies. The first indicates His gentleness and kindness, and the absence of self-advertising, noisy, demonstration. The second is His voice as a Conqueror, "the voice of the Lord," by which the foes of God are to be overthrown at the end of the age.'

The subject of the wrath of God is taboo in most of Western society; but it certainly is not taboo in the Bible. The Bible writers have absolutely no inhibitions about it. They show that it is never cruel, but always judicial. They show that the recipients of God's wrath get precisely what they deserve. People have a choice. 'But in accordance with your hardness and your impenitent heart you are treasuring up for yourself wrath in the day of wrath and revelation of the righteous judgment of God, who will render to each according to his deeds,' writes Paul in Romans 2:5. They can choose to follow the light God gives them, to lead them to Himself; or they can retreat from it. 'This is the judgment,' says John 3:19, 'that the light is come into the world, and men loved the darkness rather than the light; for their works were evil' (RV). The judgment that the enemies of God receive, is a judgment they call on themselves. This entails the full implication of the choice they make. The age of grace offers the gospel to rebels, but it will not last forever – 'The Lord shall go forth like a mighty warrior.' (Notice that in the synagogue Jesus stopped his reading of Isaiah 61:2, just before the mention of the declaration of the coming day of vengeance.)

The cry of the Conqueror will be heard (see Jeremiah 25:30). Following His Second Coming, the One who used Cyrus for the defeat of Babylon, will one day ride out of heaven and conquer His enemies in wrath (see Revelation 19:11-21). On His robe is written, 'King of Kings and Lord of Lords.' It is great news that now we can be justified by the blood of the Lord Jesus, and saved from wrath through Him (see Romans 5:9). To be justified is to be forgiven, to be accepted as righteous. How? Through faith in the Lord Jesus. The choice is ours.

FEBRUARY 27TH

"I have held My peace a long time, I have been still and restrained Myself. Now I will cry like a woman in labour, I will pant and gasp at once." Isaiah 42:14.

I s there a more difficult thing to understand than the silence of God? In this modern day we are used to getting things instantly. If a fax machine slows up, or an Email is proving truculent, we grumble. We forget that in days gone by, passing information across the earth could take a long time – sometimes weeks, months, even years. When God remains silent, though, and there is no instant answer from Him, it is hard to understand what is happening.

Have you been devastated by some tragedy in your life, and there is no obvious purpose to it? You may even wonder if God is against you. Like Job, you ask, "Have I sinned? What have I done to You, O watcher of men? Why have you set me as Your target, so that I am a burden to myself?" (Job 7:20).

Be sure of this, believer: God is not against you. He may have been silent, but silently He has been working out a purpose. In today's text, God is speaking about His purposes for the Gentiles. He has deliberately restrained Himself over many centuries of time; but like the growing of a baby in the womb now coming to birth, so His purposes eventually brought the Messiah, the Saviour, into the world.

In the 266 days from conception to birth, the single fertilized egg becomes a staggering complex organism of 200 million cells, having increased its original weight one billion-fold! As in the birth of a child, so God has been guarding the seed of the woman through the Jewish race, to bring a light not to them only, but also to the Gentiles.

Like a woman crying out and panting in childbirth, so God has feelings. He has felt the pains of His people; and though they thought He had forgotten them, the opposite was the case. Now His feelings are revealed. His self-imposed silence had caused Him pain. He is the all-feeling God. Now He will speak.

So, in this great passage of Scripture, there are two powerful points of comfort. One is that God is working out a purpose in our lives; and the other is that He has felt the pain over His self-imposed silences, every bit as much as we have. If you doubt it, just meditate on His Perfect Servant in the Garden of Gethsemane, and you will have your doubts removed.

FEBRUARY 28TH

"I will lay waste the mountains and hills, and dry up all their vegetation; I will make the rivers coastlands, and I will dry up the pools. I will bring the blind by a way they did not know; I will lead them in paths they have not known. I will make darkness light before them, and crooked places straight. These things I will do for them, and not forsake them. They shall be turned back, they shall be greatly ashamed, who trust in carved images, who say to the moulded images, 'You are our gods.'" Isaiah 42:15-17.

Looking at these verses, in the wider context of the gospel coming through the Messiah, they are saying that things are going to change completely. The things that sustained God's people in the past will pass away; and under a new Covenant a new and better way will come. The 'terrain' will change; the 'vegetation' and 'water supply' will be different. The spiritually blind will be led into a new, unknown way, by paths they have never walked. Darkness will become light. Crooked places will be made straight. People who once trusted in false gods will be ashamed that ever they did.

Let this beautiful verse remind you of the power of the gospel. It is true that the old order has passed. 'For you are all sons of God through faith in Christ Jesus. For as many of you as were baptised into Christ have put on Christ. There is neither Jew nor Greek, there is neither slave nor free, there is neither male nor female; for you are all one in Christ Jesus' (Galatians 3:28). The rich panoply of the Old Testament Tabernacle and all it contained, spoke in minute and graphic detail of the coming One. After His death and Resurrection, every Christian would be a priest as part of a new body, the church; and the long-hidden mystery would be gloriously revealed. It would all come about through the declaration of the gospel of the perfect Servant. The change from the ritual of the temple and synagogue to Christian worship, would be as big a change as a transformed landscape and environment.

As we go through this year, let us remember that the gospel can change the landscape of people's lives, not only a pattern of worship. People who once looked for their sustenance to drugs, money, academia, or social status of one kind or another, can find a new, lasting source of satisfaction. That source is the Lord Jesus. All around us are people who are bitterly disappointed with the gods they have worshipped. I have never, ever, met anyone who was disappointed with the Lord Jesus. Have you? Tell folks about Him; some of them will thank you eternally.

FEBRUARY 29TH

"Hear, you deaf; and look, you blind, that you may see." Isaiah 42:18.

There is huge encouragement in this little verse. It is speaking of the spiritually deaf and blind Gentile people. In a future day, they will hear, and they will see. God's perfect Servant, the Messiah, will bring this about. On one occasion, after Jesus had healed a man by the pool of Bethesda, He said something truly astounding. "Most assuredly, I say to you, he who hears My word and believes in Him who sent Me has everlasting life, and shall not come into judgment, but has passed from death into life. Most assuredly, I say to you, the hour is coming, and now is, when the dead will hear the voice of the Son of God: and those who hear will live" (John 5:24-25).

How can dead people hear? This is the miracle of the gospel of Jesus Christ. People who are spiritually dead (those who have not the slightest interest in worshipping God or in obeying His Word) can hear the gospel, and be quickened by the Spirit, convicted of their need, and become believers. That person who works in the office beside you, the farmer on the next farm, that fellow-student in your tutorial, that son or daughter of yours, your teacher – perhaps they all show no interest in the things of God. Though spiritually dead, all of them can become spiritually alive through a word of gospel witness. Notice that Jesus did not say, 'those that live shall hear,' but 'those that hear shall live'. There is a glorious difference! Through the power of the gospel, the dead and deaf shall hear, the blind shall see.

So, don't be discouraged by the spiritual deadness of people around you. Don't give up your witness for Christ. Even years after your witness, the Lord can use it to bring about spiritual life. It's a miracle that happens all the time, all over the world. However, speaking to the spiritually dead and deaf can be a very discouraging business! I know, for I often do it, and sometimes feel like a fool. The world, the flesh, and the devil have voices that millions love. There is an offence in preaching the message of the Cross. 'For the message of the cross is foolishness to those who are perishing, but to us who are being saved it is the power of God' (1 Corinthians 1:18). So, keep going, discouraged one! Some of those spiritually dead and deaf will hear you, and live!

March

This photograph shows long fibres of line-flax. In earlier times line flax was made into fine yarns on hand wheels on farms by 'spinsters'. This followed the process of stooking, retting, breaking, scutching and hackling. The Bible tells us that 'Samuel ministered before the Lord, even as a child, wearing a linen ephod.'

MARCH 1ST

"Who is blind but My servant, or deaf as My messenger whom I send? Who is blind as he who is perfect, and blind as the Lord's servant?" Isaiah 42:19.

In the immediate context, the spiritually blind and spiritually deaf Gentile world is asked to look at Israel, God's servant. Sadly, there is no spiritual illumination, for Israel is but the blind leading the blind. Only Israel's Messiah will ultimately lead the Gentiles to spiritual light. The nation whom God had sent as His messenger, specifically given the great honour and duty of bringing God's truth to a darkened world, had failed.

Is there any more penetrating question in all of the Scriptures than, "Who is blind but my servant . . .?" It wasn't that they never had any light. They had been given plenty. In his final great speech to Israel, Moses lamented, "He found him in a desert land, and in the wasteland, a howling wilderness; He encircled him, He instructed him, He kept him as the apple of His eye . . . so the Lord alone led him, and there was no foreign god with him . . ." "but," said Moses, " . . you have forgotten the God who fathered you" (Deuteronomy 32:10,12,18). Now Isaiah speaks out against the foolishness of Israel. These stubborn people had been given the privilege of 'seeing many things,' but Israel did not observe. These people had had their ears opened, but they did not hear.

The old song is accurate, when it says that there is none so blind as one who will not see. The Lord Jesus made a famous statement, explaining that 'the sons of this world are . . . wiser than the sons of light' (Luke 16:8). What did He mean? He meant that, with an opportunity staring them in the face, the sons of this world will take it and use it to their advantage; but those who follow Him often see an opportunity, and for reasons of laziness, stubbornness, or downright disobedience, they do not follow through to spiritual and eternal advantage. He had just told the story of the shrewd manager who, knowing that he would soon lose his job, had spent the interim making himself some friends to have after he was redundant. He was commended for his shrewdness.

So, in the service of God, Jesus urges us not to use the privileges and possessions we have as an end in themselves. Let us not waste them, for they are only on loan. Let us use them to God's glory and we will find ensuing eternal advantages.

MARCH 2ND

The Lord is well pleased for His righteousness' sake; He will exalt the law and make it honourable. But this is a people robbed and plundered; all of them are snared in holes, and they are hidden in prison houses; they are for prey and no one delivers for plunder, and no one says, "Restore!" Isaiah 42:21-22.

Here we have a huge contrast between the law, and Israel to whom God revealed it. God exalted His law and was well pleased with it, for it revealed His righteous character. There was, of course, only one who fulfilled it perfectly, and that was the Lord Jesus. He delighted to do God's will, and God's law was in His heart. There was not one detail of the law that Christ did not fulfil. He also took the full weight of the law on the cross, when He died in our place. 'For He made Him who knew no sin to be sin for us, that we might become the righteousness of God in Him' (2 Corinthians 5:21).

However, the people who were to uphold that law often failed to do so, and they were to reap the results of that failure. They were to be snared in holes, hidden in prison houses; they were to become prey and plunder. Great expectations were to tumble into misery.

It reminds me of a visit I once made to a park in the highlands of Scotland. There on display was an eagle in a cage. Meant to soar and glide effortlessly at altitudes of over 2,000 feet, it was a pathetic sight. Here was a bird, that could dive at speeds of up to 200 miles per hour, hopelessly entrapped. No matter how furiously he might beat his wings, tear with his beak, clutch with his talons, the azure blue was no longer his habitat. A caged eagle looks the saddest of birds.

Trappers, putting out 'easy fish,' often entrap eagles. We all love something for nothing, but everything has its price. The bird is lured by the pattern of free fish being set out by the trappers, and then, having accepted the structure as part of the established order, one day he finds he is no match for a trap once it has sprung. Neither are we. Let this passage of Scripture, which is filled with deep sadness, be a warning to us. Instead of upholding the glorious teaching of God's Word, we too, like Israel, can be trapped by the easy ways of the world that does not make the demands of us that God does. We too can become cowed victims, trapped in a cage, licking our wounds, when we should be soaring for God.

MARCH 3RD

Who among you will give ear to this? Who will listen and hear for the time to come? Who gave Jacob for plunder, and Israel to the robbers? Was it not the Lord, He against whom we have sinned? For they would not walk in His ways, nor were they obedient to His law. Isaiah 42:23-24.

Isaiah is truly a faithful prophet. He powerfully addresses Israel with some questions, which they will find both penetrating and challenging. He is asking them if there is any one of them who will be moved and exercised as to who is behind their circumstances. There is a hand, which brought about the circumstances that had led to them being robbed, plundered, snared and empowered. He had always warned Israel that if they did not obey Him there would be serious consequences, but they did not obey Him or listen to what He had said. Nobody was interested in asking the simple question, "Who?" They could not see the hand of God in it all. Nor could they hear His voice in their circumstances.

It is a dreadful thing to become insensitive to the voice of God. In my experience I have found that, when God speaks, He speaks clearly. We cannot make the excuse that we have not heard; yet we walk away from His call and refuse to listen to His voice in our circumstances. A great fish had to vomit Jonah on to a beach before he really listened to the word of God, calling him to minister to the people of Nineveh. An earthquake, a fire, and then a still small voice found Elijah cowering in a cave at Horeb. "What are you doing here, Elijah?"

God asked (1 Kings 19:13). The emphasis was on the word 'You.' It took a vision from God, and a straight word from Paul, before Peter understood that God wanted him to stop communicating the gospel to the Jews only! How many times did God have to speak in the temple, before the disobedient Eli realised that the Lord was calling the little boy, Samuel? And it took quite a time before the two on the way to Emmaus recognised that the Stranger explaining the Scriptures to them was God incarnate.

Somewhere today, in your circumstances, God will speak to you. Be ready to listen. He will be saying something important that will guide you in your walk with Him. Let the Holy Spirit use part of today's text to speak to you. It is a question: "Who will listen and hear for the time to come?"

MARCH 4TH

Therefore He has poured on him the fury of His anger and the strength of battle; it has set him on fire all around, yet he did not know; and it burned him, yet he did not take it to heart. Isaiah 42:25.

The anger of the Lord was poured out against Israel for her disobedience. History rolled across her, bringing war, deprivation, suffering and loss. It eventually led to exile. Let us remember that God is not impatient to act in His severity. He is, in fact, 'slow to anger' (see Nehemiah 9:17; Psalm 103:8; 145:8; Joel 2:13; Jonah 4:2), and 'longsuffering' (see Exodus 34:6; Numbers 14:18; Psalm 86:15). It appears that God even waited 120 years for the disobedient people of Noah's day to repent (see 1 Peter 3:20; Genesis 6:3). God is willing that all should come to repentance (2 Peter 3:9). But Israel did not repent, so the fury of God's anger fell on her.

Yet, incredibly, even with the fire of war raging around them, these people did not 'get it.' It even burned them, but neither their mind nor heart was touched by the realisation that God was trying to bring them to repentance and blessing. The servant of God was blind and deaf, and unmoved by the punishment of the Lord.

Let us apply this verse to our lives. We are not being punished for our sins: that was dealt with at Calvary. But the Lord chastens us from time to time. It was the great Christian leader, George Whitefield, who spoke of God putting 'thorns in your bed.' Do not despise Him for doing it. His purpose is to awaken you to a wrong direction you have taken, which will lead you to grief and disappointment if you stubbornly continue. 'My son,' says the Book of Proverbs, 'do not despise the chastening of the Lord, nor be discouraged when you are rebuked by Him; for whom the Lord loves He chastens, and scourges every son whom He receives' (Proverbs 3:11-12). 'No chastening,' says the Book of Hebrews, 'seems to be joyful for the present, but painful; nevertheless, afterward it yields the peaceable fruit of righteousness to those who have been trained by it' (12:11). Do you find those 'thorns in your bed' painful? God is educating you, and if you are teachable those 'thorns' will lead you to a better way, a greater future, and a harvest of righteousness in your life. Please, please do not miss the handsome harvest that can and will be yours if you are an educable Christian.

March 5th

But now, thus says the Lord, who created you, O Jacob, and He who formed you, O Israel: "Fear not, for I have redeemed you; I have called you by your name; you are Mine." Isaiah 41:1.

If ever there was a word of comfort, this is it! The Lord turns from His anger to consolation. Israel has received double for all her sins, her warfare is ended, her iniquity is pardoned, and she is now to receive comfort. 'But now, thus says the Lord' – and we hold our breath to hear a final word which may lead to Israel being wiped out by the Almighty. But no; it does not come. They have been punished, but there is a tie between them and the living God that His fingers have tied. He created them, He formed them, and He has a purpose for them. He knows what He is doing.

There follows some of the most tender, comforting, encouraging, and moving words that God has ever spoken to His people. "Fear not!" says God. It seems a trite word in the face of all they were experiencing. They had every reason to be afraid; but notice that God's call for them to be without fear is valid. The reason for the call is based, first, upon the supernatural act in His predetermined council to create and form them; secondly, by His redeeming power that brought them out of Egypt. All through their existence, God insists that at all times He regards these people as His redeemed possession. Notice what God thought of the sons of Korah, when they insisted that the redeemed were not special, and they rebelled against the whole concept (see Numbers chapter 16).

The third reason for this call is based upon the fact that He has called them by name. "You are mine," He says. This is no mere, mundane act; it is something that brings delight to God's heart. Any parent knows the feeling behind this. If a parent heard the name of an injured child belonging to their neighbour, being read out on the media, they would be touched and moved. If, though, they heard the name of their own child being read out, they would be touched and moved in a very different way. Why? Because that child is their own. Creation, redemption, and a personal relationship, are all good reasons for God's people not to be afraid.

And you, too, Christian, as part of the church, grafted into the vine that is Israel, have the same reason not to be afraid. We are 'created in Christ Jesus,' 'redeemed through His blood,' and 'called by name.' Really? – called by name? Certainly! Speaking of Himself as the Good Shepherd, Jesus said, 'He calls His own sheep by name and leads them out' (John 10:3). What stopped Mary Magdalene in her tracks, as she turned away from the supposed gardener at Christ's tomb? "Mary!" He said. That was all, but it was enough! The sheep knew the Shepherd's voice, and she fell at His feet and worshipped Him; and then went to tell the world the good news.

March 6th

"When you pass through the waters, I will be with you; and through the rivers, they shall not overflow you . . ." Isaiah 43:2a.

I once preached at the Baptist Church in Port St. Mary on the Isle of Man, and afterwards an older lady approached me. She said something that I have long remembered. "If Christians led charmed lives," she commented, "then people would become Christians in order to lead charmed lives." God does not tell His people that, in their pilgrimage to the Celestial City, they will never pass through deep waters. Notice that the verse does not say 'if' you pass through the waters and rivers, but 'when.' It is inevitable that we will face all kinds of trouble in our lives. Like rising waters, trouble often threatens to overflow us. We feel we are going to be in over our heads and swept away by its force.

The promise in this verse is that, no matter how threatening the water, it will not overflow us. We will not be spared 'out' of the rising water, but 'in' it. The hand that held the sinking Peter is as strong as ever it was. The Children of Israel passed through the Red Sea and the Jordan, and we will pass through the troubled waters of our circumstances. Sorrow, illness, war, whispering campaigns, tragedy, the wickedness of muggers and thieves, the horror of desertion by a wife or husband, the fickleness of the crowd, the dirty tricks of politics, the heartlessness of the critic, the bantering sarcasm of the light-headed, the collapse of a business: on and on troubles rise around us, but even death itself cannot wipe us out. We have the highest Friend in the Universe: we are accepted in Him, and we have nothing to fear. "I will be with you," He said.

The famous writer, Thomas Carlyle, born in Ecclefechan in Scotland, once told how his father had taken him on his back across a river in spey. They crossed safely, but he made the comment that if it had been his mother carrying him, she would have carried him face-to-face. If the Lord has not come, when the time comes to cross the final river of death, I like to think that I will be carried face-to-face across its freezing, dark, and daunting waters. Selah.

March 7th

" . . . when you walk through the fire, you shall not be burned, nor shall the flame scorch you." Isaiah 43:2b.

Trials – we all face them. Yet they are good for us! They will not consume us. 'You have been grieved by various trials,' wrote Peter, 'that the genuineness of your faith, being much more precious than gold that perishes, though it is tested by fire, may be found to praise, honour, and glory at the revelation of Jesus Christ' (1 Peter 1:6,7).

Bring your mind forward, from the time of Israel's trial of fire at Babylon and her subsequent deliverance, to the time when Nebuchadnezzar cast Daniel's three friends into the fiery furnace. We are told that they 'fell down bound into the midst of the burning fiery furnace,' and that a fourth figure, described by Nebuchadnezzar as 'like the son of God,' walked with them in the fire. When they came out of the fire, 'the hair of their head was not singed nor were their garments affected, and the smell of fire was not on them.'

It is worth noting, though, what Nebuchadnezzar asked his counsellors: 'Did we not cast three men bound into the midst of the fire?' 'True, O king,' they answered. 'Look!' he answered, 'I see four men, loose, walking in the midst of the fire.' Loose? Of course! That's what your trials do for you. God allows them to loosen you from that which binds you.

Trials, when they are finished, yield the gold of freedom. What price, freedom? The price of trial! We are stronger as a result; we are kinder; we are easier to live with; we are less critical; we are less impressed by the phrase, 'You need to know key-people.' Now we would rather say, 'All you need to know is the One who holds the key.'

Show me a believer who has come through trial, and I will show you ability without instability, attractiveness without vanity, cheerfulness without lightness, gift without lording, courage without rough-handling. I will also show you someone who has learned not to wait for some great occasion, but who seeks now, by God's grace, to make every occasion great.

MARCH 8TH

"For I am the Lord your God, the Holy One of Israel, your Saviour; I gave Egypt for your ransom, Ethiopia and Seba in your place. Since you were precious in my sight, you have been honoured, and I have loved you; therefore I will give men for you, and people for your life." Isaiah 43:3-4.

This is a remarkable prediction: given as if it had already happened. When the Hebrew people returned from captivity in Babylon, God rewarded Cyrus (the Persian king who allowed them to go home), by permitting him and his son, Cambyses, to possess Egypt (including Seba, which lay between the White and Blue Nile). Ethiopia too was part of the 'kopher,' or, price that was paid. In fact, God valued Israel so much that He was willing to give nations for them. With the whole world at His disposal, it is not an exaggeration to say that, if necessary, He would have given the whole world for them. These people were precious, honoured, and loved, even though they had behaved abominably.

When we compare God's love for Israel with His love for the world, it could be put this way: He was prepared to give the world for Israel; but He was prepared to give His own Son for the world (see John 3:16). The ransom was not to be paid in nations, but in Christ's own blood.

I shall long remember a visit I once made to Edinburgh castle. There, in a glass case, I saw the crown of Scotland. A tall custodian stood by the case, and innocently I asked him how much it was worth. I was surprised when he turned on me quite indignantly. "How much is it worth?! Three thousand men died in one day to put that crown on the head of Robert the Bruce," he said. "If you are willing to put a price on human blood, you are welcome to try. That crown is priceless." I came down the Royal Mile in Edinburgh thinking long thoughts!

If human blood is priceless, what value will we put on the blood of Christ? No wonder we call it precious. Not all the treasures of Egypt – and they are considerable; nor all the wealth of Ethiopia, combined with any other nation we could think of, could ever pay the ransom we owed for the debt of sin. We are redeemed, 'not with corruptible things, like silver or gold . . . but with the precious blood of Christ, as of a lamb without blemish and without spot' (1 Peter 1:18, 19). If any proof were needed, that we are valued, loved, and honoured by God, this would surely be enough. So, walk today in the conscious knowledge of that love.

"Fear not, for I am with you; I will bring your descendants from the east, and gather you from the west; I will say to the north, 'Give them up!' and to the south, 'Do not keep them back!' Bring My sons from afar, and my daughters from the ends of the earth."
Isaiah 43: 5-7.

It is always wise to take a long look at the far-reaching purposes of God. What God decided before the world was created, is not going to be abandoned by Him; like we do, when some whim makes us abandon something we set our hearts on. God chose Israel, created her for His own glory, formed her, and called her by His name. God's purposes for her are not abandoned, even though, because of disobedience, she is scattered worldwide, and looks as if she is no longer a people. Today's verse tells us that God can re-gather His people from the four corners of the earth and bring them home. God can, and will, compel nations to give up His sons and daughters. The power that scattered is the same power that can restore; be it from Babylon or Moscow.

The promise to re-gather is to 'everyone who is called by My name.' The grace of God will not be thwarted. Wherever they are found when Christ returns, 'the dead in Christ will rise first. Then we who are alive and remain shall be caught up together with them in the clouds to meet the Lord in the air. And thus we shall always be with the Lord' (1 Thessalonians 4:16-17). It is understandable, then, that Paul adds, 'Therefore comfort one another with these words.'

"Fear not!" says God through Isaiah: He shall re-gather His people from exile. "Comfort one another," says God through Paul: He shall raise the dead in Christ, and the remaining Christians shall be caught up into the air with them. The purposes of God, decided in 'eternity past,' shall be fulfilled to the letter. No problem is too complex, no country too far away, no circumstance too narrow, no person or persons too intimidating, no barrier too high, for God not to be able to fulfil His purposes for you. As F. B. Meyer put it, 'Read the whole book; step back and consider the perspective; get a glimpse of the mighty roots that moor the slight tree of thy life.' The God who first made Israel, was able to get her out of Babylon and home to Jerusalem. He will get you out of the corner that you are in, too, and fulfil His purposes for your life. Fear not!

Bring out the blind people who have eyes, and the deaf who have ears. Let all the nations be gathered together, and let the people be assembled. Who among them can declare this, and show us former things? Let them bring out their witnesses, that they may be justified; or let them hear and say, "It is truth." Isaiah 43:8-9.

We are back in the courtroom. God calls out the blind and deaf as witnesses. But this time it is not the false gods of wood and stone, who are called 'blind' and 'deaf.' It is God's people! They had ears, of course, but they would not hear; and they had eyes, but they would not see. Their obstinacy was deliberate. Will the Lord's case be made to look ridiculous because of them? No! Standing before the assembled nations of the world, even these people can witness to the truth. The truth to which they can witness is God's ability to predetermine events, speak of His intention before the events happen, and then carry them out perfectly.

We can all take heart from this text. Thinking of the witness of the church in this present age, who among us has not failed in the service of the Lord? Having heard His word, have we not at times come miserably short of obeying it? Having seen spiritual reality (Ephesians 1:18), who has not deliberately lived for the immediate and the transient, without keeping a constant eye on the eternal? Who has not allowed the 'Vesuvius' in us to erupt, said the hasty word, and then pined for the occasion to return, so that this time we could give a gentle response? The Christian has never lived, who has not felt himself or herself to be, at best, a flawed witness.

But do these failures mean that God will never use us to be a witness for Him? If that were so, Peter would never have been used on the Day of Pentecost. David would never have become 'the sweet psalmist of Israel.' Paul would never have been used to spread the gospel across Europe. Jonah would never have been sent to tell Nineveh to repent. Moses would never have been able to witness to the hard-hearted Pharaoh. Solomon would never have been allowed to have his Proverbs published. Samson would never have achieved the fulfilment of God's purposes for him. And, make no mistake, Samson did fulfil his ministry (see Judges 13:5; 16:30). Despite their heated disagreement, both Barnabas and Saul went on to have fruitful ministries. Despite our failures to be rôle models, we can all point to the perfect Rôle Model, our Lord Jesus Christ. There is no flaw in Him. Deliberately blind and deaf as we often are, it is of great comfort to know that we are still His witnesses. In spite of our failures, by His grace He can still use us. Even today.

MARCH 11TH

"You are My witnesses," says the Lord, "and My servant whom I have chosen, that you may know and believe Me, and understand that I am He. Before Me there was no God formed, nor shall there be after Me. I, even I, am the Lord, and besides Me there is no Saviour." Isaiah 43:10-11.

Imagine witnesses needing a prod! Chosen by God to know, believe, and understand that God is the One who carries through on all his predictions, Israel needs to be prodded to say so! Before the assembled nations, they still seem to be reticent to declare the attributes of Deity. So much so, that God Himself declares them; and they are awesome indeed! God was not formed by anyone. He never had a beginning. He will never have an end, and no one will succeed Him. From His very first involvement with humankind, He has been a saviour. The theme of the saving Lamb of God runs through Scripture as a blood-red line: from Abel's offering (Genesis 4:10), to the Lamb as it had been slain, in the midst of Heaven (Revelation 5:6). But His chosen people had to be reminded and prodded to declare Him.

Why are we so reticent to speak? I remember travelling with a man in a railway carriage from Glasgow to Aberdeen. I felt a deep urge to witness to him of Christ, but was extremely reticent to do so. Eventually I was just beginning to get around to it, when he took a heart attack right in front of my eyes. I ran to find help, and watched as he was carried off the train on a stretcher to hospital. That night my conscience pricked me. With the help of a friend, the next day I searched until I found the man. And this time, I witnessed.

Is God prodding you to speak up for Him in your office, where He is often, perhaps, the butt of derision? Maybe you are being asked to speak up in the media, where gospel truth is often on the scaffold? It could be that God is prodding you to write songs to His praise, that would then soar over the airwaves of the world? Or it could simply be that He is prodding you to come out of your silent corner, and speak to your children of His deeds, past and present, and of His declarations about the future. I had a mother who did this in our home, and without her witness I reckon I would not be writing this book today. Speak up, Christian; please speak up! We need to hear your witness. The world needs to hear it. 'Let the redeemed of the Lord say so' (Psalm 107:2).

MARCH 12ᵀᴴ

"I have declared and saved, I have proclaimed, and there was no foreign god among you; therefore you are My witnesses," says the Lord, "that I am God." Isaiah 43:12.

I f we are going to be witnesses to God, then we must have confidence in Him. As a friend of mine used to put it, "Does your God <u>do</u> anything?" Grasp the meaning of the statement in today's text: God says, "I have declared (or revealed) . . . saved . . . proclaimed." At the burning bush, long before the redemption of Israel from Egypt, God told Moses exactly what He was going to do. Then God saved His people from their bondage, and through Moses He declared what He had done, and why He had done it. No foreign god had done this.

Only an hour ago I was in a shop, and a lady said to me, "I believe we all pray to the same God." I pointed out to her that in Japan there are 30 million gods. "Don't confuse me," she said, with a smile. Only the Lord reveals, redeems, and then expounds what He has done. He did it in Egypt. Through Isaiah He tells Israel that He is going to do it in Babylon; and, supremely, of course, He promised to do it in the Lord Jesus. Has He done as He said He would?

A few days ago I sat in a classroom in Northern Ireland with a friend of mine, whose life had once been filled with incredible hatred. He had been deeply involved in terrorism in this land and had been in prison for his crimes. I quizzed him about his life, and the lies that the Devil had sown, which had brought a horrendously frightening harvest. He spoke of how he used to wake up in the mornings drenched with sweat. Since he had come to know the Lord Jesus, now he wakes up in the mornings with peace in his heart. I asked him about the hatred in his heart, particularly against others of a different persuasion to himself. That hatred had gone. I found, in effect, a man whose name had been 'Legion,' sitting, clothed, and in his right mind, with Christian joy written all over his face!

As we sought to witness for Christ to those young people in the Religious Instruction class in that school, the girls burst into applause for my friend. There, sitting in their classroom, the young people could see the evidence before their very eyes. What was the basis for our witness? God had done something in my friend's life that He had said He would do (see Isaiah 53:5). For Israel, He did something that the New Testament Scriptures explain (see Acts 7:17-36). Of course, the very existence of Israel is a witness in itself. It is actually one of the reasons why I believe in the one, true and living, God.

MARCH 13TH

"Indeed before the day was, I am He; and there is no one who can deliver out of My hand; I work, and who will reverse it?" Isaiah 43:13.

Here is a truth to brighten your day. We have seen how God declares that He will do something, He does it, and then He explains and expounds what it is that He has done. Now God asks who will reverse His work. It is a wholesome question to consider.

Satan has certainly tried to reverse God's work. Introducing sin, he caused the fall of humankind. It all looked so impossible, but the Saviour came and faced Satan at Calvary. Something happened that day which began a process that will lead to a new earth (see Romans 8:18-25). But is that not a reversal of God's creation? Peter tells us, 'the elements will melt with fervent heat; both the earth and the works that are in it will be burned up' (2 Peter 3:10). The sceptic will say, 'There you are, the earth will be burned up; so God was defeated, His work has been reversed.'

My friend, Professor David Gooding, once pointed out to me that one might burn a table, but the atoms of the table will remain. There will be something of the old earth in the new earth; else why would it be called a 'new earth'? God's work will not be defeated, when it comes to our bodies either. There will be a day when we get new bodies (see 1 Corinthians 15:42-58). Just because we get new bodies, that does not mean there is nothing of the old in the new; else why would they be called 'bodies'? It is because of this truth that I believe we shall know one another in heaven. 'Then,' says 1 Corinthians 13:12, 'I shall know just as also I am known.' Satan will not have the final word.

Has God done a work in your life? Has He opened a door for you? His word says that no person can shut it. Are you saved by God's grace? Then remember that the Scriptures say, 'No one is able to snatch you out of My Father's hand' (John 10:29). Got it? Isaiah says it in his prophecy; Christ said it when He was here on earth, so why should you doubt it? Heartening, isn't it?

MARCH 14TH

Thus says the Lord, your redeemer, the Holy One of Israel: "For your sake I will send to Babylon, and bring them all down as fugitives – the Chaldeans, who rejoice in their ships. I am the Lord, your Holy One, the Creator of Israel, your King." Isaiah 43:14.

Part of the population of this great city were Chaldeans. They navigated the great river Euphrates, that flowed through Babylon into the Persian Gulf. Using ships built by the Phoenicians, the Chaldeans navigated the Euphrates and the Gulf in time of war, and also for commerce. They loved their ships: they 'rejoiced' in them, says Isaiah.

The Lord now makes a prophecy. He says He will bring judgment to the Chaldeans; and those who had rejoiced in their ships would now use them as a means of escape. The Chaldeans would become refugees. Let us be careful about what we glory in. Babylonians gloried in their Navy, and many another nation has done the same. Let us never forget that regimes and empires pass, and with them their weapons of war. Only our Redeemer, the Holy One, remains unchanged.

It may not be a Navy in which you glory, but some social circle in which you move, some material thing you possess, some achievement you have experienced. It is so easy to be proud of something, to look at it, to trust in it, and then to find that it does not deliver on what it promised; to find that it is transitory. To trust in the Lord will never cause you to blush. He will see you through the toughest times, and you will not be disappointed.

There is a section of Hebrews 11 that speaks of Abraham going out from Ur of the Chaldees, at the call of God. He did not trust in the gods of the Chaldeans, or have pride in their culture. He trusted in the Lord. Hebrews 11 says of such people, 'And truly if they had called to mind that country from which they had come out, they would have had opportunity to return. But now they desire a better, that is a heavenly country. Therefore God is not ashamed to be called their God, for He has prepared a city for them' (Hebrews 11:15-16).

Imagine Abraham, in heaven, and being disappointed. Imagine him giving up all that he did, and then finding that the end result simply was not worth it. Hebrews 11 is teaching that, if such a thing were to happen, then God would be ashamed. Abraham was not disappointed. Nor will any who live by faith. In fact, the end result of their faith will be even greater than they imagine. Note that today's text highlights the personal relationship of God to His people: 'your Holy One . . . your King.' Believer, rest on the fact that your God will not be ashamed that what He promised will not be delivered. Never! Ever!

MARCH 15TH

Thus says the Lord, who makes a way in the sea and a path through the mighty waters, who brings forth the chariot and horse, the army and the power (they shall lie down together, they shall not rise; they are extinguished, they are quenched like a wick) . . .
Isaiah 43:16, 17.

So, you face insuperable odds? Mountainous seas of unexpected trouble rise on your horizon, and you are frightened. People criticise you, misunderstand you, gossip about you, and even despise you. You got up this morning, and said in your heart, 'There is no way out of this; I'm finished.' No, you are not! God is about to do new things for you: things you never dreamt would happen. You are going to be used by Him in places you never thought possible. You will go to new places, you will meet new people. There will be new opportunities for God to display His grace, His power, and His love, through you. He has awesome ability to turn situations around, to bring the possible out of the seemingly impossible. You see a difficulty in every opportunity, but He sees an opportunity in every difficulty. He has started a process of redemption in your life, and He will not be stopping it because of the aggression of any opposing force, no matter how strong.

To bolster our faith, He reminds us of what He did with Israel at the Red Sea. The sea in front of them was made into 'a way.' Let that be a word from God for you today. The waters of the Red Sea piled up like a wall to Israel's left and right, and a path of dry land was formed in the midst of the sea. The thing that seemed to bar progress, was made into a path for progress. Understand it, and understand it well: the thing you fear most will be the very thing that will be used to take you forward. It will be made into 'a way.' The mighty power of Egypt, based on chariots, horses, and army, did not find the sea to be 'a way.' They found it to be a place of death. They thought they could tread the same path as Israel with immunity, but in trying to do so they were drowned. The God who did not quench the 'smouldering flax' that was His people, quenched their enemy, 'like a wick.'

Grasp it, then. That person who hurts you will become 'a way' to advance your maturity. The seeming disaster in your business, that was not of your making, will lead you through doors of opportunity, and provide greater scope for your gifts. Whether it is a sea in front and an enemy behind, or you between the Devil and deep Red Sea, God will make a way for you.

MARCH 16TH

"Do not remember the former things, nor consider the things of old. Behold, I will do a new thing, now it shall spring forth; shall you not know it? I will even make a road in the wilderness and rivers in the desert." Isaiah 43:18-19.

God is full of surprises! As at Creation He did new things on each new day, so throughout history He has been doing new things. Here, a new Exodus is being promised to Israel. God is not tied to the past. As He leads His people to new days, He is to act in the new circumstances in a fresh way. In the first Exodus, the waters of the Red Sea parted. In the new Exodus, He is to make 'rivers in the desert.' Different circumstances, different methods, the same God.

It is so easy to be tied to the past, even, at times, to live in it. The 'old days' are often looked upon as being so much better than the present. At the building of the new temple, we are told that the old men wept and the young men rejoiced. Why do we often feel that the 'old days' were better than what God is doing now, or will do in the future? It is because we idealise them and are being unrealistic about them. In truth, there were just as many obstacles to be overcome then, as the present or future days will present. As God brought us through the past, He will bring us through what we face now. God is not planning your past; He is planning your future.

Notice God's instruction to His people: "Do not remember the former things, nor consider the things of old." He is warning them not to keep going over their past, but to turn their eyes to the new thing that He is doing. He is challenging them to move on. Depending on which direction they took, the journey home to Jerusalem could be up on 900 miles. It would be quite an undertaking, but God would be as faithful to them as ever He had been. They must stop 'hanging their harps on willows' by the rivers of Babylon, and go forward with God.

Is this God's word to you today? Are you stuck in your past? Come on! Embrace what the Lord is doing in you and through you right now. Move on with God. The new thing is springing up in front of you. Shall you not experience it? You won't, if you don't act. It will mean change; it will be an exercise of faith; but it will lead you to a new thing that will be every bit as touched and blessed by God as anything in your former days. Paul could have stayed and watched the sunsets at Miletus; but he told the elders there, "See, now I go bound in the spirit to Jerusalem, not knowing the things that will happen to me there, except that the Holy Spirit testifies in every city, saying that chains and tribulations await me. But none of these things move me; nor do I count my life dear to myself, so that I might finish my race with joy" (Acts 20:22-24). He moved on, and the rest is incredible spiritual history.

The new thing before you may involve tough times, but be sure that in it there will be indescribable joy. It is better to endure the tribulations of God's new thing and have His joy, than to try to work up old joys that are past, and miss it.

MARCH 17TH

"The beast of the field will honour Me, the jackals and the ostriches, because I give waters in the wilderness and rivers in the desert, to give drink to My people, My chosen."
Isaiah 43:20.

There will come a day when the Lord will reign over a restored world, and 'the wolf also shall dwell with the lamb, the leopard shall lie down with the young goat. The calf and the young lion and the fatling together; and a little child shall lead them. The cow and the bear shall graze; their young ones shall lie down together; and the lion shall eat straw like the ox. The nursing child shall play by the cobra's hole, and the weaned child shall put his hand in the viper's den. They shall not hurt nor destroy in all My holy mountain, for the earth shall be full of the knowledge of the Lord as the waters cover the sea' (Isaiah 11:6-9).

This future day is pointed to in today's text. Obviously, it is a day when the law of the jungle is reversed. Can God do it today, or is this process only to be seen in the future? This question is answered by the story given in Daniel chapter 6. For his faithfulness in prayer, Daniel is thrown into a den of lions. 'Then a stone was brought and laid on the mouth of the den, and the king sealed it with his own signet ring and with the signets of his lords, that the purpose concerning Daniel might not be changed' (Daniel 6:17). And was it changed? Early next morning, the king rushed to the door to see if Daniel's God had been able to deliver him from the lions. To the king's shock and amazement, Daniel answered, "My God sent His angel and shut the lions' mouths, so that they have not hurt me." The law of the jungle had been reversed! Hungry lions, that normally would have devoured a human being, found that their instinct was changed. Even an animal can unwittingly give honour to God.

Once Jesus said to two of His disciples, "Go into the village opposite you; and as soon as you have entered it you will find a colt tied, on which no one has sat. Loose it and bring it. And if anyone says to you, 'Why are you doing this?' say, 'The Lord has need of it,' and immediately he will send it here" (Mark 11:2-3). And Jesus taught that no sparrow falls to the ground without the Lord's knowledge. If animals can, and do, unconsciously honour Him – how about you, His chosen one, consciously doing it today? Somewhere in your talk or actions today, make a conscious effort to honour God.

MARCH 18TH

"This people I have formed for Myself; they shall declare My praise. But you have not called upon Me, O Jacob; and you have been weary of me, O Israel." Isaiah 43:21-22.

It was Lowell, who said, "To the spirit select there is no choice. He cannot say, 'This will I do, or that.' A hand is stretched to him from out the dark, which grasping without question, he is led where there is work that he must do for God." What did he mean? He certainly did not mean that you and I have no choice in whether or not we respond to God's will for us. We can walk away from it, but it is God who chooses the work for us to do. He will make it very clear what that work is, and if we walk away our loss is incalculable.

Three times Israel deliberately walked way. They murmured against God in the wilderness, and were sent back to wander in the wilderness for 40 years. After they entered the Promised Land, 19 kings ruled over them before they were exiled for around 70 years to Babylon. After they rejected the Messiah, they have been scattered to the ends of the earth. But, as a people, they will yet be saved (see Romans 9:27).

Today's texts are piercing. Israel was formed by the Divine potter for Himself, to declare His praise, and to attract people to His beauty and power, so that they, too, might know Him. But, instead of praising God, Israel came close to cursing Him. Instead of leading people to a deeper appreciation of God, they gave a false conception of His character by their attitude and behaviour. They were prayerless, and grew weary of God. Imagine, they were tired of God!

In this age of the church of Jesus Christ, exactly who forms that church? Peter tells us that we are, '. . . a chosen generation, a royal priesthood, a holy nation, His own special people, that you may proclaim the praises of Him who called you out of darkness into His marvellous light; who once were not a people but are now the people of God, who had not obtained mercy but now have obtained mercy' (1 Peter 2: 9-10).

The piercing question is: are we fulfilling God's purposes for us, or are we preventing Him from getting the results for which He saved us? When the Lord comes to me looking for fruit, does He find me unfruitful? (See Titus 3:14.) Wouldn't it be dreadful to have had my silent heart redeemed, my tongue untied to express His praise, and for me to remain silent?

One day, as Christ came into Jerusalem on a colt, 'the whole multitude of the disciples began to rejoice and praise God with a loud voice for all the mighty works they had seen.' The Pharisees got very annoyed, and called to Him from the crowd, "Teacher, rebuke your disciples." 'But Jesus answered and said to them, "I will tell you that if those should keep silent, the stones would immediately cry out."' Selah.

March 19th

"You have not brought Me the sheep for your burnt offerings, nor have you honoured Me with your sacrifices. I have not caused you to serve with grain offerings, nor wearied you with incense." Isaiah 43:23.

God is probing deeply into the very heart and nature of Israel's worship. These people begrudged things being given to God. They wanted a cheap religion. Matthew Henry comments, 'They had not brought, no, not their small cattle, the lambs and the kids, which God required for burnt offerings, much less did they bring their greater cattle.' He had not asked expensive sacrifices from them, but they were stingy even with what was required. The Lord delighted in these sacrifices. Indeed, they were a 'sweet savour' to Him, and brought Him satisfaction; but not if they were given by a tight-fisted people. These people did not care to delight the heart of God.

The saying goes, 'There was a man, they called him mad; the more he gave, the more he had.' A generous spirit is a beautiful thing to observe. Big heartedness is long remembered. When someone dies, what is it that you fondly remember about him or her? Their bank balance? The car they drove? The places they went on holiday? The academic degrees they had? How many clothes they had in their wardrobe? Often, the thing that springs to mind is some act of kindness. "He was good to me," is a phrase that is often repeated. Or, "she once wrote me a comforting letter;" "he visited me in hospital;" "when I was at my lowest point, she encouraged me." Big heartedness is remembered with delight and appreciation; a mean spirit, with disgust.

Is God good? Yes! Is He good all the time? Yes! He is the God of all grace. In all their teachings, the religions of the world have nothing like it. You can do nothing more to make Him love you more; and nothing less to make Him love you less. There is no stinginess in His character. Did He not show us awesome kindness in the gift of His Son? There never was a more expensive gift. Why, then, should we be close-fisted with God? If He asks for something, give it to Him. If God asks you for spoonfuls, you will find that He will give you back shovelfuls. Jim Elliot was right, when he said, 'he is no fool who gives what he cannot keep, to gain what he cannot lose.'

March 20th

"You have bought Me no sweet cane with money, nor have you satisfied Me with the fat of your sacrifices . . ." Isaiah 43:24a.

'Also take for yourself quality spices – five hundred shekels of liquid myrrh, half as much sweet-smelling cinnamon (two hundred and fifty shekels), two hundred and fifty shekels of sweet-smelling cane, five hundred shekels of cassia, according to the shekel of the sanctuary, and a hin of olive oil. And you shall make from these holy anointing oil, an ointment compounded according to the art of the perfumer. It shall be a holy anointing oil' (Exodus 30:23-25).

The holy anointing oil of Exodus 30 was to be poured out on the sacred things within the Tabernacle, and it must have had a beautiful smell. In fact, the law said, 'Whoever compounds any like it . . . shall be cut off from his people' (v.33). In the ingredients of that spicy, perfumed oil, was two hundred and fifty shekels' worth of sweet-smelling cane. Reckoned to be sweet calmus, it was a very important ingredient in the anointing oil, and it was to be poured on Aaron and his sons, who were to serve as priests. But the people brought God no sweet smelling cane. There was, generally, a great lack of sweetness in their worship.

Did not Judas think that Mary's pound of very costly spikenard, poured out on the feet of Jesus, was wasted? He certainly did, and protested about it. But Jesus said, "Let her alone; she has kept this for the day of My burial." What did He mean? At burials in the Middle East, spices were used to take away the stench of death. Mary had sat at Jesus' feet, and heard Him tell of His resurrection. She believed Him, and knew that He would not need the spices at His burial; so she gave it to Him while He was living! Including His disciples, of all the entourage around Jesus, Mary of Bethany was the only one who believed Him! She poured out her spikenard for sheer love of Him. She begrudged Him nothing. What about you?

MARCH 21ST

" . . . but you have burdened Me with your sins, you have wearied me with your iniquities. I, even I, am He who blots out your transgressions for My own sake; and I will not remember your sins." Isaiah 43: 24-25.

The gospel lies at the heart of today's texts. There is no gospel like it anywhere, or in any era. Here is the living God, burdened with His people's sins, and His patience exhausted. As the bitter fruit of the seeds of sin that they have sown, they have been exiled to Babylon. God is weary of their iniquities and their lawless perversity. Could any situation be darker? "You have not called upon me," says God, ". . . you have not brought me the sheep for your burnt offerings nor honoured me with your sacrifices . . . you have brought me no sweet cane with money." It is a very miserable predicament: a sinful people, and a burdened, weary God.

Suddenly, right into the darkness, comes the light of the gospel. The light that exposes is the light that saves! "I, even I, am He who blots out your transgressions for My own sake; and I will not remember your sins." The only explanation for this incredible action is that God says He does it for His own sake! We do not merit such blessing, any more than Israel did. It comes from the very heart of God, and originates with Him alone. It is the mystery of grace: love stooping to show kindness and favour to one who does not deserve it, and can never earn it. It is a many-splendoured thing.

Today's text points to Calvary, where God in Christ took on the burden of human guilt. How heavy was it? Incalculably heavy! The wrath that we deserved from God, fell on God Himself, and our transgressions were blotted out. Our sins can never be brought up against us: '. . . by His wounds we are healed' (Isaiah 53:5).

Tell me, Christian, are you enjoying this grace? Are you full of its contagious joy, or are you full of rigidity and dullness? If God has forgiven your sins, and set you free from any accusation that could take away your freedom (see Romans 8:31-39), are you enjoying your condition, or enduring it? Is this 'new life in Christ Jesus' grim, or glorious? Leave 'the rivers of Babylon' behind you: you are on your way to the heavenly Zion. 'For you have not come to the mountain that may not be touched, and that burned with fire, and to blackness of darkness and tempest, and the sound of a trumpet and the voice of words, so that those who heard it begged that the word should not be spoken to them anymore . . . but . . to Jesus the mediator of the new covenant, and to the blood of sprinkling that speaks better things than that of Abel' says Hebrews 12:18-24. Come on, grim-face, cheer up!

MARCH 22ND

"Put Me in remembrance; let us contend together; state your case, that you may be acquitted. Your first father sinned, and your mediators have transgressed against Me. Therefore I will profane the princes of the sanctuary; I will give Jacob to the curse, and Israel to reproaches." Isaiah 43:26-28.

We are back in the courtroom again. God calls on Israel to remind Him if they have any merit that might acquit them. He takes them back to Adam, their first father, and finds that he sinned. Adam believed the lie of Satan, that he would be as God. Many people who follow 'New Age' thinking today, believe themselves to be divine; but it is not really 'New Age' teaching, it is 'Old Age' teaching. It is as old as the Garden of Eden! What, then, of Israel's history? Is there any merit in their mediators? The word 'mediators' implies their spokesmen in each generation.

I have often counselled people whose lives are marked, even wrecked, with sin. With downcast eye and broken spirit, they feel there is no hope for them. I remind them that the Bible is full of stories of people just like themselves. As this courtroom reviews Israel's spokesmen, they look in vain for one who is faultless.

What of Noah, who preached righteousness for 120 years? Once he was found in a very embarrassing drunken state. What of Abraham, the father of their nation? He lied, and had to be thrown out of Egypt by Pharaoh. What of Moses? He was one of the greatest leaders in history; but, because of bad temper, he was refused entrance to the Promised Land. What of Joshua, Moses' successor? See him at Ai, falling to the ground in unbelief. What of the great judges who were raised to correct Israel's backsliding? Gideon set up an ephod and led Israel into idolatry. What of Jephthah? He made a tragically rash vow. What of Samson? He carelessly fooled around, wasting his gift. What of the High Priest, Eli? God chose to tell State secrets to a little boy rather than to Israel's High Priest, because of the disastrous state of Eli's leadership. As Eli's daughter-in-law was dying in childbirth, she renamed her child Ichabod, meaning, 'the glory has departed from Israel.'

What of Saul, Israel's king? He disobeyed the Lord's command, and the kingship was given to his neighbour, David. And what of David himself, the wonderfully gifted musician, writer, and leader? His sins had a devastating effect on his family and the nation. And Solomon, the wisest representative Israel ever had? 'Then Solomon built a high place for Chemosh the abomination of Moab, on the hill that is east of Jerusalem, and for Molech the abomination of the people of Ammon. And he did likewise for all his foreign wives, who burned incense and sacrificed to their gods. So the Lord became angry with Solomon, because his heart had turned from the Lord God of Israel' (1 Kings 11:7-9).

Were the prophets perfect? No! What was Elijah doing, cowering in a cave at Horeb, far from his sphere of ministry? On and on, it was a tale of failure and sin. Israel did not have a spokesman who was able to disprove that the verdict they are given is justified. As a nation, they are disqualified and discredited. 'Jacob' does not deserve pardon, but a divine curse.

So, failed and sinful one, like me, you are not alone in deserving God's wrath. Yet, as we are about to see, we can know complete and absolute forgiveness!

MARCH 23RD

"Yet hear now, O Jacob My servant, and Israel whom I have chosen. Thus says the Lord who made you and formed you from the womb, who will help you: 'Fear not, O Jacob My servant; and you, Jeshurun, whom I have chosen.'" Isaiah 44:1-2.

Fear not? Why? Condemned rightly and justly out of court and by history, why should Israel not fear? Certainly, she has every right to fear. Yet there is an unassailable truth that she must learn. God meant it, when He said that Israel would declare His praise. Our text tells us that God had formed Israel from the womb to be His servant; and His purpose will not be reversed, even by their gross sin. God still calls Israel 'Jeshurun,' meaning, 'beloved.' It is a term of endearment (see Deuteronomy 33:26).

There is a great challenge to all of us in this section of Isaiah's prophecy. As believers, we can co-operate with God's purposes for our lives, and know His strength for each task; His blessing along each winding turn, and joy in it all. Or we can be obstinate, full of complaints, and incur His discipline. He will accomplish His purposes with these people; but it will be at an enormous cost to them. It will be the same with us.

So, tell me, are you co-operating? Ever since you have tasted of Christ, you know in your heart that you are spoiled for the world. So, why are you courting it? Did the world ever give you the peace that the Lord Jesus has given you? Why try to have a foot in both camps? It will not work; in the end no one but Christ can satisfy. Obstinacy will lead you to heartache and wasted years. It led Israel to wander for 40 years in the wilderness. If only she had obeyed, she would have known possession of a land flowing with milk and honey. She would not have been trouble-free; but she would have been free to serve God in and through her troubles, and to know sweet victory.

So, Christian, yield to God's ways with you. Repent, and He will blot out your transgressions: your past sins will not be raised against you. God will do things with you as great and greater than ever He did with you in the past. Would it not be better to let God have His way with you and accomplish His will easily, than to have it accomplished through severe discipline? Yield!

MARCH 24TH

"For I will pour water on him who is thirsty, and floods on the dry ground; I will pour My

Spirit on your descendants, and My blessing on your offspring; they will spring up among the grass like willows by the watercourses." Isaiah 44:3-4.

Don't you love this word, 'pour'? The Holy Spirit gives of Himself to God's people. Who is He? He is God. He is personal. He is holy, eternal, omnipotent, omniscient, omnipresent, and able to be blasphemed against. In Scripture He is described as being like wind, breath, fire, oil, a dove, and a guarantee. He authenticates, comforts, empowers, counsels, leads, indwells, and prays. He strengthens, removes fear, assures, instructs, and fills.

In today's text He is described as being like water poured out on a thirsty land. Its benefits are clearly seen: grass grows, and willows spring up by the watercourses. Authorities consider that the willows mentioned here belong to the true willows of Israel, of which there are four species. It is a fast growing tree, found in moist places and on the margins of rivers and streams.

Here we have cause and effect. The water is poured out, and up comes beautiful, luscious growth. So it is with the Holy Spirit. He cannot give of Himself to a person and that person not be aware of the benefits. The fruit in a person's life of the outpouring of the Spirit is: love, joy, peace, longsuffering, kindness, goodness, faithfulness, gentleness, and self-control. I like the way Peterson's translation of Galatians 5:22-23 puts it: 'He brings gifts into our lives, much the same way that fruit appears in an orchard – things like affection for others, exuberance about life, serenity. We develop a willingness to stick with things, a sense of compassion in the heart, and a conviction that a basic holiness permeates things and people. We find ourselves involved in loyal commitments, not needing to force our way in life, able to marshal and direct our energies wisely.'

Let us never forget that there are other, very different, fruits from another source. 'For the flesh lusts against the Spirit, and the Spirit against the flesh: and these are contrary to one another' (Galatians 5:17). The works of the flesh are very different. 'It is obvious what kind of life develops out of trying to get our own way all the time: repetitive, loveless, cheap sex; a stinking accumulation of mental and emotional garbage; frenzied and joyless grabs for happiness; trinket gods; magic-show religion; paranoid loneliness; cut-throat competition; all-consuming yet never-satisfied wants; a brutal temper; an impotence to love or be loved; divided homes and divided lives; small-minded and lopsided pursuits; the vicious habit of depersonalising everyone into a rival; uncontrolled and uncontrollable addictions; ugly parodies of community. I could go on.' (Galatians 5:19-21, Peterson's translation).

Which fruit would you rather have? The fruit of the Spirit for sure! Then let's remember the advice of Scripture: 'Walk in the Spirit, and you shall not fulfil the lust of the flesh' (Galatians 5:16).

MARCH 25TH

"One will say, 'I am the Lord's'; another will call himself by the name of Jacob; another will write with his hand, 'The Lord's,' and name himself by the name of Israel."
Isaiah 44:5.

76

Another result of the outpouring of the Spirit of God is a new identity. People suddenly see who they really are. In Israel's case, they personally reclaim four names. David McKenna helpfully divides them: 1. A spiritual name: 'I am the Lord's.' The Spirit-filled person is not ashamed to tell everyone who he or she worships and serves. 2. A parental name: they reclaim the name of their father, 'Jacob.' They are not ashamed to show that they have a history. Joseph was not ashamed before Pharaoh of Jacob his father, even though shepherds were despised by the Egyptians; and so these people are not ashamed of one of the great fathers of their nation. 3. A relational name: these Spirit-touched people love 'the Lord.' In the context of this time, we understand that a young lover would write the name of the one he or she loved on the palm of their hand with indelible ink. It is a touching image of an Israelite, opening the palm of his or her hand and revealing the Lord's name written there. 4. A national name, 'Israel.' Their national identity is reclaimed: they are God's chosen people.

As Christians, can we not draw inspiration from this beautiful verse? Of course we can! Where do you plan to go this month? Where will you travel? What will you see? What do you hope to accomplish? All our movements have importance and significance in the eyes of God. Will we own that we are the Lord's, in all that we do? When our 'hand is opened,' will it be revealed that we are in a deep love-relationship with the Lord? To further apply the image: will that insignia be indelible, or easily washed off? Said Paul to the Corinthians, 'You are Christ's . . .' (1 Corinthians 3:23); but, by the way they behaved at the Lord's Supper, you would never have thought so. He told the Galatians: 'If you are Christ's, then you are Abraham's seed, and heirs according to the promise' (Galatians 3:29). So, let's show who we really are; but be sure to take heed to Paul's warning to Timothy: 'Let everyone who names the name of Christ depart from iniquity' (2 Timothy 2:19).

MARCH 26TH

"Thus says the Lord, the King of Israel, and his Redeemer, the Lord of hosts: 'I am the First and I am the Last; besides Me there is no God. And who can proclaim as I do? Then let him declare it and set it in order for Me, since I appointed the ancient people. And the things that are coming and shall come, let them show these to them.'" Isaiah 44:6-7.

I don't know what you are facing today. It may be the worst day of your life; or it may be one of the very best. These verses are saying that God is in the detail of your life. Don't be saying, 'the Devil is in the detail.' It is God who knows everything from the beginning of history to the end. His is the hand behind history, moving it according to His purposes. He is working it out for good. I once put this truth into a little poem. Let me share it with you.

Just as he was having his toughest day,
And Goliath was coming with a lot to say,
And Israel was silent; come what may,
God was working it out for good!

Just as they thought it would never come,
And thick walls surrounded Babylon,
And the people of God were sick for home,
God was working it out for good!

Just when the times were dark and dread,
And the Assyrian hosts by a fiend were led,
The angel moved, and the foe lay dead:
God was working it out for good!

Just when they thought their case was lost
They heard a knock, and said, 'It's a ghost.'
But Peter arrived when they needed him most:
God was working it out for good!

Just stop today and bow your knee,
Though you're fit to scream and ready to flee.
Lift your heart to Him and say with me,
God is working it out for good!

MARCH 27TH

"'Do not fear, nor be afraid; have I not told you from that time, and declared it? You are My witnesses. Is there a God besides Me? Indeed there is no other Rock; I know not one.'" Isaiah 44:8.

Here God gives Himself another name. For the fourth time, He calls upon Israel, 'Do not fear nor be afraid.' Why shouldn't they fear? Because He is their 'Rock.' If God says He does not know of any other Rock that can be compared to Him, be assured there isn't one! What does this name tell us about God? It tells us that He is an unchanging place of refuge. These Israelites lived in an unmechanised world, of primitive agricultural tools and transport. You might drive a car, use a mobile phone, Email your friends, jet to any destination; but the God they went to for refuge in their troubles is the very same God whom you serve. Their Rock is your Rock.

Today, as you turn to God in prayer, try to remember that, when you drive down the highway with the fast lane surging past, your God is the very same God that Moses turned to in the wilderness centuries ago. The God to whom you pour out your heart, is the very same God to whom Hannah prayed in her distress. "O Lord of hosts, if You will indeed look on the affliction of Your maidservant," she vowed, "and remember me and not forget Your maid-servant, but will give your maidservant a male child, then I will give him to the Lord all the days of his life . . ." (1 Samuel 1:11). Eli saw it differently. One translation puts his reaction to Hannah's praying as, "How long will you go on, you drunken creature? Away with you, go and sleep off your drunkenness" (v.14). But Hannah did not flinch. Why? Even though a storm of accusation raged around her, she had been hiding in the 'Rock of Ages.' So she gave him a gentle answer, and, says Scripture, 'the woman went her way and ate, and her face was no longer sad' (v.18).

On the day that the Lord delivered David from the hand of Saul, he spoke to the Lord in the words of this song; 'I will love you, O Lord, my strength. The Lord is my rock and my fortress and my deliverer; my God, my strength, in whom I will trust . . .' (Psalm 18:1-2). And Isaiah wrote, 'A man will be as a hiding place from the wind, and a cover from the tempest, as rivers of water in a dry place, as the shadow of a great rock in a weary land' (Isaiah 32:2). Notice the different conditions: wind, tempest, driving rain, or burning heat. In every kind of condition, in every age and generation, the Lord is the place of refuge.

I think of Francis Ashbury, the great Christian leader of a past generation. He received an abusive anonymous letter. In his journal he wrote about it with these words: "I came from my knees to receive the letter, and having read it I returned whence I came." Good to have such a refuge, isn't it? Are you hassled, misunderstood, frightened, confused, anxious, petrified, and in despair? Run for it! To the 'Rock in a weary land!' Rest, and be refreshed under its awesome shadow.

March 28th

Those who make an image, all of them are useless, and their precious things shall not profit; they are their own witnesses; they neither see nor know, that they may be ashamed.
Isaiah 44:9.

Imagine considering something to be precious; and in the end it has no true profit whatsoever. Millions of people do just that. Idol-makers produce their useless idols; and they eventually have to hide their faces in shame, knowing very well that the gods they create cannot do anything. Yet millions worship these gods, believing them to be of great value, when in fact they are valueless.

At the time of writing, I have been visiting schools across the island where I live, addressing hundreds of young people about their dreams and ambitions. I have been speaking about a book which I have written, *A Voice Full of Money: The Parable of the Great Gatsby*, in which I applied the Scriptures to the moral and ethical themes raised by F. Scott Fitzgerald in his novel, *The Great Gatsby*. It is an evocative novel, in which Fitzgerald looks at the United States in the 1920's, as people gave themselves to the god of hedonism. The central character, Jay Gatsby, goes after a dream that does not deliver on what it promises. It is a hauntingly sad novel, and all the more because it reflects Fitzgerald's own life. At the end of the novel there is a very well known paragraph, one of the most famous in American fiction. In fact, Bill Gates has a quotation from it etched on to the portico of his house. Basically, it states that all of our dreams elude us, because we are like boats beating against the current, being borne back ceaselessly into the past.

But this is a hopeless view of life and eternity. It is not unlike the sad epitaph which John Keats asked to be inscribed upon his grave in the Protestant Cemetery in Rome: 'Here lies one whose name was writ in water.' After her experience of hedonism, Marie Antoinette said, "Nothing tastes." Fitzgerald knew only too well the emptiness of the hedonism which millions were chasing. And in today's text, the ancient prophet, Isaiah, said that all the gods of earth will bring no true profit.

Compare the hopelessness that Fitzgerald is speaking about, with what the Lord Jesus says: "I am come that they might have life, and that they might have it more abundantly" (John 10:10). What did He mean? He meant that we may have more life than we can handle! Meditate on these promises of Christ: "I am the living bread which came down from Heaven. If anyone eats of this bread, he will live forever . . ." (John 6:51). "Whoever drinks of this water will thirst again, but whoever drinks of the water that I shall give him will never thirst. But the water that I shall give him will become in him a fountain of water springing up into everlasting life" (John 4:13,14). "Come to Me, all you who labour and are heavy laden, and I will give you rest. Take My yoke upon you and learn from Me, for I am gentle and lowly in heart, and you will find rest for your souls. For My yoke is easy and my burden is light" (Matthew 11:28-30).

So, bring the gods of this world out into the open, and compare them with the living Lord. Sell your soul to them and, should you should gain the whole world, you will profit nothing. Trust, worship, and follow Christ, and you will have something better than gold, land, fame, or fortune. You will have something beyond price.

MARCH 29TH

Who would form a god or mould an image that profits him nothing? Surely all his companions would be ashamed; and the workmen, they are mere men. Let them all be gathered together, let them stand up; yet they shall fear, they shall be ashamed together. Isaiah 44:10, 11.

We are not big enough to be the goal of our own existence! The same truth applies to any idol we might create with our hands. No matter how large, beautiful, or intricate, it cannot be any bigger or more beautiful than the capacity of its human creator. In modern times, this can be truly awesome, particularly with special effects on film. Human ingenuity can soar, with imagination capable of fascinating creativity. Yet, in the end, it is finite and limited; and only makes one ask that if humans can invent and create so awesomely, what must God be like, in whose image we are created?

This verse calls for an appraisal. All those gifted but limited workmen, who create the idols of earth, are commanded to come together. It would make quite an international conference! What is the agenda? To assess what they are doing. They make gods, whose eyes are sightless, whose mouths are speechless, and whose ears are deaf. The idols are the witness to their own uselessness. God is saying that, if these idol-makers were only to appraise their efforts properly, they would become afraid and ashamed together. They would see the profitless, useless, work into which they pour their lives. They would be afraid of the anger of God, at their creation of such pointless puppet-gods. They would be ashamed of such a waste of talent and time.

As we think about these idol-makers appraising their work, what about you and me, appraising ours? Deep in our hearts, is there a flirting attitude with the gods of earth? Are we wasting precious time and energy, chasing what they seem to offer: fame, fortune, money, status, the praise of people, and the acclaim of the world? I assume that I do Christian work out of love to the Lord, but is it a safe assumption? Let me make sure that I do. Ezekiel once wrote: "Now some of the elders of Israel came to me and sat before me. And the word of the Lord came to me, saying, 'Son of man, these men have set up their idols in their hearts, and put before them that which causes them to stumble into iniquity . . . I the Lord will answer him who comes, according to the multitude of his idols, that I may seize the house of Israel by their heart, because they are all estranged from Me by their idols'" (Ezekiel 14:1-5). Outwardly, these men led Israel; inwardly, their hearts worshipped other gods. May God search your heart and mine today, and find that He, and He only, reigns there. Selah.

MARCH 30TH

The blacksmith with the tongs works one in the coals, fashions it with hammers, and works it with the strength of his arms. Even so, he is hungry, and his strength fails; he drinks no water and is faint. Isaiah 44:12.

When I was a lad, I used to go to a blacksmith's forge and watch him work. He once made some wheels for our soap-box-guider, and we had the fastest one in town! It was always fascinating to watch him hammer the red-hot iron. It was hot, tiring, and thirsty work. In today's text the blacksmith is hard at work, fashioning an idol with his tongs and hammers, purporting to create something which is divine, that needs no nourishment of any kind outside of itself. The living God never grows weak. His strength is limitless. The Creator and the idol-maker are contrasted; and the latter is just as ludicrous as he looks! How can the faint produce One who cannot faint? How can strength that fails produce the strength that never fails? No effect can be greater than its cause.

As the idol-makers are being withered by Isaiah's sarcasm, comfort raises its beautiful head. All of us, idol-makers included, find our strength waning at times. We grow weary of the road, tired of the constant hassle, worn down by the relentless stress of modern living. As believers, though, in a world-weary way, we do not say, 'Is that all there is?' As F. B. Meyer points out, we remember that God has a set of scales. On one side of the scales is the word 'as,' and on the other is the word 'so.' As the pressures of your day bear down on you, the scales are tipped. Do they remain that way? No! The Scripture says, 'As your days, so shall your strength be' (Deuteronomy 33:25). The part with 'so' upon it now fills up, and the scales become perfectly balanced. The metaphor is apposite. Whatever your day, God will send you the strength to meet its challenges. Remember, it was even when we were without strength, that Christ died for us. There is nothing you will face today, but God will send strength to meet it, and the source of this strength is eternal.

I was visiting in the small American town of Warm Springs, Georgia. Nearby in a forest was the Little White House that F. D. Roosevelt had built, close to the special springs that eased his polio. One day the President was being painted by a famous Russian artist; but sudden illness struck, and in a very short time he died. I talked to an elderly disabled lady there, called Susan Pike. One day in Warm Springs, at a centre for the disabled with which the President was associated, she was struggling to walk in her callipers. The President saw her difficulty, and said to Susan, "If I can do it, you can do it." She will always remember his encouragement. President Roosevelt's portrait still stands, unfinished, beside the chair in the room where he took ill. It is a poignant reminder that even great human strength is fragile. Somehow, I found that room a very moving and challenging place.

Turn today to the One whose strength is made perfect in weakness. Even if you have to go through the valley of the shadow of death itself, you will find that strength there to draw from. It is unfailing and infinite, and it comes into its own when you are weak.

MARCH 31ST

The craftsman stretches out his rule, he marks one out with chalk; he fashions it with a plane, he marks it out with the compass, and makes it like the figure of a man, according to the beauty of a man, that it may remain in the house. Isaiah 44:13.

There is a beauty in humankind. 'We are fearfully and wonderfully made,' says Psalm 139:14. Take any part of the human body – the ear, for example. It is made up of three parts: the outer, middle, and inner ear. The ear can pick up the sound of a jet or birdsong, the howling wind, or the faint tick of a watch. In the outer ear there are small glands, protecting the ear from dust and other harmful things. The middle ear is joined to the back of the nose by the Eustachian tube, which allows air to reach through a membrane to the eardrum inside the middle ear. Being sensitive to sound waves, it vibrates. The inner ear contains very fine nerves that communicate with the brain, and it has three semi-circular canals filled with fluid that, together with sight, give us a sense of balance.

Or, take the brain. A boy was said to have begun an essay on the subject of the brain, by saying, 'The brain is a solid lump of nine cells, with hair on top, an ear on either side, and me underneath!' In fact, the brain is not solid, but soft. It has something like fifteen million cells, and they never all work at the same time. The brain controls everything that happens to a human being: nerve fibres carry messages to and from all parts of the body. Without it, we couldn't breathe, our hearts would not beat, and we would not be able to sit, walk, or stand. We could have no thoughts, and no memories. It is probably the most wonderful object in all of creation.

And what about the human eye, or feet, or heart? The whole human being is an extraordinary creation of God. What, then, shall we say of a man, choosing a piece of wood, measuring it, drawing a pattern on it with chalk, fashioning it with a plane, marking it out with a compass, making the figure of a man, setting it up in his house and worshipping it? Man is certainly made in the image of God; but God is not made in the image of man. There are no bounds to His presence, no limits to His knowledge. "Your thoughts of God are too human," said Luther to Erasmus. We grow old, but God is immutable. God's beauty and majesty are untainted and eternal. His thoughts are not man's thoughts, and His ways are not man's ways. It is time we got back to believe in the majesty of God. People take His name and make it common: the name of God has become an exclamation-mark in everyday speech. Let's abhor such abuse of His sacred name, and worship Him in all His majesty. I trust this month's readings have helped you to do just that.

April

The Industrial Revolution brought huge changes to the linen making process. Here we have pallets of machine-heckled line-flax being drawn into the spinning frame. The virtuous woman of Proverbs 31 was commended because she made linen garments and sold them.

He cuts down cedars for himself, and takes the cypress and the oak; he secures it for himself among the trees of the forest. He plants a pine, and the rain nourishes it. Then it shall be for a man to burn, for he will take some of it and warm himself; yes, he kindles it and bakes bread; indeed he makes a god and worships it; he makes it a carved image, and falls down to it. Isaiah 44:14-15.

T rees are the largest living things on earth, and they are able to grow for many years. The giant Californian sequoia may live for more than 3,000 years. From tiny plants they become mighty forests. Who amongst us has not walked through a wood and marvelled at the beauty of the trees? You may see a bird feeding on acorns which it had buried for its winter store; the acorns it leaves behind become mighty oaks! It is incredible to think that oak-wood – used in the construction of everything from Viking long-boats, to Nelson's battleships; and house-beams a thousand years old, to pulpits and pews – came from the little acorns the birds forgot to eat!

Pine woods are a very special natural phenomenon. In the Scottish Highlands, they spring up in about thirty glens, which are quite a distance from one another. In April the buds break, and soon clouds of golden pollen are scattered on the wind, to form yet more trees! The mighty, fragrant cedar of Lebanon, with its warm, red timber, free from knots, often grows to 120 feet in height and 40 feet in girth. It is said that it was the hard, durable wood of the Cypress tree that was used in the construction of the ark. All species of trees have been appreciated for domestic firewood; though some burn better than others.

Beech-wood fires are bright and clear,
If the logs can be kept a year.
Oaken logs burn steadily,
If the wood is old and dry.
Chestnut's only good, they say,
If it has long been laid away.
But ash, whether it's new or old,
Is fit for a Queen with a crown of gold.

Birch and fir logs burn too fast:
They blaze up bright, but do not last.
By the Irish it is said, that
Hawthorn bakes the sweetest bread.
But ash, whether it's green or brown,
Is fit for a Queen with a golden crown

Elm-wood burns like churchyard mould:
Even the very flames are cold.
Poplar gives a bitter smoke,
It fills your eyes, and makes you choke.

Apple-wood will scent your room
With sweet, incense-like, perfume.
But ash, whether it's wet or dry,
Is fit for a Queen to warm her slippers by.

But, no matter which tree is best for burning, imagine the logic of a man warming himself by a fire of wood, and then taking what wood is left over and falling down and worshipping it! It has been pointed out that the wood will do him more kindness in its natural use as fuel, and bring him more satisfaction, than ever it will when he carves it into a god.

For sources of spiritual nourishment, why do we turn to things which cannot satisfy the hunger that we have in our hearts? Don't try to substitute anything for God. Fall down before Him, and you will rise nourished, refreshed, and inspired.

APRIL 2ND

He burns half of it in the fire; with this half he eats meat; he roasts a roast, and is satisfied. He even warms himself and says, "Ah! I am warm, I have seen the fire." And the rest of it he makes into a god, his carved image. He falls down before it and worships it, prays to it and says, "Deliver me, for you are my god!" Isaiah 44:16-17.

We may think that this man is illogical; but to whom do we turn for our deliverance? Do we depend on our wits, our social network, our money, or perhaps we turn to the philosophers? Intelligence, good government, money, and wise thinking are useful, but we must always make sure that we correct all human thinking with biblical thinking.

Let's go to the New Testament, to underline the liberating truth of the Lord as our deliverer. All who have trusted the Messiah as their Saviour are described as being '. . no longer strangers and foreigners, but fellow citizens with the saints . . . ' (Ephesians 2:19). That means they belong to a kingdom, to a State. You could live in a kingdom, and be ignorant of the advantages available to that community, and all its cultural possibilities. You could be there as a foreigner, and have no ultimate rights: you could be living on a passport. Your birth certificate would not constitute you as a citizen of that country, with legal rights. If you are a citizen of a kingdom it affects your status: you are linked to your fellow-citizens, and protected by the laws of that kingdom.

As a believer, you belong to a kingdom whose king is the King of all kings and Lord of all lords. Its capital is New Jerusalem; your fellow citizens are all believers. And who is your protector? Mark these lovely words in Psalm 3:1-7:

'Lord, how they have increased who trouble me! Many are they who rise up against me. Many are they who say of me, "There is no help for him in God." Selah. But you, O Lord, are a shield for me, my glory and the One who lifts up my head. I cried to the Lord with my voice, and He heard me from His holy hill. Selah. I lay down and slept; I awoke, for the Lord sustained me. I will not be afraid of ten thousands of people who have set themselves against me all around. Arise, O Lord; save me, O my God!'

Come on then, distressed one, be comforted! The Lord will lift up your head. The King of the new kingdom to which you belong delivers on all His promises. Is your head bowed in sorrow? Is it bowed under the taunt of critics? Is it bowed under the seeming impossibility of business success? Is it bowed under the pressure of exams? Is it bowed under the realisation of your limitations and faults? Have you taken a wrong turning in your life? Has a relationship broken up?

George Matheson (1842-1906) was a Scottish minister, who suffered from sight impairment. His engagement to the woman he loved had just broken up, and he found himself alone in his family home. Everyone had gone out for the evening. In his loneliness he lifted his pen and, in ten minutes, he wrote the hymn of his life. It was entitled 'O Love that will not let me go.' He wrote of the Light that followed all his way; of the Joy that sought for him through pain; of the rainbow he could trace through the rain; and of the Cross that lifted up his head. Remember that on the Cross, Christ's head was bowed in death, in order to lift up your head. This fact is beyond all human comprehension. So, away with misery; and come in, joy!

APRIL 3RD

They do not know nor understand; for He has shut their eyes, so that they cannot see, and their hearts, so that they cannot understand. And no one considers in his heart, nor is there knowledge nor understanding to say, "I have burned half of it in the fire, yes, I have also baked bread on its coals; I have roasted meat and eaten it; and shall I make the rest of it an abomination? Shall I fall down before a block of wood?" Isaiah 44:18-19.

These are chilling verses. God is allowing these idolaters to have what they had chosen. They worshipped a carved block of wood, the other half of which they used as domestic fuel – and God left them to it. Spiritual blindness has fallen, so they do not understand the absurdity of what they are doing. They do not know the difference between right and wrong, between truth and error. The Lord has shut their eyes, so that they cannot see; and their hearts, so that they cannot understand.

We all have to make choices. There is a light that crosses everyone's path. The Scriptures teach that this is 'the true Light which gives light to every person coming into the world' (John 1:9). These idolaters have turned to that which their very reason would tell them is absurd. Persistently, willingly, and stubbornly, they denied the light that God had given them; so He gave them over to it. God asks a powerful question: "Shall the potter be esteemed as the clay; or shall the thing made say of him who made it, 'He did not make me'?" (Isaiah 29:16). These people are answering with a resounding 'Yes!' so they got what they wanted. In their opinion, the carved wood is the creator, not the one who carved it. Indeed, they think that the wood is divine: 'you are my god!' (v.17).

The New Testament's commentary on today's verses could not be more relevant to our modern world.

'For since the creation of the world His invisible attributes are clearly seen, being understood by the things that are made, even His eternal power and Godhead, so that they are without excuse, because, although they knew God, they did not glorify Him as God, nor were thankful, but became futile in their thoughts, and their foolish hearts were darkened. Professing to be wise, they became fools, and changed the glory of the incorruptible God into an image made like corruptible man . . . Therefore God also gave them up to uncleanness . . . who exchanged the truth of God for the lie . . .' (Romans 1:20-25).

What was the result? '. . . God gave them over to a debased mind, to do things which are not fitting; being filled with all unrighteousness, sexual immorality, wickedness, covetousness, maliciousness, full of envy, murder, strife, deceit, evil-mindedness; they are whisperers, backbiters, haters of God . . . those who practise such things are deserving of death, not only do the same but also approve of those who practise them' (vs.28-32).

The light of God's truth is a wonderful thing; but to choose to turn away from it will have dark consequences. Just look around you, and those consequences are plain to be seen. Choose God's way, for His way is best.

APRIL 4TH

He feeds on ashes; a deceived heart has turned him aside; and he cannot deliver his soul, nor say, "Is there not a lie in my right hand?" Isaiah 44:20.

The young student had a superb brain, he got first class honours in his exams. Then he was offered meat, which had first been offered to idols, and he point blank refused to eat it. King Nebuchadnezzar had put this 'University of Babylon' student on a three-year course, so that he might serve before the king; but the student and three of his fellow-Jews refused to eat the king's meat.

Why? Because of Jewish food-laws. One of the main tenets of those laws was symbolic. God said to His people, 'Be holy, for I am holy' (Leviticus 11:44, 45). The physical rule was given to teach them deeper lessons. Some ways of satisfying our appetites are unclean; and not just our physical appetites, but also our moral, spiritual and psychological appetites. The world is full of abominable things being served up. Daniel and his friends took their stand for holiness of appetite.

And these idolaters in today's text? They are feeding their spiritual appetite through their idolatry. On what are they feeding? On ashes! Their appetite is perfectly healthy in itself, but they feed on that which does not satisfy. Instead of eternal truth, these idolaters nourish their souls by worshipping the figure of a man carved out of wood, that is in reality nothing more than dead embers.

The ultimate idol-factory isn't on the edge of some forest, but in the human heart and mind. Those hearts and minds might be well educated and extremely sophisticated. In Ephesians 5:5 and Colossians 3:5, Paul states that such things as lust, evil desires, greed and covetousness are idolatry. Millions of modern minds and hearts feed on these things, which are just about as satisfying as ashes. One has only to read F. Scott Fitzgerald's novel *The Great Gatsby*, and note his use of a 'valley of ashes' in the story, to see that the worship of hedonism leaves a very nasty taste in the mouth.

So, from the ashes of idolatry, we turn to feed on the Living Bread. The Lord Jesus said, "I am the living bread which came down from heaven. If anyone eats of this bread, he will live forever" (John 6:51). The God who gave us a spiritual appetite has also given that which will satisfy it. By faith, let us feed on Christ, and on the feast in His Word: 'Taste and see that the Lord is good;' 'He forgives all your iniquities;' 'He heals all your diseases;' 'He redeems your life from destruction;' 'He crowns you with loving kindness and tender mercies;' 'He satisfies your mouth with good things, so that your youth is renewed like the eagle's.' In our meditation on that cold day in January, we saw that the eagle sheds its feathers one at a time, thus enabling it to continue to fly during the moulting season. You, too, can keep going, as God renews your life for each new stage. So, get up and away from those ashes, Christian, and soar! There is no god but God.

APRIL 5TH

"Remember these, O Jacob, and Israel, for you are My servant; I have formed you, you are My servant; O Israel, you will not be forgotten by Me!" Isaiah 44:21.

T alk about contrasts! The Lord now calls His people to remember some very important truths. First, they are His servant. This is in direct contrast to those who are
the slaves of idolatry, held in spiritual darkness, feeding on ashes. The servant of
God serves One whose truth is light, and whose nourishment satisfies beyond all earthly
resources. There is no service greater than the service of God, and no work done for Him is
insignificant. So, do all your work as unto the Lord. One day, 'Little acts you had forgotten,
He will tell you were for Him.'

Second, these people had been formed and shaped by God. This is in direct contrast to
idolaters, who have formed and shaped their own god. What does this tell you? There will
never be another you! The living God formed you in all your own uniqueness. One morning
I addressed hundreds of children in a 'Rooftop School' in Hong Kong. I was invited back to
speak to the children at lunchtime, and I asked if anyone could remember what I had said in
my first address. Not a hand stirred! I was confused, until the headmaster touched me on the
shoulder and gently informed me that this was a different group of children! The first group
had gone home at lunchtime. They all looked the same to me! But they were not all the
same: each was a unique individual. Please do not spend your life wishing you were someone else. God has formed you for a purpose.

Israel, God's servant, formed specifically by Him, is now told that God will not forget her.
Is there anything more comforting than to be remembered? Just yesterday, as I was writing
this book, I got a letter from a friend of mine in Bournemouth, called George Wilcocks. He
wrote to thank me for another Daily Reading Book that I had written. In it I had mentioned
Isaiah 42:3, that refers to 'a bruised reed and smoking flax.' Not knowing that I was deep
into this present book, George wrote, '. . . thinking today about bruised reeds and smoking
flax. . . what a marvellous Saviour we have!' My, with that line, he hit the bull's eye of
encouragement. This morning I lifted my pen with fresh vigour. You see, my friend had
remembered me, and gone out of his way to let me know. It is good to be remembered.

But God always remembers me! His thoughts about me are more than the sand on the seashore (see Psalm 139:17,18). Should I forget Him, He will never forget me. He is guiding, comforting, sometimes challenging, sometimes chastening, sometimes warning; but He has me before Him every moment of every day.

In exile, overwhelmed with an alien culture and far from home, Israel said 'My way is hidden from the Lord, and my just claim is passed over by my God' (Isaiah 40:27). But they could not have been more wrong. If you are tempted to think or to say the same, don't! Never, ever, say 'I think that God has forgotten about me.' Such talk is downright unbelief. What's more, it is a lie.

April 6th

"I have blotted out, like a thick cloud, your transgressions, and like a cloud, your sins. Return to Me, for I have redeemed you." Isaiah 44:22.

The young man was a gambler. He was the paymaster in one of the barracks of the Russian army. Sadly, he had gambled away a great deal of the Government's money, as well as his own. As it happened, his father was a friend of the Tsar, Nicholas I. Eventually the young man received notice that a representative of the Tsar was coming to check the accounts. That evening he got out the books and totalled up what he owed, knowing only too well that he was ruined. He determined to take his own life, and pulling out a revolver he placed it on the table before him. At the bottom of the ledger where he had totalled up his illegal borrowings he wrote, 'A great debt! Who can pay?' He decided that on the stroke of midnight he would die.

As the evening wore on, the young soldier got drowsy and fell asleep. That night the Tsar, as was sometimes his custom, made a round of this particular barracks. He saw a light and, looking in, he saw the young soldier asleep. On entering the room he immediately recognised him, and looking at the ledger he realised what had happened. He was about to awaken him and put him under arrest, when his eye fastened on the young man's message: 'A great debt! Who can pay?' With a surge of compassion and kindness, he reached over and wrote one word at the bottom of the ledger and slipped away.

The young soldier eventually awoke. He looked at the clock and realised that it was long after midnight. Reaching for his revolver to take his life, his eye fell on the ledger, and the one word which the Tsar had written: 'Nicholas.' He could hardly believe it, so he went to a file, found a signature of the Tsar on some Government document, and checked it. It was the real thing! Sure enough, in the morning a messenger came from the palace with exactly the right amount needed to pay his debt. Only the Tsar could pay and, mercifully, he did.

Imagine, then, Israel's sin; or your sin and mine. Imagine the debt that we owe, when we realise the moral requirements of God's righteousness, as found in His law. Then imagine the name, 'Jesus Christ,' written against that debt. Israel was redeemed through the death of the sacrificial lamb, which typified Christ. We are redeemed through the blood of the Lamb of God in person, 'as of a lamb without blemish and without spot' (1 Peter 1:19). On that basis, our sins are 'blotted out,' meaning, 'wiped clean.' 'As a thick cloud,' our sins came between us and God. Now that cloud has been swept away. On the basis of redemption,

God's people are called back to a close walk with Him. There is no better ground to walk on than 'redemption ground.' There is no better forgiveness to enjoy than forgiveness on the basis of redemption. Rejoice in it, Christian! And if you are not a Christian, repent towards God, and put your faith in Jesus Christ. Then you will rejoice in it too.

APRIL 7TH

Sing, O heavens, for the Lord has done it! Shout, you lower parts of the earth; break forth into singing, you mountains, O forest, and every tree in it! For the Lord has redeemed Jacob, and glorified Himself in Israel. Isaiah 44:23.

The Lloyd-Webber musical, *Jesus Christ Superstar*, presents the cross of Christ as a good mission gone wrong, a tragedy. The Bible presents the cross of Christ as a triumph, a mission gloriously accomplished. "It is finished," the Saviour cried on the cross, and died. The veil in the temple was rent from the top to the bottom: a new and living way to the very heart of God was opened (Hebrews 10:20). The resurrection of Christ was God's seal upon that perfect work of redemption, which Christ accomplished for us.

Isaiah calls on the heavens and the earth to sing, 'for the Lord has done it.' All of the glory is the Lord's due. It is using poetic language, to call on the sky and the stars to sing; but in a very real way, they do! Have you ever stood on a hill somewhere of an evening, and gazed at the stars? I often do; and they speak to me! It is a speechless speech, a wordless word; but they tell out a message. 'The heavens declare the glory of God,' says David. What is glory? It is the outward shining of God's inner being. Without using words, the stars tell out the glory of God, and we recognise the message. '. . the firmament (expanse of sky) shows His handiwork. Day unto day utters speech, and night unto night reveals knowledge. There is no speech nor language where their voice is not heard. Their line (sound) has gone out through all the earth, and their words to the end of the world' (Psalm 19:1-4).

Isaiah wants the sky and the stars to sing to the glory of God. What a choir! Once, when God was talking with Job, He asked Job if he had been present 'when earth's foundations were laid . . . when the morning stars sang together.' When the Lord had finished talking, it's no wonder Job answered, 'I have heard of you by the hearing of the ear but now my eye sees you' (Job 42:5).

Now Isaiah calls on the mountains and every tree of the forest to break into song. The idolater worships the tree, and Isaiah calls on the tree to sing to God's praise (see Psalm 96:10-13). Just as I could walk into your room, and tell your tastes and interests by the things you have in it, so in God's earth and universe I can see what kind of mind He has, what His interests are, and what His glory is like. The stars, the mountains, and the trees, 'sing' it! Pity if they 'sing' of it, and I am silent, isn't it? Are you redeemed and silent? God forbid.

APRIL 8TH

Thus says the Lord, your Redeemer, and He who formed you from the womb: "I am the Lord, who makes all things, who stretches out the heavens all alone, who spreads abroad the earth by Myself." Isaiah 44:24.

90

The One who formed me as a tiny embryo in my mother's womb, also 'stretches out the heavens all alone.' Sometimes I think about the question of how far He stretches them out. Spacecraft may travel deep into space, but their scope is limited. How far does space extend? Forever? Was it not Einstein, who taught that gravity bends space? If that is so, does it mean that space is round like the earth, and that if I start from a certain point I can keep going until I come right back to where I started? God is infinite – that is, He is unlimited, and of endless extent. Is His creation the same? I simply do not know. Yet Isaiah tells me that, no matter how far God stretches the heavens, nobody helps Him to do it. He does it alone.

Why should I get all worked up today with matters over which I have no control? The road to life and eternity stretches out before me. The God who stretches out the heavens alone, also plans my life alone. He did not consult anyone about whether I should have blue eyes or brown, whether I should lean towards the arts rather than the sciences, or whether I should have no children, three children, or five. This verse tells me that the God who formed me is my Redeemer. There is not a single detail of my life that He does not know or care about. He knows what is around the next corner; and I am not afraid, because He is already there. When I get round it, I will find that He planned what is best for me; even if it did mean going through difficult times.

One of the best illustrations of this truth comes from the story of the Apostle Paul. He was arrested, charged by the Jews with treason against the Emperor, and given into the charge of the palace guard, the personal bodyguard of the Emperor. So here he was in Rome, a prisoner of Caesar, awaiting trial. Amazingly, he never once said he was a prisoner of Caesar; he always referred to himself as a 'prisoner of Jesus Christ' (see Ephesians 3:1). When one reads his letters, the reason is obvious. He saw that Caesar did not have the final say about him: the Lord Jesus did. The length of his confinement was not determined by Caesar, but by the Lord. The more Paul came to understand the One whom He served, the more he realised that the Lord Jesus was in control of history. He is the One who holds the keys; the One who opens, and no one can shut, who shuts and no one can open (Revelation 3:7). Paul knew that he would be set free when the Lord decided his imprisonment was of no further benefit. When the Lord spoke, Caesar acted; and not the other way around. It is a comfort to remember this truth, especially when we become worried and anxious about what today's political powers are doing in this world. It is not the Caesars who stretch out the heavens, and spread abroad the earth. It is your Lord, and mine. He is in ultimate control of the world's history, and ours.

APRIL 9TH

"Who frustrates the signs of the babblers, and drives diviners mad; who turns wise men backward, and makes their knowledge foolishness; who confirms the word of His servant, and performs the counsel of His messengers; who says to Jerusalem, 'You shall be inhabited,' to the cities of Judah, 'You shall be built,' and I will raise up her waste places."
Isaiah 44:25-26.

If you want to make God smile, at the end of this year tell Him how you thought your year would turn out!' Even since you read those words in our meditation for 27th January, I guess you have had a few surprises! And if we continually discover how far off the mark our predictions are, what about the predictions of the fortune-tellers? The Chaldean soothsayers obviously had all sorts of predictions for the future glory of Babylon; but they were to be frustrated and made to look foolish.

What about those who practised divination? Divination was an attempt to obtain knowledge (especially of the future) by inspiration, or by reading and interpreting certain signs, called omens. Those who practised it believed that the gods could be induced to impart their secrets. Omens, dreams, hydromancy (foretelling from the appearance of water), astrology, necromancy (consulting the dead), and even the sacrifice of children, were all associated with divination. The Scriptures condemn the practice outright (see Deuteronomy 18:10-14). Whilst the Babylonians listened to their soothsayers and diviners, Israel was called upon to listen to the Lord. He guaranteed them that His word would be confirmed: they would be restored from captivity, and Jerusalem would be rebuilt.

Does the Lord confirm His word to us, in our day and generation? Of course He does! One has only to look around to see it confirmed every day. The rainbow in the sky confirms God's covenant-promise never again to completely destroy the earth with a flood. God instituted marriage and the family to be the backbone of society. But what happens when people tinker with God's blueprint? The social fabric of a nation begins to come apart, and those who are hurt most are the children. A while ago, a sign appeared in a jeweller's window, 'We rent wedding rings!' The warnings of Proverbs 5 and 6 are implicit, regarding unfaithfulness in marriage and the satiation of lust. The end result of ignoring those warnings is spelt out in no uncertain manner. How often have you seen it confirmed? Every day the media is full of it.

The Lord says that if we acknowledge Him in all our ways, He will direct our paths (Proverbs 3:6). Does He? Have you ever found Him to fail? He confirms His word day by day. As you share His word with others, He confirms all that it teaches in the hearts and lives of those who hear it, whether they obey it or not. Later in Isaiah, we shall see that the Lord says, 'So shall my word be that goes forth from My mouth; it shall not return to me void, but it shall accomplish what I please, and it shall prosper in the thing for which I sent it' (55:11). Since God's word is so certain, make sure you sound it out. When you counsel people who are in need, use the counsel of His word sensitively and wisely, declaring His promises. They will soon find that He delivers on them all.

APRIL 10TH

"Who says to the deep, 'Be dry! and I will dry up your rivers'; who says of Cyrus, 'He is My shepherd, and he shall perform all My pleasure, saying to Jerusalem, "You shall be built," and to the temple, "Your foundation shall be laid."' Isaiah 44:27-28.

The God who dried up the Red Sea to let His people pass through, can also dry up rivers. Later we shall see that, during a siege of Babylon, Cyrus, the king from the East, diverted the waters of the river Euphrates. His army walked up the oozy channel into the city. It was God who was behind his actions. He calls Cyrus 'My shepherd,' even though Cyrus was an idolater. In the recent passages we have studied together, idolatry has been roundly condemned. So, what is happening? Here we have a clear example of the sovereignty of God. He condemns idolatry, but uses an idolater. Indeed, He can use whomever He chooses.

It is not hard to imagine how Israel would be terrified of another king waging war against their captors. They probably thought it was the worst thing that could happen; but it turned out to be their liberation. This 'shepherd' would release those 'sheep'. God would use the Emperor of Persia to guide and care for His people: 'He shall perform all My pleasure.'

A man once urged me to consider full-time Christian ministry. He saw it as 'the bent of my life,' and he was used to guide me into my life's work. He was not in it himself, and I don't think he would have seen it as his passion in life; but he sought to persuade me to think seriously about it. God uses all kinds of people to bring about His purposes: surprising people, people who only see the immediate goal they are after, never realising that God's greater purposes are being accomplished through them. In promoting Joseph, Pharaoh did not realise that he was preserving the seed of the Messiah. Pharaoh was thinking of the good of Egypt; but God was thinking of the greater good of the whole world, for in the Messiah every family on earth would be blessed.

I often think of Nehemiah. Deep in his heart, he wanted to rebuild Jerusalem; but he was in a far-off land, butler to a heathen king. Yet, on finding out the desire of Nehemiah's heart, it was that very heathen king who gave him letters of authorisation, permitting him to pass through the many regions en route to Jerusalem. He also gave him a letter to the keeper of his forests, enabling him to get timber to make beams for the gates of the citadel connected to the temple, for the city wall, and for the house where he would live.

What is the lesson? It is that you should cheer up, Christian; for the Lord often makes a straight line with a crooked stick.

APRIL 11TH

"Thus says the Lord to His anointed, to Cyrus, whose right hand I have held – to subdue nations before him and loose the armour of kings, to open before him the double doors, so that the gates will not be shut: 'I will go before you and make the crooked places straight; I will break in pieces the gates of bronze and cut the bars of iron. I will give you the treasures of darkness and hidden riches of secret places, that you may know that I, the Lord, who call you by your name, am the God of Israel.'" Isaiah 45:1-3.

Today we begin a study of the passage in Isaiah, which runs from 45:1 – 46:13, dealing with the fact that it is King Cyrus whom God has chosen as the instrument to free His people from captivity. Why is there so much detail? Because God's people were not so keen on the idea as God was! In fact, they recoiled from it; but they could not see the big picture. So God is determined to show them that His way is best.

God calls Cyrus, 'His anointed.' This was a title normally given to Israel's kings; particularly to David and his descendants, through whom the Messiah was promised. Later we read of God making an everlasting covenant with His people, called 'The sure mercies of David' (Isaiah 55:3). Was God going to set all this aside, and use a pagan king? This was a hard pill for them to swallow.

Of course God had not forgotten His promise to use the Davidic line. However, in 587 BC, Zedekiah, the last Davidic king, was blinded and taken captive to Babylon (2 Kings 25:4-7). God's promise would still hold, and God would see to it that, when the Messiah was eventually born at Bethlehem, He would be 'of the house and lineage of David' (Luke 2:4). Meanwhile, in the dark days when that promise seemed to be almost wiped out, God was going to take hold of a Persian king, and 'subdue nations before him, loose the armour of kings, open the double doors, break padlocks, make crooked places straight; gates would open to him (Babylon had 100 bronze gates); and iron bars would be cut. Buried treasure and secret caches of valuables would be his.' (It is reckoned that Cyrus got as much as £126 million as a result of His conquests.)

If God could do all that for a pagan king, He can clear the way for His will in your life. No barrier is too great, no obstacle too complex. Cyrus freely acknowledged that his success was down to the hand of the living God (Ezra 1:2). As you face the complex problems of your life, let the active verbs of today's verses inspire you. Meditate on them: God will 'hold,' 'subdue,' 'loosen,' 'open,' 'go before,' 'straighten,' 'break,' 'cut,' and 'give.'

Are you frightened? He will hold you steady through the present storm in your life. Do the defences of the enemy seem impenetrable? God will loosen those defences. Are doors, even double doors, closed before you? Do you simply not know where to turn? He will do the impossible. Are your circumstances deeply complex? You couldn't explain them if you were asked! He will straighten out those circumstances. Are you faced with people, whose opposition to you is like closed, locked gates of iron and brass? You are shut out. Fear not, God will break and cut through those unyielding gates. Are you without resources, even financially? Peter found that God can bring money from a fish's mouth, and send an angel to open closed doors. Remember you have access to Him at this very moment. Everything changes when you turn to the Lord.

April 12th

"For Jacob My servant's sake, and Israel My elect, I have even called you by your name; I have named you, though you have not known Me. I am the Lord, and there is no other; there is no God besides Me. I will gird you, though you have not known Me."
Isaiah 45:4-5.

In front of me on my desk I have a photograph of the famous Cylinder of Cyrus, that tells of his capture of Babylon and liberation of the captives. This cylinder, produced by the priests of the god Marduk, gives Marduk all the credit for what happened. Cyrus acknowledged Marduk as the cause of his success, just as he acknowledged the Lord in Ezra 1:2. If nothing else, Cyrus was a politician! Even after all his experiences, Cyrus did not know the Lord.

I find this a very sad fact. "I have named you,' says God, 'though you have not known me . . . I will gird you, though you have not known me." How about us? Do we know God? J. I. Packer makes two very challenging points in his great work, *Knowing God* (Hodder and Stoughton, 1973). Firstly, we can know a great deal <u>about</u> God without much knowledge <u>of</u> <u>Him</u>. We can be interested in theology, know Christian history and creeds, give out opinions in private and in public on the Christian standpoint, lead study groups, and know much about God; and all the time hardly know Him at all! Secondly, we can know a great deal about <u>godliness</u>, without much knowledge of <u>God</u>. We can read books on how to pray, read the Bible, witness, tithe, and be effective Christians. We can apply this knowledge, and do good pastoral work; yet hardly know God at all.

We were made to know God. Eternal life is the knowledge of God (see John 17:3). The Bible teaches that we can know God, as a son knows his father, as a wife knows her husband, and as a sheep knows its shepherd. It is through knowing Jesus Christ, that we can know God in this way. It is very personal, and will affect every area of our thinking. Once we enter into a relationship with Jesus Christ, we discover that it is a deeply emotional relationship. We will also find out that not only do we know Him but that He knows us, down to the very number of hairs on our head. He knows the most about us, yet He loves us still. Here is comfort and relief beyond anything. So, let us heed the words of Jeremiah regarding the personal knowledge of God: "Let not the wise man glory in his wisdom, let not the mighty man glory in his might, nor let the rich man glory in his riches; but let him who glories glory in this, that he understands and knows Me" (Jeremiah 9:23,24).

APRIL 13TH

"That they may know from the rising of the sun to its setting that there is none besides Me." Isaiah 45:6a.

W hat God was going to do, in using Cyrus to free His people, was to have universal implications. The main point of the exercise was that the whole habitable world might know that Jehovah was the only true God. In it lay the seed of the gospel of the Messiah, that today is proclaimed across the whole earth.

There is something deeply comforting about knowing that, from the sun's rising to its setting, there is no god but God. If I know Him, it does not matter where He places me in His service. In whatever culture, city, town, or village, He is the very same God. Whatever job of work I do, in school or office, in hospital or university, in business or farming, whether I pilot an aircraft or make one, I am called and equipped by Him to face what I have to face today. Of course, it is not easy when God moves you on to another place of service. It often means learning new social skills, getting to know new people, even learning a new language. Have you had to move in recent times? Do not be afraid.

I was teaching God's Word in Japan – where the sun rises. My interpreter told me that he had been raised in a family, where his father was believed to be a god and was followed as such. My interpreter had come to know God in Christ; and what a privilege it was to serve the Lord with him. In the mountains of Kyusyu, we were preparing the Bible teaching I was about to give. As together we talked of the deep things of God, it was as though I was at home talking about the same things to my Christian friends in Belfast. There was the same joy, the same deep sense of being in the body of Christ, and filled with the same Spirit. No move that you ever have to make will take you away from the nearness of your Heavenly Father.

We have only to think of Elijah the prophet. God moved him on from the mountains of Gilead, to stand before a king in his court and declare God's word. Then God moves him to live by a brook, where daily he is fed fresh food by the ravens. One day the ravens do not come. Now God moves him to Zarephath in the land of Zidon, to a culture foreign to his own, and where his God is not worshipped. A widow gives him her last meal, and thus finds she is sustained in a famine by a resource that is beyond her knowledge. Elijah is moved on to Mount Carmel, where he is used to reaffirm before the nation that the Lord is God. Unfortunately, he believes the threats of the wicked queen, Jezebel, and he runs away. The angel of God finds him, sleeping under a juniper tree in the wilderness, and feeds him. Cowering in a cave on Mount Horeb, this servant of God is reached by the still, small voice of God, restored, and set back on track in his ministry. The latter part of that ministry was most fruitful, and ended with a final, dramatic flight in a chariot of fire to Heaven. From the hills of Gilead, to the hills of Glory, Elijah found God faithful in every place. So, too, will you and I find that, from the rising of the sun to its setting, in every place and at every time, there is no one like God.

APRIL 14TH

'I am the Lord, and there is no other. I form the light and create darkness, I make peace and create calamity; I, the Lord, do all these things.' "Rain down, you heavens, from above, and let the skies pour down righteousness; let the earth open, let them bring forth salvation, and let righteousness spring up together. I, the Lord, have created it."'
Isaiah 45:6b-8.

L et's be clear in our thinking about today's text. The word 'calamity' is the Hebrew word, 'ra'. It occurs about 640 times in the Bible and, says Alec Motyer, 'it can range in meaning from a nasty taste, to full moral evil. There are about 275 cases where it refers to trouble or calamity.' Here it refers to the consequent calamity that fell in the wake of the judgments of war, brought about by Gentile powers through King Cyrus, God's chosen instrument. It is very important that we interpret this verse in that context.

In this Lord, whom we follow, all things consist. He formed day and night by the word of His power. Take Him out of the universe, and it would collapse. He who energised the actions of Cyrus to bring war, also energised his actions to bring peace. And He can still do it; He is a God of action. He brought about righteousness in the midst of His people's exile in Babylon: it came down like rain, and sprang up with salvation, like a crop in springtime.

So, be comforted today, Christian. The rain of righteousness, which God sent to His people before, can come again; the crop of salvation, which they knew, can grow again.

Here in Europe, where I live, the desert of godlessness is frightening. Nothing seems to be absolute. Indeed, the only absolute law that a lot of people follow nowadays, is that there is no law which must be absolutely followed! To find someone with a value system, and to see them stick to it, is rare in our generation.

Value systems seem to be based on the question, 'What can it do for me?' Selfishness seems to rule under the maxim, 'Look out for number one.' Yet, through the declaration of the gospel of Jesus Christ, lives can be transformed. As I mentioned before, I am currently travelling across Northern Ireland and into the Republic of Ireland, to speak in schools about the Lord Jesus Christ. Norman Craig, who is travelling with me, testifies to the young people about how he was involved in terrorism, drugs and alcohol. He went to prison, and his life became such a mess that his wife was going to leave him. He had severely neglected his children. Then he met Jesus Christ, and his life was transformed. He lost his bigotry and hatred. Peace now reigns in his heart, where once was restlessness and violence. I find that the young people are gripped and deeply moved by his story – and so am I! They often burst into applause at the end of his message. In this land of tragic beauty, Norman's message falls like refreshing rain; and we pray it will bring a crop of salvation. "I, the Lord, do all these things," says our text. He might do it through your witness today, and bring about a delightful harvest beyond all you could ever have asked or thought. Onward!

APRIL 15TH

"Woe to him who strives with his Maker! Let the potsherd strive with the potsherds of the earth! Shall the clay say to him who forms it, 'What are you making?' or shall your handiwork say, 'He has no hands'? Woe to him who says to his father, 'What are you begetting?' or to the woman, 'What have you brought forth?'" Isaiah 45:9-10.

Ahead of the time, God has declared that He is going to use King Cyrus to free Israel. This chieftain of an obscure Persian tribe, unknown beyond the narrow confines of his native hills, would begin a course of conquest which would sweep from the frontier of India to the Aegean Sea, subjugating even Croesus, king of Lydia, whose wealth was legendary. God promised to open doors of opportunity for him, and to guide and use him to free His people from Babylon. But would you believe it – small-minded Israel quibbled and quarrelled about it? They criticised the ways of God!

Of course, Israel could only see that they were being liberated by a heathen king. He would probably subjugate them; they would be under his authority in the rebuilding of Jerusalem and its temple. They felt that this was a fate even worse than exile in Babylon! Where was the promise to King David's line?

What's new? Through long ages, God's people have behaved in the same way. Are you and I guilty, too? God brings about certain circumstances, and we moan about them! We ask, 'Where are His promises now?' God knows that we even doubt Him at times. In these verses, then, see God's remonstrance of His people. "You are like an earthen vessel among other earthen vessels, questioning the potter who made them!" says God. When we think about it, such an action would be absurd. The potter knows best. Perhaps He has a plan to take that clay, and fashion it as a vessel for a widow of Zarephath, or for a King Solomon in his palace. Or the vessel may be fashioned simply to hold oil, to give light to a man and his family in their home on dark evenings. The divine Potter has all sorts of plans for the clay. But now that it is made, and His plan is in action, the vessel complains! Come off it! The Potter is sovereign, not the clay! This is as ridiculous as sperm saying to a father, 'Who gave you permission to use me to make a baby?'; or a foetus asking a mother, 'Why have you cooped me up in this belly?' (*The Message*, NavPress Publishing Group, 2000.) Search your life today, and ask, 'Am I behaving like that clay, that sperm, that foetus?' Yield, Christian: yield to the Potter's hands.

APRIL 16TH

Thus says the Lord, the Holy One of Israel, and his Maker: "Ask Me of things to come concerning My sons; and concerning the work of My hands, you command Me. I have made the earth, and created man on it. I – My hands – stretched out the heavens, and all their host I have commanded. I have raised him up in righteousness, and I will direct all his ways; He shall build My city and let My exiles go free, not for price nor reward," says the Lord of hosts. Isaiah 45:11-13.

J ust think about the scope of the work of God, presented in these verses. God asks us to discuss with Him the nature of His work. He asks us to question Him. But He is saying, 'Ask.' He is not saying, 'Criticise.' The Bible shows that we are allowed to reason with God; we are allowed to ask, 'Why?' Is not this the way Isaiah's prophecy begins? "Come now, and let us reason together," says the Lord, "though your sins are like scarlet, they shall be as white as snow; though they are red like crimson, they shall be as wool" (Isaiah 1:18).

God is asking the moaners, complainers, and grumblers to drop their reactions to what He is doing, and enter into discussion with Him as regards Israel's future, and the work of His hands in general. God points out that He made the earth in the first place, and put people on it. He crafted the skies and directs the constellations. He shall raise up and direct King Cyrus to build Jerusalem, and free His people from exile in Babylon. God will direct all his ways – He will not negotiate with Cyrus, nor hire him, and Cyrus will not be motivated by reward. You and I, too, are allowed to talk to Him and to question Him about it all. From the beauties of the earth, to human beings; from the heavenly constellations, to kings – the scope of God's work is awesome.

Of course, if we want to know what God is like, we must look at the Lord Jesus. Do you remember the historic night in the Upper Room, when He instituted the memorial feast with His disciples? In order to visualise what was happening on that occasion, it is important to understand the seating arrangements. The table was low and V-shaped, with the place of honour in the centre of one side. At table Jewish people reclined, resting on the left elbow, leaving the right arm and hand free to eat food. They reclined on couches, and a person's head was literally on the breast of the person to the left. As they were eating, Christ pointed out that one of the disciples at the table would betray him. The disciples were perplexed. 'Now there was leaning on Jesus' bosom one of His disciples whom Jesus loved. Simon Peter therefore motioned to him to ask who it was of whom He spoke. Then, leaning back on

Jesus' breast, he said to Him, "Lord, who is it?"' (John 13:23-25). To this day, Christians talk of John as 'the disciple who leaned on Jesus' breast.'

Why do I raise that story at this stage of our readings in Isaiah? Because both the story and today's text show that we, too, can come with our questions, close to God's very heart. Study the story, and you will see that John, Philip, Peter, and Thomas all questioned Christ in the Upper Room. This Teacher is approachable. This God can be questioned, and He will give the answers.

Thus says the Lord: "The labour of Egypt and merchandise of Cush and of the Sabeans, men of stature, shall come over to you, and they shall be yours; they shall walk behind you, they shall come over in chains; and they shall bow down to you. They will make supplication to you, saying, 'Surely God is in you, and there is no other; there is no other God.'" Isaiah 45:14.

Now, here is something! The day is now anticipated when the whole world will acknowledge that there is no god but God. Already we have learned that God declared, 'from the rising of the sun to its setting . . . there is none besides Me' (45:6); and here we learn that the world will accept this fact. The pronoun, 'you,' in today's verse is feminine singular. In the Hebrew language, cities are referred to in the feminine gender. In our very first meditation in this book, we found that Jerusalem refers to the people of God (40:1-2). Now they are scattered, but are soon to return. It is from Jerusalem that their Messiah shall eventually rule the world. So, in this text today, we move from the coming of Cyrus, to the future coming of the Lord Jesus.

Here we learn that nations, in all their wealth and in the full vigour of health, will submit themselves. Isaiah prophecies, '(they) shall come over to you,' – that is, of their own will, after serious contemplation; 'they shall walk behind you,' – the Lord will lead His people, and the nations will come along behind them. 'They shall come over in chains; and they shall bow down to you. They will make supplication to you . . . ' – they are in earnest. What is the issue? They have recognised one unassailable truth: 'Surely God is in you, and there is no other; there is no other God,' they say.

That future day will be great. But what about now? Is there a practical application here to the everyday life of the Christian? Of course there is! I remember one evening at Cambridge University, hearing Dr. Martyn Lloyd Jones speak on the subject, *The Man on the Outside.* Who is he? He is the person mentioned in 1 Corinthians 14 who, if he comes into a church service and finds people speaking in tongues without interpretation, will declare that they are all mad. Paul calls for order in the church: 'If anyone speaks in a tongue, let there be two or at the most three, each in turn, and let one interpret' (v.27).

Dr. Lloyd Jones told us about a woman who was a Spiritualist. One rainy day she followed the people into a Christian service in Westminster Chapel, and it led to her conversion. How did it happen? Later she stated that, where she had been previously, there had been a power present, just as she had felt a power present in the Christian service. The difference, she said, was that one was an 'unclean power,' and the other was a 'clean power.'

Is that what people feel, when they come into the Christian gatherings with which we are associated? May it ever be the case. If we faithfully speak out God's Word in language people can understand, then, through the power of the Spirit, they will encounter God's truth. That truth will reveal the secrets of their hearts. 'The man on the outside,' coming in and hearing this truth, will 'fall down on his face, he will worship God and report that God is truly among you' (1 Corinthians 14:25).

APRIL 18TH

Truly You are God, who hide Yourself, O God of Israel, the Saviour! Isaiah 45:15.

William Cowper, England's great poet, caught it perfectly when he wrote of God's mysterious ways being like 'planting His footsteps in the sea, and riding upon the storm.' The storms of exile and obscurity, the destruction of national institutions – the overwhelming experience of captivity would be the very storm that God would ride upon, to bring about Israel's recognition of His glory and power. But He was hidden from them in it.

Think about it. Does God guide nations and individuals in ways that are contrary to what we would naturally expect? When Lot split up from Abraham, headed down the well-watered plain, and the enemies in Sodom took him captive, he never dreamt that God would use Abraham to rescue him. When the two little twins began struggling with one another in Rebecca's womb, she was worried. So she did a wise thing, she enquired of the Lord. 'If all is well, why am I like this?' she said (Genesis 25:22). He told her that two nations were in her womb: 'Two peoples shall be separated from your body; one people shall be stronger than the other, and the older shall serve the younger' (v.23). When they were being born, the younger twin grabbed the heel of the older one! The rest is history – God's history; but Rebecca would not have known if she hadn't asked.

As he lay in an ark of bulrushes in the river Nile, the tears of a tiny baby did not seem to have world history mingled in them, when Pharaoh's daughter first saw them on the face of baby Moses. Yet on those tears hung the destiny of nations! History was hidden in a young shepherd's sling; and in the words of a little servant girl in the home of an army commander called Naaman. History was hidden in the flight of a raven with food in its mouth; in the headache of a Shunammite's son; and in a rumour heard by the mighty and cruel Assyrian king, Sennacherib.

History was hidden in the heart of an eight-year-old king called Josiah; in the woes of Job; in the moral stance of the student, Daniel; and in the life of the sheepbreeder, Amos. Awesomely, it was hidden in the womb of Mary of Nazareth; and uniquely in the heartless and bloodstained crucifixion at Calvary.

The mysterious ways and purposes of God were hidden in all of these things; unintelligible, even to the most brilliant mind; unseen, but very real. Always remember, too, that they are hidden in the twists and turns of our lives. The hand of God, moving in His unerring ways, is in our heartaches and delights, our frustrations and joys. Is there any greater comfort than knowing this, and living by it? Onward!

They shall be ashamed and also disgraced, all of them; they shall go in confusion together, who are makers of idols. But Israel shall be saved by the Lord with an everlasting salvation; you shall not be ashamed or disgraced forever and ever. Isaiah 45:16-17.

L et me ask you a question. Have you ever been caused to blush with shame, because you put the Lord first, or obeyed Him? Has the Lord ever caused you to squirm, because you sacrificed your own will for His will? Often we have blushed with shame and squirmed painfully, because we gave in to the temptations of our 'adversary the devil' (1 Peter 5:8). Following in his path, we find that there is a foul dust blowing in his wake.

Recently I have been reading a biography of the famous naval hero, Lord Nelson. Although killed in action, he will always be remembered for his great victory at Trafalgar. Unfortunately, there is a disgraceful thing in Nelson's life, which mars his memory. When they were both 28, he was married to Frances Herbert Nisbet, the daughter of a judge, and the widow of a physician. She was an heiress, and Nelson was an unknown captain. Frances was an exceptionally faithful wife who deeply loved her husband. Sadly, Nelson was notoriously unfaithful to Frances. Nelson's father was a minister in the Church of England. He wrote to his son after the Battle of Copenhagen, pleading with him to change his ways, 'while it is called Today.' He was alluding to the Bible verse, which goes on to warn, 'lest any of you be hardened through the deceitfulness of sin' (Hebrews 3:13).

Three times Frances bravely tried to make reconciliation with him, as he continued his affair with Emma Hamilton. Her last letter was sent back marked, 'Opened . . . but not read.' The way in which both Nelson and Emma Hamilton treated Frances was disgraceful and cruel. Frances outlived Emma by twenty-six years. Nelson was certainly a great naval commander, but the shame of what he did to an innocent and devoted woman besmirches his life.

Doesn't sin do that to all of us? 'All have sinned and come short of the glory of God' (Romans 3:23). Sin may appear to be lovely, but before it is finished it is frighteningly dark. In today's text Isaiah is warning those who do not follow the Lord, but make idols of their own, that they will find their legacy will be disgrace and confusion. He is also underlining the truth that Israel shall be saved with an everlasting salvation; and that His leadership will never let them be ashamed or disgraced. Not now, or in the future – not ever! Let's follow that leadership today.

For thus says the Lord, who created the heavens, who is God, who formed the earth and made it, who has established it, who did not create it in vain, who formed it to be inhabited: "I am the Lord, and there is no other. I have not spoken in secret, in a dark place of the earth; I did not say to the seed of Jacob, 'Seek Me in vain'; I, the Lord, speak righteousness, I declare things that are right." Isaiah 45:18-19.

God never does anything in vain. In bringing about the Fall, with the consequent introduction of thorn and briar, disaster and death, the devil has wrought havoc on the earth. But he has not conquered. There will be a new earth, in which righteousness will dwell (2 Peter 3:13). He who formed and established the earth will see to it that there will be something of the old earth in the new one (see March 13th). The devil will never be able to say, 'God created the earth in vain.' God will have the last word.

Our text tells us that not only did God not create the earth in vain, but He did not ask Israel to seek Him in vain. He is a God who can be found; no earnest seeker will ever be turned away. 'Ask, and it will be given to you; seek, and you will find; knock, and it will be opened to you' (Matthew 7:7).

In Psalm 119:150, the psalmist writes, 'They draw near who follow after wickedness; they are far from Your law.' Then immediately he adds, 'You are near, O Lord . . .' Are those devotees of 'every trick in the book,' who unashamedly break the rules, coming into your space and threatening your life and principles? Have they said things about you that are untrue, manipulated people and turned them against you? Have they cheated and made a lot of money? 'Pride serves as their necklace . . . their eyes bulge with abundance' (Psalm 73:6, 7). Are they healthy, while your health is breaking down? Are they 'always at ease'? (Psalm 73:12). Are you tempted to think that 'seeking the Lord' is in vain; 'following after righteousness' is just not worth it?

Let me remind you of Asaph, whose experience is recorded for us in Psalm 73. He was almost overwhelmed by the prosperity of the wicked and the difficulties of the righteous. But on visiting the temple, his problem was thrown into the correct Biblical perspective, as he was suddenly reminded of how close the wicked are to destruction (v.18). He realised that they are only a heartbeat away from Hell. In contrast, the believer is but a heartbeat away from Heaven. Asaph found great comfort in the Lord: "I am continually with You; You hold me by my right hand . . . My flesh and my heart fail; but God is the strength of my heart and my portion forever" (vs. 23, 26).

Do the wicked draw near? Then remember that the Lord is near. After the resurrection, Thomas got a very big surprise when the Lord appeared to him, and was able to tell him what he had said in a former conversation, even though the Lord had not physically been there at the time. Small wonder that Thomas fell at His feet, saying, 'My Lord and my God.' So remember, He is the Lord who is near.

APRIL 21ST

"Assemble yourselves and come; draw near together, you who have escaped from the nations. They have no knowledge, who carry the wood of their carved image, and pray to a god that cannot save. Tell and bring forth your case; yes, let them take counsel together. Who has declared this from ancient time? Who has told it from that time? Have not I, the Lord? And there is no other God besides Me, a just God and a Saviour; there is none besides Me." Isaiah 45:20-21.

The Lord is now renewing His protest against idolaters. Again He reminds His people that the idols of earth cannot foretell the future, and now He emphasises His great ability to save. The people that carry the gods of wood in the processions have no knowledge of the future, and they pray to a god who cannot save. The living God is the mightiest Saviour, and He is gathering out a people (lit. 'escapers'). God did not hide His intention, that His salvation would extend world-wide. He told Abraham, 'In you all the families of the earth shall be blessed' (Genesis 12:3). In the book of Isaiah we have this priceless stanza:

'For unto us a Child is born, unto us a Son is given; and the government will be upon His shoulder. And His name will be called Wonderful, Counsellor, Mighty God, Everlasting Father, Prince of Peace. Of the increase of His government and peace there will be no end, upon the throne of David and over His kingdom, to order it and establish it with judgment and justice from that time forward, even forever. The zeal of the Lord of hosts will perform this' (9:6-7).

Idolaters pray to a god who cannot save; believers pray to 'a just God and a Saviour.' In the Bible, the word 'salvation' denotes deliverance. God delivered His people from Egypt, and He delivered them in their national battles. He also delivered the individual. David says, 'I sought the Lord, and He heard me, and delivered me from all my fears. They looked to Him and were radiant, and their faces were not ashamed. This poor man cried out, and the Lord heard him, and saved him out of all his troubles. The angel of the Lord encamps all around those who fear Him, and delivers them. Oh, taste and see that the Lord is good; blessed is the man who trusts in Him' (Psalm 34:4-8).

In the New Testament we read that Jesus came to seek and to save that which was lost (Luke 19:10). Here is deliverance, not just from Hell, but also from sin's present power (see Romans chapter 6). This deliverance through Christ brings conversion, regeneration, justification, adoption, sanctification and glorification! By faith in Christ, believers become a new creation. This deliverance is all by God's grace: it is entirely undeserved. It also extends to the deliverance of the universe (see Romans chapter 8; 1 Corinthians 15:28; Ephesians 1:10). Not only will our bodies be delivered from corruption, the very earth and the heavens will be delivered and redeemed. The gods of wood, and those who worship them, know nothing of this work of salvation. Happy are you, if you are among the 'escapers.'

APRIL 22ND

"Look to Me, and be saved, all you ends of the earth! For I am God, and there is no other." Isaiah 45:22.

For very many people, this verse is deeply associated with the great Victorian preacher, Charles Haddon Spurgeon, who has often been called 'the prince of preachers.' On Sunday morning, January 6th 1850, he was prevented from going to a church service by a severe snowstorm, so the 16 year-old Spurgeon stepped into a Primitive Methodist Chapel in Artillery Street, Colchester. Inside there were only a few people. The minister did not turn up, and a thin-looking man – 'a shoemaker, or tailor, or something of that sort,' Spurgeon later recalled – went up into the pulpit to preach. Spurgeon longed to know the salvation of his soul, but none of the preaching he had previously listened to told him how this could come about. He had heard that the Primitive Methodists sang so loudly they made people's heads ache; but he so much wanted to know how he might be saved, if they could tell him, he did not care how much they made his head ache!

Spurgeon later commented that the speaker that morning was obliged to stick to his text, for the simple reason that he had little else to say. It was our text for today: 'Look to Me, and be saved, all you ends of the earth! For I am God, and there is no other.' The thin-looking man could not even pronounce the words right. "My dear friends, this is a very simple text indeed. It says, 'Look.' Now lookin' don't take a great deal of pa'n. It ain't liftin' your foot or your finger; it is just 'look.' Well, a man needn't be worth a-thousand-a-year to be able to look. Anyone can look, even a child can look." He then urged his listeners to look to Christ. After about ten minutes, when his sermon was at its end, he looked at Spurgeon sitting under the gallery, and said, "Young man, you look miserable, and you will always be miserable. Miserable in life; and miserable in death, if you don't obey my text. But if you obey now, this moment, you will be saved." Spurgeon 'looked,' and was converted on the spot!

When eventually his great ministry came to an end, he was buried in Norwood cemetery in London. A hundred thousand people lined the route, and admission to the graveyard was by ticket only. They put a sash around the coffin. What did it say on the sash? 'Look unto me, and be ye saved, all the ends of the earth: for I am God, and there is none else.' Selah.

APRIL 23ʳᵈ

"I have sworn by Myself; the word has gone out of My mouth in righteousness, and shall not return, that to Me every knee shall bow, every tongue shall take an oath. He shall say, 'Surely in the Lord I have righteousness and strength. To Him men shall come, and all shall be ashamed who are incensed against Him. In the Lord all the descendants of Israel shall be justified, and shall glory.'" Isaiah 45:23-25.

When God makes a promise, surely His mere word is enough for us to rest upon with confidence? In today's text, God is not content to simply make a promise, He swears by an oath as well: 'I have sworn by Myself.' There is no higher source by which God can swear an oath, than by Himself. Here He swears that one day every knee will bow to Him. Just as surely as when God made a promise to Abraham, again swearing by Himself that with blessing He would bless him (Genesis 22:16,17), so here He swears that one day there will be a universal submission to Him.

This submission will be through an acknowledgement by knee and an acclamation by tongue. People will say, 'Surely in the Lord I have righteousness and strength.' Some, however, are not willing to submit. They still love their gods, and are enraged against the Lord. Theirs is an enforced submission, and their lot will be an everlasting shame. Which will you be: one who gladly submits to the Lord now, or one who will ultimately be forced to do so? All who do, are counted as the descendants of Israel. 'In the Lord' all are justified – made righteous – and shall glory in Him.

We have here, then, Isaiah's vast evangelistic vision. His message goes out to 'the ends of the earth.' In the final analysis, it involves every knee and every tongue. It is so easy to slip into a denominational view of spiritual things. Meditate on the vast scope of the message of Isaiah, which, as we shall see, has the Lamb of God at its heart. It is not some little thing, done in a single corner. Bowing to the Lord's authority and sovereignty over your life has profound implications: ultimately, it touches every corner!

There are superb truths in today's text: the promise of God, sworn on an oath; the ultimate, universal submission to God; the shame of idolatry; the truths of justification and glorying in the Lord. Yet, note the lovely practical truth linked right into it all: those who do submit to the Lord say, 'Surely in the Lord I have righteousness <u>and</u> strength.' Don't you love that touch from God? In Christ, you stand righteous before God; and you also get strength for the journey. How I need it! Don't you? Strength to face the foe, strength to witness, strength to deal with life's complexities, strength to face the unknown future, strength to keep my mind clean, strength to find the right word of compassion, strength to give the word of warning, strength to be good. Only in the Lord can such strength be found. Draw on it today, because it is inexhaustible.

APRIL 24TH

Bel bows down, Nebo stoops; their idols were on the beasts and on the cattle. Your carriages were heavily loaded, a burden to the weary beast. They stoop, they bow down together; they could not deliver the burden, but have themselves gone into captivity. Isaiah 46:1-2.

From history, it would appear that these verses do not apply to King Cyrus at the time when he besieged and invaded Babylon. There is no historical record of Cyrus taking the Babylonian gods into captivity. In fact, he had a policy of restoring them to their temples. On the Cyrus Cylinder (see April 12th), it says that he asked that the gods, Bel and Nebo, would be requested to grant him a long life. Isaiah is here, therefore, taking God's people forward to a distant day, when untold millions will worship the Lord. With His wonderfully graphic writing, he is asking them to grasp the futility of all man-made gods.

'Bel' means 'lord,' and was an alternative name for Marduk, the chief god of the city of Babylon. 'Nebo' was the patron god of wisdom and the art of writing. His function was to write the fates of people for the coming year on 'tablets of destiny,' as decreed by the gods. At every New Year festival he was brought from his own temple at Borsippa, South West of Babylon, and carried in procession with his father, Bel, through the streets of Babylon to the great Esagila shrine. All this would have been viewed by the captive Israelites, among them Daniel, Shadrach, Meshach and Abed-Nego.

Isaiah contemplates the end of these gods. The day comes when they are taken down from their pedestals and loaded on to the backs of, say, elephants, or pitched into the ox-wagons, and taken into captivity. It is, surely, an ignominious sight.

What can we learn from Isaiah's undoubted sarcasm? Some people have to carry their gods through life; they are burdened by the ritual, observances and creeds connected to their worship. I have seen them, by the million. Others have an entirely different experience; they yield their lives to the living God, and He carries them! Meditate on these words of Moses to the Children of Israel in the wilderness, before they passed over into the Promised Land: 'Do not be terrified, or afraid of them. The Lord your God . . . will fight for you, according to all He did for you in Egypt before your eyes, and in the wilderness where you saw how the Lord your God carried you, as a man carries his son, in all the way that you went until you came to this place' (Deuteronomy 1:29-31). The same God, who carried them, also carries you.

APRIL 25TH

"Listen to Me, O house of Jacob, and all the remnant of the house of Israel, who have been upheld by Me from birth, who have been carried from the womb: even to your old age, I am He, and even to grey hairs I will carry you!" Isaiah 46:3-4a.

When I first read F. B. Meyer on these verses, I confess to feeling somewhat like John Keats on first discovering Chapman's *Homer*. I am indebted to him for his observations.

He points out, firstly, that we all have the burden of existence. We did not ask to be born, but we were; and the life we have will last forever, somewhere. We all bear the burden of sin: would you be free of it? Christ bore our sins in His own body on the tree (1 Peter 2:24). Secondly, there is the burden of responsibility for others. Your family is dependent upon you, and it is no easy burden. Perhaps you have employees, and you care deeply for them: they are also dependent upon you. You may be a teacher, a doctor, a nurse, a nursery assistant, a chemist, a police officer – these all carry responsibility for others. Or you may be responsible for the care of aged parents. Thirdly, there is the burden of your life's work. It is a work only you can do. God gave you talents, for which you must give an account.

We all have heavy responsibilities placed upon us. Humanly speaking, we bear our own burdens in a solitary way. It is, and always will be, a lonely business. But we are not alone. The Lord has assumed the responsibility to carry us. He is the great burden bearer. He has carried us from the womb, and He promises that He will continue to do so, even to our old age.

So, then, weary one, 'Cast your burden on the Lord, and He shall sustain you' (Psalm 55:22). Says Christ, "Come to Me, all you who labour and are heavy laden, and I will give you rest" (Matthew 11:28). Remember, you don't carry Him – He carries you!

APRIL 26TH

"I have made, and I will bear; even I will carry, and will deliver you." Isaiah 46:4b.

Why does God assume the responsibility for carrying us? Because He made us. He made Israel as a very special people; and, despite all her wanderings and disobedience, He has not given up on her. He will carry and deliver her. God also made the world; and, despite what the Fall has done, He will carry and deliver it, for there will most certainly be a new earth. He made you, and put you in Christ. Despite all kinds of pressures that come upon you, and the times when you feel overwhelmed with failure, do not despair. Paul wrote, 'being confident of this very thing, that He who has begun a good work in you will complete it until the day of Jesus Christ' (Philippians 1:6).

Look around you. People leave work unfinished and abandon their projects. But in God's workshop, what He starts, He finishes. His strength will complete the work of grace, which He has begun in your life. God is not just reforming you – He is transforming you! It is the life of God working out in your soul. He awakened a desire in you for Himself, He revealed the work of Christ to your soul, He showed you the real meaning of Calvary, He forgave your sins and created a new person. Still He continues to work in you through His Word, using people and circumstances to smooth the rough edges. It is like the person who said to the sculptor, as he was sculpting a horse from a huge block of stone, "How do you get a horse from that?" "Everything that isn't horse has to come away," he replied.

The culmination of the mighty work that God has begun, is the day when there shall be 'new heavens and a new earth in which righteousness dwells' (2 Peter 3:13). The Lord Jesus will reign as King in that new earth. That is the day of ultimate redemption. It is called 'the day of Jesus Christ' (Philippians 1:6). On that day you will receive your reward for service to Him, and enter into your inheritance, which is 'incorruptible and undefiled and that does not fade away, reserved in heaven for you' (1 Peter 1:4). The work that He has begun in you will be completed to absolute perfection.

God has made you, and He will bear you. Whatever circumstances you face, He will carry and deliver you.

APRIL 27TH

"To whom will you liken Me, and make Me equal and compare Me, that we should be alike? They lavish gold out of the bag, and weigh silver on the scales; they hire a goldsmith, and he makes it a god; they prostrate themselves, yes, they worship. They bear it on the shoulder, they carry it and set it in its place, and it stands; from its place it shall not move. Though one cries out to it, yet it cannot answer nor save him out of his trouble." Isaiah 46:5-7.

God is unequalled and incomparable. It is absurd to put Him on a level with idols. They are made from earthly substances, which He made in the first place! The goldsmith takes the gold, and shapes a god out of it – God made the gold! Men then fall down and worship the god! In the wilderness, even the Children of Israel did the very same thing with the golden calf. It is human energy that bears, carries and sets the gods in their place; but the transcendent God is independent of all human activity. And aren't you glad that He is? He cannot be manipulated or moulded according to human desire. God is working out His own purposes, and He will have His way. When the Saviour of the world was crucified, even the cruel grave could not hold Him. Nothing can stay God's purposes: no army, political party, government, dictator, king, or queen; no school of philosophy or thought. When He moves to protect His people, or lead them into new ways, He will not be thwarted.

The gods of earth are lifeless. In the days of Elijah, do you recall the prophets of Baal calling out to their god on Mount Carmel? 'They called on the name of Baal from morning even till noon, saying, "O Baal hear us!" But there was no voice; no one answered.' Can we ever forget the scorn of Elijah? "Cry aloud," he said, "for he is a god; either he is meditating, or he is busy, or he is on a journey, or perhaps he is sleeping and must be awakened." They cut themselves with knives, and 'prophesied until the time of the offering of the evening sacrifice. But there was no voice; no one answered, no one paid attention' (1 Kings 18:26-29).

When you pray today, remember one great thing that links you with people like Isaiah and Elijah: the God who answered their prayers is just the same today. They did not live in a mechanised age. They had no satellites, mobile phones, aircraft, or cars. Elijah never had a personal computer! Yet their age and ours are linked by the fact that God is unchanging, and the gods of earth are still just as lifeless. Turn to the living God in prayer, and He will do what they cannot do: He will answer, and save you out of your trouble.

APRIL 28ᵀᴴ

"Remember this, and show yourselves men; recall to mind, O you transgressors. Remember the former things of old, for I am God, and there is no other; I am God, and there is none like Me, declaring the end from the beginning, and from ancient times things that are not yet done, saying, 'My counsel shall stand, and I will do all My pleasure.'"
Isaiah 46:8-10.

M y mother was very ill, and near to death. I was a schoolteacher at the time, and I recall one day coming home from work and standing at the foot of her bed. I asked her a very serious question: "What is it like to be where you are now, as a Christian?" "See that text on the wall," she said. It read, 'Thou wilt keep him in perfect peace, whose mind is stayed on thee' (Isaiah 26:3). She then mentioned a friend who had been a missionary in China, who told her that the Mandarin translation of the verse reads, 'You will keep him in perfect peace, whose mind stops at God.' "That's what I have got," she said.

This is exactly what Isaiah is driving at in today's text. God's people had a very different attitude to that of my mother. They were in a state of rebellion against God, particularly regarding His use of the heathen king, Cyrus, to bring about His purposes. God calls them 'transgressors,' rebels. He commands them to think through the immediate situation, and to let their minds stop at Him. Had He ever let them down? What is the record of His care for them? He challenges them to own up to the fact that, in all their long and rich history, even from the beginning He had always told them what was going to happen to them, and He would fulfil to the letter all that He had set out to do. Again He reminds them that He is unique, no idol can ever replace Him.

Whatever, then, the difficulties you face today, look past the problem to God. Perhaps you have failed? Then remember He is the God of Peter. Have you lost your temper? Remember

He is the God of Moses. Have you sinned sexually? Remember He is the God of David. Have you lied? Remember He is the God of Abraham. Have you run away from His will? Remember He is the God of Elijah. Are you facing tragedy? Remember He is the God of Job. Have you been stubborn? Remember He is the God of Jonah. Have you been bereaved? Remember He is the God of Ruth. You will be kept in perfect peace, if your mind stops at God.

APRIL 29TH

"Calling a bird of prey from the east, the man who executes My counsel, from a far country. Indeed I have spoken it; I will also bring it to pass. I have purposed it; I will also do it." Isaiah 46:11.

"Don't get a swelled head if the Lord uses you," said Stuart Briscoe, "because He has used some mighty strange people!" Like a successful bird of prey, Cyrus came from the east, guided and empowered by God to fulfil His purposes. Let this fact induce you to praise the Lord. Let it stimulate your faith and your hope. It shows the sovereignty of God, that He can choose whomever He pleases, and use whatever circumstances He wishes, to further His purposes.

I have recently been privileged to serve the Lord with a very fine group of young people who belong to the St. Andrew's University Christian Union. They faced a very difficult problem. St. Andrew's University Students' Union banned the Christian Union because, in their opinion, they were not inclusive enough. The fact that one had to be a confessing Christian to belong to the Christian Union was frowned upon. They found that they were not included in the University Handbook, nor were they able to hire rooms in the Students' Union for meetings, or even allowed to use a photocopier!

So, what did they do? Lie down under it all? Anything but! They stood up and declared that every Society gathers around some body of truth, and that theirs was the Lord Jesus. Members must believe in Him; but even if a person was not a Christian, they could still come to all the meetings. They put up posters, saying, 'Come along and find out why we have been banned.' Crowds of students did just that! The student newspaper, ironically called 'The Saint,' gave the Christian Union a full page to explain their position. They 'went to town!'

What happened? They saw a spiritual awakening in many lives, leading to conversions. They helped organise a Day of Prayer in Scotland, which attracted hundreds of praying students. I arrived on one of their 'away weekends,' to find two double-decker busloads of students, eager to study the Epistle to the Hebrews. They presented me with a lovely water-colour painting of St. Andrew's, that now hangs on my study wall. I asked them to sign the back of it for me. The signatures are accompanied by poignant comments, like, 'Thank you for reminding me that, because I have tasted of Jesus, I am spoiled for the world;' 'You have a great High Priest, whose name is love;' 'He has made me glad;' 'Thanks for revealing God's face to me;' 'The cross has said it all.' I was inspired and encouraged by the enthusiasm which they had for the things of God.

I returned at Christmas, to take their Carol Service. It was wonderful to hear that the ban had been lifted. Despite the opposition that this group of young Christians had faced, there was an edge to their witness, a power amongst them, which I'll never forget. Blessing from God sometimes comes from rare circumstances. Keep that in mind, Christian.

"Listen to Me, you stubborn-hearted, who are far from righteousness: I bring My righteousness near, it shall not be far off; My salvation shall not linger. And I will place salvation in Zion, for Israel My glory." Isaiah 46:12-13.

This is strong language from the God who had promised to bear Israel's burdens. God's love is not indulgent, it isn't soft. His people were stubborn, doubting His goodness, questioning His methods, rebelling against His prophecy. With God's impeccable record of care for His people, one would think that they would gladly submit to His purposes. Not so! They are far from aligning themselves to that which is right with God. These people are truly hard to help, but God's patience is awesome. He will not retract His good purposes; He will bring His righteousness near, and will not hesitate to save His people. They will be placed in Zion, and He will be glorified in them. And still today, God brings His righteousness near. He does not hesitate to save. All around us, people will not align themselves with Him, yet it doesn't frustrate His plans:

"The word is near you, in your mouth and in your heart" (that is, the word of faith which we preach): that if you confess with your mouth the Lord Jesus and believe in your heart that God has raised Him from the dead, you will be saved. For with the heart one believes unto righteousness, and with the mouth confession is made unto salvation. For the Scripture says, "Whoever believes on Him will not be put to shame." For there is no distinction between Jew and Greek, for the same Lord over all is rich to all who call upon Him. For "whoever calls on the name of the Lord shall be saved" (Romans 10:8-13).

It was in a huge storm at sea, that an amazing experience overwhelmed the blaspheming John Newton. For days on end, *The Greyhound* had tossed like a bottle in the mountainous seas. Suddenly the wind blew the sails into shreds, and in a very few moments the vessel became a virtual wreck. For John Newton and the twelve men on board, death stared them in the face. As he took his turn at the ship's pumps, Newton said to the captain, "If this won't do, then may the Lord have mercy on me." Then, suddenly he thought, "Why should the Lord have mercy on me?" Looking into that awful sea, he began to think about the Lord Jesus, whom he had mocked and scorned, but who had died for him at Calvary. Later he wrote, "The more I looked at what Jesus had done on the cross, the more He met my case exactly. I needed someone, or something, to stand between a righteous God and my sinful self – between God, who must punish sin, and a blasphemer. I needed an almighty Saviour, who would step in and take my sins away."

John Newton found God right there, on those hazardous waters of the Atlantic Ocean. *The Greyhound* eventually arrived in Ireland, off the Donegal coast, and limped up Lough Swilly. On 8th April 1748 it anchored beneath Buncrana Castle. Newton went on to become a very effective Christian minister. And still today, God's righteousness is near to stubborn hearts; His salvation does not linger, even in the midst of storms. Selah.

May

Here we have part of the spinning process where the linen fibres are being made parallel. We read in the Book of Ezekiel that the Phoenicians of Tyre used fine embroidered linen from Egypt for the sails of their famous ships. They sailed to destinations as far apart as Cornwall and Ophir; and Phoenician skill led to the circumnavigation of Africa.

"Come down and sit in the dust, O virgin daughter of Babylon; sit on the ground without a throne, O daughter of the Chaldeans! For you shall no more be called tender and delicate. Take the millstones and grind meal. Remove your veil, take off the skirt, uncover the thigh, pass through the rivers. Your nakedness shall be uncovered, yes, your shame will be seen; I will take vengeance, and I will not arbitrate with a man."
Isaiah 47:1-3.

We turn now to look at a poem by Isaiah, which carries a single theme: worldly power and arrogance. All of Isaiah chapter 47 is about what happens when people become self-centred and live without God. Babylon existed in history; but she is also a potent symbol anywhere of a Godless lifestyle, and where such a lifestyle will lead. We have much to learn from this poem.

Babylon's pride will be humbled in the dust. This city, with one of the Seven Wonders of the World, will be without a throne; and her reputation for sophisticated living, which was far from the mundane tasks of everyday life, will be changed. The once tender, delicate, and protected girl will now grind at the mill, and go into exile as a naked prisoner of war, wading through rivers. The vengeance of the Lord will thus fall upon the city.

It was not that Babylon did not have a chance to repent. In Nebuchadnezzar's day, Babylon was a beautiful city. Around the city was a torrid plain, which is still there. In Daniel chapter 4, God portrayed the city as being like a beautiful tree in the midst of the earth, with food for all: its leaves were lovely, its fruit abundant. Amidst its parks and gardens lived thousands of people. Art does make a difference, that's for sure. Is God, then, against beautiful things? Certainly not. Why, then, did He judge Nebuchadnezzar so severely?

It came about because of his attitude. One day Nebuchadnezzar was walking around the Royal Palace of Babylon, and said, "Is not this great Babylon, that I have built for a royal dwelling by my mighty power and for the honour of my majesty?" (Daniel 4:30). Nebuchadnezzar had become too impressed with himself, and God set out to show him that he was not big enough to be the goal of his own endeavour. So he was humbled, and subsequently repented.

When Babylon eventually fell to Cyrus, it was on the night of King Belshazzar's feast. Belshazzar knew all about God's dealings with his grandfather, Nebuchadnezzar, but he ignored them. During the feast he made a decision: he had the sacred vessels, which were taken from the temple at Jerusalem, brought to his feast and he drank out of them. In so doing he defied God, despite His kindness. He was saying that his own amusement was more important than God. To him, pleasure was life's supreme value. He looked out for Number One – himself. Then the finger of a man's appeared on the wall of his palace, and he was "found wanting" (Daniel 5:27). There was no arbitration. Belshazzar valued God as worthless; but the day came when God valued him. Selah.

As for our Redeemer, the Lord of hosts is His name, The Holy One of Israel. Isaiah 47:4

Small wonder that the Prophecy of Isaiah has been called the 'Romans of the Old Testament.' Here is the whole panoply of God's dealings with humankind, and His purposes in history. God judges the Babylonian empire for its arrogance, a judgment that they deserved; but at the same time He is acting as the Redeemer. God's primary action is to come alongside His people, protect them, and lead them out and back to the Holy City of Jerusalem. No matter what happens in history, God always has His people in mind. He is our Redeemer. Empires rise and fall, regimes come and go; but the redeeming purposes of God remain in place, surging on to the day when all of His people will be eternally before Him (see Ephesians 1:3-14).

Notice the constant reminder in these chapters of God's redemptive purposes: '"Fear not, you worm Jacob, you men of Israel! I will help you," says the Lord and your Redeemer, the Holy One of Israel' (Isaiah 41:14). 'Thus says the Lord, your Redeemer, the Holy One of Israel: "For your sake I will send to Babylon, and bring them all down as fugitives – the Chaldeans, who rejoice in their ships"' (Isaiah 43:14).

Even amidst all the discussions about how the earth was formed, and questions regarding the existence of other universes – believer, be reminded that you were chosen in Christ before the foundation of the world. As Babylon falls from her glory and is humbled in the dust, Isaiah thunders, 'As for our Redeemer, the Lord of hosts is his name.' In the midst of such confusion, praise God for a Redeemer!

The Redeemer is called 'the Lord of hosts.' What does this name signify? It signifies that He is possessed of absolute power and authority. Dozens of times in Old Testament Scripture, we come across the phrase, 'The Lord of hosts.' In Hebrew it frequently means 'army,' and angels are often associated with it. One day, we are told, when 'Joshua was by Jericho, that he lifted up his eyes and looked, and behold, a Man stood opposite him with His sword drawn in His hand. And Joshua went to Him and said to Him, "Are you for us or for our adversaries?" So He said, "No, but as Commander of the army of the Lord I have now come." And Joshua fell on his face to the earth and worshipped . . . ' (Joshua 5:13-14).

In Psalm 103:20,21 we read, 'Bless the Lord, you His angels, who excel in strength, who do His word . . . bless the Lord, all you His hosts, you ministers of His, who do His pleasure.'

Once the King of Syria sent a great army with horses and chariots to capture Elisha. When Elisha's young servant went out in the early morning, he saw that he and the prophet were truly surrounded. "Alas, my master! What shall we do?" he asked. The glorious answer came: "Do not fear, for those who are with us are more then those who are with them." In answer to Elisha's prayers, the young man's eyes were opened, and he saw that 'the mountain was full of horses and chariots of fire all around Elisha' (2 Kings 6:15-17).

Just as the Redeemer, the Holy One of Israel, protected His people in ancient Babylon, so God is still our 'refuge and strength, a very present help in trouble. Therefore we will not fear, even though the earth be removed . . . though the mountains shake . . . the Lord of hosts is with us; the God of Jacob is our refuge. Selah' (Psalm 46).

"Sit in silence, and go into darkness, O daughter of the Chaldeans; for you shall no longer be called The Lady of Kingdoms. I was angry with My people; I have profaned My inheritance, and given them into your hand. You showed them no mercy; on the elderly you laid your yoke very heavily. And you said, 'I shall be a lady forever,' So that you did not take these things to heart, nor remember the latter end of them."
Isaiah 47:5-7.

Take your time as you read these awesome words, for they are exceedingly profound. The nation that ordered others around is now brought to silence; the ruler who put others into chains now goes into the darkness of the captive's dungeon; 'The Lady of Kingdoms' loses her position amongst the nations of earth. In His permissive and corrective will, God had allowed His people to fall into Babylonian hands. He was thoroughly disgusted with the people whom He had brought to birth; but He still held Babylon accountable for the fact that they had no compassion on Israel. They were cruel with the elderly people, putting them to hard labour. God noted that the Babylonians lived as if there was no tomorrow: they thought they would be the 'First Lady of Kingdoms' forever. They weighed nothing up, took nothing to heart, and did not look to where it would all end.

God is watching nations as well as individuals, and He holds them accountable for their actions. They will not be permitted to ride roughshod over people with impunity. Their atrocities in war, and their cruelty in ruling, are noted. They will be judged for it. 'Righteousness exalts a nation,' says the Book of Proverbs (14:34), 'but sin is a reproach to any people.' According to today's text, nations and leaders are responsible for considering carefully the consequences of their actions. A nation needs a heart that cares about its people. Could it be that God would use you to give your nation its heart? Is there someone reading these lines and, as you watch your nation plunge on like the Babylonians – heedless of people's true needs and God's laws, you feel God is calling you to become a leader?

'The Babylonian factor' is still with us. God used Shadrach, Meshach and Abed-nego to defy the king, who insisted that the inhabitants of his kingdom worship an image he had set up. Through them, the very heart of the arrogant Nebuchadnezzar was moved to worship the living God. In the days of Darius, the Mede, Daniel was used by God to do the same. Darius passed a law which demanded that, for a period of thirty days, people ask petitions only of him. If anyone asked a petition of any man or god during that period, they would be cast into a den of lions. To quote an old Jewish saying: "Ach! What things people are capable of doing for love of themselves!" In the face of such national arrogance, what could four men do in this land where they now lived? They decided to rise up in the name of God, and bring their national leaders to see that there was no god but God. They embraced the risk and took the venture of faith, for the sake of good. I seriously ask you today, 'Are you the one whom God is calling to bring about a change in your nation? Are you ready to do good for Him, and for Him alone, without any self-interest?' If so, obey Him. Stand up and be counted; and your nation may never be the same again.

"Therefore hear this now, you who are given to pleasures, who dwell securely, who say in your heart, 'I am, and there is no one else besides me; I shall not sit as a widow, nor shall I know the loss of children'; but these two things shall come to you in a moment, in one day: the loss of children, and widowhood. They shall come upon you in their fullness because of the multitude of your sorceries, for the great abundance of your enchantments." Isaiah 47:8-9.

Pride. "These new super-rich won't loosen their wads," Ted Turner was reported as saying, in the *New York Times*, "because they're afraid they'll reduce their net worth, and go down the list. That's their Super Bowl . . . My hands shook when I signed the papers (for charitable gifts), because I knew I was taking myself out of the running for The Richest Man in America." We react in disgust at what Mr. Turner says; and yet we must be careful. It was C. S. Lewis who said that if anyone would like to acquire humility he thought he could tell that person the first step. And the first step would be to realise that one is proud. He said that if you think you are not conceited, it means you are very conceited indeed. May we ever be spared the comment made of Victor Hugo, when he was described as 'a walking personal pronoun!'

Nations, too, get proud. Dr Rudi Dornbusch, an M.I.T. professor, said, "the U.S. economy likely will not see a recession for many years to come. We don't want one, we don't need one, and as we have the tools to keep the current expansion going, we won't have one. This expansion will run forever." He reckoned without September 11th. This attitude is not new, of course. Chaldea, of which Babylon was the capital, was a nation that thought she was Queen of the earth. As our text tells us, she got herself to the point where she uttered the ultimate blasphemy: "I am, and there is no one else besides me" (vs.8, 10). She did not see herself as ever being widowed, or suffering the loss of children. The blessings of life would be preserved to her, and increased, world without end. But it was a false security: God warned that one day she would know widowhood and the loss of children.

Chaldea is now described as being a seductive woman, who believes her success is found in sorcery. Her enchantments, or spells, were 'bonds,' i.e. associations with occult-powers, which she entered into with the idea of binding the future. Sex played a major role in this culture. Isthar, the sex goddess, was worshipped; and orgies were carried out in her name during the temple worship. But the practice of black art and the worship of sex would not deliver this nation or her capital city.

The counterpart to pride is what the Bible calls, poverty of spirit. Jesus said, "Blessed are the poor in spirit, for theirs is the kingdom of heaven" (Matthew 5:3). Let us also beware of false humility – of looking at oneself as a doormat. Rather, let us be among those who realise that we have nothing to boast of in this world, except God.

"For you have trusted in your wickedness; you have said, 'no one sees me;' your wisdom and your knowledge have warped you; and you have said in your heart, 'I am, and there is no one else besides me.' Therefore evil shall come upon you; you shall not know from where it arises. And trouble shall fall upon you; you will not be able to put it off. And desolation shall come upon you suddenly, which you shall not know." Isaiah 47:10-11.

Mark well the philosophy of life followed by the city and culture that had become a law to itself. Sin had become the people's way of life, they deliberately trusted in wickedness. This led them to a state where they believed they were accountable to no one but themselves. They said, "No one sees me." It was warped thinking: it led to disaster then, and it leads to disaster now.

In an interview with Associated Press, after his resignation following a scandal, President Clinton's political adviser, Dick Morris, said a very significant thing: "My sense of reality was just altered. I started out being excited working for the President. Then I became arrogant, then I became grandiose, and then I became self-destructive . . . Everybody who turns 40 should read the Greek tragedies. They all have within them the same idea: the thing that may have helped you move up, then destroys you. And I'm a living example of that."

The Chaldean culture lived by evil, and evil destroyed her. Unexpectedly and suddenly, disaster fell upon her. She could not charm it away, or buy it off. She did not know its dawn. 'That very night,' says Daniel 5:30-31, 'Belshazzar, king of the Chaldeans, was slain. And Darius the Mede received the kingdom . . .'

What, then, should our attitude be? 'Let this mind be in you which was also in Christ Jesus,' wrote Paul, 'who, being in the form of God, did not consider it robbery to be equal with God, but made Himself of no reputation, taking the form of a bondservant, and coming in the likeness of men. And being found in appearance as a man, He humbled Himself and became obedient to the point of death, even the death of the cross. Therefore God also has highly exalted Him and given Him the name which is above every name, that at the name of Jesus every knee should bow, of those in heaven, and of those on earth, and of those under the earth, and that every tongue should confess that Jesus Christ is Lord, to the glory of God the Father' (Philippians 2:5-11). God knows, we could do with people who have Christ-like minds.

"Stand now with your enchantments and the multitude of your sorceries, in which you have laboured from your youth – perhaps you will be able to profit, perhaps you will prevail. You are wearied in the multitude of your counsels; let now the astrologers, the stargazers, and the monthly prognosticators stand up and save you from what shall come upon you." Isaiah 47:12-13.

Babylon has claimed self-deification. Twice it has said, "I am, and there is no one else besides me" (vs.8, 10). As recorded in Isaiah 45:5, the Almighty One had claimed, "I am the Lord, and there is no other; there is no God besides me." Now the test had come, as it always will: in the day of evil the Almighty One calls on Babylon to save herself. Babylon had defied God, and now God gives her a chance to prove herself. With their enchantments and sorceries, astrologers, stargazers, and their monthly prognosticators, He calls the people to stand, and see if they shall prevail. They might have trusted in the multitude of predictions given over the years, but how will they fare now, as the evil day comes? We shall see in tomorrow's text; but in the meantime let us ask ourselves how would we stand in the day of testing?

Perhaps this piece, written by the broadcaster Alistair Cooke, in *The patient has the Floor*, will help:

The time was the 19th May 1780. The place was Hartford, Connecticut. The day has gone down in New England history as a terrible foretaste of the judgement day, for at noon the skies turned from blue to grey, and by mid-afternoon had blackened over so densely that, in that religious age, men fell on their knees and begged a final blessing before the end came. The Connecticut House of Representatives was in session, and as some men fell down, and others clamoured for an immediate adjournment, the Speaker of the House, one Colonel Davenport, came to his feet. He silenced them, and said these words: "The day of Judgement is either approaching, or it is not. If it is not, there is no cause for an adjournment. If it is, I choose to be found doing my duty. I wish, therefore, that candles may be brought."

Selah.

May 7th

"Behold, they shall be as stubble, the fire shall burn them; they shall not deliver themselves from the power of the flame; it shall not be a coal to be warmed by, nor a fire to sit before! Thus shall they be to you with whom you have laboured, your merchants from your youth; they shall wander each one to his quarter. No one shall save you."
Isaiah 47:14-15.

How will Chaldea fare in the coming great test? How will its capital city do in the hour of trial and evil? Its whole system of false religion will explode, like stubble in a flame. Not a warm and comforting fire, burning slowly, like logs of wood. It will not glow for a long time like coal; it will be a great flame that will quickly die out, leaving only ashes. The false religion that they have followed will burn, rather than warm and comfort, them.

Where will the traffickers of their religion be in the coming day of testing? Over many years, these merchants had made a lot of money out of it all. So, where do merchants go when the market collapses? It's every person for him or her self! 'They shall wander each one to his quarter,' says the text. Each one makes an exit, to do their own thing; and, no doubt, to look for profit somewhere else.

In the day of testing, where will Babylon, 'the daughter of the Chaldeans,' be? Isaiah 47 started by telling us that she would 'sit in the dust,' and 'sit on the ground without a throne.' To the dust is added the ashes of her false religion, and no one will save her.

The saddest thing in these verses is the fact that, from their youth up, thousands of people have followed the leaders. In fact, they have 'laboured' with them: they have worked hard at their religion, only to find it worthless.

I challenge you to consider your life. Are you building your 'house' on the sand, only to see it swept away in the coming storm? On the other hand, are you building your house on a rock, which will stand unmoved when the wind and the rain beat upon it? When a culture rejects the living God, weightlessness enters into it – it is unsubstantiated. God is the God of glory: He has weight. When Belshazzar was weighed in God's balances, he was found wanting. He had no substance. There was weightlessness in his religion: the religion of hedonism – of chasing pleasure. It was swept away in the hour of death.

As children we sang, 'Build on the rock, the rock that ever stands. Build on the rock, and not upon the sands. You need not fear the storm, nor the earthquake shock. You're safe forevermore, if you build on the rock.' That rock is Christ.

MAY 8ᵀᴴ

"Hear this, O house of Jacob, who are called by the name of Israel, and have come forth from the wellsprings of Judah; who swear by the name of the Lord, and make mention of the God of Israel, but not in truth or in righteousness; for they call themselves after the holy city, and lean on the God of Israel; the Lord of hosts is His name." Isaiah 48:1-2.

When all is said and done, there is more said than done. In their solemn oaths and personal pledges, God's people swear by the name of the Lord. They make mention of the God of Israel in their worship, and, no doubt, in their discussions about theology. They are also happy to take the name of Israel, and claim their great spiritual pedigree from 'the wellsprings of Judah.' They proudly claim their citizenship in Jerusalem. They talk the talk, for sure; but they do not walk the walk.

If all this were not hypocritical enough, they then turn to the Lord in their times of trouble or need, and 'lean on' Him. Who is this One to whom they swear allegiance? He is the Lord Almighty, the God of the angel-armies, the One who rules the world, and the One who can wipe out their enemies.

Here we have the rottenness of external religion, without inward reality. These people are not genuine or right, and the Lord of Hosts can see their hypocrisy and failure. He can see through their hearts and lives.

I can remember as a little boy listening to one of the greatest Bible teachers I have ever heard. He had been born the son of a miner; schooled in God's school, he had been called into His service as a preacher and teacher of God's Word. He was a preaching partner of my father. His name was David Craig, though I confess we all called him 'Scotch Davy.' As I sat listening to him, he started to preach about hypocrisy being like the wax that was sometimes used to fill in the cracks in the columns of Greek temples. The 'fluted' wax looked just like the real thing. Then came the day of a great fire, and the flames started to lick at the columns, melting the wax. The great columns came crashing down, exposing their 'hypocrisy.' Mr. Craig applied the message, and in memory's ear I can still hear the old clock ticking on the wall. The stillness was palpable, as the message on hypocrisy went home to our hearts. He told us that the true nature of our works would one day become clear: 'The Day will declare it, because it will be revealed by fire; and the fire will test each one's work, of what sort it is . . . If anyone's work is burned, he will suffer loss; but he himself will be saved, yet so as through fire. Do you not know that you are the temple of God and that the Spirit of God dwells in you? If anyone defiles the temple of God, God will destroy him. For the temple of God is holy, which temple you are' (1 Corinthians 3:13-17).

So, then, no more 'waxing.'

MAY 9TH

"I have declared the former things from the beginning; they went forth from My mouth, and I caused them to hear it. Suddenly I did them, and they came to pass. Because I knew that you were obstinate, and your neck was an iron sinew, and your brow bronze. Even from the beginning I have declared it to you; before it came to pass I proclaimed it to you, lest you should say, 'My idol has done them, and my carved image and my moulded image have commanded them.'" Isaiah 48: 3-5.

Is it not just incredible that Isaiah uses the same argument against Israel, as he did against the Chaldean and Babylonian people? They trusted in dead idols, but the Lord contended and proved that He could predict the future, and their idols could not. Now He shows why He had let them in on the way He worked; how He had told them what He was going to do beforehand, and then fulfilled it all to the letter. If He had not, they would have said that their idol had done it! What! Israel? The very people. They had become idolaters.

And more. God exposes their character. Metaphorically speaking, they had become people with necks like sinews of iron, and their foreheads like bronze. God saw their pride and their closed minds. In temperament they were stubborn, obstinate, difficult and cantankerous. And all the time God had been planning for them in love!

It reminds me of David, when he sinned with Bathsheba. He became so hardhearted. The shepherd boy who defeated Goliath, the songwriter whose psalms are still enjoyed by millions, the man who longed for God's glory more than anything else, had stolen another man's wife and arranged his death. David fell morally, and committed the sin of his life. For a whole year he tried to hide his sin, closed his lips, and refused to confess it. Then David defeated the king of Rabbah, and the king's crown was set on David's head. He brought out the people of Ammon from every city, and put them to work with saws, iron picks, and axes. But the tough ruler was a hypocrite. Through Nathan the prophet, the Lord, who still loved him, moved to expose his sin and bring him to repentance. If ever anybody was sorry for his sins, that person was David. The horror of what he had done almost overwhelmed his very sanity. His penitential psalms are truly restorative material.

As we shall see, the love of God for His erring people was as great in Isaiah's time as it was in David's. And it still is. Can I explain it? – "I know not why, I only cry, 'Oh how He loves me!'"

MAY 10TH

"You have heard; see all this. And will you not declare it? I have made you hear new things from this time, even hidden things, and you did not know them. They are created now and not from the beginning; and before this day you have not heard them, lest you should say, 'Of course I knew them.'" Isaiah 48:6-7.

'**K**now-alls' are arrogant people. They think there is nothing more you can tell them. Even God has to confront them about their attitude. God is doing something here that He did not do in the exodus from Egypt, where His intentions were plainly laid out beforehand. The announcement of His choice of Cyrus to be Israel's Saviour took them by surprise: they had no idea it was going to happen. Not one of them could say that they had known all along that it was going to happen, and arrogant Israel was humbled by this news. Here was something completely new, and the 'know-alls' were exposed.

It may sound trite, but don't you think we ought to acknowledge that God knows some things that we don't? Some people have to know a reason for everything that happens to them. I have written it before, and I write it again: God is full of surprises. He can do a completely new thing in a way of His own choosing, and we don't have to be told – do we? If we don't know immediately what ultimately He is up to, is that any less reason for not trusting Him?

Don't you think promises are much better than explanations? Imagine yourself in hospital over an extended period, with broken bones and serious injuries. One day a doctor arrives and tells you in great detail what he has given you by way of overall treatment. Would that deeply inspire you? It would be interesting and helpful, but it would not compare to the doctor saying to you that you were going home tomorrow! One is an explanation, the other is a promise.

God knows it all, not us. His knowledge is awesome. In His wisdom He does not explain everything from the beginning; but He does give us promises, as we trust Him for the future. Then, in that future, it is His prerogative when He springs some surprises. Let's be glad and rejoice in it, and tell others about this glorious characteristic of our God. Let's not be like Israel who heard and saw this, but sulked, argued, and criticised God for His actions.

MAY 11TH

"Surely you did not hear, surely you did not know; surely from long ago your ear was not opened. For I knew that you would deal very treacherously, and were called a transgressor from the womb. For My name's sake I will defer My anger, and for My praise I will restrain it from you, so that I do not cut you off." Isaiah 48:8-9.

Treachery in the people of God? In what way were they treacherous? They went over to false gods and served them, at the same time as they professed their allegiance to the Almighty God (Isaiah 48:1-2). They were poor listeners to what the Lord had to say. Right from the start they were called 'a transgressor' from the ways of the Lord. God knew exactly what He was taking on.

Here we see the awesome patience of God. How easy it would have been for Him to pour out His anger upon them! 'Our God is a consuming fire' (Hebrews 12:29). The Scriptures speak of the time when the Lord Jesus will be 'revealed from heaven with His mighty angels, in flaming fire taking vengeance on those who do not know God, and on those who do not obey the gospel of our Lord Jesus Christ. These shall be punished with everlasting destruction from the presence of the Lord and from the glory of his power' (1 Thessalonians 1:7-9). God opened the ground, and it swallowed the rebellious sons of Korah (Numbers 16:31-33). Uzzah perished when he dared to touch the Ark of the Covenant (2 Samuel 6:6-7). The judicial, righteous 'wrath of God is revealed against all ungodliness and unrighteousness of men, who suppress the truth in unrighteousness' (Romans 1:18).

Despite all Israel's treachery and transgressions, God restrains and defers His anger. Why? For His name's sake, and for His praise. This is not an attempt by God to justify Himself; it is God being true to Himself. This is what He is like. We do not need to wait until New Testament times to find out that it is in God's nature to be a saviour. Through the blood of a lamb He saved Israel from the avenging angel in Egypt; and it spoke of the day when He would save us through the blood of the Lamb at Calvary. Christ said that He had not come to condemn the world but to save it (John 3:17). He was only revealing the heart of God.

The second reason for restraining His anger towards His people was because praise was due to Him. After the golden calf debacle, Moses stood between the people and God's anger. He contended that the Egyptians would mock God if He abandoned His people: 'Why should the Egyptians speak, and say, "He brought them out to harm them, to kill them in the mountains, and to consume them from the face of the earth"?' (Exodus 32:12). Moses reminded God of His promises to Abraham, Isaac and Jacob.

Believer, there is a deep mystery in today's texts; but the bottom line is that God will keep you, for His name and for His praises' sake. You can be assured of it, and people will praise His name for what He has done in your life.

May 12ᵀᴴ

"Behold, I have refined you, but not as silver; I have tested you in the furnace of affliction. For My own sake, for My own sake, I will do it; for how should My name be profaned? And I will not give My glory to another." Isaiah 48:10-11.

In the end, the Lord's purposes will be accomplished. He chose Israel, and He will not be diverted from His choice. If He is faced with treachery, transgression, and downright obstinacy from His people, then He will refine them through the furnace of affliction. It is a different process from the refining of silver. Alec Motyer points out that silver endures the heat until all the impurity is gone. But Israel would not be able to endure the heat, she would perish under it. So the Lord set a limit to the furnace of affliction. Whether in Egypt or Babylon, a point is reached where the refining process stops, and the Lord lets His people go.

Let me share a poem I wrote when preaching once at the Keswick Convention in England's beautiful Lake District. My wife Margaret and I went into nearby Ambleside, and ambled into a shop, where a glass-blower was at work. Here is the experience I had:

The craftsman of Ambleside

I watched him at work in Ambleside,
As he made that sand into glass.
And what I learned that afternoon,
I feel I must not let pass

The molten liquid he stretched and pulled,
His measuring rod he applied.
He cut and smoothed and rolled it along –
It's natural shape he defied

As slowly, so slowly, its new shape emerged,
He frequently left his seat,
And took his creation to the furnace door,
And moved it into the heat

It was at 1,400 degrees, they said –
And I'm sure they had not lied.
He did not spare the white-hot heat,
That craftsman of Ambleside

As I quietly watched that master at work,
My Master gently said to me,
"There are things I do now that you don't understand,
That one day you'll eventually see."

Do you know what that craftsman is truly about,
Do you know what he'll finally make,
And how useful it will be in palace or home,
For a king or a mother to take?

A beautiful plate on which to place food,
A vase to put flowers in place,
A lampshade to focus an evening glow –
An entrance-table to grace?

A chalice to drink from, a paperweight,
An anniversary piece of true pride,
A figurine, or sculpted face,
And many other creations beside?

So now from the heat may I not turn away.
Though against it I've often cried,
May I cry no more, because of what I learned
From the craftsman of Ambleside.

MAY 13TH

"Listen to Me, O Jacob, and Israel, My called: I am He, I am the First, I am also the Last. Indeed My hand has laid the foundation of the earth, and My right hand has stretched out the heavens; when I call to them, they stand up together." Isaiah 48:12-13.

In my memory I can still hear my mother calling me as a child. I can recollect many a teacher's call in school. In this island of tragic beauty, I have heard many a community leader's call for peace. I have known love's call, in a look, a movement, and an inflection. I have known the call of duty, demanding a very steady hand. I have certainly heard temptation's call – subtle, luring, and deadly. I have known the call of our children – as babies, juniors, teenagers – and I am amazed and touched that as adults they still give us a call! Who of us have not known the call of the heavens, as 'day unto day they utter speech, and night unto night they reveal knowledge' (Psalm 19:2)? Yet, above all the calls I have ever heard, the most distinct and unmistakable is the call of God.

In today's text we learn that when God calls, the heavens stand to attention. He who starts things and finishes them only has to speak, and from His creation there is immediate reaction. Each part moves to fulfil its purpose. Whether they liked it or not, this very same God also called Israel: "Israel, My called," He says. They may deny His call or try to get away from it, but the Lord will fulfil His purposes for them. Their refining will lead to their usefulness.

My friend Os Guinness has recently been writing, speaking and teaching about the call of God to us as individuals. "If there is a call, there must be a caller," he affirms. He draws attention to the huge, seismic shift in Europe when, in 1520, Martin Luther wrote and published his work, *The Babylonian Captivity*. The captivity in question was the church's denial of spiritual rights to the laity. His writing heralded the recovery of the Biblical view of 'calling.' In one move, Luther undermined the medieval world's distinction between the secular and the sacred, and between a life of contemplation and one of action. He was used by God to highlight the truth that everyone, everywhere, and in everything, can act by faith and glorify God. Whatever we do, we should all live with a sense of calling. As George Herbert put it:

This is the famous stone
That turneth all to gold;
For that which God doth touch and own
Cannot for less be told.

MAY 14TH

"All of you, assemble yourselves, and hear! Who among them has declared these things? The Lord loves him; He shall do His pleasure on Babylon, and His arm shall be against the Chaldeans. I, even I, have spoken; yes, I have called him, I have brought him, and his way will prosper." Isaiah 48:14-15.

The word of God is behind all that happens in history and eternity. From the calling of creation, to the calling of Cyrus standing at the gate of Babylon; from the vast detail of outer space, to the tiny details guiding an earthly king to free a people – the sovereignty of God is a great comforting factor, as in our day and generation we contemplate the world scene. "I, even I, have spoken," says God.

Notice the phrase, 'The Lord loves him.' Alec Motyer points out that where it is hyphenated the phrase becomes, as it were, a title: 'The-Lord-loves-him.' Cyrus never had a better title. All through his career the Lord was at his side, ordering his affairs, clearing his way across valley and hill, until he fulfilled to the letter precisely what the Lord had predicted he would do.

People and nations respond to titles. In business, in politics, in the judiciary, in the military, and in education, titles are important. What business card, for example, does not give a precise description of who the person is, in terms of the position he or she holds in their company? Here, for any individual, is the title above all titles: 'The-Lord-loves-him.' Is this not the factor that brings sanity in a world filled with selfishness and hatred? You can claim it, because the Scripture states, 'God so loved the world that He gave His only begotten Son, that whoever believes in Him should not perish but have everlasting life' (John 3:16).

Franklin Graham tells the story of being in Africa at a time of crisis, where the utter devastation of war had broken into the lives of the people. He saw a little girl sitting in the midst of a camp, rocking herself as children do when they are distressed. She was singing. He asked a soldier who was standing by what she was singing, so he leaned down to listen. She was singing in French. And the words? 'Yes, Jesus loves me. The Bible tells me so.'

You may be confused, you may be heartbroken. You may be surrounded by people who do not have your good at heart, and you can see no way out. But exult in the title, 'The-Lord-loves-me.' If you were to swim in the ocean of God's love for a thousand years, you would never come to the shore. Why? Because there is no shore.

MAY 15TH

"Come near to Me, hear this: I have not spoken in secret from the beginning; from the time that it was, I was there. And now the Lord God and His Spirit have sent Me." Isaiah 48:16.

Who is this speaker? He is unnamed, but He carries the name that is above all other names. The interjection comes as a surprise: why should the Messiah speak here? Because King Cyrus is about to fade from the scene, his work having been accomplished, and the One who is the object and climax of history is about to be revealed. Earlier in the chapter, God had spoken of 'new things from this time, even hidden things, and you did not know them.' Now the One who would bring about those 'new things' interjects to say that God has sent Him. I find my own spirit soaring as I hear Him moving by the rivers and gates of Babylon, saying, "Come near to Me." My heart responds, "Gladly, Lord, gladly."

And what would He say to me? "I have not spoken in secret from the beginning," He says, "from the time that it was, I was there." To be quite honest, this fills me with the deepest awe. It makes me cast my mind forward to the prologue to John's Gospel. Just as the eagle is the only living creature that can look straight at the sun and not be dazzled, so John penetrates his gaze into eternity past and, without a flinch, says that there never was a time when Christ did not exist. A literal translation reads, 'In the beginning was continuing the Word' (John 1:1). At the beginning of the earth He was there, for John says, 'All things were made through Him.' There is 'not a flower but shows some touch, in freckle, streak or strain, of His unrivalled pencil.'

There are probably ten octillion stars in space. One thousand million is one billion; one thousand billion is one trillion; one thousand trillion is one quadrillion; one thousand quadrillion is one quintillion; one thousand quintillion is one sextillion; one thousand sextillion is one septillion; one thousand septillion is one octillion – and there are at least ten of those in space! In this very week of writing, NASA scientists, using a sophisticated new camera on the Hubble Space telescope, have unveiled the most spectacular views of the rest of the Universe ever seen by human beings. The first pictures taken for the surveys by the £52-million Advanced Camera show the Cone and Omega nebulae, or gas columns, in our Milky Way. The first is 2,500 light years away, and the second is 5,500 light years away! The farthest object observed is the Tadpole galaxy, which is 430 million light years way! The Gospel of John tells us that Christ was there when the Universe was first formed.

"And now the Lord God and His Spirit have sent me," says Isaiah 48:16. I have often sung the old evangelistic hymn with the children, about the gypsy boy who first heard the gospel on his deathbed. When he believed the message, the lad was heard to say, "I am so glad that for me He was sent." And so am I. The One who was there at the beginning, never ends with an end: He always ends with a beginning. Whatever you face in life, as sure as the sunrise, the Lord will bring you fresh, new, invigorating beginnings. Christian, when time ends for you, it will be the beginning of an eternal day.

MAY 16TH

Thus says the Lord, your Redeemer, the Holy One of Israel: "I am the Lord your God, who teaches you to profit, who leads you by the way you should go." Isaiah 48:17.

Here is a teacher whom the Harvard Business School would do well to observe. He guides people to that which truly profits. In order to lead Israel away from unprofitable living, He had just disciplined them. They had been going down paths that led them to waste their precious talents and lives. God wanted them to profit, not lose.

In all chastening by God, it is 'for our profit, that we may be partakers of His holiness' (Hebrews 12:10). Eternal profit is so much better than transitory, material profit. To underline how worthwhile it is, let me share a well-known story.

John Bunyan was a tinker's son, born in 1628 in the little English village of Elstow in Bedfordshire. As a boy he was idle, heavily into lying and blaspheming. For a time he became a soldier in the Civil War. He was eventually led to Christ by his wife, and in 1653 he joined a group of nonconformists in Bedford, and became a great preacher. Nonconformists disagreed with the disciplines and some of the teachings of the established Church, the Church of England. When King Charles II ended the freedom that the nonconformists had enjoyed, Bunyan was jailed for over 12 years in all. In 1678, from the prison in Bedford, Bunyan published his famous work, *The Pilgrim's Progress*. He was so uncertain about whether or not it was a good book, that he wrote a little rhyme of apology:

Some said, "John print it." Others said, "Not so."
Some said, "It might do good." Others said, "No."

I found it a moving moment, when reading the published Order of Service for the funeral of Queen Elizabeth the Queen Mother, that she had personally chosen a beautiful section of *The Pilgrim's Progress*. Part of it read,

I see myself now at the end of my journey, my toilsome days are ended. I am now to see that head that was crowned with thorns, and that face that was spit upon for me. I have formerly lived by hearsay and faith, but now go where I shall live by sight, and shall be with Him in whose company I delight myself. I have loved to hear my Lord spoken of; and wherever I have seen the print of His shoe in the earth, there have I coveted to set my foot to. His name to me has been as a civet-box; yea, sweeter than all perfume. His voice to me has been most sweet; and His countenance I have more desired than they that have most desired the light of the sun. His word I did use to gather my food, and for antidotes against my fainting. 'He has held me, and hath kept me from mine iniquities: yea, my steps hath He strengthened in His way.'

Is it not fascinating, that a Christian preacher, imprisoned by King Charles II, should publish a Christian book in 1678, and 324 years later Queen Elizabeth, the Queen Mother, would deliberately arrange to have part of it printed in the Order of Service for her funeral? Over 200 million people heard it read live, across the worldwide media. This is what I call eternal profit! Bunyan never would have dreamt that such profit lay in store, through a book that some Christians told him not to print. Christians are not always right in their assessment, that's for sure. Selah.

MAY 17TH

"Oh, that you had heeded My commandments! Then your peace would have been like a river . . . " Isaiah 48:18.

Yesterday we read of profit to be gained; today we read of profit that was lost. If these people had only obeyed the Lord's commandments, they would have had one of the greatest gains anyone could know: peace like a river. Are there sadder words in any language than, 'It might have been'? With his writer's gift of the masterful use of imagery, here we have Isaiah, under God, wistfully taking the image of a river to epitomise peace.

Again, I deeply appreciate F. B. Meyer's exposition of this verse. He points out that the image is not that of a brook. A brook is a small stream. You can hear it as it gushes musically over the stones. Nor is it the image of a stream. A stream is a small river. It may not even be able to afford enough water for fish to pass to its higher reaches. Rather, it is the image of a broad, deep river, sweeping along far down its course with a calm current, heading for the depth and volume of the open sea.

'Oh, rivers that minister perpetually to man – not swept by storm, nor drained by drought, not anxious about continuance. Always mirroring the blue of the azure sky, or the stars by night, and yet content to stay for every daisy that sends its tiny root for nourishment – in your growth from less to more, your perennial fullness, your beneficent ministry, your volume, your calm, you were meant to preach to man, with perpetual melody, of the infinite peace that was to rise and grow, and unfold with every stage of his experience! Such at least was God's ideal for Israel, and for all who swear by His name and make mention of Jehovah as God' (F. B. Meyer, *Christ in Isaiah*, Marshall, Morgan & Scott, 1950, p.77).

My reader, how about you? What about your ministry? To borrow Isaiah's image, are you flowing through your community like a deep, peaceful river – nourishing, calming, and refreshing all who know you or touch your life? Or are you going to spend the rest of your life overwhelmed with the cares of this world and the deceitfulness of riches, with your thoughts wholly concentrated on how to make more money in the shortest possible time?

Are you going to obey your Lord's commandments, follow His call upon your life, and radiate the peace that passes understanding, which will point others to the Prince of Peace? May our prayer be, 'Lord, make me a channel of Your peace.'

MAY 18TH

" . . . *and your righteousness like the waves of the sea.*" Isaiah 48:18.

Again I am indebted to F. B. Meyer for his interpretation of this verse. He maintains, I think with some justification (as we shall see when we get to the last verse of chapter 48), that Isaiah is not here referring to the waves along the seashore. He is referring rather, to the waves of mid-ocean, where they reach to the horizon on every side, and beneath them lie miles of seawater.

'No-one can look upon the majestic roll of the Atlantic breakers, in purple glory, crowned with the white crest of foam, chasing one another as in a leviathan game, without realising the magnificence of the Divine intention that all who have learnt to call God Father, should be possessed of a moral nature as fresh, as multitudinous, as free in its motion, as pure in its character, as those waves, which, far out to sea, lift up their voice and proclaim the wealth of the power of God' (F. B. Meyer, *Christ in Isaiah*, Marshall, Morgan & Scott, 1950, p.77).

If we obey God's commandments, conforming to what is right before the Lord, and level our lives to the light we have, then powerful, overwhelming, refreshing blessing will be seen. It comes in waves: one rises and passes, but then another comes, equally as powerful.

Don't you think that we desperately need righteousness in our lives? The seven deadly sins are all around us: pride, envy, anger, sloth, avarice, gluttony and lust. Compare these to what Christ presented in the Sermon on the Mount. Was it not Gandhi who said that if Christians lived out the Sermon on the Mount, there would be no Hinduism? Gandhi's version of the seven deadly sins was: 'politics without principle, wealth without work, commerce without morality, pleasure without conscience, education without character, science without humanity, worship without sacrifice.'

As Os Guinness has pointed out, Christ's beatitudes present a contradiction to the seven deadly sins:

Humility instead of pride;

Sharing in the happiness of others instead of envy;

Refusing to do harm to others, and a desire for peacemaking, instead of anger;

Passion for, and a pursuit of God and good, instead of sloth;

Mercy, which leads us to share with others, even the undeserving, instead of avarice;

Dedication that can surmount persecution, even though it may bring a loss of even the basic necessities of life, instead of gluttony; and

Purity of heart, instead of lust.

All these qualities can come like waves in your life. Who wouldn't be glad to see such waves rolling towards them?

MAY 19TH

"Your descendants also would have been like the sand . . . His name would not have been cut off nor destroyed from before Me." Isaiah 48:19.

Here is, perhaps, the saddest result of Israel's disobedience: they lost their identity. As promised to Abraham, if they had obeyed the Lord's commandments, their descendants would have been like the abundance of the grains of sand. There would have been no need for dispersion into exile, and Israel would still have been identifiable as a nation. If they had been faithful to the Lord, He would have been faithful to them. Now the city of Jerusalem is laid waste, and Israel is diminished and broken up as a nation. If only they had listened and obeyed, their history would have been very different.

In Isaiah chapter 48, notice God's call to His people to listen to Him: "Hear this, O house of Jacob" (v.1); "Listen to Me, O Jacob, and Israel, My called" (v.12); "Oh, that you had heeded My commandments! Then your peace would have been like a river . . ." (v.18).

Is God calling for your attention? Are you turning away? Please, please listen to Him. You don't want the words, 'If only,' written across your life, do you? It was Churchill who said, 'The further backward you can look, the further forward you can see.' So, let's look back for a moment – not as far back as Israel's exile to Babylon, but to the 19th century – and consider the daughter of a wealthy English family.

Against a wall of convention but with the support of a family friend, Dr Fowler, she desperately wanted to learn the rudiments of Nursing. Nurses at the time were unskilled, and famous for drunkenness and immorality. Hospitals were filthy and filled with stench. Only the poor and destitute went there. Because she saw it standing between her and becoming a nurse, this lady turned down two proposals of marriage. In order to relieve the tension in her home, she was taken on a trip to Egypt, Greece and Europe. On-board ship she sensed God calling her, and asking if she would do good for Him, and for Him alone, without self-interest? She recalled how a friend, advising her how to listen to God, had said, "Can you hesitate between the God of the whole earth, and your little reputation?" She settled the question with God and, despite her family doing everything possible to distract her and to thwart her plans, she determined to go into Nursing training. In October 1851, and with her parents' permission, she enrolled at a Nursing school in Kaiserworth, Germany.

Eventually she went to the Crimea and gave service in the Battle of Inkerman, where there were neither beds nor other amenities for the wounded. There were 10,000 under the care of this single woman. The death rate, 42% on her arrival, immediately came down to 31%, and ultimately fell to 5%. Few in history could have triggered what became a world-wide alleviation of suffering. Her name was Florence Nightingale.

The lesson is clear. If God is calling you to do some work for Him, then listen to Him and do what He tells you. Then your experience will be entirely different to the experience of having 'If only' written across your life. Let Henry Wadsworth Longfellow have the last word:

> The wounded from the battle-plain,
> In dreary hospitals of pain,
> The cheerless corridors,
> The cold and stony floors.
> Lo! In that house of misery
> A lady with a lamp I see
> Pass through the glimmering room.
> And slow, as in a dream of bliss,
> The speechless sufferer turns to kiss
> Her shadow, as it falls
> Upon the darkening walls . . .

MAY 20TH

Go forth from Babylon! Flee from the Chaldeans! With a voice of singing, declare, proclaim this, utter it to the end of the earth; say, "The Lord has redeemed His servant Jacob!" And they did not thirst when He led them through the deserts; He caused the waters to flow from the rock for them; He also split the rock, and the waters gushed out. "There is no peace," says the Lord, "for the wicked." Isaiah 48:20-22.

We now reach the climax of the prophecies of deliverance. God has told His people that they are to be delivered, and that, despite their grumbling about His choice, King Cyrus is to be the deliverer. God now tells them to get out of Babylon and flee from the Chaldeans. The second Exodus has come; and they are to announce it to the world, as a witness to the faithfulness of their God. It is a huge historic event. Cyrus made a proclamation, saying, "All the kingdoms of the earth the Lord God of heaven has given me," and he called on the people of God to "go up to Jerusalem . . . and build the house of the Lord God of Israel . . . which is in Jerusalem" (Ezra 1:1-3).

So this stubborn, iron-necked, bronze-browed, transgressing people have come through the furnace, and are, at last, to be set free by the overthrow of Babylon – one of the mightiest cities in history. We read that 42,360 of them came out (Ezra 2:64), and returned to Jerusalem.

As this great prophetic section ends, God reminds Israel of what happened in the first Exodus. They had camped in the wilderness at a place called Rephidim, but there was no water to drink. So they complained bitterly to Moses, railing against him for bringing them out of Egypt in the first place. Moses remonstrated with them to no avail, and he cried out to the Lord, "What shall I do with this people? They are almost ready to stone me" (Exodus 17:4). God told Moses to strike the rock in Horeb, and as a result the people had all the water they needed. Moses called the place Meribah, 'because the people tempted the Lord, saying, "Is the Lord among us or not?"'

Sadly, in Isaiah's day, things were not much different. They were still a complaining people (see 45:9-10), yet God would still provide for their needs. If only they had listened to God and obeyed His commandments, their righteousness would have been like those mid-ocean waves (see May 18th); but now they are like the waves on the seashore.

Have you looked on the shores at an ebb tide? What did you find? Muddy ooze, black rocks, and wastes of sand, with debris from the ocean cast along the shoreline. 'The wicked are like the troubled sea,' says Isaiah 57:20-21, 'when it cannot rest, whose waves cast up mire and dirt. "There is no peace," says my God, "for the wicked."'

Is it not incredibly sad that this majestic section of prophecy should end with the words, "There is no peace," says the Lord, "for the wicked"? Israel was as a shoreline-wave, not a mid-ocean one, and she missed so much blessing. Compare this with the Lord's word to the church in Philadelphia: "I know your works. See, I have set before you an open door, and no one can shut it; for you have a little strength, have kept My word, and have not denied My name" (Revelation 3:8). It seems that the open door was not a reward for faithfulness, but the opportunity through which this church proved its faithfulness. God opened the door, they went through it, and used what little strength they had to 'seize the day' for His glory. It was not the greatness of their strength that brought them the reward, nor even the greatness of the opportunity, but faithfulness to the opportunity given, and full use of whatever strength they possessed.

Has God opened a door of opportunity to you? Quit stalling! Put away time-wasting excuses, and go through it. God is bigger than any one of your excuses. When the Lord first called him, Isaiah confessed to being a foul-mouthed sinner; but that did not disqualify him from God's service (see Isaiah 6:1-8). The Lord touched his profane lips and cleansed him; and we have been feeding on his spiritual food for five months' readings already! Carpe Diem, my friend, Carpe Diem.

"Listen, O coastlands, to Me, and take heed, you peoples from afar! The Lord has called Me from the womb; from the matrix of My mother He has made mention of My name." Isaiah 49:1.

If ever a people needed comfort after an extremely sharp rebuke, Israel was that people. Does it come? And how! There is no antidote to sin, failure and lost opportunity, like the sinless, victorious and perfect Servant, the Messiah. But not only does Israel need Him, the whole world needs Him. Receive, then, the opening overture to this, the second great Servant Song in Isaiah. (The first, being Isaiah 42:1-4).

A summons goes out to the farthest corners of the earth, the 'coastlands' – meaning, literally, the islands of the earth. Whether it was the Greek islands, where democracy was cradled, or the Aran islands, where the Celts lived: no matter how obscure the tribe or people, how great the nation, or how diverse the culture, here is a word for everyone, everywhere, and for all time. And, again, who is the speaker? He is God's ideal Servant. As His servant, Israel had failed. This is the One who will accomplish all that Israel should have done in the world. In the synagogue at Antioch, Paul quotes from Isaiah 49, and shows that Christ has become the light to the Gentiles that Israel should have been (Acts 13:47). He fulfilled to the letter all that the Servant Nation was meant to do. Israel was the root, Christ is the flower.

Our text tells us that the Messiah was called by appointment of God. And notice, while He certainly was born, He was not created, as Israel had been. Honourable mention is given to His mother: Isaiah 7:14 had prophesied, 'the virgin shall conceive and bear a Son, and shall call His name Immanuel.' As Matthew Henry puts it, 'The God who took a motherless woman out of the side of a man, took a fatherless man out of the body of a woman' (quoted by John Blanchard in *Gathered Gold*, Evangelical Press, 1984, p.330).

What were the attributes of Christ's remarkable mother? She certainly needed a Saviour, and said so when she referred to the Lord as "my Saviour" (Luke 1:47). For her to be made whole, she had to watch her Son being rent. Yet she had wonderful attributes: her mind was stored with the Scriptures, her heart was endued with a love for Israel, her life was filled with deep humility, the hope of her life and soul was in the great promises of the Covenant, and the fear of the Lord was always before her.

Remember, to make a person, God begins with his or her mother – and she who rocks the cradle rules the world, for good or ill.

"And He has made My mouth like a sharp sword . . . " Isaiah 49:2.

Words! Without them, comfort cannot be spoken. A baby cannot be sung to sleep. An ambassador cannot plead his country's cause. A defending lawyer cannot present the case before a jury. A fellow cannot tell his girl that he loves her, or vice versa. A teacher cannot describe a subject in depth. Nation cannot speak peace with nation.

Have we any idea of the power of words? When his teacher tells him that he has written something good, Johnny's next essay is always better. On the suicide note were written two words: 'They said.'

Let us never forget that God can use our words. So let your words be brought under the influence of the Lord, and the result can be incalculable. Our text tells us that the Father made the words of the Messiah incisive. He submitted to His Father and He filled His mouth with the awesome words which we now feed upon. God promised the stammering Moses that He would be with his mouth (Exodus 4:12). When Moses kept protesting that he wasn't capable of speaking, the blessing passed to Aaron. Christian, don't miss the blessing! Speak up for the Lord: remove sarcasm with words of encouragement; replace bitter words with beautiful words; instead of cutting everybody down with your words, use words that will build them up. Take the truth you have learned from God's Word and unfold it to others. Nothing inspires like it, so they will bless you for it. Use words to challenge the evils of your day. Maybe you will be used to drive back the gates of Hell, for those gates are defensive weapons, not offensive. Incisive speech could reach more people than you could ever dream of.

Don't forget that Christ is the Perfect Servant, and He is not ashamed to be called 'The Word.' If Christians quoted His word more, what we have to say would be appreciated all the better. Selah.

MAY 23ʳᵈ

". . . In the shadow of His hand He has hidden me . . . " Isaiah 49:2.

Here we have the image of the skilled archer. The responsibility for feeding his little family depends on his accuracy. The support he is able to give to the infantry against the enemy depends on his prowess. Archers were as important in battle in Israel's day as they were at Agincourt. Isaiah here uses the image of the arrow in the archer's quiver to represent service. The arrow lies in the archer's quiver, waiting for its opportune moment. Until that time, it is in the shadow of the archer's hand.

Meditate on this powerful image, and consider what it is saying. Think of Joseph in an Egyptian prison, because of the lie of a woman. What hope had he of ever getting out of such a narrow circumstance? How could his gift ever flourish? The truth was that he was hidden in the Lord's quiver, covered by the shadow of His hand. When the moment came, he was taken out and sent on his way to accomplish a great thing for the Divine Archer. In the Lord's hand, he was an arrow in a sure place.

Think of Ananias, the devout Christian of Damascus. We never read that he held public office, nor do we read that any gift that he had brought him into high public profile. 'Now there was,' says Acts 9:10, 'a certain disciple at Damascus named Ananias; and to him the Lord said in a vision "Ananias." And he said, "Here I am, Lord." Notice how he was in the shadow of the Lord's hand, and when in a strategic hour the Divine Archer reached for him he was ready and waiting. The results reach us even in the 21st century. Ananias was taken from the Lord's quiver, and sped on his way to the street called Straight, where he enquired for one called Saul of Tarsus. Knowing full well Saul's former antipathy to the Christian church, Ananias had to overcome any prejudice which he had, in order to carry to him a message from the Lord. He informed Paul that he was a chosen vessel to bear the Lord's name before Gentiles, kings, and the children of Israel. Ananias may not have been capable of writing the famous Letter to the Romans, but he could encourage the one who did. He was another arrow in a sure place.

As you head out to face another day, or turn to go to sleep, it would be very worthwhile to meditate further on other characters in Scripture who come to mind when you think of today's text. Make sure, though, that you too are ready at any moment, to be taken out of the shadow of the Divine Archer's hand, put into His bow, and sent speedily to a sure place, to His glory. As Alecander Solzhenitsyn said, "One word of truth outweighs the whole world." You might be sent to give that word today.

MAY 24TH

"*. . . and made Me a polished shaft; in His quiver He has hidden Me.*" Isaiah 49:2.

In archery, what use is a rusted arrow-point? It will simply glance away from the target. The rusted hulks of even modern weapons of war soon deteriorate, if left strewn for years on, say, an Afghan or Gulf battlefield.

As sandpaper or a file is used to remove rust, so the Lord uses his 'sandpaper' and 'file' to remove the 'rust' in his 'arrows,' so that we will continue to have the cutting edge in our service for Him. Don't forget that we are 'training for reigning.' One day we shall reign with Him (see Revelation 5:10). In the meantime, our lives are interrupted by all kinds of frets, burdens, annoyances, problems, trials and hassles. If we only knew it, God is using these to train us for reigning.

Can that really be true? Well, take the example of David. When he was a young man, the Lord told him through Samuel that one day he would reign over Israel. It was a promise. David must have wondered about that promise when he was being hunted like a partridge on the mountains by King Saul and his men. For years he was hassled almost beyond endurance, but notice how he reacted. When given the opportunity to kill Saul, he refused. He treated him with respect, even kindness, because he was the Lord's anointed. All this encouraged him to be patient, and to encircle any ambition he had with mercy. It taught him to wait for the Lord's time. It was his training for reigning. God's 'file' and 'sandpaper' made him a polished arrow, which went to a sure place when the moment came to reign.

'Do you not know that the saints will judge the world? And if the world will be judged by you, are you unworthy to judge the smallest matters? Do you not know that we shall judge angels? How much more, things that pertain to this life?' (1 Corinthians 6:2, 3). If the day is coming when we shall judge the world and angels, don't you think that God is impelling us

133

to judge everyday affairs in our homes, family and business, in order to 'polish us' for a greater day? Because they were unwilling to make fair and wise decisions amongst themselves, the Christians in Corinth were taking each other to Court. The unconverted, before whom they brought these cases, were not impressed.

Do you feel hassled today, as you are forced to make a decision about, say, what video your child should, or should not, watch? Do you have to decide, between some very good candidates, which person to hire for your company? You hate change, but you have to decide whether to move on to that new job and opportunity. Is God asking you to lay down some cherished work, and you have to decide? Remember, making that decision is part of your training for reigning. Awesome, isn't it?

May 25th

"And He said to me, 'You are My servant, O Israel, in whom I will be glorified.' Then I said, 'I have laboured in vain, I have spent my strength for nothing and in vain; yet surely my just reward is with the Lord, and my work with my God.'" Isaiah 49:3-4.

As the perfect servant, here the Lord is given the name, 'Israel'. He is the One who embodies all that Israel was called to be. The name, 'Israel,' was first given to a man, namely Jacob. It means 'a Prince with God.' Now the name is given to the Perfect Servant, the Messiah. Through Him the Father's glory will be displayed, as Jacob and the nation never could. He is 'the brightness of His glory and the express image of His person' (Hebrews 1:3). Everything that He does will be for the glory of His Father.

We have traced the introduction of the Perfect Servant through from chapter 42. In today's text we have the introduction of Him as the Suffering Servant. For the Lord Jesus, the shadow of coming suffering now falls ominously on the pages of Isaiah.

At some point, the phrase, "I have laboured in vain, I have spent my strength for nothing and in vain," is the language of all who serve God. Outwardly, our work may appear to be a failure, as it did for the Lord Jesus. The words of the critics bit deeply into His consciousness: '. . . they shoot out the lip, they shake the head, saying, "He trusted in the Lord, let Him rescue Him; let Him deliver Him, since He delights in Him!"' (Psalm 22:7-8). Echoing the words of Psalm 22:1, He cried at Calvary, "My God, My God, why have You forsaken me?" But these were not words of doubt, unbelief, or despair. As Isaiah 53 will later explain, Christ knew why He was forsaken by His Father: 'But You are holy,' says Psalm 22:3; 'He made Him who knew no sin to be sin for us, that we might become the righteousness of God in Him,' says 2 Corinthians 5:21. Today's text says, "Yet surely my just reward is with the Lord, and my work with my God." In the service of God, that is where true comfort lies. It is ultimately for the Father to judge whether work done for Him is in vain, or for His glory.

Just after His death, our Lord's work would certainly not have shown any sense of accomplishment. The crowds had gone. The two on the way to Emmaus thought it was all over. Even the disciples seemed to want to go back to their fishing boats. The Romans thought, 'that was that.' Unbelieving Israel sneered. But three days later, God raised the

Lord Jesus from the dead, demonstrating what He thought of that perfectly finished work. And Christians now glory in the work of the Cross.

And how is your work for God? Are you discouraged because there is no sign of a harvest? Do you feel that all you have done is a failure? Recently I have been thinking of the gospel seed sown in the city of St Petersburg in the 18th Century by the third Baron Radstock. It is reckoned that at least two million souls eventually found Christ through the initial sowing of Radstock, as he quietly presented the gospel in St. Petersburg, particularly in the homes of the aristocrats. They formed, in part, the Baptist Churches of Russia, and with other evangelical Christians they became hugely influential in the Human Rights movement, that in turn brought down the old Soviet Union. A process was set in motion that, just this month, led to the cutting back of nuclear weapons between the United States and Russia! All this was never envisaged by Radstock, when he first presented the truth of justification by faith to those spiritually-starving people of an elitist regime. Christian, please do not underestimate your work for God. Just get on with it, and God will one day prove to you that your labour was not in vain. The strength you put into it was not wasted – anything but.

MAY 26TH

"And now the Lord says, who formed Me from the womb to be His Servant, to bring Jacob back to Him, so that Israel is gathered to Him (for I shall be glorious in the eyes of the Lord, and My God shall be My strength)." Isaiah 49:5.

There never has been a servant like the Lord Jesus. He was perfect in all respects. From before His birth He knew what His mission in life was. He was being prepared to be that polished arrow, hidden in the shadow of the hand of the Almighty. His purpose was to bring Jacob (Israel) back to God – as promised in Isaiah chapters 43 and 44.

Having a purpose in life is very important. A conference was once held in Oxford University, and a prominent businessman rose to speak. He pointed out that he had been very fortunate in his career, and had made a lot of money. He said that, if he was being honest, one of his motives for making money was simple: he wanted to have the money to hire people to do what he didn't like doing himself. A single tear began to roll down his cheek as he confessed that there was one thing he had never been able to do: he had never been able to hire a person to find his own sense of purpose and fulfilment. He said he would have given anything in order to discover that.

It was Thomas Carlyle who wrote, 'a person without a purpose is like a ship without a rudder.' A lot of people have too much to live with, but too little to live for. The Christian has discovered that the final aim and ultimate meaning of life are to be found beyond life altogether. Jesus says, "Follow me;" and as you go forward by faith, tremendous things can happen. Despite all the trials you may face, God will strengthen you for every situation. When finally you see His face, you will discover all that God has been doing in and through you. If your aim is to live for His glory, one day you will see it.

MAY 27TH

"Indeed He says, 'It is too small a thing that You should be My Servant to raise up the tribes of Jacob, and to restore the preserved ones of Israel; I will also give You as a light to the Gentiles, that You should be My salvation to the ends of the earth.'" Isaiah 49:6.

We talk about the importance of 'seeing the bigger picture.' Here we see that Christ's work is not merely to restore Israel. He has an even greater task; and what He does will encompass the ends of the earth. He will reach out beyond the tiny and precious land of Israel and, as a light to the Gentiles, He will bring God's salvation to the ends of the earth. Together with many millions of people, I have found out that the light that exposes my sin, is the light that saves me!

One day the Lord made a mudpack, and with the clay anointed the eyes of a man who had been blind from birth (see John chapter 9). Then He told him to go and wash in the pool of Siloam. So he went and washed, and came back seeing. A huge argument erupted with the Pharisees about the whole matter. They even accused the Lord Jesus of being a sinner. Slowly, amidst the mudpack, the pool, and the religious arguments, it began to dawn on the man that the One who had healed him was no ordinary person. He reminded the Pharisees that in all history no one had ever been healed of congenital blindness, i.e. blindness from birth. He began to realise that what had happened to him was a miracle from God; and the man who had done the miracle must be from God. He also realised that, since God does not answer the prayers of unrepentant people, this man could not be the unrepentant sinner that the Pharisees were calling Him!

The man's spiritual sight was now dawning. He refuted the Pharisees on their own ground, but they threw him out of the synagogue. They literally excommunicated him. But Jesus found him – what a moment! Being excommunicated from dead religion, to be found by the living Saviour, is no mean swap. "Do you believe in the Son of God?" asked Christ. "Who is He, Lord, that I may believe in Him?" said the man. "You have both seen Him and it is He who is talking with you," said Christ. Immediately the man said, "Lord, I believe!" and he worshipped Him.

Have you left moribund, decadent, organised religion, for a living Saviour? Then you'll know that there is no comparison. Thank God for the Light of the World.

MAY 28TH

Thus says the Lord, the Redeemer of Israel, their Holy One, to Him whom man despises, to Him whom the nation abhors, to the Servant of rulers: "Kings shall see and arise, princes also shall worship, because of the Lord who is faithful, the Holy One of Israel; and He has chosen You." Isaiah 49:7.

The self-humbling of the Lord Jesus is prophesied clearly in today's text. So, too, is His exaltation. People will despise Him, His very own nation will abhor Him, He will make Himself subject to the Roman authorities, and He will be the servant of rulers. He will actually hand Himself over to the Romans and to their will, in order to fulfil the greater purposes for which He has come. Through an act of mercy He will even show kindness to one of their centurions.

Here is the One who was co-equal with God, who took the status of a bondservant, and suffered all the indignities which people heaped upon Him, even to the point of death. But God has exalted Him: 'Kings shall see and arise, princes also shall worship.' Scripture is very accurate. Just today my wife and I attended a special service for the Golden Jubilee of Queen Elizabeth II. In the presence of Her Majesty, it was just thrilling to hear Dr. Alistair Dunlop exalt the Lord Jesus in the preaching of the gospel. Later, to the ancient Irish tune, Slane, we sang the Recessional hymn, 'Be thou my vision.' It includes these apposite words:

> Riches I heed not, nor man's empty praise.
> Thou mine inheritance through all my days.
> Thou, and Thou only, the first in my heart,
> High King of heaven, my treasure Thou art!
>
> High King of heaven, when the battle is done,
> Grant heaven's joy to me, O bright heaven's Sun,
> Heart of my own heart, whatever befall,
> Still be my vision, O Ruler of all.

We are deeply grateful for the sincere Christian faith of our Queen; but what will the day be like, when the glory of the New Jerusalem will be seen?

'I saw,' wrote John, 'no temple in it, for the Lord God Almighty and the Lamb are its temple. The city had no need of the sun or of the moon to shine in it, for the glory of God illuminated it. The Lamb is its light. And the nations of those who are saved shall walk in its light, and the kings of the earth bring their glory and honour into it. Its gates shall not be shut at all by day (there shall be no night there). And they shall bring the glory and the honour of the nations into it' (Revelation 21:22-26).

I can't wait!

MAY 29TH

"I will make each of My mountains a road, and My highways shall be elevated. Surely these shall come from afar. Look! Those from the north and the west, and these from the land of Sinim." Isaiah 49:11-12.

Here, a world-wide gathering together of God's people, is prophesied. Some say that Sinim is the name often given to China, others say it refers to Aswan. Obscurity, distance of location, or obstacles of terrain, will not prevent the Divine Gatherer. Ultimately, a massive flow of people will come into the Kingdom of God. In the immediate context, it is the exiles returning from Babylon to Jerusalem; but when the Light to the Gentiles will come, people from every tongue and nation will enter His kingdom.

"I will make each of My mountains a road," says God. Meditate on this beautiful phrase for a moment. It means that God will make a way through each of His mountains. Do you face a 'mountain' of a problem in your life this week? It towers above you and dominates your thinking. You feel you will never conquer it. Not only will you get over the mountain, but as you go up its steep slopes you will find that God will use the experience to bring you closer to Himself, and you will have communion with God that you could never have imagined. The mountain may open up a way to a new ministry for you, to new and fresh experiences in His service. Even if that mountain brings death itself, you will then experience a new day of service.

I heard the famous singer, Sting, tell how he and his friends had gone to do a performance in the United States. They arrived at the venue, but only three or four people turned up. Instead of quitting, they gave the best performance they could. It so happened that some DJ's were present, who then played Sting's music in their radio stations. Millions know the rest of the story. If someone like Sting does not baulk at such a 'mountain,' then why should you, Christian? In God's hands, it will be a way to blessings that you would not otherwise experience. Notice that God does not say He will remove the mountains. He put them there in the first place, to prove to you His power and grace. Not one of them is a waste of time and energy in the crossing. So, get climbing, and you will not believe what you will find on the other side.

May 30TH

Sing, O heavens! Be joyful, O earth! And break out in singing, O mountains! For the Lord has comforted His people, and will have mercy on His afflicted. But Zion said, "The Lord has forsaken me, and my Lord has forgotten me." Isaiah 49:13-14.

God has given all these wonderful promises to His people. Now He looks for a response. He calls on the heavens to sing, the earth to be joyful, and the mountains to break out into singing. Creation is called upon to respond to the comfort that God has brought to His people. The full scope of these promises, of course, will not only bring about the restoration of His people, but of the very earth and heavens themselves.

So how did His people respond? They maintained that the Lord had left them: He had completely forgotten them! Is that how you feel? You have become so engulfed by your problems and difficulties that you think God has withdrawn from you completely. Have you done something very wrong, and the pain is such that you are saying, "God loathes me. He can't bear me anymore. As far as my life is concerned, He has decided to 'throw in the towel.' I'm on my own now. God is no longer involved in my life, and I don't blame Him. I deserve it"?

Tell me, whom do you think all these promises were for? A perfect people, who faithfully obeyed His Law in every respect? You know that is not true. They were the very opposite. Israel brought the exile on herself. She was entirely to blame. Yet it was to such a people that

God brought all His mighty, comforting promises. But they did not 'get it,' did they? No matter how comforting the promises, they were still defeated and despondent. Whilst God is calling on His creation to sing in response to His promises, His people are grumbling! Are you going to be like them?

Let me remind you of how John Bunyan put it. Hopeful and Christian are caught sleeping in the grounds of Doubting Castle by the owner, Giant Despair. They are put in a dungeon and fearfully beaten by the giant. He then advises them to commit suicide: "For why," he says, "shall you choose life, seeing it is attended with so much bitterness?" Then in the castle-yard he shows them the bones and skulls of those pilgrims he had already dispatched!

They were in the dungeon from Wednesday morning until Saturday night. On Saturday, about midnight, they began to pray. Suddenly, a little while before day, Christian broke into passionate speech: "What a fool am I, thus to be in a stinking dungeon, when I may as well walk in liberty! I have a key in my bosom, called Promise, that will, I am persuaded, open any lock in Doubting Castle."

It did just that, and the noise of the opening gate wakened Giant Despair – 'Who hastily rising to pursue his prisoners, felt his limbs to fail, for his fits took him again, so that he could by no means go after them.' They went on and came again to the King's Highway, and so were safe, because they were out of the Giant's jurisdiction. Then they erected a pillar, engraved with a warning to any pilgrims coming after them. It told of the dangers of going along the way to Doubting Castle, and of the intents of Giant Despair to destroy pilgrims who were faithful to the King of the Celestial Country. So, reader, heed the warning of Christian and Hopeful, and be away about the King's business!

MAY 31ST

"Can a woman forget her nursing child, and not have compassion on the son of her womb? Surely they may forget, yet I will not forget you." Isaiah 49:15.

One day when I was on a train in the London Underground, a mother and her child were sitting opposite me. The affection between them was most touching to observe. As the train rolled along under the great metropolis, this verse suddenly flashed into my mind. There is no human love more pure or so unselfish as a mother's love for her child. What depths of sacrifice would she not go to, so that her child might be well and flourish? When we were in pain or distress, who has not known the comfort of a mother's hug? Which of us has not benefited from a mother's warnings or counsel, and been sustained by a mother's prayers? That love, which delights in us as a helpless infant, stays with us through our lives. We rise up and call it blessed.

By and large, what I have just written is true. But can a mother ever fail in her relationship with her child? It does happen. Only F. B. Meyer could describe it thus: 'maddened with frenzy, sodden with drink, flushed with unholy passion, infatuated with the giddy round of gaiety . . .' – it has been known for a woman to forget her child. While it is not by any means normal, the fact is that it does occur.

One of the most pathetic things I have ever read is the record of the haunting pleas written to his mother by Winston Churchill as a child from boarding school. He pleads with her to come and see him. He would give her a billion kisses, if she would only come; but again and again he was to be disappointed. His mother had plenty of time to entertain society, of course. In fact, she planned feasts for others; but to her son she had given a stone.

With God, no such neglect or forgetfulness will ever occur in His relationships with His children. It would be utterly impossible. "Surely they may forget, yet I will not forget you," He says. Here is love that will not let you go. In the midst of all the demands made upon it, it will never forget you. No matter where you go, or what happens to you, God's love for you and His interest in you will never cease.

June

Spinning of the long linen fibre produces exceptionally strong, fine yarns. Here we have spun linen on bobbins. King Solomon had linen yarns brought out of Egypt. We are told that the King's merchants received the linen yarn 'at a price.' Twentieth century excavations suggest that Egyptian fine linen was made of a quality of fibre and spinning that is unobtainable today.

"See, I have inscribed you on the palms of My hands; your walls are continually before Me." Isaiah 49:16.

I think of a beautiful house that I know just outside Monaghan town in Ireland. It once belonged to a man called Montgomery, who emigrated to the United States and eventually had a town named after him: Montgomery, Alabama. When I visited the house one Sunday afternoon, its present owners, Mr. and Mrs. Graham, showed me an engraving on the kitchen window, written by a woman who once lived there. Her name was Mary, and she engraved her name on the window the night before she emigrated to South Africa. Sadly, she and her husband disappeared one evening during their honeymoon, and were never seen again. It is thought that wild animals killed them. This makes the engraving on the window so poignant. As I sat there in that kitchen looking towards that window, drinking my afternoon tea, my thoughts were long and sad.

What is this about God – using the illustration of Babylonian idol-worshippers, tattooing the name of their gods on their palms? Or, as we noticed earlier in this book, people writing the name of their beloved in indelible ink on their palms? God does not say that the name of His people is tattooed, or written, on His palms. Rather, He says, it is engraved (NIV). The name, 'Mary,' on the window in Monaghan, cannot be erased from the glass. Engraving is permanent. So is the name of God's people on the palms of His hands.

Think of the day after the resurrection, when the Lord appeared to His disciples. 'He showed them His hands' (John 20:20). They saw the wounds, inflicted by the nails of His crucifixion. Were those wounds eventually erased? No – they will never be erased. 'And I looked,' says John, 'and behold in the midst of the throne . . . stood a lamb as though it had been slain' (Revelation 5:6). Every time the Lord reaches out His hands to you, Christian, He has in them the marks of His love for you.

"Your walls are continually before me," says God. I take it that this does not mean that He keeps an image of the wrecked and ruined 'walls' of our lives before Him; but in Christ He sees us as we were meant to be. It is a more glorious view than when we were 'ruined' by Satan; that's for sure.

"Your sons shall make haste; your destroyers and those who laid you waste shall go away from you." Isaiah 49:17.

Out go the wasters and destroyers, and in come the builders! The destroyers laid waste a city steeped in history, containing the beautiful temple in which the living God had dwelt. The wasters pillaged and carried the sons of Israel into captivity. The 'sons' of Israel (alt. reading 'your builders') are now coming back to restore what had been ruined.

I'd rather be a builder than a destroyer, wouldn't you? But it is much more difficult to build than to tear down. It takes planning and patience and time. Builders come in for criticism, too. Under Nehemiah, when the work of restoring the ruined walls of Jerusalem had commenced, pitiless criticism was levelled at the builders:

'. . . when Sanballat heard that we were rebuilding the wall, that he was furious and very indignant, and mocked the Jews. And he spoke before his brethren and the army of Samaria, and said, "What are these feeble Jews doing? Will they fortify themselves? Will they offer sacrifices? Will they complete it in a day? Will they revive the stones from the heaps of rubbish – stones that are buried?" Now Tobiah the Ammonite was beside him, and he said, "Whatever they build, if even a fox goes up on it, he will break down their stone wall."' (Nehemiah 4:1-3).

Nehemiah went on building, anyway. Anyway? There was a sign found on the wall of Mother Teresa's Children's Home in Calcutta, entitled 'Anyway.' Under that title were these words, which I recommend to you:

People are unreasonable, illogical and self-centred. Love them, anyway.

If you do good, people will accuse you of selfish ulterior motives. Do good, anyway.

If you are successful, you win false friends and true enemies. Succeed, anyway.

The good you do will be forgotten tomorrow. Do good, anyway.

Honesty and frankness make you vulnerable. Be honest and frank, anyway.

What you spend years building may be destroyed overnight. Build, anyway.

People really need help, but may attack you if you help them. Help people, anyway.

Give the world the best you have, and you'll get kicked in the teeth. Give the world the best you've got, anyway.

JUNE 3ᴿᴰ

"Your sons shall make haste; your destroyers and those who laid you waste shall go away from you." Isaiah 49:17.

In our text today, I see a word of challenge. The wreck and ruin of the destroyers of Jerusalem is contrasted with its builders (again, the alternative reading for 'your sons,' is 'your builders'). The prophecy states that the destroyers are to 'go away,' and the builders are to 'make haste' to rebuild.

Don't you think it is time to 'make haste' and rebuild what the enemy has destroyed? Indeed, is it possible? AIDS campaigners across the African continent, for example, have found the disease almost impossible to assuage. It destroys lives and threatens nations. Recently I talked with Mr. David Tucker, the current President of Trans World Radio, the Christian radio network that broadcasts the gospel across the world. He told me that one day when he was in Africa he had an appointment with the President of a certain African country, but he found that the tyres of his car had been let down. When eventually he got to the President's 'palace,' he was half an hour late. He was deeply embarrassed, and said to the President's secretary that he would return at another time. No, said the secretary, the President wants to see you today. So, rather flushed, and not a little surprised, David was ushered in to see the President. What he heard was of incredible encouragement to him. The President pointed out that the Government had tried everything to thwart the AIDS epidemic that was threatening the very life of the nation, but it had all failed. He then began to commend Trans World Radio, for its presentation of the moral truths of the Christian faith on its programmes. He applauded its non-political stance and its focus on the gospel. He said that the Government would be happy to pay for the programmes to be broadcast to his nation, as it was felt that the preaching and teaching of the gospel was the answer to the deep moral problems lying behind the epidemic. David went away most encouraged as to the power of the gospel in contemporary society.

Christian, 'make haste' to build what has been destroyed. In the gospel there is an inherent power to overcome ethnic divisions within society, power to transform lives that are being destroyed by drug addiction and alcohol abuse, power to deepen relationships between husband and wife, between parents and children. Here is a message that can provide an armour to withstand all the fiery darts and intents of the evil one. But the challenge is that we must 'make haste' and build for God where the enemy has sought to destroy. There is an urgency about it because, as Jesus said, ". . . the night is coming when no one can work" (John 9:4). Today's word is clear: make haste, Christian, make haste.

JUNE 4TH

"Lift up your eyes, look around and see; all these gather together and come to you. As I live," says the Lord, "you shall surely clothe yourselves with them all as an ornament, and bind them on you as a bride does." Isaiah 49:18.

All believers should address the present in light of the future. This was certainly the practice of all the Old Testament prophets, including Isaiah. It must not have been easy to project down through the years, and promise the emancipation of a people who were currently in exile. Prophetically, Isaiah now calls on these exiles to look by faith, and see crowds of people gathering in Jerusalem. The image he uses is that of people putting on jewellery, and these exiles will be as the precious jewellery that a woman uses on special occasions, sparkling and flashing in the light.

I have long loved the words from the book of Malachi: 'Then those who feared the Lord spoke to one another, and the Lord listened and heard them; so a book of remembrance was written before Him for those who fear the Lord and who meditate on His name. "They shall be mine," says the Lord of hosts, "on the day that I make them My jewels. And I will spare them as a man spares his own son who serves him"' (Malachi 3:16-17). God finds His jewels scattered far and wide: some of them are hidden in obscure places, with their worth not recognised by the society around them. But on the day that God gathers them, their true worth will be seen clearly. I look forward to that day with all of my heart, for 'many who are first will be last, and the last first' (Matthew 19:30). The divine jeweller will have a display that will be unique. I've seen the treasures of the Tsars in Moscow, the Crown Jewels in the Tower of London, and the jewellery at Tiffany's on Fifth Avenue, but I anticipate this display as no other. 'You shall also be a crown of glory in the hand of the Lord, and a royal diadem in the hand of your God' (Isaiah 62:3) – such is the status of the believer.

But there is more! The second image is of a bride adorned for her wedding day. All eyes are on the bride as she enters the ceremony, her every adornment is carefully noted. It is her day. It will be Israel's day, on her return from exile; and the Church's day, when she is presented as the bride of Christ. Husbands are called upon to love their wives, '. . . just as Christ also loved the church and gave Himself for her . . . that He might present her to Himself a glorious church, not having spot or wrinkle or any such thing, but that she should be holy and without blemish' (Ephesians 5:25, 27).

Why will our Heavenly bridegroom present His bride to Himself? When, on 2nd December 1804, Napoleon Bonaparte crowned himself in Notre Dame in Paris, there was something distinctly arrogant about it. And yet, when we come to the truth of Christ presenting His church to Himself, we have no aversion to it. Why? Because nobody else is adequate to do it. In the first place, He died for her. Then, through the past two millennia, day after day, from every corner of the earth, He has been adding to her number. From every climate, every culture, speaking in different tongues, from all walks of life, He has been calling His church. He has become for her wisdom and righteousness and sanctification and redemption (1 Corinthians 1:30). He has clothed her with His righteousness: all her salvation is all of Him, so He alone is adequate to present her to Himself. What a moment it will be!

JUNE 5TH

"For your waste and desolate places, and the land of your destruction, will even now be too small for the inhabitants; and those who swallowed you up will be far away. The children you will have, after you have lost the others, will say again in your ears, 'The place is too small for me; give me a place where I may dwell.' Then you will say in your heart, 'Who has begotten these for me, since I have lost my children and am desolate, a captive, and wandering to and fro? And who has brought these up? There I was, left alone; but these, where were they?'" Isaiah 49:19-21.

Transformation! If ever there was a comforting and encouraging word from God, this is it. Do you despair that you will ever see any spiritual progress amongst those to whom you minister? Has the enemy so swallowed up lives around you, that you feel there is no point in going on with your work?

It is easy to despair. In the United Kingdom, a huge problem of drug addiction has emerged. Just the other day I listened to a young boy of fourteen describe his heroin addiction. One could sense the overwhelming power of his addiction, trying to throttle his very life before it has hardly begun. Other addictions abound, and Satan's influence seems unstoppable. You might wonder if great days of spiritual awakening shall ever be seen again.

God promises Israel that her devastated and ruined land will one day be too small for the number of people who will live in it, and her enemies will be far away. After the loss of children in exile, other children will be born to her, who will say that they want more room. They want to move forward in their lives to something bigger. Only a little while ago they faced a decimated land, now the place of their desolation becomes the place of a new, burgeoning, and positive, lifestyle.

Our God is the God who turns things around. That is His prerogative. You cannot do it by yourself. Young Leonardo da Vinci copied a verse into his notebook that read:

Let him who cannot do the thing he would, will to do the thing he can.

To will is foolish, where there is no power to do;

That man is wise who, if he cannot, does not wish he could.

Get on with what you can, and let God do the transforming. He can turn the desert into a rose, the desolation into something that overflows. God called His people to go home from exile, and they went. He fulfilled all that He promised. They were full of questions as to how such an amazing restoration could ever come about. How could a desolate, captive people ever be surrounded by such a multitude of her children? "Where were they?" asks Israel. The mystery is about to be revealed. The Lord was behind it all. Praise God – as with them, so it is with us. "For I know the plans I have for you," declares the Lord, "plans to prosper you and not to harm you, plans to give you hope and a future" (Jeremiah 29:11 NIV). Selah.

JUNE 6TH

Thus says the Lord God: "Behold, I will lift My hand in an oath to the nations, and set up My standard for the peoples; they shall bring your sons in their arms, and your daughters shall be carried on their shoulders; kings shall be your foster fathers, and their queens your nursing mothers; they shall bow down to you with their faces to the earth, and lick up the dust of your feet. Then you will know that I am the Lord, for they shall not be ashamed who wait for Me." Isaiah 49:22-23.

This is a view of world history that you will not hear in most television discussions, magazines, or newspaper articles. History books do not usually say that it is the hand of God that guides the course of history. But Isaiah is not afraid to do so. God 'lifts His hand,' and with the co-operation of kings and queens His people will be brought back from Babylon. Nations do His bidding, and bow in subservience to His people.

To help us understand these verses, let us go back for a moment to Isaiah 37:29. The background is the story of Sennacherib, coming to take Jerusalem. Isaiah depicts him as a horse charging in all its pride, power and vigour; but there is a rider on the horse's back, giving direction to all that vitality. That rider is the Lord. Although Sennacherib's impulses are sinful, the origins of his pride and sin are not from the Lord. Nevertheless, the Lord is working out His purposes through him. God is not passive regarding this world, but active. He is so active that He says, "I also withheld rain from you, when the harvest was still three months away. I sent rain on one town, but withheld it from another. One field had rain; another had none and dried up" (Amos 4:7, NIV). Talk about God being into detail! As a foster father cares for his child and a nursing mother for an infant, so kings and queens will devote themselves to the good of God's people. They will actually do drudgery, like scrubbing the floors. All God has to do is to raise His hand and it will happen; and to raise His flag and nations will rally.

We cannot help but think of Joseph, raised as God's standard in Egypt for the good of God's people. Pharaoh said that no one in Egypt 'would lift a hand or a foot' without Joseph's consent (Genesis 41:44). What an extraordinary statement! So let me repeat the truth: God is into the nitty-gritty of your life. When He moves on your behalf, neither the Pharaohs nor the nations of this world can stop Him. In fact, they become the 'horse' that He rides upon as He comes to your aid.

"Then you will know that I am the Lord, for they shall not be ashamed who wait for Me."
Isaiah 49:23.

Let me ask you a question. Have you ever been caused to blush with shame because you hoped in the Lord? For three and a half years Elijah hoped in God, that He would send rain (see Luke 4:25). In the meantime Elijah had to 'sweat the small stuff,' as the Americans say. Eventually, a cloud 'as small as a man's hand' appeared in the sky, and Elijah said to the king who was standing near him, "Prepare your chariot, and go down before the rain stops you" (1 Kings 18:44). Then the heavy rain fell. Elijah actually ran ahead of him to the entrance of Jezreel, where the king had his palace. Was Elijah ashamed that he had waited for God? I think not.

To wait for God, means, to hope and have faith in God whatever your circumstances. Despite the unspiritual behaviour of Eli, Hannah waited for God. Where did she get the strength to stay in the temple and pray, instead of walking out? She hoped in the Lord, and the little boy who was born to her eventually became a spiritual tower of strength to the nation of Israel. Even when Noah's ark rested on Mount Ararat, Noah still had to wait for seven months before he and his family got out. For someone who had preached regularly for 120 years to an unyielding people, what was a wait of seven months?! He had learned to wait for God, and he was not ashamed.

Think of Hagar who, smarting under the hatred of Sarah, fled into the wilderness, heading for Egypt. The Angel of the Lord met her and told her to return and submit to her mistress. It was not easy, but she submitted and waited for a further thirteen years. Then God set her free. In a fit of impatience it is easy to have our own plans, and refuse to wait for God. But if we do, like Hagar, we will not be ashamed.

Are you impatient? Are you about to rush into what you think is an exciting new experience? Are you about to give up a commitment that seems unspectacular, mundane and troublesome? Remember what Uncle Remus said: 'You can't run away from trouble, because there ain't no place that far.' Are your activities born out of communion with God? No matter how impressive they may appear, if God has not initiated them they will not bring true happiness.

How, then, do you know whether or not something you want to do is pleasing to the Lord? Remember the man who asked his wife whether his shirt was dirty or clean: 'If it's doubtful, it's dirty,' she replied. In all ages believers are categorically called to wait for God

– to wait and wait, and wait again. Then they are called to wait some more. If you doubt the wisdom of all this, ask Eve.

JUNE 8TH

Shall the prey be taken from the mighty, or the captives of the righteous be delivered? But thus says the Lord: "Even the captives of the mighty shall be taken away, and the prey of the terrible be delivered; for I will contend with him who contends with you, and I will save your children." Isaiah 49:24-25.

Isaiah writes now about another court scene. This time, those who hold God's people captive are in court. God will contend, or plead, His case with them. There have been, and will be, many through history who have held the people of God. It does not matter if it is a despotic king, or some regime that claims to hold them lawfully, in the end they will be defeated, and ultimately all will know that the Lord is His people's Saviour and Redeemer.

One day we will all meet God and give an account of our lives. Even Christians will face the Judgment Seat of Christ. What then? The true story is told of the old minister, Dr. Davidson, in Drumtochty, Scotland. It was Christmas Day and, after a busy time of preaching and visiting, he was having supper at the manse with one of his elders, a man called Drumsheugh. Suddenly he became very thoughtful, and said: "You and I, Drumsheugh, will soon have to go on a long journey, and give an account of our lives at Drumtochty. Perhaps we have done our best as men can, and I think we have tried; but there are things we might have done otherwise, and some we ought not to have done at all. It seems to me now that the less we say of the past on that day, the better. We shall wish for mercy rather than justice, Drumsheugh, and we would be none the worse of a friend to say a good word for us in the great Court."

It turned out to be Dr. Davidson's last conversation. He showed his elder to the door and watched him walk away in the snow. The next morning the Doctor was found dead in his chair.

To be 'in Christ' is to have a friend in that unseen world. We need Him now as we live in this world, and we will need Him then, when we enter that amazing world where the final word will be given on how we have served Him. No wonder the term, 'in Christ,' was one of the Apostle Paul's favourite expressions (see Ephesians chapter 1). It is still gloriously applicable to Christians, from Ephesus to Drumtochty, is it not?

JUNE 9TH

Thus says the Lord: "Where is the certificate of your mother's divorce, whom I have put away? or which of My creditors is it to whom I have sold you? For your iniquities you have sold yourselves, and for your transgressions your mother has been put away." Isaiah 50:1.

148

The Lord stood in a very special relationship with Zion, and Israel looked on Zion as its mother. The Lord had betrothed Himself to Zion, and now Israel was haunted by a deep fear: had the Lord walked away from Zion and abandoned their relationship? Were the transgressions and iniquities of the Israelites so great that the Lord had decided to divorce Zion? (See Isaiah 49:14). Had it already happened? With Zion ruined and Israel in exile, it certainly looked like it.

Which of us has not had a similar feeling? I know I have. As I look into my own heart, I know its dark side only too well, and I am aware that my life is deeply flawed. In times of failure the stabbing question comes: has God decided that His special relationship with me is over? Has He left me? Has He abandoned me?

In ancient Israel, a husband had the exclusive power to hand an unfaithful wife a writ of divorce (Deuteronomy 24:1-4). The divorced woman had no right of appeal, and a reconstitution of the original marriage was impossible. In response to Israel's fear, God now asks, "Where is the certificate of your mother's divorce, whom I put away?" But the certificate cannot be found. Why? Because He had never issued it. A divorce was not complete in Israel without this piece of writing, so the husband could take his wife again without reproach. Zion was still His, and Israel had no need to fear.

Israel also had fears relating to another law, which provided for a debtor to sell his dependants, if all other sources for repayment were exhausted (see Exodus 21:7; 2 Kings 4:1; Nehemiah 5:1-5). The rights lay with the creditor, not the debtor. Had the Lord sold Zion and her children to clear a debt? No, they were sold because of their sins. They had wilfully rebelled against the Lord, and they were now reaping the results. However, allowing Zion to be ransacked and her children exiled by a Gentile power was not the Lord's way of discharging a debt. Zion was not divorced, nor were she and her children to be sold.

Coming into the New Testament, and its teaching regarding Christ and His church, one thing is certain: Christ will never divorce His church. His bride will not be sold into slavery to pay a debt that she owes Him. When I become conscious of the debt of my sins, I am constantly made aware of the fact that the debt was paid by Christ at Calvary, and I am part of the church that He will never divorce. Look for a Bill of Divorcement anywhere in the earth or universe and you will never find it, for such a bill will never be issued. Nor will a Bill of Sale ever be found. This is called 'the eternal security of the believer.'

JUNE 10TH

"Why, when I came, was there no man? Why, when I called, was there none to answer? Is My hand shortened at all that it cannot redeem? or have I no power to deliver? Indeed with My rebuke I dry up the sea, I make the rivers a wilderness; their fish stink because there is no water, and die of thirst." Isaiah 50:2.

Can you believe it? After all God had done for Israel, especially in neither divorcing nor selling them, there was not a single person who responded to His call to come back to Himself! No one said a word; nobody stirred with emotion and said, "Yes, Lord!" Was it because the Lord was short of money to redeem the slaves who had sold themselves into slavery? (The meaning of 'shortened hand' has to do with financial resources: it literally means 'the hand that cannot reach'). Did He not have the power to deliver His people from exile? Was there silence, because the One who had promised to deliver them could not do so? He had dried a path through the Red Sea. He had dried the rivers of Israel in Elijah's day, so that the fish died. He had enveloped the land of Egypt with blackness, and caused mourning through the death of Egypt's firstborn sons. He did have power and had proved it, but nobody wanted to lean on it.

Does this incredible verse remind you of the church at Laodicea? The Christians thought they were rich; but the truth was, they were far from God. The Lord said they were 'wretched, miserable, poor, blind, and naked' (Revelation 3:17). He counselled them to buy of Him 'gold refined in the fire, that you may be rich.' God's 'gold' could not be bought with money, but had to be purchased through repentance and yielding to the Spirit of God. So God waited. He stood and knocked, and if anyone in the Laodicean church would hear, He would come in and have fellowship with that person. Sadly, like Israel, there was not a single person who had so far responded.

God has not changed. His wealth is unlimited and His power is awesome. He calls us to have fellowship with Him: to walk and talk with Him, and draw on His vast resources. As He calls, will you also be silent? God calls you on an adventure beyond all other adventures. But will you enter on it?

JUNE 11TH

"The Lord God has given Me the tongue of the learned, that I should know how to speak a word in season to him who is weary. He awakens Me morning by morning, He awakens My ear To hear as the learned." Isaiah 50:4.

We come now to the third Servant Song. These songs are exquisite in every way; and this one is exquisite in the way it describes the inner life of the Lord Jesus when He was here on earth. Have you ever wondered as to the secret source of all the wonderful things He said? Hassled in public by venomous Pharisees, He found the right thing to say to expose their false view of God. Surrounded by people who were physically and emotionally weary by all that life threw at them, the Lord Jesus sustained them with words that still encircle the earth every day and bring comfort to millions in nations with vastly diverse cultures. How did He do it?

His Father educated Him, and gave Him the gift of an instructed tongue. He actually said so Himself when here on earth: "I do nothing of Myself; but as My father taught Me, I speak these things . . . a Man who has told you the truth which I heard from God" (John 8:28, 40). This was education like no other.

To speak a word that sustains people who are weary takes a very special skill. It needs to be timely; for there are occasions when weary people, worn down with care and sorrow, will not respond to any words. On such occasions, it is usually better to say nothing. Yet a 'word in season' – a word given at the right moment – is deeply inspirational. The timing and approach of a sustaining word is vital.

The Lord Jesus was schooled by His Father for His special ministry of words that would not break 'bruised reeds' nor quench 'smouldering flax.' How did He go about it? His Father wakened Him in the morning, and the Lord Jesus listened to His instruction; and what He learned, He later shared. Morning by morning – whether it was on the hillside, or at His friends' home in Bethany, or in the fishing boat – the Lord Jesus was touched by His Father, awakened, and given a new lesson for the day ahead. Each new day brought different problems and fresh suffering for people, and the Lord Jesus was given instruction as to what He was to say in these circumstances. No matter how demanding those instructions, He did not turn away from them. They would ultimately lead him to Calvary; and in the midst of indescribable suffering He would speak a word to a weary thief, so timely that it reached him on the edge of death.

In our day and generation, we have the inspired Word of God. The promises in that Word are new every morning, as sure as the sunrise. The principles which it teaches are timeless. Its insights are relevant from Bangkok to Belfast, and from Baltimore to Bahrain. The comfort it brings sustains the weary as nothing else can. But it needs to be passed on – it needs to be communicated. It is not to be read, studied and learned, as an end in itself. We must pass on the Word in a timely, sensitive way, to sustain those weary people all around us. If a doctor has the answer to a disease, would it not be a crime if he sat in his study further analysing that answer, and did not pass it on to those who are suffering? Some weary person needs a word from you today. Don't fail to give it.

JUNE 12TH

"The Lord God has opened My ear; and I was not rebellious, nor did I turn away. I gave My back to those who struck Me, and My cheeks to those who plucked out the beard; I did not hide My face from shame and spitting. For the Lord God will help Me; therefore I will not be disgraced; therefore I have set My face like a flint, and I know that I will not be ashamed." Isaiah 50:5-7.

From the beginning, our Lord knew that He must die. We die, because we have been born; He was born that He might die. In those morning experiences with His Father, there was discussion as to what it all entailed. His listening ear absorbed the detail of the coming flogging, torture, shame and spitting, but He never questioned the necessity of His obedience to all God asked of Him. Indeed, He was vehemently opposed to all those who sought to deflect Him from the object of His life, which was His death.

As the awful hour approached, we read that the Lord Jesus was overwhelmed with sorrow. He was hemmed in on every side, and 'deeply distressed' (Mark 14:33). His acute emotional pain caused His sweat to become 'like great drops of blood falling down to the ground' (Luke 22:44). Was He afraid of pain, insult and death? Certainly not. He was no coward. Why, then, was He in such distress? It was because He had to drink the cup of God's wrath. His distress was in anticipation of enduring God's judgment against your sins and mine. He asked that, if possible, the cup might be taken from Him (Luke 22:42). But it was not possible. He must drink it all. There was not a flicker of rebellion, because it was His

Father's will that mattered, not His own. And so, with undying love, He laid down His life for His sheep.

How can I write adequately of such sacred things? Our Lord deliberately chose to give His back to those who flogged Him, and His cheeks to those who plucked out His beard. He resolutely set out to finish the work of redemption. He knew that in the end His Father would help Him, and that He would not be ashamed – He would not regret what He had done.

Are you called to suffer for Christ's sake? Perhaps you have had to face fierce antagonism for the cause of Christ. Have you been overlooked for promotion in your job, or lost value in the eyes of your colleagues, because of your faithfulness to the Lord? The promise is, you will not be disgraced, nor will you be ashamed. Those who are identified with Christ and His sufferings will share in His glory. It is guaranteed.

JUNE 13TH

"He is near who justifies Me; who will contend with Me? Let us stand together. Who is My adversary? Let him come near Me. Surely the Lord God will help Me; who is he who will condemn Me? . . . " Isaiah 50:8.

The court scenes of Isaiah would make a separate and very special study. This court scene has the Lord Jesus in the dock, and many charges are being brought against Him. It is astonishing to read this prophecy, written hundreds of years before Christ's public ministry. It foresees and foretells the accusations that became part of His everyday life on earth. The chief priests of His day accused Him of many things. Even when Christ healed the blind man, controversy raged around His kind act. The Pharisees accused Him of Sabbath-breaking, while others accused Him of being a sinner. Some said that He had cast out demons by Beelzebub, the ruler of demons.

When eventually Pilate sat on his judgement seat, and offered the crowd the choice of the thief, Barabbas, or Christ, they chose Barabbas. Mystified, Pilate asked one of the most penetrating court questions in history: "Why," he asked, "what evil has He done?" (Matthew 27: 23). Pilate admitted that he could find no fault in Christ, but still the accusations came. The crowd, who hated the Romans, accused Christ of being against Rome. To His enemies, He could do no right.

But there was One who would vindicate the Lord Jesus: Jehovah would be near Him. Mark this truth well, for our justification depends on it. It has been pointed out that they accused Christ of being the friend of sinners; His father justified Him by making sinners into saints. They accused Christ of being mad; His Father justified Him by making His teaching the most majestic on earth, and the supreme problem for philosophy! They said He was a blasphemer, when He said He was the Son of God; His Father raised Him from the dead and exalted Him to His right hand in glory (see Romans 1:4; 1 Timothy 3:16). Whose life has ever been vindicated like that of the Lord Jesus? Throughout history and time, He has been shown to be flawless.

If the life and death of the Lord Jesus had not been justified by His Father, then our justification would not have been possible. Now that we have fled to Christ for refuge, we now that He who justifies us is ever near. 'Therefore, having being justified by faith, we have peace with God through our Lord Jesus Christ, through whom also we have access by faith into this grace in which we stand, and rejoice in hope of the glory of God' (Romans 5:1-2). 'Who shall bring a charge against God's elect? It is God who justifies. Who is he who condemns? It is Christ who died, and furthermore is also risen, who is even at the right hand of God, who also makes intercession for us. Who shall separate us from the love of Christ? Shall tribulation, or distress, or persecution, or famine, or nakedness, or peril, or sword?' (Romans 8:33-35). As the sinless Christ delighted in being justified by His Father, so we justified sinners sing with the church throughout all ages, 'My Jesus has done all things well.'

JUNE 14TH

"Surely the Lord God will help Me; who is he who will condemn Me? Indeed they will all grow old like a garment; the moth will eat them up." Isaiah 50:9.

In 1923 a group of the world's most successful financiers met at the Edgewater Beach Hotel in Chicago. It consisted of a member of the President's Cabinet; the greatest stockbroker on Wall Street; the President of the largest independent steel company; the President of the Bank of International Settlements; the President of the New York Stock Exchange; and the owner of the world's greatest monopoly. How did they subsequently fare in life? Did they all enjoy a peaceful and comfortable retirement amidst comfort and happiness? I discovered an interesting summary of what happened to them all. Let me share it with you.

Albert Fall, the member of the President's cabinet, was released from prison to die at home. The stockbroker, Arthur Cullen, died abroad, bankrupt. The steel man, Charles Schwab, lived on borrowed money and died five years later, broke. The President of the Bank of International Settlements, Leon Fraser, committed suicide. The President of the New York Stock Exchange went to Sing Sing prison. Ivor Kruger, the owner of the world's greatest monopoly, committed suicide.

The transience of wealth is attested by time. Century after century affirms that it does not last. Alexander the Great left instructions that his hand should be left hanging out of his coffin, to prove that his wealth could not be taken with him. Jesus distinctly taught that a person's life does not consist in the abundance of the things which one possesses (see Luke 12:15).

The subject of transient things is extremely pertinent. When I got up this morning, a moth was flying about in my home. As I watched it, I thought of today's text. It shows the transience of something else in our world – the transience of all the Lord's accusers and enemies. Like a garment wears out and falls to pieces, to become a prey to the moth, so all those who oppose the Lord will fall apart. As the moth begins to eat the fading garment and bring about its destruction, so all those who accuse and condemn our Lord Jesus will not survive their 'moth-eating time.'

Meanwhile, our Lord Jesus and the truths He taught are indestructible. Everything that opposes Him is inadequate to answer eternity's deepest questions, and will fail. Don't let the wrath of those who oppose God and His ways cause you to doubt the final vindication of His cause. Follow the Lord and do what He did, as prophesied by Isaiah: He 'set His face like a flint,' to do God's will; He committed His cause to His Father; He believed that His Father would justify and vindicate whatever He did; He knew that all opposition would eventually be destroyed, and that He would not be confounded. God will do the same for you: 'He shall bring forth your righteousness as the light, and your justice as the noonday' (Psalm 37:6). High noon will reveal all.

JUNE 15TH

"Who among you fears the Lord? Who obeys the voice of His Servant? Who walks in darkness and has no light? Let him trust in the name of the Lord and rely upon his God. Look, all you who kindle a fire, who encircle yourselves with sparks: walk in the light of your fire and in the sparks you have kindled – this you shall have from My hand: you shall lie down in torment." Isaiah 50:10-11.

Once more the call comes to a reluctant and stubborn Israel. Nobody, we have been told, has answered the Lord's call; and when He came no one greeted Him, or opened the door. Now in grace He calls again. He asks if there is anyone who fears Him: anyone who will listen and obey the voice of His Perfect Servant. Notice the realism in this call, as God acknowledges that those who do listen and obey will have dark days.

Is there a reader who is having one of those dark days? You simply do not understand what is happening to you. Your plans have been thwarted, and you are in the dark. The unconverted may even be scoffing at you, saying, 'Where is your God, now?' Are the tears blinding you? Have people been cruel, and their tongues cutting? Have you been misunderstood? Are you deeply depressed, because there seems to be no way out? Are you groping in the dark? Have you lost the sense of wonder that you once had? Are you afraid?

Come then, says the Lord, lean on Me. Trust in the name of the Lord, and rely on your God. Let the name of the Lord be as a guiding light. As long as you have a light, you can keep going on in the dark. I once got lost while canoeing across a lake in New York State. I simply could not find my way back, because darkness had fallen and I had no light of any kind to guide me. I couldn't read the stars, and there was no silvery moon. I was afraid. Eventually, the light of a building on the shore came in sight and guided me in.

The Lord's name is our light when things get dark. He is called 'Elohim': the mighty, strong, prominent, covenant-keeping God. 6,823 times in the Old Testament He is called 'Jehovah,' which means, the One who possesses essential life, permanent existence – 'the existing One.' He is called 'El-Shaddai,' meaning the God who is mighty to nourish and satisfy. Approximately 300 times in the Old Testament He is called 'Adonai,' meaning 'Master of Masters.' He is also called 'Jehovah-Jireh': 'The Lord will provide'; 'Jehovah-Ropheca': 'The Lord who heals'; and Jehovah-Nissi: 'the Lord my banner.' He is the One we rally to, for the battle belongs to the Lord. He is called 'Jehovah Mekaddeshcem,' meaning 'The

Lord sanctifies'; and 'Jehovah-Shalom,' meaning 'The Lord is peace.' He is 'Jehovah-Tsidkenu,' meaning 'The Lord our righteousness'; and 'Jehovah-Shammah,' meaning 'The Lord is there.' To crown it all, He has that most precious designation, 'Jehovah-Rohi,' meaning 'The Lord is my Shepherd.' Walk in the light of His name and you will never be led astray.

JUNE 16TH

"Listen to Me, you who follow after righteousness, you who seek the Lord: Look to the rock from which you were hewn, and to the hole of the pit from which you were dug. Look to Abraham your father, and to Sarah who bore you; for I called him alone, and blessed him and increased him." Isaiah 51:1-2.

We are now approaching Isaiah's sublime prophecy of the death and resurrection of the Messiah. First, though, we are asked to look back. It has been said that the further back you can look, the further forward you can see; and that all good teaching begins with history. God now calls all those among His people who pursue righteousness and seek His presence, to learn the lessons of retrospection.

God asks them to remember that their nation began with just one man. Eventually, millions of people were to make up the nation; but it all began when God called Abraham. How obscure and alone Abraham must have felt, when Lot left him for the fertile plains near Sodom. His faith was sorely tried. Consider the aged Abraham and Sarah and the birth of their son, Isaac. God had promised, "I will make you a great nation; I will bless you and make your name great" (Genesis 12:2). Then reflect on his journey up Mount Moriah with Isaac, in whom the whole future lay. Abraham's faith triumphed, but it was deeply tested. All his life, Abraham was a pilgrim and a stranger. Transience constantly marked the Father of the nation. He only saw from a distance what God had promised. At times he was like the bruised reed and the smouldering flax. When there was a famine, he went down into Egypt. The rains had failed, and the crops were burnt up. As a stranger in a strange land, surrounded by hostile people and bearing the responsibility for huge flocks and herds, it is understandable that he went to Egypt. But, paralysed by fear, he went there out of the will of God. Instead of looking at his difficulties through God, he looked at God through his difficulties. To protect himself he was to enter into deceit; but he was restored and went on to great spiritual triumph.

Is there not a lesson in all of this for you? Trace the history of faith, and you will find that God has always done His greatest work through individuals. Here, a Noah; there, an Enoch. Here, a Sarah; there, a Dorcas. Here, a Moses; there, a Joseph. Here, a Samuel; there, a David. God saw in you a raw but precious thing: a jewel that could shine. It was He who found you, hewed you out, polished you, and made you what you are. Do not boast in yourself. He transformed you; He made you a blessing. His work goes on, and nothing can stop that work until you arrive, perfected, in His immediate presence. So give Him the praise, the honour and the glory.

There was a fascinating evangelist of a past generation, called Gypsy Smith, who served Christ through many years. He died on board a ship, on his way to yet another evangelistic tour in the United States, and was buried at sea. Someone once asked Gipsy Smith what kept him going through his many years of service. He gave a very precious reply: "I have never lost the wonder," he said. His testimony illustrates today's text, perfectly.

"Listen to Me, you who follow after righteousness, you who seek the Lord: Look to the rock from which you were hewn, and to the hole of the pit from which you were dug." Isaiah 51:1.

People forget their roots so easily. They get carried away. A poor boy becomes a rich man, and pride makes him forget his past; he becomes ungrateful and a pain to know. A woman from an obscure village rises to a place of power in a metropolis, and begins to despise her humble origins. The great academic forgets that once he had a patient teacher.

There is a story that has surfaced across the world recently, of Mitch Albon, ten times voted America's No.1 sports columnist. After he left college he promised to stay in touch with his favourite professor, but he became so immersed in his profession that he buried himself in his accomplishments and did not bother. Then one night, years later, he was watching his big television screen, when suddenly he saw an old man being interviewed. It was his old professor, Morrie Schwartz. He was dying, and sharing reminiscences with the interviewer. Mitch's conscience challenged him. He felt ashamed of what he had done, so he contacted his old teacher and flew 700 miles to be alongside the dying man. A very special relationship developed, as Tuesday by Tuesday Mitch Albon flew to see Morrie. Their relationship rekindled, and generated a million-seller book, entitled 'Tuesdays with Morrie.' Mitch found it a privilege to be able to pay his old professor's medical bills. He got a second chance to honour the teacher who had inspired him, and he took it.

Yesterday we looked at this text in the context of Israel's roots in Abraham. Today I simply want to emphasise from it the importance of remembering the people who have played such an important part in our lives and development. Think of parents who loved us, teachers who taught us, mentors who inspired us, encouragers who lifted us up when we were down, doctors who cared for us in illness, perhaps firemen who rescued us from a raging fire, faithful individuals who warned us when we were going wrong, neighbours who took an interest in our lives – the list is enormous. From bus drivers to canteen ladies, from house painters to church pastors, all kinds of people have come into our lives and done us good. Why not say hello to someone by Email or phone today, who would just love to hear from you again.

Don't forget 'the rock from which you were hewn.' Acknowledge your roots, and be thankful for what was good about them. I know it may not all have been good or perfect; and there were people whose impact was negative. Nevertheless, all of us can look back and be thankful for those people who made a very positive difference to our development. Let's be grateful, not forgetful.

JUNE 18TH

For the Lord will comfort Zion, He will comfort all her waste places; He will make her wilderness like Eden, and her desert like the garden of the Lord; joy and gladness will be found in it, thanksgiving and the voice of melody. Isaiah 51:3.

Again and again in these superb chapters of Isaiah, the Lord underlines the certainty of His comfort. One day God's people will be comforted, when they see arid, dead, unproductive land transformed into luscious, fertile, rich, cultivated earth. Eden will be restored. There will be a new earth. Joy and gladness, thanksgiving and melody, will be characteristics of this new earth. Satan will not win. What God always intended will be accomplished.

One is again reminded of Paul's inspiring teaching: 'The Spirit Himself bears witness with our spirit,' he writes, 'that we are children of God, and if children, then heirs – heirs of God and joint heirs with Christ, if indeed we suffer with Him, that we may also be glorified together. For I consider that the sufferings of this present time are not worthy to be compared with the glory which shall be revealed in us . . . the creation itself also will be delivered from the bondage of corruption into the glorious liberty of the children of God' (Romans 8:16-18, 21).

When we think of all that is entailed in the phrase, 'the sufferings of this present time,' it makes a formidable list. We face temptations, pressures, and conflicts of all kinds in our Christian pilgrimage. The world, the flesh, and the devil constantly harass the believer. God allows frustrating circumstances and burdensome things to enter our lives, and we are not protected from trouble in this world. In all these things we learn to lean on God, and are comforted.

This comfort does not tranquillise us, nor does it make us self-indulgent or unreal. It nerves us to face the present difficulties with confidence. There may be tribulation, distress, persecution, famine, nakedness, peril or sword, and it is through many trials that we will enter the kingdom of God. Yet, because God is for us, and His truths are indestructible, all that opposes us will fail. Follow and do what the Lord Jesus did, as prophesied in Isaiah: He set His face like a flint to do God's will, He committed His cause to His Father, and He believed that His Father would justify and vindicate Him. He knew that all opposition would eventually be destroyed, and that He would not be confounded. God will do the same for you. So don't let the wrath of those who oppose God and His ways make you doubt the final vindication of His cause.

JUNE 19TH

"Listen to Me, My people; and give ear to Me, O My nation: for law will proceed from Me, and I will make My justice rest as a light of the peoples. My righteousness is near, My salvation has gone forth, and My arms will judge the peoples; the coastlands will wait upon Me, and on My arm they will trust." Isaiah 51:4-5.

Isaiah's prophecy is full of references to the Lord's arm. 'Be their arm every morning,' is the prayer of Isaiah 33:2. 'His arm shall rule for Him,' says Isaiah 40:10. We have read of God as a shepherd, gathering 'the lambs with His arm,' in Isaiah 40:11. The question is asked in Isaiah 53:1, 'To whom has the arm of the Lord been revealed?' What, then, does the phrase, 'the arm,' or 'arms,' of the Lord, signify?

The first reference in today's text is to the 'arms' of the Lord – the only other reference in the Bible to the plural is in Deuteronomy 33:27, where we read, 'The eternal God is your refuge, and underneath are the everlasting arms; He will thrust out the enemy from before you.' The phrase has to do with the might of God's power. In the plural, as Alec Motyer suggests, it is 'the fullness of divine personal action.' When the Lord's arm or arms move, His awesome power is seen. Notice the contrast in the use of God's power, seen, first, in His power to judge nations, and, second, in His power to keep and protect all who trust Him.

These verses remind me of two women with whom I had fascinating conversations. The first worked for NASA, and she told me that she was an astrophysicist. Her work involved watching the earth via satellites, and checking continents and countries for pollution of the environment. As a result of what they saw, they would talk to the appropriate governments. If NASA judged a nation to be causing pollution through its industrial policy or whatever, I reckon a phone call from them would certainly cause that government to sit up – NASA has a 'strong arm.' If a satellite can find wrongdoing, what must God find as He surveys nations? 'Shall not the judge of all the earth do right?' asks Abraham in Genesis 18:25.

The second woman I talked with was Dr. Helen Lewis, a Jewish survivor of Auschwitz. She told me how her Nazi captors had brought their prisoners with them as they fled from the approaching Russian army. The roads were extremely icy, and if anyone fell they were shot immediately. Helen was wearing clogs, and had a fever. Two women held her by the arms as they left the camp. "She's a liability," said one to the other, and they decided to let her go. Helen fell into a snowdrift, the guard did not see her, and she made her escape. After some amazing adventures she arrived back in her home city of Prague. I remember talking to Helen at length at a friend's house, and afterwards helping her walk to her home nearby. The road was icy, and Helen leaned on my arm. I had a strong feeling that I was touching history.

So our text tells us that God's arms will judge the nations: He will judge them in the fullness of divine personal action. Yet we see from Isaiah 53:1 that the phrase, 'the arm of the Lord,' can refer to the Lord Jesus. 'On my arm,' says our text, 'they will trust.' His arms are mighty to save, and they were lovingly extended wide on our behalf at Calvary. If we trust Him as Saviour, we can lean on Him, and know for a certainty that we will never be treated as a liability.

JUNE 20TH

"Lift up your eyes to the heavens, and look on the earth beneath. For the heavens will vanish away like smoke, the earth will grow old like a garment, and those who dwell in it will die in like manner; but My salvation will be forever, and My righteousness will not be abolished." Isaiah 51:6.

Isaiah presents us now with another contrast, as the Lord compares the material with the spiritual: one is temporal and the other is eternal. He asks us to lift up our eyes to the heavens, and to look on the earth beneath. It is difficult to imagine that one day these will disappear. The mountains that people have looked upon through the medieval and other ages, are the same mountains that we look upon today. Yet our text tells us that the heavens above them and the earth beneath them will vanish as quickly as smoke carried away by the wind.

The beautiful earth in which we live, with its changing seasons, its seedtime and harvest, day and night, will grow old and fall apart like a worn garment. People, too, will quickly pass on in the same way.

Contrast all this with the unchanging God and His immutable salvation and righteousness. His word will be fulfilled, Babylon will fall; and the salvation of all those who trust in Him is eternally secure. Shattering world events do not change His purposes. Even the passing of the earth and the heavens will not bring disaster on the soul that has leaned on His arm. His throne is permanent.

To know God through Christ is to have righteousness assimilated into our lives. Such righteousness is no passing fad. Think through the righteous life depicted in the Sermon on the Mount. Instead of pride, there is humility; rather than envy, there is sharing in the unhappiness of others. For anger, there is meekness. Sloth is replaced by a passion for God and good. For greed, there is mercy; for gluttony, courage under suffering; for lust, purity of heart. Such righteousness will be established forever.

I was intrigued to read in a newspaper extract from the autobiography of the tennis player, John McEnroe, that his biggest regret was never having been able to 'turn the other cheek.' Those melt-downs of temper at Wimbledon – screaming at the umpire, "You guys are the absolute pits of the world," – brought astonishment to the millions of people who heard it. He now admits that it brought pain to himself, and he says that he often apologized for it. Isn't it interesting that his biggest regret is that he didn't follow what the Bible outlines as a good standard of behaviour? If we are honest, who doesn't have similar regrets?

Let's not sacrifice our lives for what is but passing smoke, or give our energy to what will eventually fall apart. See, then, the transient for what it really is, and live out your life for the permanent.

June 21st

"Listen to Me, you who know righteousness, you people in whose heart is My law: do not fear the reproach of men, nor be afraid of their insults. For the moth will eat them up like a garment, and the worm will eat them like wool; but My righteousness will be forever, and My salvation from generation to generation." Isaiah 51:7, 8.

When you are opposed by people for the Lord's sake, and reproached for standing up for righteousness, you must not be afraid of their insults. You might say, "that's easier said than done." It is! So, what is the secret of overcoming such opposition?

It is to remember that those who oppose you are but mortals; only a breath separates them from death. They pass, 'but the Lord's righteousness will be forever, and His salvation from generation to generation.'

This time, the call to listen to the Lord is not given to people who are seeking after Him nor to those who pursue righteousness (see Isaiah 51:1); but to those who know righteousness and in whose heart is God's law. From Isaiah 50 we learned how the Lord Jesus would be hassled and insulted by His adversaries, and His response was to set His face as a flint to do God's will. He spoke of how He would have the help of His Father, and that those who condemned Him would grow old like a garment, and the moth would eat them up.

Now, those who would follow the Lord are being asked to respond to their critics in the same way. They must get on with their work, and not be diverted by the bitter words thrown at them. They must not fear man, for that will bring a snare. One day, the critics will die they will fall apart like a garment, as the moth and the worm get to work.

I think of the work of Trans World Radio. Over fifty years ago, they bought a radio station in Monte Carlo, which had been built by Hitler for Nazi propaganda. 'Fortress Europe' had seemed impregnable, and the power of the Nazis overwhelming; but Hitler eventually committed suicide in his bunker, and Berlin and Europe fell to the Allies. The gospel began to be broadcast out of Monte Carlo, leading to the blessing of multitudes, from the very place that was built to spread poisonous propaganda. That work now stretches in a network across the world to an audience of millions.

The work of God continues, and His righteousness from generation to generation. No moth or worm will eat it up. The professed saviours of the nations of this world have risen and disintegrated, but this Saviour and His salvation are imperishable. Today I saw a poster, advertising 'Rock for all ages.' I thought I would rather hide in the 'Rock of all ages.'

JUNE 22ND

"Awake, awake, put on strength, O arm of the Lord! Awake as in the ancient days, in the generations of old. Are You not the arm that cut Rahab apart, and wounded the serpent? Are You not the One who dried up the sea, the waters of the great deep; that made the depths of the sea a road for the redeemed to cross over?" Isaiah 51:9-10.

Promises are one thing, but action is another. The Lord has given His people a lesson in retrospection: they have looked to the rock from which they had been hewn, and they have been reminded of their huge journey from the moment God called Abraham as a single individual until now. They have also heard the promises of future comfort and of the desert becoming the garden of the Lord. All of this has created a fervent desire for the fulfilment of what God has promised, and the cry goes up for action.

This cry may be from Isaiah, or it may be the voice of the faithful amongst God's people. Whoever the speaker may be, the intensity is unmistakable. God loves us to come to Him upon the basis of His promises; and this speaker is doing just that. The appeal is for God to clothe Himself with His almighty power to act. What He has done before, He can do again.

Was it not His power that intervened and cut Egypt apart, as it sought to decimate Israel? 'Rahab' is Isaiah's nickname for Egypt, says Motyer. It means 'loudmouth.' It has been suggested that the wounded serpent was Pharaoh, who was not drowned in the Red Sea, but was 'pierced.'

The mighty, restless, often monstrous sea is no barrier to the Lord. He dried up the waters of the Red Sea and made the bottom of the ocean a road for the redeemed to cross over. Don't you love the holy boldness in this petition: "Are you not the One who dried up the sea?" God just loves such talk, and responds to it.

In my own land there was a man who read a book by that great 19th century servant of God, George Muller. He was thrilled by Muller's account of what God had brought about in his life. This man then asked himself, 'If God can do it for Muller, can He not do it for us?' So he gathered some friends together in a little schoolhouse in Kells, Co. Antrim, and they prayed for a revival in Ireland. God answered their prayers, in the conversion of 100,000 people in one year. It became known as The 1859 Revival. Read today's two verses again, and then talk to the Lord about your village, your town, your city, your nation. He can do great things again.

JUNE 23RD

So the ransomed of the Lord shall return, and come to Zion with singing, with everlasting joy on their heads. They shall obtain joy and gladness; sorrow and sighing shall flee away. Isaiah 51:11.

Has God heard their appeal for help? There comes the glorious assurance that He has. The results of God's action are described now, in what is one of the most beautiful verses in the Bible. God ransomed His people: the verb means 'to redeem.' The same Hebrew word is used in the Biblical love story of Ruth and Boaz. The nearest relative to Ruth's dead husband could redeem and marry her as of right, for her protection and blessing. But he did not want to do this. So Boaz stepped in, claimed his right as the next near kinsman, and redeemed Ruth. Thus God steps in and redeems Israel from slavery, to be His own. This leads to the return of His people, and they re-enter Zion. Their sorrow is replaced with gladness, their sighing with singing, and everlasting joy is the wreath about their heads.

The same results are assured for the future of the church. Ransomed at an enormous price, bought by the blood of Christ and redeemed from sin's slavery, one day it will come to 'Mount Zion and to the city of the living God, the heavenly Jerusalem' (see Hebrews 12:22). There the church will sing a new song (see Revelation 5:9); and faithful servants of Christ will hear Him say, "Well done, good and faithful servant . . . enter into the joy of your Lord" (Matthew 25:21). That joy will most certainly be an everlasting joy.

In the interim, is there joy for the believer? In the midst of all of life's hassles and trials, can the believer know the reality of Christian joy? A look through Paul's Letter to the Philippians shows that we certainly can. The theme of Paul's letter is joy; and this from the man who tells us (see 2 Corinthians 11:25,26) that five times he received thirty-nine lashes from the Jews, three times he was beaten with rods, once he was stoned, three times he was shipwrecked, and a night and a day he spent in the deep. He tells us that his life was in danger from robbers, from his countrymen, from the Gentiles, in the wilderness and in the city. He suffered sleepless nights, was hungry and thirsty, and often was without food, in cold and exposure. In the midst of it all, he carried the daily pressure of concern for all the churches!

Now imprisoned in Rome, Paul writes to his friends in Philippi. Sixteen times in his letter he mentions the word 'joy,' or its derivative 'rejoice.' The secret of his joy was the supremacy of Christ. It adjusted his attitude to what was happening to him. Life is 10% what happens to me, and 90% how I react to it. Christian joy is more than a feeling: it is an attitude of mind. Since I believe that Christ is supreme, and all His promises will be fulfilled, then my attitude to all my trials is changed and it doesn't really matter what happens to me. Like Paul, I can take this joy with me; and one day it will no longer be tested, but eternally experienced.

JUNE 24TH

"I, even I, am He who comforts you. Who are you that you should be afraid of a man who will die, and of the son of a man who will be made like grass? And you forget the Lord your Maker, who stretched out the heavens and laid the foundations of the earth; you have feared continually every day because of the fury of the oppressor, when he has prepared to destroy. And where is the fury of the oppressor?" Isaiah 51:12-13.

Fear comes in all sorts of ways. Many people are frightened long before their feet hit the floor in the mornings. On any one day, they think they could be in an accident, fired from a job, the victim of a personal attack, mistreated, robbed, slandered, or threatened with a lawsuit.

One evening I was to speak to several hundred people. As they came in I gave them all a piece of paper. There were worried glances at the paper, but they soon discovered what it was all about. I asked them to write down a single problem in their lives at that particular time. No names were to be written on the paper, just the problem. I told them I would read out some of the contributions halfway through the service.

When the time came, a hush fell over that crowd. I told them that I wanted to prove that, in what appeared to be an average crowd of people, the hidden problems were greater than anyone would expect; and that, in truth, I did not really know who I was talking to.

The list was an eye-opener. Let me share some of the things written on those pieces of paper. 'Broken marriage.' 'My organisation appears to be ruthless, uninterested in its individual members of staff and more inclined to expediency than integrity.' 'An alcoholic father.' 'Feeling far from God.' 'Having a stammer which hinders freedom of thought and expression.' 'My brother doesn't speak to me, ever.' 'Leukaemia.' 'After fourteen years worshipping in a certain church, I have been ostracised by many members.' 'I have not the means to provide for my wife and four children.' 'Compulsive gambling.' 'Deep spiritual depression.' I could go on!

In the midst of life's pressures, when fear comes rolling in on your life, like fog off the sea, it is so easy to forget God. Notice, then, the constant reminder from God to His people, that He who created the world and the universe is present in our circumstances. To allow fear of a mere mortal oppressor to make you forget God, will constantly lead you to defeat, and hinder your progress. Notice the double affirmative from God: "I, even I, am He who comforts you."

God reminds us that, even though a furious oppressor might want to destroy us, He who made the skies above and the earth beneath created us also. 'Here you are,' God says, 'every day full of fear of someone whose very fury will soon be expended, and whose life is as grass that will wither and die.' Ask yourself, 'what is the opposition in comparison to the One who defends me?' and ultimately there is no contest. Faith in such a God will overcome your fear. As those first courageous students at the beginnings of the Cambridge University Inter Collegiate Christian Union used to declare:

> It's better to shout than to doubt.
> It's better to rise than to fall.
> It's better to let the glory out,
> Than to have no glory at all!

JUNE 25TH

"The captive exile hastens, that he may be loosed, that he should not die in the pit, and that his bread should not fail. But I am the Lord your God, who divided the sea whose waves roared – the Lord of hosts is His name." Isaiah 51:14-15.

Walking past a wall in Romania one day, I suddenly heard some children singing on the other side of it, 'Our God is so big, so great, and so powerful, there's nothing that He cannot do.' Eighteen months previously, the evil perpetrated by Ceaucescu had forced a revolution. In Bucharest I saw the (misnamed) Palace of the People. It was a monstrosity, raised by Ceaucescu at enormous cost to his country. Along the esplanade leading to the palace were the apartments of the Party-faithful. I entered one of them, and 'the faithful' were there all right; only they weren't the Communist-faithful. They were Christians, running Bucharest's first Christian bookshop in 45 years.

An older man was printing Christian literature in a large room at the back of the apartment. He told me that the printing press had come from the former East German Communist propaganda headquarters. In that very apartment some years before, Pastor Richard Wurmbrand had been tortured. Now it was a Christian bookshop. What a turn-around! "What do you put it down to?" I asked. "The finger of God," he replied. "There is a verse in the Bible," he said with a smile, "about Him who sits in the heavens laughing!" Indeed there is, and as I walked out on to the esplanade I could almost hear the laughter of God.

Today's verses underline this truth. They present images of people being released from deep trouble, as the Lord sets the exiled captives free. People who are doomed to be sent to a dungeon and then put into a common grave, find the Lord opening the door. Others who fear hunger, find that their bread does not fail. And this God is your God too. Raging seas are no barriers to His power. The sea's roar is a mighty and powerful thing to hear; it is awesomely frightening. This very day, the roar of the sea of trouble, the turbulence of sorrow, misunderstanding, and seeming chaos in your life, may be deafening you! If you can listen to them they are saying that your God is so big, so great, and so powerful, there's nothing that He cannot do. 'The Lord of the angel armies' is His name, and He who divided the waves at the Red Sea also spoke to the raging storm in Galilee. As He spoke, those mighty waves rested. The seas do not terrify Him: He terrifies them!

JUNE 26TH

"Awake, awake! Stand up, O Jerusalem, you who have drunk at the hand of the Lord the cup of His fury; you have drunk the dregs of the cup of trembling, and drained it out. There is no one to guide her among all the sons she has brought forth; nor is there any who takes her by the hand among all the sons she has brought up." Isaiah 51:17-18.

There are many images in Isaiah, but these verses show one of the saddest. Jerusalem is graphically described as being drunk. The potion she has taken has been drained to its dregs. She has staggered, fallen over, and lies asleep, dead drunk. As she lies in her drunken stupor, she has no sons to pick her up and lead her home.

What is going on? The imagery is highlighting the fact that God's people have had to drink out of the cup of God's wrath; and drain it to the last drop. The punishment of God has fallen on His people, and they have had to pay dearly for their sins.

In the image, the whole city succumbs to the potion that has been taken. But all is not lost. Suddenly, a voice comes across the city crying, "Awake, awake! Stand up, O Jerusalem!" The people who look hopeless and wiped-out, lying like a drunken woman in the street, are not beyond redemption. The Lord comes with good news to waken them up and set them on the path to holiness and blessing. In fact, we are soon to come upon the most sublime pages of good news ever written in all literature, and one of the highest peaks in sacred truth. But first, see the setting! Things could not look worse. Who would not be tempted to give up on God's people as they are described in today's texts? Helpless, unaided, embittered, stupefied; and it has all been brought on their own heads – it is entirely their fault.

Do I write this today for some frustrated believer? Are you devastated as you survey the scene in your town or city? Are the people of God around you divided, cantankerous, and power-mad? Are they even 'drunken,' not on the wrath of God, but on lust, money, and pleasure? Is their prayer life ineffective? Is their interest in the Scriptures virtually nil? Like the disciples in the Garden of Gethsemane, are they heavy with sleep? Does the Lord say to them, 'Could you not watch with me one hour?' Is their enthusiasm for the things of God waning? Do not despair. If they are the Lord's, He can waken them up and draw them to Himself. David could write of the One who restored His soul. God often begins with a divine wake-up call. Your church may be in for one very soon.

These two things have come to you; who will be sorry for you? – desolation and destruction, famine and sword – by whom will I comfort you? Your sons have fainted, they lie at the head of all the streets, like an antelope in a net; they are full of the fury of the Lord, the rebuke of your God. Isaiah 51:19-20.

This is a dismal scene. Desolation has come to Jerusalem; assault and battery has left the city in ruin. The people face famine and hunger, and many have been killed under the sword of the enemy. At this point, the prophet raises two penetrating questions: 'Who will be sorry for you?' 'By whom will I comfort you?'

Maybe I write today for someone who is feeling very isolated. All kinds of problems have invaded your life, and the sickening thing is that you have brought them down on your own head. By disobedience to God's word – an act of quick temper, a self-indulgent moment, a proud spirit, a stubborn attitude in your relationship with your boss at work, or with your husband or wife at home, or by spoiling your children – somewhere you have yielded to the call of temptation. Now you are reaping the harvest of that choice. To add to your troubles, no one feels sorry for you. There are no phone calls, no knocks on the door; nobody contacts you to sympathize with your dilemma. The feeling is that you deserved what was coming to you, and you too are aware of the fact. Who, then, should be sorry for you?

Israel was in such a sad situation that even her sons could not assist her. They had drunk of the wine of God's fury, and were lying 'at the head of all the streets, like an antelope in a net.' They had been captured by the hunter, and were exhausted by their vain efforts to be free; so they too were suffering because of their disobedience to the Lord.

Isaiah wants to know who will be sorry for Israel, and who will be able to comfort them? The beautiful answer is that the Lord is sorry for them, and He will comfort them. When no one else cares, He cares. When no comfort is to be found anywhere in the world, the Lord comforts like no one else can.

If you feel isolated, I am certain that the empathy and comfort of the Lord will be yours today, if you will but turn to Him in repentance and faith. He bore your sins in His own body on the Cross, so He knows how heavy the burden of your sin can be. He died under its weight, and yet rose over it victorious. Enter into that victory today.

Therefore please hear this, you afflicted, and drunk but not with wine. Thus says your Lord, the Lord and your God, who pleads the cause of His people: "See, I have taken out of your hand the cup of trembling, the dregs of the cup of My fury; you shall no longer drink it. But I will put it into the hand of those who afflict you, who have said to you, 'Lie down, that we may walk over you.' And you have laid your body like the ground, and as the street, for those who walk over." Isaiah 51:21-23.

The Lord now addresses His people in their devastating situation. Here is hope for the hopeless and light to dispel darkness. The best news that the world has ever heard is about to be highlighted in prophecy. Isaiah 53 will declare it; but our text today is among the last of the foothills leading to the summit.

The afflicted – those with hangovers and headaches, which they did not get with drinking wine – are reminded that the Lord is the One who has taken up their case and the One who pleads their cause. The Lord, who is the defender and advocate of His people against all-comers, now declares that He has taken away the cup of trembling from the drunkard's hand. Israel deserved God's wrath, but now it has gone. It is over, and they will not drink it again. The cup will be given to their enemies.

God's wrath is taken away from Israel, but it falls on the Babylonians. It has been pointed out that, in the first Exodus, when the wrath of God was removed from Israel, it fell on the Egyptians. But there was still the necessity for Israel to have a Passover lamb. Babylon, who lived by the sword, would die by the sword. Those who, as a sign of conquest, forced their prisoners to lie on the ground while they walked over their backs, will now find that the worm has turned. But what about Israel?

Are there not here shades of Calvary? The righteous demands of God must be met: there must be a draining of the cup of God's wrath on their behalf. No doubt they will still keep the Passover, but it will point to another lamb, the Lamb of God. It will point to the One who will be handed the trembling cup of God's wrath, and who will drink it until it is all gone. Isaiah is about to write of how the Lord Jesus will be put to grief and His soul made an offering for sin, so that all who trust Him will find that they have escaped the wrath they deserved. Is there any message like it? The God whose wrath is raised against the sinner takes the punishment of that wrath to Himself in the person of His Son, and sets the sinner free. It is called grace.

> Jehovah bade His sword awake;
> O Christ, it woke 'gainst thee!
> Thy blood the flaming blade must slake,
> Thy heart its sheath must be;
> All for my sake my peace to make,
> Now sleeps that sword for me.

JUNE 29TH

Awake, awake! Put on your strength, O Zion; put on your beautiful garments, O Jerusalem, the holy city! For the uncircumcised and the unclean shall no longer come to you. Isaiah 52:1.

Israel felt that God was asleep (Isaiah 51:9); but now she has discovered that she is the one who is asleep. God has awakened Zion, and she finds that two garments have been prepared for her to wear. One is called strength, and the other is called beauty.

Let this ancient text speak into your own life today. Has God awakened you from sleep? Has the world been lulling you into spiritual sleep, and the Lord has graciously spoken into your situation and opened your eyes? Be glad, then, that you are now awake to spiritual life with all its possibilities. Life is passing quickly, and so much of it can be wasted in lethargy. If we are alert, we can respond to the Lord's will for us, and accomplish great things for His glory.

Zion had the garment of strength available to her, and the New Testament believer also has a garment of strength to wear. It is called 'the whole armour of God' (Ephesians 6:13). There is 'the belt of truth,' comprising the truth of doctrine and integrity of heart. There is 'the breastplate of righteousness,' which is our standing in Christ. There is covering for our feet in 'the preparation of the gospel of peace.' The peace that the Christian knows gives a firm standing against the enemy, and makes him or her ready for combat. Sluggishness, lethargic attitudes, slowness to react, thoughtless, unintelligent living will make no impact on the enemy. So, having our feet 'shod with the preparation of the gospel of peace,' we will be mobile in the service of God. Then there is 'the shield of faith,' which, of course, has to be taken up. This shield will be 'able to quench all the fiery darts of the wicked one.' And 'the helmet of salvation.' Salvation is a gift from God, and when this is received it gives us huge confidence in the spiritual battle. There is no better helmet in the entire world than the helmet of salvation. And to augment all these things that we put on, there is also the attack weapon: 'the sword of the spirit, which is the word of God.' These, then, are the garments of strength available to the New Testament Christian.

God's Old Testament people were to be a kingdom of priests; and these verses are a call for the awakened Zion to fulfil their priestly responsibilities. In the New Testament, we are taught that believers are priests (see Revelation 1:6); and they too have beautiful garments to wear. We are called upon to 'put on the new man who is renewed in knowledge according to the image of Him who created him . . . put on tender mercies, kindness, humility, meekness, longsuffering ... put on love, which is the bond of perfection' (Colossians 3:10-14). How can we do all this? By 'putting on the Lord Jesus' (Romans 13:14). Put Him on, and all these beautiful garments will be available in your wardrobe.

June 30th

Awake, awake! Put on your strength, O Zion; put on your beautiful garments, O Jerusalem, the holy city! For the uncircumcised and the unclean shall no longer come to you. Shake yourself from the dust, arise; sit down, O Jerusalem! Loose yourself from the bonds of your neck, O captive daughter of Zion! For thus says the Lord: "You have sold yourselves for nothing, and you shall be redeemed without money." Isaiah 52:1-3.

What an awakening! Zion is drunk, but not on wine, and is lying in the street. Now she is awakened and commanded to stir herself. God has removed those who wanted no part of Him – as we know, God only goes where He is wanted. Babylon was asked to descend from her throne and sit in the dust (Isaiah 47:1); and Jerusalem is commanded to shake herself from the dust, arise, and sit on her throne. The God who commands her to do this is the God who 'raises the poor out of the dust, and lifts the needy out of the ash heap, that He may seat him (or her) with princes – with the princes of His people. He grants the barren woman a home, like a joyful mother of children' (Psalm 113:7-9). The captive daughter of Zion is told to throw off her chains.

I deeply appreciate Barry Webb's wonderful exposition of the phrase, "You have sold yourselves for nothing." He maintains that the second call to awake is to counter a sense of utter worthlessness, which is a deadly cause of spiritual paralysis. Egypt, Assyria and Babylon had treated Israel as nothing; and if you are treated as nothing you will eventually come to feel that you are nothing. But the truth is very different. No money had changed hands, God had not given up His people, and they were still His possession. They are being challenged to see themselves as God sees them, not as their enemies see them. They were to be redeemed at a price; but the price would not be money.

What, then, is the price of their redemption? Once again we can see an indirect reference to the Suffering Servant, the coming Messiah. 'You were not redeemed,' writes Peter, 'with corruptible things, like silver or gold, from your aimless conduct received by tradition from your fathers, but with the precious blood of Christ, as of a lamb without blemish and without spot. He indeed was foreordained before the foundation of the world, but was manifest in these last times for you, who through Him believe in God, who raised Him from the dead and gave Him glory, so that your faith and hope are in God' (1 Peter 1:18-21).

Do you ever feel worthless? Maybe some individual has been harassing you this very day; and, because they treat you as of no value, you feel you are of no value. If God thought you to be of such value, that He gave that which was of the greatest value in the Universe, to die for your redemption, how can you go on feeling valueless? In God's eyes you are beyond price. So, walk in the conscious knowledge that you are precious to the Lord.

July

Here spinning bobbins have been rewound on to larger packages, and cleared of any defects. The linen yarn is now ready for further processing, including dyeing or weaving. When Joseph of Arimathea received the body of the Lord Jesus under the command of Pilate, he and his friend Nicodemus 'bound it in strips of linen with the spices, as the custom of the Jews is to bury.'

For thus says the Lord God: "My people went down at first into Egypt to dwell there; then the Assyrian oppressed them without cause. Now therefore, what have I here," says the Lord, "that My people are taken away for nothing? Those who rule over them make them wail," says the Lord, "and My name is blasphemed continually every day. Therefore My people shall know My name; therefore they shall know in that day that I am He who speaks: behold, it is I." Isaiah 52:4-6.

The Sovereign Lord now reviews long years of the history of His people. As He looks at it all, He asks, "What have I here?" It is a good question. Is God saying, 'What advantage do I have here?' or 'What can I have been thinking of, to let all this happen?' or 'Do I care?' I think, the last one. Of course, He cares: these people have been kept as the apple of His eye (Deuteronomy 32:10). What can be more sensitive than the eyeball or the pupil at its centre, protected by the eyelids automatically closing when anything comes too near? It is a symbol of something that is precious, and has to be protected. To touch God's people is as if you are touching the pupil at the centre of God's eye, and He will automatically protect it. What touches His people touches Him.

First, God speaks of Israel's experience in Egypt. They "went down at first," peaceably, simply to live there. As the years passed, however, they were 'ethnically cleansed' by a Pharaoh who did not know Joseph. The Lord delivered them from Egypt. Later, in the Promised Land, they were invaded by Assyria, and some were taken into captivity. Sennacherib very nearly captured Jerusalem, except that the Lord once again delivered His people by sending His angel. 185,000 of the enemy were smitten, followed by the assassination of Sennacherib (Isaiah 37:36-38).

Then came the Babylonian captivity, and there is something going on now that touches Him deeply. Scholars disagree over the meaning of the phrase, 'those who rule over them make them wail.' Some say it is a reference to the weeping of God's people under opposition; but others point out that the Hebrew literally means, 'their rulers wail, or howl.' I lean towards the second interpretation. It seems it is not the howling of Israel in their misery, but the constant 'whooping it up' of the Babylonians day by day, as they cast a slur on that which is associated with Israel's God, and daily blaspheme His name. God promises that He will make His name known, even in these circumstances. He, Himself will speak (see Isaiah 63:1).

The message in these verses is still relevant to our hearts. God still regards His people as the apple of His eye. Whoever touches you, touches Him. Even though you are surrounded by a culture that uses your Lord's name in conversation as an exclamation mark, and constantly 'whoops up' derision of the things of God, all is not lost. Your Lord will manifest His name in all its power in your circumstances. The opposition will fade, and one day 'every tongue shall confess that Jesus Christ is Lord, to the glory of God the Father' (Philippians 2:11).

How beautiful upon the mountains are the feet of him who brings good news, who proclaims peace, who brings glad tidings of good things, who proclaims salvation, who says to Zion, "Your God reigns!" Your watchmen shall lift up their voices, with their voices they shall sing together; for they shall see eye to eye when the Lord brings back Zion. Isaiah 52:7-8.

This scene is achingly beautiful. Watchmen are anxiously looking out from the ruined walls of Jerusalem, and they see a runner in the distance. His body language is very clear as he nears that city, charred and wrecked as it is by the oppressor. Something joyful is going on in the runner's heart, which is displayed in the beauty of his movements, and the swiftness of his feet. He is bearing good news. As God had promised, the mountains that should have been a barrier have become an open way.

What is the nature of the good news borne by this swift-footed messenger? It is good news of peace: God's wrath against His people is over, the enmity is finished. They are now to enter into the good of their redemption; they are to rise from the dust and sit among princes. It is good news of salvation: deliverance from all that interferes with the enjoyment of God's highest blessings. It particularly means deliverance from sin, as well as from the various evils that are a consequence of sin. The messenger brings 'glad tidings of good things' – including the news, "Your God reigns." They had sung about this truth in their temple songs, but now they are to experience the reality.

It is fascinating how Paul picks up on this quotation: 'How then shall they call on Him in whom they have not believed?' he writes, 'and how shall they believe in Him of whom they have not heard? and how shall they hear without a preacher? and how shall they preach unless they are sent? As it is written: "How beautiful are the feet of those who preach the gospel of peace, who bring glad tidings of good things!"' (Romans 10:14, 15).

Paul is teaching that those who are sent to preach the gospel are just like that swift messenger of Isaiah 52 running toward a ruined Jerusalem. They preach justification by faith, which brings peace with God. When faith is exercised in the Lord Jesus, the enmity between the sinner and God is broken down, the fierce wrath of God is assuaged, war gives way to peace. Through believing the good news of the gospel, the past is dealt with, and grace is given to contend with all present circumstances. Salvation is by grace: it is through Christ that the believer has 'access by faith into this grace wherein we stand' (Romans 5:2). And what of the future? As Isaiah looked forward to the day when the Lord would 'bring back Zion,' so Christians 'rejoice in hope of the glory of God' – and look forward to the time when the church will reign with Christ.

Christian, as you go about your business today, may you be a swift messenger of the good news of the gospel to someone who desperately needs to hear it.

Your watchmen shall lift up their voices, with their voices they shall sing together; for they shall see eye to eye when the Lord brings back Zion. Isaiah 52:8.

L et's pause, to study the ministry of the watchmen. You will find it beneficial. The watchmen of Israel are in a fellowship. What they have been looking for, they have found; and it is so good that they sing about it. How beautiful is their song! How precious is their fellowship!

But who are these watchmen? They work on a very wide front. In fact they are the prophets of Israel, Isaiah being one of them. They were a very special body of people, who received messages from God and declared them to the people, sometimes orally, and sometimes in writing. When they spoke concerning the distant future, their messages could be believed every bit as much as when they were speaking about the present, or the immediate future. Why? Because their prophecies came to pass, thus proving their reality (Jeremiah 28:9). The penalty for being a false prophet was death (Deuteronomy 13:5).

Again and again over the centuries, they prophesied about the coming Messiah. In the entire ancient world there was nothing like it. The prophets of Israel all spoke in unison of a future deliverance by the Messiah. Right from Adam's time, we are told that the seed of the woman would bruise the serpent's head (see Genesis 3:15). All Messianic prophecy is based on that promise. Again and again we read of this Messiah, the 'anointed one.' He is the King, in Psalms 2, 4, 5, 72 and 110. Isaiah tells us that He is to be born of a virgin (Isaiah 7:14). The Lord Jesus said that even Abraham 'rejoiced to see My day, and he saw it and was glad' (John 8:56).

In the New Testament there is a helpful commentary by Peter on the work of these watchmen. It sums up their ministry, as they looked far into the distance for the Messiah:

'Of this salvation the prophets have inquired and searched carefully, who prophesied of the grace that would come to you, searching what, or what manner of time, the Spirit of Christ who was in them was indicating when He testified beforehand the sufferings of Christ and the glories that would follow. To them it was revealed that, not to themselves, but to us they were ministering the things which now have been reported to you through those who have preached the gospel to you by the Holy Spirit sent from heaven – things which angels desire to look into' (1 Peter 1:10-12).

Following the running herald, the Lord comes to restore Zion. The watchmen burst into song at the sight of it all. It was a sight so clear, that they see 'eye to eye' – that is, as vividly as one person sees another by looking into his or her eyes. With their own eyes, the watchmen see their prophecies being fulfilled to the letter. Imagine each one saying to the others, 'Look, there He is – just as I said He would be, away back in such and such a century!'

I know that, as believers, people are saying to us in our day, 'Where is the sign of His coming?' Daniel, one of the world's greatest civil servants, was exiled in Babylon. Zion was in ruins, but he still believed that the 'Ancient of Days' would come (Daniel 7:22), and Zion would be restored. So we, too, believe that the Messiah will come, and our faith will be rewarded by sight. We shall see 'eye to eye,' and shall burst into song with a people whose number no computer could calculate. It is guaranteed.

Break forth into joy, sing together, you waste places of Jerusalem! For the Lord has comforted His people, He has redeemed Jerusalem. The Lord has made bare His holy arm in the eyes of all the nations; and all the ends of the earth shall see the salvation of our God. Isaiah 52:9-10.

When I read these verses, I think of an old man, who lived hundreds of years after Isaiah had written these verses depicting the glory of restoration after the years of ruin.

Isaiah writes of joy that replaced despair, singing that replaced many tears, and of the Lord making bare His holy arm. This is a metaphor of a soldier removing all the coverings from his arm in order to exert his power to the full. In modern times, the metaphor is of a man 'rolling up his sleeves,' to accomplish a task. Isaiah looks away across the future, and anticipates the day when all the ends of the earth shall see God's holy arm at work – even those who opposed the salvation of our God shall see it. He tells us that one of the reasons for all this joy and singing is the fact that the Lord has comforted His people. Right through this section of Isaiah, we see the Lord bringing comfort to His people (40:1; 49:13; 51:3, 12). His comfort is incomparable.

Why, then, should I think of an old man? Because he, too, was a watchman in Jerusalem. His name was Simeon. Dr. Luke tells us that he was waiting for the 'Consolation of Israel' (Luke 2:25-35). He knew that precious comfort would come; but he also knew that it must come at a huge price. The Holy Spirit revealed to Simeon that he would not die before he had seen the Messiah. When Mary brought her firstborn to the temple, Simeon approached her, took Jesus in His arms, blessed God, and said, 'Lord, now You are letting Your servant depart in peace, according to Your word; for my eyes have seen Your salvation which You have prepared before the face of all peoples, a light to bring revelation to the Gentiles, and the glory of your people Israel' (Luke 2:29-32).

Simeon was obviously well versed in Isaiah chapters 40-55. He could see that Israel would be comforted, and the whole world would be affected by the child in his arms. But Simeon gently reminded Mary that her child must suffer, and 'a sword will pierce through your own soul also.' Yet the death of her son would bring about the eternal purposes of God. Salvation would be through this child: with such a promise the old man could die in peace. Can you? If you must go through 'the valley of the shadow of death,' then, like Simeon, you can know peace, because the promises of God are sure. If he enjoyed that peace before the actual death and resurrection of the Lord Jesus, how much more can you and I know it now?

Break forth into joy, sing together, You waste places of Jerusalem! For the Lord has comforted His people, He has redeemed Jerusalem. Isaiah 52:9.

L et me stay with this verse for another day. Why? Because it reminds me of another watchman, or, should I say, watchperson! Her name was Anna (see Luke 2:36-38). She, too, was well versed in the content of Isaiah's writings. Simeon's emphasis was on the comfort of Israel, and the salvation of God reaching to the ends of the earth through the death and resurrection of Christ. Based on today's text, Anna's emphasis was on the redemption of Jerusalem. Let's reflect on her witness.

The Law required two things from Mary. First, she had to bring a sacrifice in connection with the purification of a woman after childbirth. Second, the Law required that she present her firstborn to the Lord. In Israel, the whole emphasis in the presentation of a firstborn to the Lord was on redemption. On the night that the avenging angel went through Egypt, Israel's firstborn were saved by the blood of the Passover lamb. In recognition of the saving of their lives, all subsequent firstborn males had to be consecrated to God. This meant a life of religious service. Hannah's presentation of Samuel was an example of this consecration (see 1 Samuel 1-2). Parents could redeem their firstborn from that life of service when they were one month old, by paying five shekels of silver (see Numbers 18:15-16).

It was on this occasion of the presentation of her firstborn to the Lord, that Simeon approached Mary, to gently indicate to her that Israel's redemption depended on the sacrifice of Jesus. Just as he finished praying, Anna joined them. 'And coming in that instant she gave thanks to the Lord, and spoke of Him to all those who looked for redemption in Jerusalem' (Luke 2:38). The eighty-four year old widow seemed to spend her life in the temple, where she served God with fastings and prayers day and night. She believed in Isaiah's promise of the redemption of the city of Jerusalem, and at the very moment it was needed, she comforted Mary with its truth.

Professor David Gooding has helpfully pointed out: 'Had Anna appeared first, delivered her message and then left Simeon to finish the story, Mary might have concluded that Simeon's announcement annulled Anna's enthusiastic message; that Israel's rejection of God's Son, although it meant that salvation would go to the Gentiles, made it doubtful that Jerusalem city would ever be restored. But Anna had come up after Simeon; and in spite of all that Simeon had said, she had still assured her listeners that Jerusalem city would be redeemed. Remembering this, Mary would be prepared to hear the worst without losing heart' (*According to Luke*, Leicester, Inter-Varsity Press, 1987, p.60).

One of the most thrilling of all God's activities is His timing in people's lives. Abraham found a ram caught in a thicket at the very time he needed it. On request, the beautiful Rebecca gave a drink of water to a stranger. When he had drunk it, she said, "I will draw water for your camels also, until they have finished drinking." She did not realise that her destiny hung on what she had just done, and her marriage to Isaac was assured. Joseph was kind to two prisoners, and found his action to be God's highway to the premiership of Egypt. In a time of war Gideon kept the food supply going for his family, and discovered his action symbolised what God wanted to do for his nation, and he was chosen to bring it about. David faithfully shepherded His father's sheep, and soon he was shepherding Israel. At the precise second that the king wanted to exalt Mordecai, Haman walked into the court of Ahasuerus. Haman wanted Mordecai hung, but instead he was used to bring about Mordecai's exaltation. The little boy found his picnic lunch useful at the very moment Christ wanted to feed five thousand people.

God's timing is perfect. You may find that, walking through a certain door, receiving a phone call, reading an article, bumping into a friend on the street today, may lead to the most incredible time of your life. Remember, God is never late.

July 6th

Depart! Depart! Go out from there, touch no unclean thing; go out from the midst of her, be clean, you who bear the vessels of the Lord. Isaiah 52:11.

The climax is now reached, and the call comes for the second exodus. God's people are commanded to depart from Babylon. They must not touch any unclean thing, so that they will not contaminate themselves. In the first exodus, the children of Israel, 'asked from the Egyptians articles of silver, articles of gold, and clothing . . . thus they plundered the Egyptians' (Exodus 12:35-36). The implication seems to be that some of those articles were associated with the worship of other gods. Isaiah had strongly condemned those who contaminated the worship of the true God by having anything to do with the worship of idols. Now that the remnant is returning to Jerusalem to restore the temple, no idols, or anything associated with them, are to be taken away.

Nebuchadnezzar had brought the vessels of the Lord from Jerusalem to Babylon. He did not destroy them, but 'brought the articles into the treasure house of his god' (See Daniel 1:1-3). He recognised that the Israelite vessels were the vessels of a god. When he placed those vessels in the house of his god, Marduk, Nebuchadnezzar was saying that Marduk had overcome Jehovah. Now these vessels were to be restored to the temple at Jerusalem; and those who carried them were not to be contaminated with idol worship (see Ezra 1:7-11). 'Be clean, you who bear the vessels of the Lord,' writes Isaiah. It is a challenge to holiness of life.

F. B. Meyer points out, 'in all our lives there are Babylons, that have no claim on redeemed people.' Too right! But how easy it is to get contaminated. Things that we once abhorred, we now embrace. Things that we once found extremely suspicious, now fascinate us. We once cringed at certain language that people use; now we laugh at it. Business practices that we never would have dreamt of using, we now use all the time. God says, 'Depart! Depart! Go out from there, touch no unclean thing.' Like Lot, we linger; we hang on in there. We hold back, when we should be gone; we embrace what we should shun.

Come on then, Christian! Be done with your 'Babylon.' Switch off that untoward programme. Break away from the influence of that ungodly companion: 'Be not unequally yoked together with unbelievers' (2 Corinthians 6:14). If the one whom you intend to marry does not love the Lord Jesus, you will be bringing a yoke into your life that you will regret. We have only to look at the life of Solomon, once the wisest man in all the earth, to see what can happen. 'His wives turned his heart after other gods; and his heart was not loyal to the Lord his God, as was the heart of his father David' (1 Kings 11: 4). There was a 'Babylon' in Solomon's life, which turned him into an effeminate fool.

Remember, however, that what you renounce for God you will be compensated for one-hundredfold (Mathew 19:29). Nobody who has left 'Babylon' for a closer walk with God has ever lived to regret it.

For you shall not go out with haste, nor go by flight; for the Lord will go before you, and the God of Israel will be your rear guard. Isaiah 52:12.

The exodus from Babylon was to be unhurried and orderly. Cyrus would give these people an honourable discharge. They would not be pursued across the wilderness by an opposing power; they were to go with decorum. God promises that He will go before them and behind them. In this beautiful text, there are good lessons for us today.

When things are done in the midst of feverish living, there are all kinds of dangers. In a generation that has been accused of having the attention span of a flea, we need to be careful to take time over what we are doing. It is so easy to go rushing here and there. In a parable told in 1 Kings 20, we read of a man who forfeited his life by letting a person escape who was in his charge. The reason given for the man's carelessness was business: "While your servant was busy here and there, he was gone" (1 Kings 20:39-43). Mark those words, and let me repeat them: "While your servant was busy . . . he was gone." Don't let even legitimate business divert you from the main purpose for which you have been called. You must give up doing good things, to do a better thing.

The perfect Servant, our Lord Jesus, is the best example of unhurried service for God. To put it in plain and simple terms, Jesus was never in a hurry. His brothers urged Him to speed things up, by going up to the feast at Jerusalem and doing some spectacular miracles to reveal Himself to the world. But the Saviour refused. His Father regulated His time, and He refused to go anywhere until His will was known. His public entry into Jerusalem was still six months ahead. His hour had not yet come.

How can a steady, unfevered pace mark our lives? To use a military illustration, they must be governed by an assurance that God is our sapper and our rearguard. The sapper clears obstacles for the advancing army, and the rearguard protects it from attack from behind. The promise in our text is that the Lord will go before and come behind us. Are you frightened about the future? Have you have arrived at a point in your life, where there is no visible support? Your path is hidden by the long grass; so, what do you do? Whatever you do, be sure you do not rush on. Your Lord says, 'Be quiet; stand still. Bring all your questions and anxieties to Me in prayer. Listen for My voice, and I will speak to you. Ignore other voices and follow Me – I call My own sheep by name. I will lead you forward, and I will also guard your back. So, there is no need to hurry. I have gone on ahead, and when you need to move, I will call you. There will be no doubt about what you should do. Trust me.'

Behold, My Servant shall deal prudently; He shall be exalted and extolled and be very high. Isaiah 52:13.

While Israel's deliverance from Babylon is implied and alluded to in the section that we have recently been studying together, there has been a wider dimension to Isaiah's writing. Commentators are agreed that, from chapter 49 forward, Isaiah is also speaking of a spiritual deliverance – Babylon is not mentioned again by name. The spiritual deliverance that Isaiah is speaking of would be impossible without God's Perfect Servant. As we come now to the third Servant Song, our attention is gripped by an unexcelled perspective of Him, introduced by the words, 'Behold, My servant.' It is a song of suffering, in which we learn that our spiritual deliverance was not possible without profound grief and sorrow.

In its original language, this song did not read as prose; but as superb Hebrew poetry. It consists of what is known as completive parallels: it comes in pairs of couplets, in which the second member of the pair extends, or completes, the thought of the first. So, now we have the first couplet: 'Behold My Servant shall deal prudently; He shall be exalted and extolled and be very high.' We are commanded to watch how the Lord Jesus behaves; and we see that He acts prudently, i.e. with care and foresight. Think of each careful step of His mission to, and on, the earth. His mother is from among the peasant folk of Galilee; He is born in Bethlehem, and laid in a manger; His boyhood is spent in Nazareth where He worked in the carpenter's shop, submitting to His parents; as a youth, He is found in the temple, in deep discussion with Israel's leaders; and then at thirty He begins His public ministry. With each careful step He is moving on, unflinchingly, to Calvary.

Then Isaiah calls on us to watch and see what Christ's prudent actions led to: prosperity, such as the universe has never known. First, came His mighty resurrection: He rose up in exaltation. The best news the world ever heard came from a graveyard. Then came His ascension: He was gloriously lifted up. His present position is at the right hand of God: 'He shall be . . . very high,' says Isaiah. Paul expands this for us in Philippians 2:9: 'Therefore God also has highly exalted Him and given Him the name which is above every name.' Says the writer to the Hebrews, '. . . when He had by Himself purged our sins, He sat down at the right hand of the Majesty on high' (Hebrews 1:3).

In our lives, let us be like our Lord Jesus, and ask Him for grace to act wisely, so that we might do His work with care and foresight. As we follow in His steps, we shall find a spiritual prosperity beyond all that we could ever ask or think. So, Christian, carefully as it goes.

JULY 9TH

Just as many were astonished at you, so His visage was marred more than any man, and His form more than the sons of men; so shall He sprinkle many nations. Kings shall shut their mouths at Him; for what had not been told them they shall see, and what they had not heard they shall consider. Isaiah 52:14-15.

In a home in Northern Ireland one evening, a sceptic spoke up in the conversation: "Other people have suffered as much as Christ," he maintained. Someone whom I know was present. He was a converted drunkard, and certainly knew little of Academia; but he had personal experience in God's school. With deep pathos, he reminded the sceptic of today's verse. He pointed out that Christ's face was more marred than any individual, and His form more than all individuals.

Prophetically, Isaiah is pointing out that, when Christ would be crucified, many would look upon His marred face and His body, disfigured beyond recognition, and be astonished. In Hebrew the word means to be 'appalled.' There is another side to the extremity of Christ's grief: there is reward in it. Many people looked upon Him and were appalled; yet multitudes will come into the rich reward. 'He shall sprinkle many nations' – many people will be cleansed and atoned for by Christ's death. 'Kings shall be dumbfounded by it,' but they shall see and understand something that they had never heard of before. Its significance will dawn on them: the Cross had to come before the crown, and shame and ignominy before glory – but what glory!

Have you found that there is offence in the Cross of Christ? We speak of Christ's blood being shed, His back being opened by the scourging, His hands being pierced by the nails and His side by the spear; but when we seek to point out that His death is the means of salvation and redemption, we discover that it is still an offence and a stumbling block. Yet, in the preaching of Christ crucified, have you not found there is a drawing-power like no other? While the preaching of the cross appals many people, many others, by believing its message, are cleansed and atoned for. So, let's never be ashamed to preach the cross: to those who are perishing it is foolishness, but to those who are being saved it is the very power of God (1 Corinthians 1:18).

The story is told of a local church that had a text displayed on its building. It read, 'We preach Christ crucified.' Ivy began to grow over it, and soon it read, 'We preach Christ.' As the ivy continued to spread, it read, 'We preach.' Soon all that was left was the word, 'We' – and in time that disappeared too. Ironically, what was happening physically on the outside was happening spiritually on the inside, and that local church died. Selah.

JULY 10TH

Who has believed our report? And to whom has the arm of the Lord been revealed? For He shall grow up before Him as a tender plant, and as a root out of dry ground. He has no form or comeliness; and when we see Him, there is no beauty that we should desire Him. He is despised and rejected by men, a Man of sorrows and acquainted with grief. And we hid, as it were, our faces from Him; He was despised, and we did not esteem Him.
Isaiah 53:1-3.

Ever since it was first told, the report of a disfigured, marred Messiah, beaten beyond recognition, has seemed incredible. It has always appeared a thought beyond all thoughts, that God would send His Son to the womb of a peasant woman in Galilee. His Son growing up on earth before His Father as a 'tender plant,' and as 'a root out of a dry ground,' was not something that people believed easily. In fact, the populace in His own town regarded Christ as the illegitimate son of Mary. "Can anything good come out of Nazareth?" asked the guileless Nathanael (John 1:46). There was nothing physically attractive about Him. In the eyes of His contemporaries, His background was shameful, and His surroundings exceptionally humble. This is far from the popular image of Christ's birth and childhood that millions have in their minds today. To most of my readers, however, I know He is beautiful beyond description. They believe that the hinge of history was on the door of that Bethlehem stable. They thrill to the fact that God was 'contracted to a span, incomprehensively made man' – as Charles Wesley put it. So, what makes the difference?

A revelation has taken place. 'The arm of the Lord,' is a reference to the Lord Jesus. With all my heart, I believe that conversion is a revelation of Christ to the soul: 'the arm of the Lord is revealed,' and those who believe are saved. Why have you believed 'the report'? Because the loveliness, beauty, and intrinsic worth of the Reported One was revealed to you by God the Holy Spirit.

In their blindness, the nation of Israel turned away from the Lord Jesus when He was living on earth: 'He came to His own, and His own did not receive Him' (John 1:14). They placed no value on Him. The ghastly disfigurement, the awful sight of His ignominious death on the accursed cross, made them hide their faces from Him. His nation did not hold Him in esteem. In the past two thousand years, many have followed their example. And today, millions still do not see that He identified Himself as the 'Man of Sorrows.' They have written Him off, and totally rejected Him. Yet, as the hymn puts it so poignantly: *He took our sins and our sorrows, and made them his very own.*

Be glad, then, Christian, that 'the arm of the Lord' has been revealed to you; and that you have believed the 'report.' Without that revelation, Christ in all His exquisite beauty would simply be to you 'as a tale that is told.'

JULY 11TH

Surely He has borne our griefs and carried our sorrows; yet we esteemed Him stricken, smitten by God, and afflicted. Isaiah 53:4.

S in has brought grief and sorrow into our world, but the Lord Jesus came and took up that grief and sorrow. He shouldered it for us. Look at Him in Capernaum, entering into Peter's house and seeing his mother-in-law 'lying sick with a fever.' He touches her hand, and the fever leaves her. In the evening, 'they brought to Him many who were demon-possessed and He cast out the spirits with a word, and healed all who were sick, that it might be fulfilled which was spoken by Isaiah the prophet, saying: "He Himself took our infirmities and bore our sicknesses"' (Matthew 8:14-17).

As we trace the Saviour's steps throughout His earthly ministry, we see how closely He carried our griefs and sorrows. Of course, He was completely misunderstood by those around Him. They considered His suffering to be a mark of God's displeasure upon Him. They thought that His suffering was inflicted on Him by God – that God was smiting Him. Just as we need a special revelation from God to see beauty in that 'root out of dry ground,' so we need a special revelation to understand His sufferings. Notice that the verbs, 'bore,' and 'carried,' emphasise the idea that, in bearing our griefs and sorrows, Christ consciously endured a pressure of weight. The passage in Matthew quoted above tells us that, in healing the people, He was fulfilling this prophecy in Isaiah; and yet it is also telling us that, in some mysterious way, Christ Himself suffered even as He dispensed the healing. Long before the Saviour reached Calvary, He consciously suffered as a Man of Sorrows, because of His complete identification with our griefs and sorrows.

I read an interview by Oliver Burkeman in *The Guardian* newspaper (18.6.2002), of CNN's Ted Turner. Turner has a charity called The United Nations Foundation, which gives a lot of money to help solve world problems in the 21st century. In 1997 he pledged $1billion to the United Nations. During the interview, Turner began talking about some problems in the Middle East, and said he found it all very depressing. Suddenly it became apparent that he was crying. Burkeman reported that it only lasted for a few moments, and then Turner continued to outline his solutions. But it was obvious that the man cared. At times, the world's problems do get to us all at a deep level. Most of us shrug them off, and move on with our own agenda. Christ took up our griefs, and shouldered our sorrows. He did not throw them off. When we face problems, it is deeply comforting to know that we have such a shoulder to cry on.

JULY 12TH

But He was wounded for our transgressions, He was bruised for our iniquities; the chastisement for our peace was upon Him, and by His stripes we are healed. Isaiah 53:5.

What can I write about this immortal text? It beggars words – the harrowing truth of the piercing of the side of the Perfect Servant by a spear, and the iron spikes piercing into His hands. When I read that the cause of His wounding and bruising was my transgressions and iniquities, I am dumbfounded. And when I discover that His wounding and bruising results in me being made whole, I say with Donald English, 'The wonder of the Cross is not the blood, but whose blood, and to what purpose.'

This text makes me think of two people. I remember talking many years ago with my friend Dr. Victor Glasgow of Newtownards. He told me how that, as a boy of eight years and ten months old, he was sitting in a special meeting for children in a little Gospel Hall on Scrabo Hill, listening to a speaker talking about Calvary. "He broke my heart with his presentation of the Cross of Christ," Dr. Glasgow told me. Suddenly, he broke down in tears. "That's fifty years ago," he said "and, Bingham, Calvary still breaks my heart!" The speaker then told the story of a dying sea captain, called Captain Coutts. He was shown how he could put his own name into the lovely words of Isaiah 53:5: 'He was wounded for Captain Coutts' transgressions, He was bruised for Captain Coutts' iniquities; the chastisement for Captain Coutts' peace was upon Him, and by His stripes, Captain Coutts is healed'. The Captain did so, and believing the truth of those words he was converted on the spot. Sitting in that little hall, Victor slipped his name in there too. Have you done that?

The second person this text makes me think of is Gina. She hosted a radio programme, called *Personally Speaking*, in the great city of Geneva. Anyone being interviewed on her programme had no idea what they might be asked; there was no set agenda. If a mistake was made during the interview, it was not edited out. Gina told me that quite often people 'hung themselves' on her programme! Among her former guests was the Dalai Lama; but now it happened to be me. Nervously, I tried to answer her many questions, and we got so deeply into the conversation that she decided to make it into two programmes. Towards the end, she looked at me and asked how I would sum up the message which I preached. She highlighted the fact that the Headquarters of the United Nations is in Geneva, so people from all kinds of cultures and beliefs lived in the city. "Have you got a Bible, Gina," I asked. She went and found one, and slowly and deliberately, I read all of Isaiah chapter 53. It was moving, then, to be able to emphasise that, in order to secure peace with God for sinners, our punishment was borne on the cross by the Saviour of the world: 'by His stripes we are healed.' Somehow that day I realised, as never before, that the gospel message is international. It is as relevant in Newtownards as it is in Geneva, and as relevant to your heart as it is to mine.

July 13TH

All we like sheep have gone astray; we have turned, every one, to his own way; and the Lord has laid on Him the iniquity of us all. Isaiah 53:6.

In a letter dated 10th November 1854, the pre-Raphaelite painter, William Holman Hunt, described to his fellow-artist, Sir John Everett Millais, the story of the scapegoat in Leviticus 16:21 and said that he would like to do a painting of it. Bearing all the sins of the children of Israel, the scapegoat was sent away into the wilderness.

Hunt eventually went to Israel. At risk to his own life from robbers (also, at one point, he almost sank to his death in a pit of slime), he painted each day until sunset at the edge of the Dead Sea. His painting *The Scapegoat*, was exhibited at the Royal Academy in 1856. In general, it was much criticised and misunderstood.

I love Hunt's painting. It presents an awesome vision of desolation, and calls me to worship the One whom it typifies. (If you ever get a chance, you can view it at the Lady Lever Gallery at Port Sunlight near Liverpool.) I can well understand how his painting was criticised and misunderstood: is that not what always happens when the message of the cross is presented? It is a universal reaction. Like sheep without a shepherd, we have all gone astray and deliberately turned to our own way. The message of God making to meet upon one Person the iniquity of us all, is still misunderstood and criticised by many. However, Isaiah has not misunderstood the reason for Christ's sufferings. He tells us that Jehovah placed on Him the full weight of our iniquities and the wrath that was due for them. As the hymn says:

It was my sin that held Him there,
Until it was accomplished.
His dying breath has brought me life.
I know that it is finished.

The reality of it moves me to rest on His perfect, finished work, and to serve Him all my days in gratitude.

July 14th

He was oppressed and He was afflicted, yet He opened not His mouth; He was led as a lamb to the slaughter, and as a sheep before its shearers is silent, so He opened not His mouth. Isaiah 53:7.

In his book, *The Master Theme of the Bible* (Tyndale House Publishers, 1973), J. Sidlow Baxter explains that there are completive parallels in Isaiah 53. As explained already, completive parallels are when the second member of a pair extends, or completes, the thought in the first member. He shows that the exact centre of these twenty-four parallels is, 'He was led as a lamb to the slaughter, and as a sheep before its shearers is silent.' Here is the centrality of the Lamb.

Yesterday, we looked at the image of the Lord bearing our sins: like the scapegoat being sent into the wilderness. Today, we look at Him as the sacrificial lamb, going silently to the slaughter, and as a sheep lying passively in the hands of its shearers. Willingly, we have strayed into our sinful ways. Willingly and voluntarily, the Lord Jesus walked the path of obedience, silently accepting all that it meant. The lamb and the sheep are silent because of lack of knowledge as to what is happening to them; but the Lord Jesus is silent, even in the full knowledge of what is happening to Him.

Certainly, Christ was 'led as a lamb to the slaughter;' but He knew exactly what it would entail, and He went voluntarily. That is exactly what John says in his Gospel:

'Then Judas, having received a detachment of troops, and officers from the chief priests and Pharisees, came there with lanterns, torches, and weapons. Jesus therefore, *knowing all things that would come upon Him*, went forward and said to them, "Whom are you seeking?" They answered Him, "Jesus of Nazareth." Jesus said to them, "I am He." And Judas, who betrayed Him, also stood with them. Now when He said to them, "I am He," they drew back and fell to the ground. Then He asked them again, "Whom are you seeking?" And they said, "Jesus of Nazareth." Jesus answered, "I have told you that I am He. Therefore, if you seek Me, let these go their way"' (John 18: 3-8).

There is no way they could have led Christ to the slaughter without His permission. The silent, voluntary submission of the Saviour to the will of God is unmistakeable. There was not a word of protest or rebellion. This is the Perfect Servant. Do I submit to the will of God in my life like that; or am I full of words of protest, because it is proving to be sacrificial and costly? May I be like the Lord whom I profess to follow. Before He left the Upper Room to face the cross, He sang a hymn with His disciples. Not only did He go voluntarily, He went singing. Selah.

July 15th

He was taken from prison and from judgment, and who will declare His generation? for He was cut off from the land of the living; for the transgressions of My people He was stricken. Isaiah 53:8.

By an oppressive judicial sentence, Christ was taken away to Calvary. It was a mock trial, with false witnesses and horrendous beatings; but Christ refused to confess to those tormentors, sins that He had never committed. It was unashamed injustice, pretence, and duplicity. These people showed no restraint whatever. Despite the pleas of the Roman Governor, as to Christ's absolute innocence; despite Pilate's judgment that Christ was a just person, they cried, "Let Him be crucified" (Matthew 27:22) The judgment of the Sanhedrin and the people was that the Lord Jesus should die. So Pilate, just to keep his job, let them have their way. Poor, wretched man, shortly afterwards he lost his job anyway.

'Who will declare His generation?' writes Isaiah, 'for He was cut off from the land of the living.' Some say this means that Christ died in the prime of life, leaving no children; but others suggest that a better rendering is, 'Who of His generation considered . . .?' It is asking, who of those around Christ in His day of suffering really understood what was happening? 'He was cut off': it is the same word used by Solomon, when he suggests to the two women arguing over the child that it should be cut in two. It is the same word used of felling a tree – it is a very savage word indeed. In reality, it was a very savage act. Why? Because of the rebellion of sinful people.

Then comes one of the finest details in all prophecy. Isaiah deliberately chooses two words, one in the plural and the other in the singular. He says that the Perfect Servant 'made His grave with *the wicked*,' – plural; but 'with *the rich* in His death' – singular. There were two thieves crucified with Christ; and there was one rich man who gave Him his tomb for burial. The sinful rulers of Israel intended to have Christ buried with the two robbers (see John 19:31); but the Roman authorities granted the body to the rich man, Joseph of Arimathea (see Matthew 27:57-60). Such detail makes me bow my head and worship.

As I face my life, with all its problems and joys, I am deeply comforted by such detail. Why? Because the God who made such fine details come together in history, orders my steps also. Despite the daily swirl of chaos in Jerusalem and the West Bank at the time of writing, I know that God is working out His purposes. I am not saying that I know how He is working them out; I cannot explain how He does it, but He does it. So, calm your mind and heart, Christian. Be still. The Lord is at your side, guiding you to His desired end, which will be glorious.

July 16TH

And they made His grave with the wicked – but with the rich at His death, because He had done no violence, nor was any deceit in His mouth. Isaiah 53:9.

Here we have even more detail about the Perfect Servant. Every word yields up deeper truths regarding Him. Isaiah tells us that Christ's honourable burial was appropriate, because He deserved it. No sin of violence had ever stained His life. No deceitful thought was ever in His heart, so no deceitful word ever came out of His mouth.

In my imagination, I am going back to that momentous day in history, when the Messiah was crucified. I see Joseph of Arimathea making his way through the streets of Jerusalem, and passing through the security surrounding the resident Governor, so he must have had influence in those circles. I watch him broach one of the most sensitive questions of that hour, and in all of history. 'He went to Pilate,' says the Authorised Version of the Bible, 'and begged the body of Jesus.' What compelled Pilate to give it to him, when the authorities of Israel intended to put Christ in a criminal's grave? Had Pilate not given in to those authorities to have Christ crucified, in the first place? What made Him defy them now? It was a power he knew nothing about. He was ignorant of the fact that a prophet, around 750 years before, had written that Christ would be with the rich in His death. 'When Joseph had taken the body, he wrapped it in a clean linen cloth, and laid it in his new tomb which he had hewn out of the rock; and he rolled a large stone against the door of the tomb, and departed' (Matthew 27:59, 60). Precious man! Precious body! Precious action! Precious prophecy fulfilled!

Where was the field of flax, which produced the linen that made the shroud for Christ? It was *fine* linen (see Mark 15:46). Who gathered it? Who processed it? How could they ever have known that this linen cloth would soon lie in Joseph's tomb, as part of the proof to the awesome truth of the resurrection of the crucified Messiah?

The Scriptures tell us a fair bit about Joseph. He was from Arimathea, which lay in the hills of Ephraim; he was a member of the Sanhedrin; he was looking for the kingdom of God; and he was a secret disciple of the Lord Jesus. He had not consented to the counsel and actions of his colleagues regarding Jesus. Amongst many fascinating questions regarding him, and his singularly sacred role at the tomb of Christ, one question arises. What made him come out so publicly? What turned this secret disciple into a fearless one? The answer is: it was the Cross that drew him out to identify publicly with Christ, and to witness fearlessly for Him, as it has drawn out millions since. What about you? What about me?

JULY 17TH

Yet it pleased the Lord to bruise Him; He has put Him to grief. When You make His soul an offering for sin, He shall see His seed, He shall prolong His days, and the pleasure of the Lord shall prosper in His hand. Isaiah 53:10.

We must be very careful how we think about the phrase, 'it pleased the Lord to bruise Him.' The terms, God's 'will' and God's 'pleasure' are synonymous here. This verse is pointing out that it was God's will and purpose to bring about the salvation of sinners, and the bruising of the Saviour was the necessary means to that end. The offering of Christ's soul as an offering for our sins satisfied the demands of a righteous God perfectly, and cleared the sinner.

The difference between the trespass offering of Leviticus 5:1-7, and the offering of the Lord Jesus, was that the first sacrifice died, but the second sacrifice died and rose again! Here Isaiah is prophesying about His resurrection. The Redeemer shall see His seed, the offspring of His mighty work; and Jehovah shall prolong His days – He is alive for evermore. God's will shall prosper in His hand – every soul to be saved shall be saved, not one of them shall be lost. He shall bring all His sheep safely home. As Alec Motyer has pointed out, 'Christ is the Executor of the salvation that He achieved . . . the Lamb's Book of Life is His prayer list.'

Let us never forget the present High Priestly work of the Lord Jesus: 'He is also able to save to the uttermost those who come to God through Him, since He always lives to make intercession for them' (Hebrews 7:25). The blood of Christ saves us from the guilt of our sin; the prayers of Christ save us in our ongoing Christian lives. It is a deep comfort to know that the Lord Jesus is praying for me today. Just as the Saviour told Peter that he would deny Him, He also told him, "I have prayed for you, that your faith should not fail" (Luke 22:32). Peter's faith did not fail, and neither shall ours, because Christ lives to intercede for us.

July 18th

He shall see the labour of His soul, and be satisfied. By His knowledge My righteous Servant shall justify many, for He shall bear their iniquities. Isaiah 53:11.

This matchless prophecy foretells how the Lord Jesus will feel about the outcome of His perfectly finished work at Calvary. Calvary's work was the labour of His very soul; and after the darkness of it all, and the death that followed, the Saviour would see the light of life. He will be alive for evermore. What kind of result would He perceive from the inordinate cost of His sacrifice? He would see the redemption of lost people, who would become His possession. And how would He feel about them? In His heart, He would be perfectly satisfied.

The story is told of a brave lieutenant in the United States army, who crawled in the face of Viet Cong fire to rescue a fellow-soldier who had been hit. He saved the soldier, but was fatally wounded himself. Sometime later, as an act of kindness to the one whose life their son had saved, the parents of the dead lieutenant invited the soldier to their home for a special meal. He arrived drunk, and behaved disgracefully. When he left, the mother of the lieutenant fell into the arms of her husband, and said, 'to think that our darling son had to die for that!'

When all the redeemed of earth are gathered home, will God, who 'so loved the world that He gave His only begotten Son,' say, 'to think that I gave My beloved Son for that'? Never, and His Son will not say or feel it, either. They will both be satisfied.

Is there someone reading this, and you feel too wretched to be accepted by God, and to become His delight? Are you like the Korean banker who came to hear me preach in Seoul, and invited me to his home for a talk. He explained that he went at times to the Buddhist temple, and sat there thinking peaceful thoughts. He said he could do so, because he knew that the Buddha had sinned just like he had done, and it was the same with Confucius and his temple. Now he had heard the Christian message that told him that he was a sinner, but Christ was sinless and he did not see how he could approach a sinless Saviour. It was a real pleasure to be able to tell him that only a sinless Saviour could redeem a sinner! 'You are not redeemed with corruptible things, like silver or gold, from your aimless conduct received by tradition from your fathers, but with the precious blood of Christ, as of a lamb without blemish and without spot' (1 Peter 1:18-19). No one is too great a sinner to be redeemed. You and I have a great need for a Saviour, but we have a great Saviour for our need. Let's trust Him.

JULY 19ᵀᴴ

He shall see the labour of His soul, and be satisfied. By His knowledge My righteous Servant shall justify many, for He shall bear their iniquities. Isaiah 53:11.

In Isaiah 11:2 we read, 'The Spirit of the Lord shall rest upon Him, the Spirit of wisdom and understanding, the Spirit of counsel and might, the Spirit of knowledge and of the fear of the Lord. Our Saviour is an all-knowing Saviour; and because He knows what is needed to save sinners, He is able to provide righteousness for all those who come to God by Him. He will 'shoulder' their iniquities.

We can have a wonderful ministry of pointing people to this perfect Saviour, so that they may be made right before God and lead a whole new life. Forgive the intrusion of a very personal incident here, but there is a point to it. One day I was walking down Hollywood Boulevard, and my hosts took me to the famous spot where the 'stars' left the imprint of their hands or feet in concrete. We had fun putting our feet into the imprint of this 'star' and that one. As we went around, I began to ask myself, 'what is a true 'star' in a Biblical sense?' My mind turned to the book of Daniel, 'Those who are wise shall shine like the brightness of the firmament, and those who turn many to righteousness like the stars forever and ever' (Daniel 12:3). It sure beats an impression in concrete, does it not?

As you pass through life, why not ask the Lord to guide you in a ministry of turning many to righteousness. I'd rather have such influence as affluence, any day. You and I have the privilege of pointing people to a Saviour who knows exactly what is needed to save sinners, and whom to know is eternal life. Surely, this is one of the greatest privileges of the Christian life. There are plenty, whose influence turns many to cynicism. Others, whose lives turn many to drugs, immorality, hedonism, love of money, and lust for power and position. So, why not be someone whom God can use to 'turn many to righteousness.' You will 'shine like the brightness of the firmament, and like the stars forever and ever.' The soul-winner is wise, says Proverbs 11:30.

JULY 20ᵀᴴ

Therefore I will divide Him a portion with the great, and He shall divide the spoil with the strong, because He poured out His soul unto death, and He was numbered with the transgressors, and He bore the sin of many, and made intercession for the transgressors. Isaiah 53:12.

The climax of this incomparable Servant Song is reached. The despised, rejected, stricken, afflicted, wounded, sacrificed, Man of Sorrows, the silent Lamb of God, has become the conqueror. According to Alec Motyer, the Hebrew reads, 'Therefore I will apportion to Him the many, and the strong He will apportion as spoil' (*Isaiah*, IVP, p. 339). There is no suggestion that the highest place should be shared with anybody. The One who was 'as a tender plant,' and 'as a root out of a dry ground,' now returns to heaven, leading captivity captive. The 'many' now in His glad captivity, were once in Satan's sad

186

captivity. The strong man has been plundered by the One who is stronger; and the Conqueror shares the strong man's spoils with the redeemed. The shout of victory is heard:

'. . . ten thousand times ten thousand, and thousands of thousands, saying with a loud voice: "Worthy is the Lamb who was slain to receive power and riches and wisdom, and strength and honour and glory and blessing!" And every creature which is in heaven and the earth and under the earth and such as are in the sea, and all that are in them, I heard saying: "Blessing and honour and glory and power be to Him who sits on the throne, and to the Lamb, forever and ever!"'

How did this come about? 'He poured out His soul unto death,' He gave *everything*. 'He was numbered with the transgressors,' He was identified with us, who had wilfully rebelled. To think that He, who had never disobeyed His father, deliberately allowed Himself to be numbered with the rebels. 'He bore the sins of many,' He did what He set out to do, and became the substitute on our behalf. 'And made intercession for the transgressors,' He is the perfect mediator between God and man. In every aspect, He is worthy.

As we leave Isaiah chapter 53, let me draw your attention to a beautiful division of this Servant Song by J. Sidlow Baxter (*The Master Theme of the Bible*, Tyndale, 1973, pp.49-50). He points out that the phrase, 'He is led as a lamb to the slaughter,' is at the exact grammatical centre of the chapter; but on either side of it are seven expressions of vicarious atonement, as seen from the human and divine viewpoints.

First, the preceding expressions: 'our griefs' (v.4); 'our sorrows' (v.4); 'our transgressions' (v.5); 'our iniquities' (v.5); 'our peace' (v.5); 'we are healed' (v.5); 'us all' (v.6). This envisages the human side of the cross. Second, the expressions that follow: 'My people' (v.8); 'When You make' (v.10); 'My righteous Servant' (v.11); 'He shall bear their iniquities' (v.11); 'He was numbered with the transgressors' (v.12); 'He bore the sin of many' (v.12); 'And made intercession for the transgressors' (v.12). Here, we have God's side of the cross.

And, between the two sevens? – 'He was led as a lamb to the slaughter, and as a sheep before its shearers is silent, so He opened not His mouth.' No wonder the angels sing, and the countless multitudes bring their praises. The Lamb, who is central in Isaiah's prophecy, should be absolutely crucial in our lives; and He most certainly is the focal point of all future government of the universe. Glory to the Lamb!

JULY 21ST

"Sing, O barren, you who have not borne! Break forth into singing, and cry aloud, you who have not laboured with child! For more are the children of the desolate than the children of the married woman," says the Lord. Enlarge the place of your tent, and let them stretch out the curtains of your dwellings; do not spare; lengthen your cords, and strengthen your stakes. For you shall expand to the right and to the left, and your descendants will inherit the nations, and make the desolate cities inhabited. Isaiah 54:1-3.

The imagery in these three verses has to do with the life of Abraham. 'You who have not laboured with child,' reminds us of the long frustration of Abraham's wife, Sarah, in not having any children. 'The place of your tent,' is a reminder of the long years of

Abraham's pilgrimage, when he had no permanent residence. 'Your descendants,' – the hope of the fulfilment of God's promises rested on this one man and his wife. 'I will make of you a great nation,' – God had promised, 'In you all the families of the earth shall be blessed' (Genesis 12:3).

Think of that faithful remnant of Israel, still exiled in Babylon. The promise that God gave to Abraham, that his seed would be as the 'sand of the sea which cannot be numbered for multitude' (Genesis 32:12), seemed remote. Now, through Isaiah, God promises that their 'descendants will inherit the nations, and make the desolate cities inhabited.' Those who never experienced having children would have far more children than those who did. The population of Israel that returned to Jerusalem and Judah after the captivity was 42,360, besides their male and female servants 'of whom were 7,337; and they had 200 men and women singers' (Ezra 2:64-65). These numbers would grow far beyond the boundaries of Jerusalem and Judah: they were to 'expand to the right and to the left.' Judah's desolate cities would be retaken from the occupying foreigners.

Ultimately, in a coming day, Israel shall be at the head of the nations. Did not Isaiah say, 'Now it shall come to pass in the latter days that the mountain of the Lord's house shall be established on the top of the mountains, and shall be exalted above the hills; and all nations shall flow into it'? (Isaiah 2:2; see also Psalm 2:8; Micah 4:1-3.) This international blessing for Israel will come to her entirely because of Christ's mighty work at Calvary. The suffering and sin-bearing by the Perfect Servant at the Cross is over, and Israel shall be called upon to sing and shout. The Lord has not divorced her, and she is to get ready to extend. Beautiful metaphorical language is used: 'lengthen your cords and strengthen your stakes.' Prepare to enjoy Calvary's blessings!

What can Christians learn from these verses? Just as Israel shall ultimately reap the blessings from Calvary, so Gentiles who learn what Christ's finished work is all about, and rest upon it, will come into spiritual enlargement and fruitfulness. Share the gospel with others, Christian, and you too can 'lengthen your cords' and 'strengthen your stakes.' In an age of spiritual desolation, you can see spiritual expansion and blessing. Faithfulness to the Lord and His gospel does not necessarily produce a smaller Christian church: the dynamic is there to expand it to a larger one. I challenge you to 'lengthen your cords,' rather than shorten them; and to 'strengthen your stakes.' Drive your tent pegs deep; take more, not less. Get ready for more blessings!

JULY 22ND

"Do not fear, for you will not be ashamed; neither be disgraced, for you will not be put to shame; for you will forget the shame of your youth, and will not remember the reproach of your widowhood anymore." Isaiah 54:4.

The first three verses of this deeply comforting chapter have taken us back to the time of Abraham, and the birth of the nation of Israel. At that time there came wonderful promises from God. The next four verses remind us of the youth of the nation, her time of slavery in Egypt, and the promises given on Mount Sinai when Israel left Egypt and set out for the Promised Land. God promised that Israel's future would be so great that she will forget the shame of her slavery.

It is one of God's great abilities, that His present blessings help us to forget the sad and frightening times in the past. No one found this out more powerfully than Joseph. How could he ever forget the cruelty he experienced from his brothers? As he lay in the pit at Dothan, I'm quite sure he didn't shout, 'Praise the Lord! Do you fellows not know that I am to be Prime Minister of Egypt, and that one day I will set you all free from death and starvation? This pit is marvellous, because it is the actual highway to God's plans for me.' No pit of suffering ever appears at the time to be the path to blessing. Those heartless men sold their younger brother to some passing traders for twenty shekels of silver; and they sold him into slavery in Egypt. 'This Hebrew slave . . . ' hissed Potiphar's wife, as she falsely accused Joseph of immorality. Years in prison followed, then God raised up Joseph to become Prime Minister of Egypt. He was overwhelmed with blessings, and when his first son was born he called him Manasseh – 'For God has made me forget all my toil and all my father's house.'

In the name that he gave to his son, we learn, for the first time, the depth of the hurt that Joseph had borne internally over all those years. The silence, the lack of bitter complaint, the patience with which he faced wrongdoing, were outstanding; the naming of Manasseh demonstrated the cost, mentally and emotionally, to the longsuffering Joseph, and revealed that his mind was now healed of all that he had come through. It is great to learn that God can help us forget the hurts in our lives, by the comfort that He sends. As in Joseph's case, God can use a little child to do this. The trust and affection of a little child is a very precious thing – there is nothing like it, it is sacred. A father's past life is unknown to the infant; the pain associated with events long gone, has never crossed its mind. 'Now' is the word for infants, not 'yesterday.' And it was so that God healed Joseph's memories.

I am sure that one day, somewhere, some place, sometime, someone with a tearful eye and a broken heart will lift today's Reading. You have been misunderstood, persecuted, sidelined, hurt, scorned, and mistreated. People have said things about you that still disturb your mind and subconscious thoughts. You wonder if you will ever be able to forget the awful experiences you have been through. Let me assure you that one day God will make you forget. He will bless you beyond all you could ever ask or think; and when you try to remember the details of what they did to you, you will find that the blessings of the present will have led to the obliteration of the past.

JULY 23ᴿᴰ

"Do not fear, for you will not be ashamed; neither be disgraced, for you will not be put to shame; for you will forget the shame of your youth, and will not remember the reproach of your widowhood anymore. For your Maker is your husband, the Lord of hosts is His name; and your Redeemer is the Holy One of Israel; He is called the God of the whole earth." Isaiah 54:4, 5.

Isaiah now uses the image of widowhood. Israel suffered the indignity of exile in Babylon, and it was like the blighting of a marriage through the death of the husband. The closeness of a loving marriage relationship, the sharing of joys and sorrows, the hopes and plans for the future, the security of 'two are better than one,' are all shattered when widowhood comes. Israel felt like that in Babylon; to His people, it was as if God was dead.

This statement reminds Israel that her Maker is her husband. He had entered into a covenant with His people at Sinai. He had not divorced them, and He was a husband who would never die. Israel may have felt that her husband was dead, but Jehovah was the self-existent one. He reminds them that He is 'the Lord of hosts' – the One whom the angels obey and fulfil His commands. He is their 'Redeemer' – their next-of-kin, coming alongside to redeem them. He is 'the Holy one of Israel' – in His very nature He is beautiful. He is called Elohim, the mighty, strong and pre-eminent One, the God of the whole earth. In Hebrew, Elohim is in the plural. In his Hebrew lexicon, Dr. Parkhurst defines the word 'Elohim,' as a name usually given in the Scriptures to the Trinity, by which They represent Themselves as under the obligation of an oath to perform certain conditions. It is the very first word used for God in the Bible: 'In the beginning (Elohim) created the heavens and the earth. The earth was without form, and void; and darkness was on the face of the deep. And the Spirit of (Elohim) was hovering over the face of the waters' (Genesis 1:1-2). In his little book, *Names of God* (Moody Press, Chicago, 1944, p.15), Nathan Stone states, 'the entire creation, animate or inanimate, was, then, not only the work of the Elohim, but the object of a covenant within the Elohim guaranteeing its redemption and perpetuation.'

Moses asked God, "When I come to the children of Israel and say to them, 'The God of your fathers has sent me to you,' and they say to me, 'What is His name?' what shall I say to them?" (Exodus 3:13). The Children of Israel had got so mixed up in worshipping other Gods, and become so far distant from the God of their fathers, that they did not even know what the Lord's name was! God told Moses to call him 'Elohim.'

When Paul confronted the philosophers on Mars Hill, he used the Greek equivalent of Elohim for the name of God. He told the men of Athens that the Elohim made the world and everything in it, and, since He is Lord of heaven and earth, He is not confined to temples made with hands. Paul maintained that Elohim 'is not far from each one of us' (Acts 17:27).

Isaiah is saying that the reproach of Israel's widowhood would be forgotten. The God of the whole earth, Elohim, is her husband. It is a superb perspective for the people of God of any age. With such a covenant from the eternal Trinity to you, Christian, you do not need to be ashamed or afraid.

JULY 24TH

"For the Lord has called you like a woman forsaken and grieved in spirit, like a youthful wife when you were refused," says your God. "For a mere moment I have forsaken you, but with great mercies I will gather you. With a little wrath I hid My face from you for a moment; but with everlasting kindness I will have mercy on you," says the Lord, your Redeemer. Isaiah 54:6-8.

We had as our guest to Sunday lunch this week, a university student whose home is in Israel. I asked her opinion about the spiritual state of Israel. "Only about thirty percent of them are 'religious' Jews," she said. When she was at school, she was the only Christian; and many of her fellow-pupils were into Buddhism and other religions. I thought of our studies in Isaiah – things haven't changed much, have they?

The image now used to illustrate Israel's relationship with the Lord is 'a woman forsaken and grieved in spirit, like a youthful wife when you were refused.' The picture is of a deserted wife. Things had gone wrong early in the relationship, and her husband has forsaken her. It is a metaphor for God's anger against Israel. He had been deeply displeased with her, but she was not hated. The Old Covenant allowed Him to let her go into captivity in Babylon. Israel might have thought that this time of God's forsaking of them was long; but with God it was 'for a moment,' and in His compassion He reaches out to gather them back to Himself. His wrath gives place to 'everlasting kindness.'

While the New Covenant teaches us that the punishment against our sins is over, we must remind ourselves that Christians can still know the chastening of the Lord. Like Israel, you may feel that God's present chastening seems to be unending, and He will never use you again. Let's think of how the writer to the Hebrews viewed it: 'we have had human fathers who corrected us, and we paid them respect . . . for they indeed *for a few days* chastened us as seemed best to them, but He for our profit, that we may be partakers of His holiness. Now no chastening seems to be joyful for the present, but painful; nevertheless, afterward it yields the peaceable fruit of righteousness to those who have been trained by it' (Hebrews 12:9-11). God's view of time is so different to ours: what is long to us is a mere moment to Him.

One day on the Isle of Man some friends took me to visit one of the world's greatest watchmakers. His name is George Daniels. I was told that he only makes one watch a year, and each one is worth £100,000. I asked him about his work, and found chronology to be his passion. "What is the most important thing you have learned from your study of time?" I asked. He replied, "human beings measure time because they will die one day. God knows nothing about time. He lives in an eternal now."

Mr. Daniels was right and wrong. He is wrong, in that God does know about time: He stepped into it, in the person of Jesus Christ. 'In due time Christ died for the ungodly' (Romans 5:6). He is right, though, that God lives in an eternal now. ' . . . the Father of lights, with whom there is no variation or shadow of turning' (James 1:17). He can see the chronology of your life from its beginning to its end, and He knows the eternal results of your chastening. Be glad of it.

July 25ᵀᴴ

"For this is like the waters of Noah to Me; for as I have sworn that the waters of Noah would no longer cover the earth, so have I sworn that I would not be angry with you, nor rebuke you. For the mountains shall depart and the hills be removed, but My kindness shall not depart from you, nor shall My covenant of peace be removed," says the Lord, who has mercy on you. Isaiah 54:9-10.

Already in this chapter we have been reminded of two covenants. The first was the Abrahamic Covenant, followed by the Mosaic Covenant. Now we are to consider the covenant with Noah. It too was associated with a promise. 'Then God spoke to

Noah and his sons, saying, " . . . behold, I establish My covenant with you and with yo⟩ descendants after you . . . never again shall all flesh be cut off by the waters of the floo⟩ never again shall there be a flood to destroy the earth . . . this is the sign of the covena⟩ which I make between Me and you . . . I set My rainbow in the cloud, and it shall be for t⟩ sign of the covenant between me and the earth'" (Genesis 9:9-13).

The rainbow in the sky is an awesome symbol. The word in Hebrew is *quesheth*, meani⟩ 'bow.' It means that the Lord's war-bow has been hung up ('rainbow' is contextual – Motye⟩ God will never flood the earth in the same way again. In today's text, the exile in Babylon compared to Noah's flood and its aftermath. Noah and his family were preserved, and mov⟨ on to prosper far and wide across the earth. Israel was preserved in Babylon. As we saw a previous day, they were told that they would 'expand to the right and to the left, and (the⟩ descendants will inherit the nations, and make the desolate cities inhabited' (Isaiah 54:3 Now God swears to Israel, "I would not be angry with you, nor rebuke you." God's promi⟨ to His people here goes further than the promise to Noah, to his family, and to creation.

Let us not forget that God also said that He would establish His covenant 'with eve⟩ living creature' (Genesis 9:10). The promise to God's people refers to the time when t⟩ earth itself will pass away. God's kindness to His people will (the word is) 'gush forth.' ⟩ Isaiah 54:8, we read that God's wrath 'gushed forth;' but now it is His kindness. Isn't it lovely word? It is like a huge waterfall, cascading down. Here it comes, splashing, surgin⟩ spilling, pouring and overflowing. Such is the promise of God's everlasting kindness. Ju⟩ as Noah and his family learned to trust God's 'covenant of promise,' so, as God's peop⟩ today, we learn to trust His promise of a kindness that will never end. This promise is calle⟩ a 'covenant of peace.' Rest in this assurance, Christian: the wrath of God against your sin ⟩ over, for it fell on the sacred head of Christ. And now eternal kindness gushes out to yo⟩ from the hand of God. Even the difficult things in your life will work together for good. H⟨ love toward you will never end.

July 26th

"O you afflicted one, tossed with tempest, and not comforted, behold, I will lay your stone with colourful gems, and lay your foundations with sapphires. I will make your pinnacles of rubies, your gates of crystal, and all your walls of precious stones." Isaiah 54:11-12.

I find great difficulty in understanding what these verses are saying. Is a future Jerusalem⟩ once 'tossed with tempest,' by cruel Gentile armies, 'and not comforted,' literally to hav⟩ her foundations laid with sapphires, her pinnacles made of rubies, her gates of crystal⟨ and her walls of precious stones? I do not know. The city was rebuilt under Nehemiah; ye⟩ it seems to me that we are looking here at the city of God, as seen by John (Revelation 21:9 27) – 'the bride, the Lamb's wife.' It is composed of every believer: 'living stones . . . bui⟩ up a spiritual house' (1 Peter 2:5). Its stones are all gems, formed by grace.

Look at the stones mentioned here in Isaiah 54: we have sapphires, rubies, and crystal. I⟩ Revelation 21, we read of jasper, chalcedony, emerald, sardonyx, sardius, chrysolite, bery⟩

topaz, chrysoprase, jacinth, amethyst, and pearls. When expounding these verses, F. B. Meyer asks us to consider what jewels consist of. He says they are by nature only lumps of dull and inert matter: the sapphire is clay, and the diamond is carbon. Why, then, is there a difference between their appearance, and that of ordinary soil? He admits that the answer is not easy to give, but the exquisite effect is probably due to crystallisation, conducted under exceptional circumstances of convulsion, pressure, and fire. He says a jewel is a bit of ordinary earth that has passed through an extraordinary experience.

Meyer says that in this chapter God is addressing His afflicted people. Theirs are the convulsions, the awful pressure, and the fiery baptism. They are taking it hard; they do not know why they are being treated like this. But they will understand it all one day, when they learn that God was making precious stones for windows, gates, and foundations. What they have gone through, and the victories they have seen, will bring glory to the Perfect Servant – by whose grace they are what they are. "They shall be mine," says the Lord of hosts, "on the day that I make them my jewels" (Malachi 3:17).

'Do you know the lovely fact about the opal?' writes Ellice Hopkins. 'In the first place, it is made only of a desert dust, sand, silica, and owes its beauty and preciousness to a defect. It is a stone with a broken heart. It is full of minute fissures which admit air, and the air reflects the light. Hence its lovely hues, and that sweet lamp of fire that ever burns at its heart; for the breath of the Lord God is in it. You are only conscious of the cracks and desert dust, but so He makes His precious opal. We must be broken in ourselves before we can give back the lovely hues of His light, and the lamp in the temple can burn in us and never go out.'

JULY 27TH

"All your children shall be taught by the Lord, and great shall be the peace of your children." Isaiah 54:13.

There is something special about God's school. His curriculum is very different. When God educates you, He gives lessons you will never forget. One day the Jews complained about Christ because He said, "I am the bread which came down from heaven." 'And they said, "Is not this Jesus, the son of Joseph, whose father and mother we know? How is it then that He says, 'I have come down from Heaven'?" The Lord Jesus gave a wonderful answer to these people, right out of the passage we are studying. He said, "Do not murmur among yourselves. No one can come to Me unless the Father who sent Me draws him; and I will raise him up at the last day. It is written in the prophets, 'And they shall be taught by God.' Therefore everyone who has heard and learned from the Father comes to Me" (John 6:41-45.)

It is obvious, from what our Lord said, that the Father is the teacher. He teaches us the beauties of Christ, and answers the deep questions in our hearts. He uses all kinds of things to underline truth. Are we listening? Do we obey? Do we use the truth that we have learned to help others? To whom much is given, much is expected.

The other day I was told the story about a man who, when he was a child, heard a children's sermon from an Ulsterman. He never forgot the punch line. Let me share it with you. The man told the children that, as he was driving his car out of Poyntzpass in Co Armagh, a car passed him at high speed. He watched it as it sped by. Shortly after that, he found himself being 'pulled in' by a policeman! The policeman pointed out that he had been going over the prescribed speed limit. He admitted his violation of the traffic law; but then he thought he would add something: "Did you see that man who passed me earlier?" "Sir," replied the policeman, "when you stand in the Court you will not be responsible for giving an account of the man you saw, but you will be responsible for giving an account of yourself." Selah.

JULY 28ᵀᴴ

"All your children shall be taught by the Lord, and great shall be the peace of your children. In righteousness you shall be established; you shall be far from oppression, for you shall not fear; and from terror, for it shall not come near you." Isaiah 54:13, 14.

The Bible teaches that there is a difference between 'peace with God,' and 'the peace of God.' We have peace with God when we repent of sin and put our trust in the Lord Jesus as Saviour. This is called justification by faith (see Romans 5:1). When this happens, the war and enmity with God is over. It is an eternal peace: nothing can take it away. It is a priceless possession: Christ 'made peace through the blood of his cross' (Colossians 1:20). It is a gift, and it is not conditional on our efforts: 'For by grace you have been saved through faith, and that not of yourselves; it is the gift of God' (Ephesians 2:8).

However, the 'peace of God' is conditional. When we bring our worries and cares to the Lord, by prayer and supplication, with thanksgiving, 'the peace of God, which surpasses all understanding, will guard your hearts and minds through Christ Jesus' (Philippians 4:6, 7). We can lose that peace by not taking things to God in prayer. I don't know about you, but I find that, when I finish praying, I may still have my problems, but they look very different when I have been close to God. Somehow, seen from His perspective, they are not so worrying.

Isaiah is teaching this very thing. In our text, he is saying that the more you know the Lord, the more peace you will have. For example, we might have a friend who is misunderstood by others; but when people speak against our friend, we interrupt them and say, 'Ah, but I know him!' We have become very close to that person, and know him in a deeper way than those acquaintances do; and on that basis we are at peace with him. So it is with getting to know God. The more you get to know Him, the more confidence you have in Him. When others question and criticise His actions, His silences, or His ways, you can interrupt them with confidence, and say, 'Ah, but you don't know Him!'

You can say with Job, "Though He slay me, yet will I trust Him" (Job 13:15); and even in the jaws of death affirm, "after my skin is destroyed, this I know, that in my flesh I shall see God" (19:26). This knowledge brings peace; and more knowledge brings more peace. Again, it was Job, who said, "Now acquaint yourself with Him, and be at peace; thereby good will come to you. Receive, please, instruction from His mouth, and lay up His words in your heart" (22:21-22). To be taught by the Lord, to get close to Him and to get to know Him, will result in peace.

JULY 29TH

"Indeed they shall surely assemble, but not because of Me. Whoever assembles against you shall fall for your sake." Isaiah 54:15.

There are plenty of people who would slime our 'Eden.' The peace with God that we possess, the confidence and trust that we have in the Lord, does not give Satan any joy, and he will try relentlessly to disrupt it. He will try to sow seeds of doubt, and throw all sorts of fiery darts at us. He wants us to live like paupers, when we are children of the King.

Our text tells us that, despite being established in righteousness through our relationship with the Lord, this does not exempt us from attack: "they shall surely assemble." Haven't you experienced it? The whisperers, the accusers, the liars, the gossips, and the critics gang up, and you run into opposition that you never could have imagined. At the start, to be a servant of God seems to be as harmless as a poached egg on a plate. However, you are not long in the Lord's service until you discover that an opposing force is assembled against you. It is impossible to escape such situations: they come with the occupation.

It is not the Lord who gathers these opposing forces: "Indeed they shall surely assemble, but not because of Me." He did not send them, and He will give us protection from them. Do not stain your Christian character by losing your temper with those who assemble against you; do not waste your energy in trying to vindicate yourself; do not spend sleepless nights worrying how to overcome all the opposition. The promise is, "whoever assembles against you shall fall for your sake." It is a very precious little phrase, 'for your sake.' It is saying that what matters to you, matters to Him. If they touch you, they touch Him. You are His servant, and He does not forget it. The opposition may look formidable; but, in the end, your protector is the God of the whole earth. Be still and know that God is God, and that the opposition will ultimately fall.

JULY 30TH

"Behold, I have created the blacksmith who blows the coals in the fire, who brings forth an instrument for his work; and I have created the spoiler to destroy. No weapon formed against you shall prosper, and every tongue which rises against you in judgment you shall condemn. This is the heritage of the servants of the Lord, and their righteousness is from Me," says the Lord. Isaiah 54:16-17.

As a child, I used to visit a blacksmith's forge, and I can recall the glow of the coals and the red-hot metal as it was hammered into shape. It was hot, sweaty, difficult work for the blacksmith. He was clever with his hands, and produced good work.

I did not know then of these amazing texts; and, facing them, I still feel like a child. How can I explain, in a few sentences, the awesome truth of the sovereignty of God? I cannot. Yet, with all of my heart, I believe in this truth. God uses the image of the blacksmith here, to illustrate His sovereignty. He created the blacksmith, who fires up the coals in his forge and starts to make a weapon, designed to be a weapon of war. The Lord permits what the blacksmith is doing, and overrules it. The Lord has a purpose that He is working out, through times of war and times of peace. If He only worked out His purposes in local churches, and ignored all the rest of human life in the local community and the rest of the world, where would we be?

The promise is that no weapon formed against His people shall prosper. Evil has risen against you, perhaps, in a particular form. Forged carefully and meticulously, it seems that you are finished. I don't know what the weapon is, but you do. Just remember it will not prosper, and its crash may come much quicker than you think. W. E. Sangster told the story of the annual dinner of a certain association that was opposed to religion. It met in a restaurant not half a mile from where his local church met, at Westminster Central Hall. The chairman rose to make an after dinner speech, and was lampooning religion and guffawing over the vision that the Apostle Paul saw on the Damascus Road. In the middle of a blasphemous sentence, he suddenly went pale, sat down, and died. The coroner said that it was 'heart failure.' The progress of a 'weapon' may be halted, with no prior warning.

If you have done right, no tongue that maligns you will prosper. God will vindicate you; every accusation, every whispering voice, will be silenced. So, go on for God, Christian, and God will preserve your honour against every attack.

JULY 31ST

"This is the heritage of the servants of the Lord, and their righteousness is from Me," *says the Lord.* Isaiah 54:17.

The emphasis moves now from the Servant of the Lord, to the servants of the Lord. The Cross evokes service. Count Zinzendorf of the Moravian movement, stood by a painting of the Cross and was challenged by the question, 'All this I have done for thee, what hast thou done for Me?' It led him to distinguished Christian service. How about you, and me?

This chapter finishes, with Isaiah saying that the blessings that he has listed are 'the heritage of the servants of the Lord.' As we close this month's readings, let us look at them again.

God's people were to enjoy great benefits:

They were to have a worldwide increase; so they were to get ready to expand (vv.1-3).

They were to enjoy God's compassion and everlasting kindness, despite past sin (vv.4-8).

They were to enjoy an end to God's wrath: the Covenant of peace was theirs (vv.9-10). The earthly Jerusalem would be rebuilt; the New Jerusalem shall be built also (vv.11-14; cf. Revelation 21:2).

They were to know security from every weapon and word formed against them (vv.15-17).

They would be clothed in righteousness that was not their own (v.17).

When we consider all the blessings that God gives to us, can we not hear the question that challenged Zinzendorf: 'All this I have done for thee, what hast thou done for me?' Surely, the response to God's blessings should be service for Him, given from hearts filled with gratitude. Even the smallest act of service will bring results that we could never have dreamt of. Let me share a personal story that inspires my heart to this day.

I was in the home of my good friend, Donald MacCuish in Inverness. He handed me a Bible. "Do you know whose Bible that is?" he asked. On the flyleaf I read the words, 'Mr. McCheyne's Bible.' I was thrilled to be handling the Bible of Robert Murray McCheyne – one of the greatest Christian ministers Scotland has ever known – who sadly died in his twenty-ninth year. Donald then told us the fascinating story of how the Bible came to be his.

When Mr. McCheyne was dying, he was in a delirium, and he said to Jessie Stewart, his housekeeper, "Jessie, 'Be ye steadfast, unmovable, always abounding in the work of the Lord, knowing that your labour is not in vain in the Lord.'" He was quoting 1 Corinthians 15:58. When Mr. McCheyne died, they gave his Bible to Jessie, who wrote in the margin against this verse, 'Last text given to me by my Pastor and master, Mr. McCheyne, before he slept in Jesus.' She took the Bible to South Africa and gave it to a friend, who in turn gave it to a minister. The minister eventually returned to Holland, and the Bible was in the possession of the Dutch Royal Family for many years.

One day in The Hague a man was contracted to clear the house of a minister who had died. He found lots of books in the house and, before throwing them away, the thought crossed his mind that a Christian he knew in the district might like some of them. The Christian came round, and found a Bible in the skip with the words, 'Mr. McCheyne's Bible,' on the flyleaf. It so happened that he had come to faith in Jesus Christ through reading one of Mr. McCheyne's sermons! He took the Bible home, and said in his heart, 'This Bible belongs in Scotland, so the first Scot to come through my door, who appreciates the ministry of Robert Murray McCheyne, shall have it.'

One day my friend, Donald MacCuish, arrived at The Hague for a wedding. He stayed in the home of the Christian who now had the Bible. When he was asked about Mr. McCheyne, he waxed eloquent, and the Bible promptly became his!

Lord MacKay and his wife were also guests at Donald's home that day. As the afternoon passed, Lord MacKay and I shared some of the texts that Mr. McCheyne had underlined in his Bible. Before he left their home, Lord MacKay signed the MacCuish's visitors book, and in the comments box he wrote, '1 Corinthians 15:58'! Isn't it amazing that the dying words of a Scottish minister travelled 154 years through time, to inspire the heart of the first Scottish Lord Chancellor in history?

In the Old Testament we read of Jehovah Tsidkenu (Jeremiah 23:6), meaning 'the Lord our righteousness.' During his short lifetime, Robert Murray McCheyne wrote a beautiful hymn. One of the verses states:

When treading the valley, the shadow of death,
This watchword shall rally my faltering breath.
And when from life's fever my God sets me free,
Jehovah Tsidkenu my death song shall be.

So it was that Jehovah Tsidkenu did actually become Mr. McCheyne's death song. The godly Donald MacCuish uncovered that fact for us.

August

This photograph, taken in the Irish Linen Museum in Lisburn, Co. Down, is of linen yarn on an old weaving loom. By 1272 ecclesiastical linen made from Irish yarn was in use in Winchester Cathedral in England. By the 1930's the Province of Ulster provided about two thirds of all American imports, and its position as a world provider was unrivalled. Irish Linen, with its international status, still competes in the world marketplace. In the story of the resurrection we learn that, when Christ's disciple, John, saw the way the linen cloths and the handkerchief lay in the empty tomb, he believed.

"Ho! Everyone who thirsts, come to the waters; and you who have no money, come, buy and eat. Yes, come, buy wine and milk without money and without price." Isaiah 55:1.

The promise of Christ, the Perfect Servant, to be as a 'light to the Gentiles,' to bring 'salvation to the ends of the earth' (Isaiah 49:6), was no empty promise. Calvary now past, the invitation goes out to 'everyone who thirsts,' to come and drink. It is soul thirst: a thirst that the waters of this earth could never quench. "Come buy and eat," says the Lord, through Isaiah – even though you have no money. How? The price has already been paid. Eat this food and you will be satisfied. Nothing else could assuage your hunger: it is soul hunger.

The rich often think that everything has its price. But this water and bread simply cannot be bought in human currency. It was paid for by the giving of the life of Christ at Calvary, and now it is freely given to all who come for it. "Come, buy wine and milk without money and without price," says Isaiah. When you are born again, the Holy Spirit enters your life. He is as water and wine to the thirsty soul (see Isaiah 44:3 and John 7:38, 39). The Word of God is to the believer as milk is to a child (1 Peter 2:2). Jesus said, "I am the bread of life. He who comes to Me shall never hunger, and he who believes in Me shall never thirst" (John 6:35). As bread is all-sufficient for life, and contains all the elements needed for nutrition, so in Christ we have everything we need for life and godliness. For the polluted, He is purity; for the irritable, He is patience; for the fearful, He is courage; for the weak, He is strength; for the ignorant, He is wisdom – He is enough.

From Isaiah we learned of the idolater, who lavishes 'gold out of the bag,' weighs 'silver on the scales,' hires 'a goldsmith,' and makes his God. What is the end result? 'He feeds on ashes,' says Isaiah: 'A deceived heart has turned him aside; and he cannot deliver his soul' (44:20).

There are lots of idolaters in this world, constantly producing conditions that lead to their own dissatisfaction. Imagine the taste of ashes in the mouth, and then compare it to bread and water, milk and wine. Such is the difference between knowing God in Christ, and worshipping idols of any kind, including money. "How much money does it take to make a man happy," someone asked J. D. Rockefeller, Sr. "Just a little bit more," he replied. I repeat, Christ is enough.

"Why do you spend money for what is not bread, and your wages for what does not satisfy? Listen carefully to Me, and eat what is good, and let your soul delight itself in abundance." Isaiah 55:2.

Consider this story by Count Leo Tolstoy. It is entitled *How much land does a man need?* I have abridged it, but the message is clear. The story concerns Pahom, who was told by a passing dealer about the land of the Bashk'rs. The dealer had bought thirteen thousands acres of land there for 1,000 roubles. There was more land there than one could cover, even if one walked for a year. All one needed to do was to make friends with the chiefs.

Pahom set off for this land, and gave some presents to the first chief he came across. He asked if it were possible for him to buy land, with the signed title deeds. Yes it was possible; and the price was, as always, one thousand roubles a day. Pahom thought this a strange measure. "How many acres would that be?" he asked. "As much as you can cover on foot in a day, will be yours," was the reply. There was, though, one condition: he must return the same day to the spot where he started, or his money would be lost. He could mark the spot, and they would stay there until he returned. He must carry a spade with him and, wherever he thought necessary, make a mark. At every turning he must dig a hole and pile up the turf. They would go round later from hole to hole with a plough. He could make as large a circuit as he pleased, but before the sun had set he must return to the place he started from. All the land covered that day would be his.

The very next day Pahom ascended a hillock with the Bashk'rs, and they all eventually came to a certain spot. The Chief took off his fox-fur cap, and placed it on the ground. Pahom took out his money, placed it in the cap, and set off toward the rising sun. After a thousand yards he dug a hole, placed the piles of turf one upon another, went on with quickening pace, and dug another hole. He reckoned he had walked about three miles, as it grew warmer, and he stopped to eat the food and drink that he had brought with him for breakfast. To make the walking a little easier, he decided to take off his boots, and stuck them in his belt. As the day progressed, he went on and on, now sweating constantly, and feeling thirsty. At noontime he rested a little, and then continued with his work. By the time the sun was halfway to the horizon, he had not done two miles of the third side of the square of land, and he was still ten miles from his goal.

Eventually Pahom headed towards the hillock. But now he walked with difficulty. His feet were cut and bleeding, his legs began to fail. He longed to rest, but it was impossible if he was to get back before sunset. He berated himself for trying for too much. Soon he began running, throwing away his coat, boots, flask, cap, and keeping only his spade for support. His shirt was soaking, his mouth was parched, his lungs were bursting, and he was seized by terror lest he should die of the strain.

He heard the Bask'rs yelling and shouting to him. He ran on and on, and just as he reached the hillock it suddenly grew dark – the sun had already set. But the people on the hillock could still see the sun, and they were still shouting to him. He took a long breath and ran up the hillock. It was still light. He saw the cap, and the Chief sitting by it. Pahom's legs gave way beneath him as he fell forward and reached the cap with his hands. "Ah, that's a fine fellow," said the chief, "you have gained much land." Pahom's servant came running up and tried to rouse him, but he saw blood flowing from his mouth. Pahom was dead. The Bashk'rs clicked their tongues to show their pity. Pahom's servant picked up the spade and dug a grave long enough for Pahom to lie in, and buried him in it. Six feet from his head to his heels was all he needed.

"Incline your ear, and come to Me. Hear, and your soul shall live; and I will make an everlasting covenant with you – the sure mercies of David." Isaiah 55:3.

We have already seen three covenants discussed by Isaiah; now we come to the final one. It is the covenant made with David. We read in Scripture of David's deep desire to build a house for God to dwell in, but it was not to be. Yet, despite the disappointment David must have felt, one can only imagine the amazement that must have filled his heart when God made a very special covenant with him. "And your house and your kingdom shall be established forever before you. Your throne shall be established forever" (2 Samuel 7:16).

To confirm the covenant with Noah, a sign was given, namely God's 'bow' in the sky. In the covenant with Abraham, the sign of circumcision was given. The covenant with Moses at Sinai was marked with the sprinkling of the blood of the lamb. So the Davidic covenant also had a sign. Barry Webb points out that this sign was to be a permanently-renewed Universe: 'Instead of the thorn shall come up the cypress tree, and instead of the brier shall come up the myrtle tree; and it shall be to the Lord for a name, for an everlasting sign that shall not be cut off' (Isaiah 55:13).

What was promised to David will be fulfilled in the One of whom he was the type, namely, the Messiah (see Acts 13:33-37). Notice the conditions required in order to enjoy the blessings of this incredible covenant. First, you must listen to God's Word: "Incline your ear," listen carefully to Me. Is that a profitable thing to do? Incalculably so! "Hear, and your soul shall live." I can't help remembering that, when John Knox preached in Scotland, it was said, 'the people lived.' And it is so in every age, when people seriously listen to God's Word. By feasting on it we get something that is sweeter than honey. We begin to 'eat what is good,' in comparison to eating the 'ashes' of idolatry; and our 'soul delights itself in abundance.' Through listening to God's Word, we are invited to come to the Living Word, and in Him we shall find an eternal banquet.

On the day after Jesus had fed the five thousand, He said to the crowd who were only interested in the earthly bread, and not in Him:

"Most assuredly, I say to you, Moses did not give you the bread from heaven, but My Father gives you the true bread from heaven. For the bread of God is He who comes from heaven and gives life to the world . . . I am the bread of life. He who comes to Me shall never hunger and he who believes in Me shall never thirst" (John 6:32-35).

Said Spurgeon, "I have a great need for Christ, and I have a great Christ for my need." So, listen and come.

"Indeed I have given him as a witness to the people, a leader and commander for the people." Isaiah 55:4.

Here, Christ is depicted as the leader. The idea behind the word is of the first in a file of people: the Commanding officer in an army, or the leader of a mountaineering expedition. He goes first and the rest follow. In Ephesians we are told that 'He led captivity captive, and gave gifts to men;' He invaded Satan's territory and took captive what Satan held. As the 'captain of our salvation' He is 'bringing many sons to glory' (see Hebrews 2:9-10).

The Father has given the Lord Jesus to us as our file leader. What a gift! He is an incomparable leader. He leads us from death to life, from the power of Satan to God, from defeat to victory. In Him we are overcomers. He leads us through our times of grief and suffering, showing us that it is moulding us into His image; one day we shall be presented without spot or wrinkle, or any such thing.

If my home is taken from me, I still have Christ. If my work is taken from me, I still have Christ. If my money is taken from me, I still have Christ. If my sight is taken away from me, I still have Christ. He will lead me through anything that I have to face, no matter how intimidating, frightening, manipulative, devious or threatening. He is the file leader. I am simply called to follow Him.

I remember once at a meal, speaking with Mr. Anthony Cordle, who has done sterling work for Christ amongst 'the movers and shakers' in our society. He spoke of his experience with 'church institutions.' They had often left him cold and uninspired. Then he began to say what he felt Christianity was really about. His 'yardstick' was whether or not a person was truly following Jesus. He told of one of the greatest 'personal' evangelists he had ever known. He was a very quiet man who did not raise his voice. But when he spoke people listened, and tears flowed. Their consciences were touched, their hearts moved, and many, many conversions took place. He was, Anthony said, a true follower of Jesus – not merely of church institutions.

Our File Leader has promised that the gates of Hell will not prevail against His church, and He will lead us to a world beyond this one where there is no sin or sorrow. So let's remember the old chorus, and sing it to now and again during this week: 'My Lord knows the way through the wilderness. All I have to do is follow.'

AUGUST 5TH

"Surely you shall call a nation you do not know, and nations who do not know you shall run to you, because of the Lord your God, and the Holy One of Israel; for He has glorified you." Isaiah 55:5.

Israel and her future are now being highlighted. As David's reign often served as a model to other kingdoms, so Israel would affect the world in a coming day. What shall the attraction be? Why will Gentile nations 'run' to her? The attraction is because of the Lord her God, the Holy One of Israel.

Let's recur to Isaiah 49:7: 'Thus says the Lord, the Redeemer of Israel, their Holy One, to Him whom man despises, to Him whom the nation abhors, to the Servant of rulers: "Kings shall see and arise, Princes also shall worship, because of the Lord who is faithful, the Holy

One of Israel; and He has chosen You.'" There is something about this Perfect Servant that is truly international. He is head and shoulders above all the saviours in the world. Indeed, He said of Himself that if he were lifted up, he would draw all men to Him.

When Sundar Singh was questioned by a Professor of Comparative Religion as to what he had discovered in Christianity that was not in his old religion, he answered, "I have Christ." "Yes, I know," said the Professor, "but what particular principle or doctrine have you found that you did not have before?" "The particular thing I have found is Christ," he replied (Stanley Jones, *The Christ of the Indian Road*, Hodder and Stoughton, p.64).

"You call me Teacher and Lord," Christ told His disciples, "and you say well, for so I am. If I then, your Lord and Teacher, have washed your feet, you ought also to wash one another's feet" (John 13:13, 14). They spoke of Him as Teacher first, and Lord second. In speaking to them about Himself, Christ reversed the order. Why? Because if we come to Christ first as Lord, and determine to obey Him, then our attitude to His teaching will be different, won't it? There will be no 'maybe I will obey,' or 'maybe I won't.'

Do the claims of Christ make Him a tyrant? Certainly not! After making this statement, Christ washed His disciples' feet in loving service to them. Such a Perfect Servant has drawing power across all cultures and nations of the world. He is superior to every name that is named. Multitudes of teachers of religion, and gods of men surround us in history, and in our present day. You could begin a detailed study of them, and never finish it in a lifetime. This Person towers above every one of them. Honour His name. Uplift it. Suffer for its sake, if necessary. Watch its drawing power.

AUGUST 6TH

Seek the Lord while He may be found, call upon Him while He is near. Let the wicked forsake his way, and the unrighteous man his thoughts; let him return to the Lord, and He will have mercy on him; and to our God, for He will abundantly pardon. Isaiah 55:6-7.

This is a call for the backslider to return. Is such a person reading these lines? You started out with great enthusiasm to live for Christ, but you have gradually slipped back in your commitment. You are not utterly indifferent, but you are not fully committed either. Like the Laodiceans, you are neither cold nor hot – you are lukewarm, tepid. You are evangelical, but not evangelistic. There is no emotion, no enthusiasm or urgency; and no passion or compassion in your faith.

How did you get into such a state? Are you like Noah – has alcohol been your problem? Noah was the man who 'found grace in the eyes of the Lord,' but he got drunk and was found by his sons lying naked in his tent. The Bible says, 'wine is a mocker, strong drink is a brawler, and whoever is led astray by it is not wise' (Proverbs 20:1). Or maybe you are you like Abraham – telling lies was his problem. He arrived in Canaan, found himself in a famine situation, panicked, fled to Egypt, and lied to Pharaoh that his wife was his full sister. He was afraid they would kill him and take her. As a result God sent a plague on Pharaoh's house. Abraham's lying was discovered, and he was thrown out of Egypt.

Are you like Moses? – haste was his problem. By killing an Egyptian who was beating a Hebrew, his hasty action led to him spending forty years in the wilderness. Perhaps you are like Samson? – a man with a she-weakness? Or Lot? – he settled in a place that was out of the will of God. During his time there, Lot did no good in Sodom. God sent two angels to warn him that Sodom was doomed, but he 'lingered.' Eventually they had to take hold of him and bring him out of the city.

There is a sense of urgency in today's texts. God is calling you to get back to the Lord 'while He may be found, call upon Him while He is near.' Abraham and Moses repented and got back to a closer walk with God, so much of their lives brought great glory to God. It was just at the end of his life that Samson was restored. Lot wasted most of his life.

Retrace your steps from a way of life that is following a wrong path, and get back on to the path of blessing. Forsake that way, and turn to the Lord's way. Is your thought-life impure? It all started in your mind, and has led to wrong actions. Forsake those thoughts now:

'Whatever things are true, whatever things are noble, whatever things are just, whatever things are pure, whatever things are lovely, whatever things are of good report, if there is any virtue and if there is anything praiseworthy – meditate on these things' (Philippians 4:8).

God will have compassion, and lavish pardon upon you. Go on! Return to the Lord, and don't waste another day of your precious life. Thirty days after his unbelievable backsliding, Peter was able to reach three thousand for Christ. Who can tell what God will do with you?

AUGUST 7TH

"For My thoughts are not your thoughts, nor are your ways My ways," says the Lord.
"For as the heavens are higher than the earth, so are My ways higher than your ways, and My thoughts than your thoughts." Isaiah 55:8-9.

The scientist Johann Kepler was one of the founders of modern astronomy. He held the position of Royal Astronomer to Emperor Rudolf II. 'Kepler's Laws' helped Newton develop his theory of gravity, and he was the first to suggest that tides were caused by the gravitational pull of the moon. It is told of him that one night, after spending hours observing the motions of the heavenly bodies, he said, "I have been thinking over again the earliest thoughts of God."

We know that God's thoughts go back a lot further than the making of the universe; but when he observed the heavens, Kepler was certainly thinking God's thoughts after Him. If you were to travel to the every edge of space, you would find that the heavens are incredibly high above the earth. Light from worlds far distant in space has been travelling towards us for millennia, and it has not reached us yet. God says, "as the heavens are higher than the earth, so My ways are higher than your ways, and My thoughts than your thoughts." This is a humbling fact.

Sin has polluted our thoughts, and hence corrupted our ways. We, who were made in the image of God to follow His ways, now find the gap between us as vast as the distance between earth and the far reaches of space. We all have longings that are not earthly, and we know instinctively that this world is not our final destination. But something pollutes those feelings and makes us like Esau, that we go for the immediate rather than the eternal. 'The carnal mind is enmity against God; for it is not subject to the law of God, nor indeed can be. So, then, those who are in the flesh cannot please God' (Romans 8:7-8).

How, then, can we ever bridge the gap? We cannot, but grace can. Just as God's ways and thoughts are so very different to ours, so is His forgiveness; which is as much above man's ideas of forgiveness, as the heavens are high above the earth.

So if we want our thinking to be transformed, and to follow God's ways, let us heed the exhortation of Isaiah 55:7: 'Let the wicked forsake his way, and the unrighteous man his thoughts; let him return to the Lord, and He will have mercy on him; and to our God, for He will abundantly pardon.' When you are in Christ, you are no longer rooted in the flesh, but in the Spirit. You do not owe the flesh anything (see Romans 8:12); therefore, sow to the Spirit and you will reap the Spirit. The power of the Holy Spirit will help you to control your mind and your will (see Romans 8:5-8). The purpose of the cross of Christ was not just to bring us to conversion, but also to release creation from the bondage of corruption. In a coming day, God's children will reign with Christ over it. In the meantime, He is getting us ready for that work (see Romans 8:21). So, yield to the Spirit's leading, guiding, and controlling, and God's thoughts and His ways will become your delight.

August 8TH

"For as the rain comes down, and the snow from heaven, and do not return there, but water the earth, and make it bring forth and bud, that it may give seed to the sower and bread to the eater, so shall My word be that goes forth from My mouth; it shall not return to Me void, but it shall accomplish what I please, and it shall prosper in the thing for which I sent it." Isaiah 55:10-11.

As with the rain and snow, so it is with the Word of God. Rain and snow fall from heaven, cause the earth to flourish, and eventually bread is produced for the hungry. So, God speaks and expresses His thoughts; His words begin to travel, expressing what He loves, hates, promises and purposes; those words fall into the human heart and conscience like seed, and they produce exactly what God has pleased. In whatever thing He has assigned, those words shall prosper. They never return to Him empty.

In this immediate context, the Word of God had come to Israel, telling, first, of the coming of King Cyrus the Persian to bring about their release from exile; and then of the Perfect Servant, the Lord Jesus. The Word of God had foretold Christ's death and resurrection, and the worldwide blessing that would follow, calling Israel to repentance and blessing. More would follow regarding a new world to come. All would be accomplished, and every prophecy would be fulfilled.

The living Word of God is 'profitable for doctrine, for reproof, for correction, for instruction in righteousness' (2 Timothy 3:16). This changeless, timeless Word will give us insight, beyond our fondest dreams. David could say,

'Oh, how I love Your law! It is my meditation all the day. You, through Your commandments, make me wiser than my enemies; for they are ever with me. I have more understanding than all my teachers, for Your testimonies are my meditations. I understand more than the ancients, because I keep Your precepts' (Psalm 119:97-100).

We are now hugely privileged to have the Holy Scriptures in our hands. Infallible truth lies deep within them, so let us observe the details, and let them shape our decisions. In the Middle Ages, copies of the Scriptures were chained to the pulpits, the public being kept ignorant of the soul-saving, life-changing truths within them. Nowadays, in the Western world, we have the Scriptures in hardback, paperback, leather and cloth. We have large-print editions, tiny pocket-size editions, all kinds of versions and paraphrases. However, the more the Scriptures are available, the less they are read. In those dark days biblical ignorance was forced, but in our day it is voluntary.

Are we going to allow loud, argumentative voices in society to divert us from following the divinely ordained map for getting through life's maze? If we follow their maps, we will end up confused and lost. The choice is ours.

AUGUST 9TH

"For you shall go out with joy, and be led out with peace; the mountains and the hills shall break forth into singing before you, and all the trees of the field shall clap their hands. Instead of the thorn shall come up the cypress tree, and instead of the brier shall come up the myrtle tree; and it shall be to the Lord for a name, for an everlasting sign that shall not be cut off." Isaiah 55:12-13.

Israel is going to return home. She will go out from captivity in Babylon with joy, and be led out with peace. Creation will rejoice as a result. This would have been true in these immediate circumstances, as their exile would have left a blighted environment. When Israel returned, with the renewed cultivation of the land, the cypress tree would replace the thorn. On the terraces of the hills, the brier would be removed and replaced by the myrtle tree. The mountains and hills would know a new day, and the trees of the field would show luscious growth.

Of course, Israel will one day know a perfect fulfilment of these things.

'And so all Israel will be saved, as it is written: "The Deliverer will come out of Zion, and He will turn away ungodliness from Jacob; for this is My covenant with them, when I take away their sins"' (Romans 11:26-27).

Heaven has received Christ, 'until the times of restoration of all things, which God has spoken by the mouth of all His holy prophets since the world began' (Acts 3:20). Even creation will be completely restored to her genesis. The Lord's name will be glorified by the coming times of incalculable refreshment, and the ancient curse will be removed from the earth.

I can almost hear you say, 'But what of the meantime?' I am certain you are like me, in that you experience a lot of thorns in your life. After the resurrection of Christ, thorns did not stop growing on the earth. His second coming will lead to their removal, but in the meantime they grow profusely. Even the Apostle Paul experienced 'a thorn in the flesh.' He uses them as a metaphor for those things in life that harass, rack, and buffet us. God had hugely blessed him with revelations, then something arrived in his life that was a real handicap to him. He begged the Lord three times to remove it, but the Lord refused. Satan's angel tried to use the 'thorn' to get Paul down. What now? The Lord told Paul that he would receive His grace to live with the harassment. In fact, the 'thorn' would cause the strength and power of Christ to rest upon him, and people would see what the Lord could do. The weaker Paul got, the stronger he became! He began to be thankful for thorns, for they led him to depend less on self and more on Christ. In any of our lives, that is never a bad thing.

My Scottish friend, William McClachlan, once told me of a Pastor who was sent by a good friend on a fishing holiday. Fully kitted-out, he arrived on a Scottish river and began to fish, but had no success whatsoever. A little lad who was fishing nearby was landing a lot of fish, so the Pastor asked him what his secret was. The lad informed the Pastor that he was too conspicuous – his shadow was being cast across the river. What did he advise the Pastor? "Away and hide yursel', man!" That's good advice.

AUGUST 10TH

Thus says the Lord: "Keep justice, and do righteousness, for My salvation is about to come, and My righteousness to be revealed." Isaiah 56:1.

T he implications of their redemption are now spelled out. The prophecies of Isaiah await their ultimate fulfilment; but in the meantime God expects His people to show in their lives the effects of their redemption. 'Faith without works is dead' (James 2:20). Redeemed people are 'living-between-times': facing the tensions of 'what is,' while waiting for 'what is to be.' Israel did return from exile, but the full glories of the new creation still lay ahead of her. And with the Church, the kingdom of God has come, but its full glories are yet to come. The final section of Isaiah (chapters 56-66) is all about 'life in the interim, waiting for the new world' (Barry Webb, *The Message of Isaiah*, IVP, page 220). Here is a call to be overcomers, with the power to overcome being available.

What, then, are the characteristics of people who have been redeemed? They 'keep justice, and do righteousness.' All my life, I have known the tensions between these two. There is the call to stand up for social justice; and there is also the call to lead a righteous life – to be personally holy. Can we be involved in both? Of course we can. The distinguished British politician, William Wilberforce, was convinced that he could not be a Christian and a Member of Parliament. It was the great John Newton who helped to show him otherwise. He lived with a settled faith in Christ, and helped to lead an incredibly successful campaign against slavery. Justice and righteousness flourished in his life.

Is this not the teaching of the Sermon on the Mount? Personal righteousness is vital; but Jesus taught that we are also to be as the light of the world, and as a city set on a hill. What is personal, should become very public. In a modern setting, I know no story that illustrates the tension between the two better, than the story of Ruby Bridges. It occurred in the early sixties in the United States. Ruby was a six-year-old girl, living in New Orleans. She happened to be one of the Afro-American children who initiated school de-segregation in New Orleans, against fearful odds. In the morning and in the evening as she travelled to and from school, Ruby had to brave murderously heckling mobs. The threats, slurs and accusations hurled at the child were incredible, so federal marshals accompanied her for her own protection. The mobs also threatened her parents. Ruby attended school alone for the best part of the year, because all the white families boycotted it.

Strangely, Ruby did not give up. Her teachers began to wonder how she was bearing up. Robert Coles, an eminent Harvard psychiatrist, was taking a journey to the Deep South at the time. He came across Ruby, and reckoned she would soon show signs of psychological wear and tear. But he was wrong. One of her teachers told of how she saw Ruby smile at a woman who spat at her. She saw Ruby smile at a man who shook his fist at her. Then she walked up the steps at the school, and turned and smiled at the crowd once more! The teacher told Coles that Ruby said that she prayed for all of the people who were insulting her.

When Coles asked her why she prayed for these people, she replied that she went to church every Sunday, and at church they were told to pray for everyone, even the bad people. And that is what she did. Through Coles' writing, Ruby soon became like a city set on a hill and a very powerful light across the world (Robert Coles, *The Moral Life of Children,* Boston, Houghton Mifflin Company, 1986). Ruby transcended Coles' textbooks, she transcended racism, and she faced 'what is,' whilst expressing the characteristics of 'what is to be.' Do you? Do I?

August 11ᵀᴴ

"Blessed is the man who does this, and the son of man who lays hold on it; who keeps from defiling the Sabbath, and keeps his hand from doing any evil." Isaiah 56:2.

It must have been a very sad sight to see her enter the synagogue that Sabbath day: 'there was a woman . . . who was bent over and could in no way raise herself up . . . when Jesus saw her He called her to Him and said, "Woman, you are loosed from your infirmity." He laid His hands on her, and immediately she was made straight, and glorified God' (see Luke 13:10-17).

The ensuing discussion makes for fascinating reading. The ruler of the synagogue was indignant because Jesus had healed the woman on the Sabbath day. Jesus called him a hypocrite, reminding the ruler that they would all have been happy to give their animals a drink on the Sabbath. He asked, then, "ought not this woman, being a daughter of Abraham, whom Satan has bound – think of it – for eighteen years, be loosed from this bond on the Sabbath?"

The phrase, 'a daughter of Abraham,' is significant. Did not God tell Abraham to 'walk' before Him? As Professor Gooding points out, "man's upright stance is more than a mere anatomical fact . . . it is a something distinctively human, an appropriate physical expression of man's moral, spiritual and official dignity as God's viceroy, created in the image of God to have dominion over all other creatures . . . the bent back is the typical physical posture of the burden-bearer and the slave under the yoke, and so becomes a natural and vivid metaphor for the effects of oppression and slavery" (*According to Luke*, IVP, p.252-253).

Was the Sabbath day not a celebration of freedom from slavery? Just as God brought Israel out of Egyptian slavery by a mighty hand and an outstretched arm (see Deuteronomy 5:14-15), so Jesus reached out and healed the woman. As Leviticus 26:13 puts it:

"I am the Lord your God, who brought you out of the land of Egypt, that you should not be their slaves; I have broken the bands of your yoke and made you walk upright."

In the midst of the much-heated discussions that surround the subject of keeping the Sabbath, it seems to me that the fact of it being a celebration of freedom from slavery is by and large forgotten. Let's not defile its significance by misrepresenting its whole point. Isaiah certainly didn't.

AUGUST 12TH

Do not let the son of the foreigner who has joined himself to the Lord speak, saying, "The Lord has utterly separated me from His people"; nor let the eunuch say, "Here I am, a dry tree." For thus says the Lord: "To the eunuchs who keep My Sabbaths, and choose what pleases Me, and hold fast My covenant, even to them I will give in My house and within My walls a place and a name better than that of sons and daughters; I will give them an everlasting name that shall not be cut off." Isaiah 56:3-5.

As Israel returned home, the question would arise as to their attitude to a very sensitive issue. The Old Testament law excluded certain people from joining them and worshipping with them. This included emasculated men and foreigners, particularly Moabites and Ammonites (see Leviticus 22:24-25; Deuteronomy 23:1-6). I find something written by Barry Webb very helpful on this issue: "These laws had never been meant to exclude genuine converts" (*The Message of Isaiah*, IVP, p.222). He cites the story of Rahab and Ruth, as pertinent examples. It is true that particular disciplines applied to certain nations; but the fact remained, in principle, even from the great first Exodus: the foreigner was always welcome to submit to God's laws and join Israel (see Exodus 12:48-49). The overriding phrase in today's text is 'who has joined (or bound) himself to the Lord.'

As the Lord encourages Israel to show compassion to those outside their ranks who have sought Him, our thoughts will go to a desert road at least seven centuries after Isaiah's prophecy (see Acts 8:26-40). Walking along that road is an evangelist called Philip. The Lord has called him away from a great spiritual awakening in Samaria, and told him to walk the Jerusalem – Gaza road. He did what he was told, and eventually a chariot came by. In it was an Ethiopian who was reading the Prophecy of Isaiah. The Lord told Philip to go near and overtake the chariot. As he did so, he heard him reading from what we now know as chapter 53. He told Philip that he did not understand what he was reading, so Philip was able to show him that Isaiah was speaking about the Perfect Servant, our Lord Jesus. He was converted, baptised, and went on his way rejoicing. The Scriptures unequivocally point out that the Ethiopian was a eunuch.

The lives of eunuchs must have been ghastly. They were the custodians of royal harems. God told Isaiah that some members of the royal family of Israel would be taken away and forcibly made eunuchs. Isaiah relayed the message to King Hezekiah: 'they shall take away some of your sons who will descend from you, whom you will beget; and they shall be eunuchs in the palace of the king of Babylon' (Isaiah 39:7). Eunuchs would never have any children. They must have led unnatural, and often every lonely lives. How could they become worshippers amongst God's people? Isaiah tells us that those who submitted to God and to His laws would be allowed into God's presence and given an honoured name – even more honoured than that of sons and daughters. They would be eternally secure, given an everlasting name that would not be cut off. Access! Acceptance! Recompense! Eternal security!

Think of the millions who have come to faith in Christ on the Continent of Africa. It all came out of Isaiah's prophecy being read by an Ethiopian eunuch who had gone to Jerusalem 'to worship,' and was returning. He was Jewish, an official representative of Queen Candace, who was also an observant Jew (*Eerdman's Dictionary of the Bible*, p.433). Now he had found Christ through these wonderful verses from Isaiah being explained by Philip. Ah! The sheer romance of God's Word and work.

AUGUST 13TH

"Also the sons of the foreigner who join themselves to the Lord, to serve Him, and to love the name of the Lord, to be His servants – everyone who keeps from defiling the Sabbath, and holds fast My covenant – even them I will bring to My holy mountain, and make them joyful in My house of prayer. Their burnt offerings and their sacrifices will be accepted on My altar; for My house shall be called a house of prayer for all nations." The Lord God, who gathers the outcasts of Israel, says, "Yet I will gather to him others besides those who are gathered to him." Isaiah 56:6-8.

'For all nations.' No nationality is excluded here. From every corner of the earth, those who bind themselves to the Lord to love and serve Him, who keep His Sabbath and hold fast to His covenant, will be welcome to pray in His house. He is the God who will gather the exiles of Israel, away beyond what He has already gathered.

This is truly an international attitude of God regarding Israel; but Isaiah prophesied that the day would come when a much wider group of people would be gathered with them. When He was driving the moneychangers out of the temple, from the very area to which Gentiles had limited access, the Lord Jesus quoted from today's text (see Matthew 21:13). Then He told His disciples that He had other sheep, 'which were not of this fold; them also I must bring, and they will hear My voice; and there will be one flock and one shepherd' (John 10:16). Writing to the Ephesian Christians, Paul reminds them that they were 'once Gentiles in the flesh . . . aliens from the commonwealth of Israel and strangers from the covenants of promise, having no hope and without God in the world. But now in Christ Jesus you who once were far off have been brought near by the blood of Christ' (Ephesians 2:11-13). He explains to them that God has revealed to him this great mystery, '. . . that the Gentiles should be fellow heirs, of the same body, and partakers of His promise in Christ through the gospel' (3:3-7).

There is no better cameo of the truly international nature of the church than the people in the church at Philippi. They could not have been more divergent. Three in particular are highlighted in the Acts of the Apostles: a businesswoman, a slave girl, and a jailer. John Stott points out some interesting things about each of them (*The Message of Acts*, IVP, p 268-270). They were of different national origins. Lydia was an Asiatic, in the sense that she came from Asia Minor. The slave girl was presumably Greek, and a resident. The jailer was Roman, like all officials in the legal administration of a Roman colony. They had different social backgrounds. Lydia is likely to have been wealthy, owning a large house, which eventually accommodated the church. The slave girl came from the opposite end of the social spectrum: she owned nothing, not even her own possessions. The jailer was probably halfway between the two, in the respectable middle class. They had different personal needs: Lydia had an intellectual need, the slave girl had a psychological need, the jailer had a moral need. The gospel reached them all, and unified them like nothing else could do. It still does.

AUGUST 14TH

All you beasts of the field, come to devour, all you beasts in the forest. His watchmen are blind, they are all ignorant; they are all dumb dogs, they cannot bark; sleeping, lying down, loving to slumber. Isaiah 56:9-10.

We now face one of the most difficult problems in all human life: failed leadership. We move from the soaring heights of the vision given to Isaiah, of glorious days in the future, to the reality of leaders who close their eyes to imminent danger, and live in a self-centred way. The leadership is so poor, that God's people are wide open to attack. Isaiah uses the imagery of beasts coming to attack and devour the unguarded flock. He uses bitter irony, by telling these beasts that they will find it easy to come and devour it. These watchmen of Israel are not like those mentioned in chapter 52:8; they are ignorant and like dumb dogs that cannot bark. They are lazy and love slumber, so the predator can get past them without them even making a whimper.

We have seen what lies in the future for God's people; but the reality is that, while we await the fulfilment of it all, bad leadership is going to bedevil us. It would plague Israel on their return from Babylon; and it plagues God's people to this day. As the Church awaits the return of Christ, are you in a position of leadership? Are you afraid to speak up for what is right? Is truth on the scaffold in your place of work or study? Is it facing attack in your local Church? God knows that even nations need guardians, who will warn when citizens are in imminent danger of being wiped out. But it is not a popular stance to take, as Winston Churchill discovered when he began to 'bark' of the approaching Nazi threat in the 1930's. "Tell the truth to the British people," he pleaded with the equivocating Prime Ministers of the 1930's, "they are a tough people, a robust people . . . if you have not told them exactly what is going on, you have ensured yourself complaints and reproaches, which are not very pleasant when they come home on the morrow of some disillusion" (*Hansard*: 11th/23rd/32). Churchill told the truth, and found himself in the political wilderness. Appeasement of the enemy was the order of the day. Concession to Hitler served to debilitate Britain, in the face of inevitable attack. Churchill's repeated calls for a defence build up, intending to avoid war, were not heeded by Britain's leadership, nor by Britain as a whole, until it drifted into war. Ultimately Churchill helped to transform Britain into a nation that displayed huge bravery; but he was long shunned before the Nation saw the enemy for the horrendous predator that it was.

People now make films and write books about watchmen like Churchill, but the price of actually being one is extremely costly. Maybe you are called to be a watchman, warning in the face of a predator? Again I say, speak up, and future generations will thank God for you.

AUGUST 15TH

Yes, they are greedy dogs which never have enough. And they are shepherds who cannot understand; they all look to their own way, every one for his own gain, from his own territory. "Come," one says, "I will bring wine, and we will fill ourselves with intoxicating drink; tomorrow will be as today, and much more abundant." Isaiah 56:11-12.

I am going to let the Prophecy of Ezekiel comment on Isaiah's exposé of the self-centredness of Israel's Shepherds. May this probing, powerful prophecy speak to all who have any responsibility in shepherding work amongst God's people.

"Son of man, prophesy against the shepherds of Israel, prophesy and say to them, 'Thus says the Lord God to the shepherds:

"Woe to the shepherds of Israel who feed themselves! Should not the shepherds feed the flocks? You eat the fat and clothe yourselves with the wool; you slaughter the fatlings, but you do not feed the flock. The weak you have not strengthened, nor have you healed those who were sick, nor bound up the broken, nor brought back what was driven away, nor sought what was lost; but with force and cruelty you have ruled them. So they were scattered because there was no shepherd; and they became food for all the beasts of the field when they were scattered. My sheep wandered through all the mountains, and on every high hill; yes, My flock was scattered over the whole face of the earth, and no one was seeking or searching for them."

Therefore, you shepherds, hear the word of the Lord: "As I live," says the Lord God, "surely because My flock became a prey, and My flock became food for every beast of the field, because there was no shepherd, nor did My shepherds search for My flock, but the shepherds fed themselves and did not feed My flock." Therefore, O shepherds, hear the word of the Lord! Thus says the Lord God: "Behold, I am against the shepherds, and I will require My flock at their hand; I will cause them to cease feeding the sheep, and the shepherds shall feed themselves no more; for I will deliver My flock from their mouths, that they may no longer be food for them."

For thus says the Lord God: "Indeed I Myself will search for My sheep and seek them out. As a shepherd seeks out his flock on the day he is among his scattered sheep, so will I seek out My sheep and deliver them from all the places where they were scattered on a cloudy and dark day. And I will bring them out from the peoples and gather them from the countries, and will bring them to their own land; I will feed them on the mountains of Israel, in the valleys and in all the inhabited places of the country. I will feed them in good pasture, and their fold shall be on the high mountains of Israel. There they shall lie down in a good fold and feed in rich pasture on the mountains of Israel. I will feed My flock, and I will make them lie down," says the Lord God. "I will seek what was lost and bring back what was driven away, bind up the broken and strengthen what was sick; but I will destroy the fat and the strong, and feed them in judgment" (Ezekiel 34:2-16).

AUGUST 16ᵀᴴ

The righteous perishes, and no man takes it to heart; merciful men are taken away, while no one considers that the righteous is taken away from evil. He shall enter into peace; they shall rest in their beds, each one walking in his uprightness. Isaiah 57:1-2.

These verses are saying that the Lord carefully arranges the timing of the death of His faithful servants. My father was a faithful evangelist for many years, but he died at the early age of 56.

'His place will be missed,' the death column said,
As across the country newspapers spread
The news of his passing to village and town,
And deep sorrow was felt by many around
The province, where his preaching had touched many a heart,
And in whose spiritual history he played a part.
Dozens of people came and stood in our garden,
As farewell hymns surrounded his parting,
And hundreds made their way out to Drumee,
Where the final service I can still see.
Hawthorn Bailey's Churchillian voice rose in prayer,
As Desmond and I stood silently there.
Of its solemn tone I can still hear the sound,
And our father's body was laid in the ground;
And the grave-digger's spade, as heartless as ever,
Poured the thudding soil, to immediately sever
All sight of a father, wise, gentle and true,
Whose sincerity thousands of people knew.
We filed out of that cemetery on Drumee Hill,
And the night closed in silent and still.

I shall always remember how my mother reacted to the early death of her husband. She would say to me, "his work was finished, and the Lord took him home." As a child growing up, I was aware that my mother's Christian belief gave her a sense of the reality that death for a Christian is not accidental or without purpose. The timing of that death is not meaningless, and it was a great comfort to know this.

Today's text shows this very clearly. The ungodly may not think much about the death of a Godly person. They are not aware that the Lord can spare His servants the agony of going through evil times that they would not be able to bear. For example, this happened to Josiah, who became king at 8 years of age, and reigned in Jerusalem for 31 years. He turned out to be a very Godly man, and when dire times were coming the Lord sent a message to him. He said, ". . . because your heart was tender and you humbled yourself before the Lord . . . surely, therefore, I will gather you to your fathers, and you shall be gathered to your grave in peace; and your eyes shall not see all the calamity which I will bring on this place" (2 Kings 22:19-20).

Not all the Israelites were like the unfaithful watchmen or the greedy, self-centred shepherds. These people continued to be righteous through difficult days. They continued to live with dignity in very undignified times; and then, at the very moment of God's choice, they were taken home to be with the Lord. Not only does the Lord bring meaning to our lives, He brings meaning to our deaths.

AUGUST 17TH

"But come here, you sons of the sorceress, you offspring of the adulterer and the harlot! Whom do you ridicule? Against whom do you make a wide mouth and stick out the tongue? Are you not children of transgression, offspring of falsehood . . . ?"
Isaiah 57:3-4.

Isaiah writes now about the behaviour of those who, in the generation that preceded the exile of Israel, had turned away from the Lord. God calls these spiritually unfaithful people, 'the sons of the sorceress.' A sorcerer or a sorceress is one who claims to have a supernatural power or knowledge. Such a person would often use magic potions, and was considered to be in league with evil forces. He calls the unfaithful, 'the offspring of the adulterer and the prostitute.' They were downright disloyal to the Lord, breaking their side of the covenant with Him.

God particularly picks out the way the pre-exilic generation mocked Him. He asks two rhetorical questions: "Whom do you ridicule?" and "Against whom do you make a wide mouth and stick out the tongue?" When we consider the awesome things you and I have learned together about God in the pages of Isaiah – of His power, love and grace – the pathos of these two rhetorical questions is deep. That a human being, whom God created by the incredible miracle of human birth, should stand and taunt, sneer and make fun of God, seems beyond belief. That they should then stick out their tongue in scorn, at Him who holds their breath in His hand, is sick. In Genesis we read that God asked Adam in the garden, "Where are you?" But Adam was hiding from God because of sin. Now in Isaiah we see sin in its full-blown state: people are sticking out their scornful tongues at God. These people were the 'children of transgression,' and 'the offspring of falsehood.'

According to Psalm 1:1, the truly happy person, 'walks not in the counsel of the ungodly, nor stands in the path of sinners, nor sits in the seat of the scornful.' Meditate carefully on the three triplets mentioned in this verse. 1. walking, standing, sitting; 2. counsel, way, seat; 3. ungodly, sinners, scornful. It represents the progress of evil, with each category moving to a climax, none of which holds true happiness. Let us be careful not to slip into any of these categories, lest, ultimately, we should sit in the seat of the scornful.

It led Israel to exile, and it will lead you, Christian, to the chastisement of the Lord. The truly happy person has discovered in the Bible a completely different view of life, and believing it has driven cynicism away. According to Psalm 1, "Such a person, 'Shall be like a tree': vitality. 'Planted': security. 'By the rivers of water': capacity. 'That brings forth its fruit': fertility. 'In its season': propriety. 'Its leaf also shall not wither': perpetuity. 'And whatsoever he does shall prosper': prosperity" (Dr. W. Graham Scroggie, *The Psalms*, Pickering & Inglis Ltd., 1965, p.49). The ungodly are likened to dead straw, chaff. They are not spiritually nourished; and having no roots they are blown away in the wind.

Going through a city in Eastern Europe recently, I saw two words sprawled on the wall of a building: No future. I wish I could have written another two words underneath: Psalm 1. It surely holds the secret of happiness.

AUGUST 18TH

"Are you not . . . inflaming yourselves with gods under every green tree, slaying the children in the valleys, under the clefts of the rocks?" Isaiah 57:5.

This is very different from 'going out with joy, and being led out with peace.' It is a huge contrast to children being 'taught by the Lord.' The thirst-quenching God of Israel is very different to the gods being worshipped by unfaithful Israelites. These gods demanded child sacrifice, as well as offerings from their harvest. The evergreen tree is being associated with a fertility cult. Sexual rites were associated with this god, to encourage him to bring fertility to the people, their land, and their animals. These dreadful orgies were cloaked with religion. As Alec Motyer points out, what these people were really doing was putting sheer lust in place of the Lord's will. Sexual gratification was their motivation and priority.

I remember once being asked to represent my University in a Debating Competition called 'The Observer Mace.' The subject in the first round was, 'This house believes that marriage is no longer a social necessity.' I faced a dilemma. Should I represent my University, by trying to make a tongue-in-the-cheek speech against marriage, and be popular; or should I refuse, on the grounds that as a Christian I believed very much in marriage, and be unpopular? I was very young, and needed advice. I went to an Academic who was a Christian, called Dr. David Gooding. "Are you going to use your gift for God's glory or your own?" he said.

"You might get up and make a funny speech on the subject, but people do not think very deeply about sinning. They are looking for an excuse to sin, and you might just give someone in your audience that excuse." So I said, 'No,' and have gone on to thank God for the day that I did.

We need to ask, 'is sexual pleasure a sin, or a gift from God?' Of course, it is a gift from God. Pleasure is God's creation not the devil's. We must also realise that pleasure is a by-product in life, not its goal. The modern world, just like the ancient world before it, has made a god out of sensuality. A Christian is not a hedonist – a person who goes after pleasure at all costs. Sigmund Freud saw man as a creature, whose every action is controlled by the pursuit of pleasure and the avoidance of pain. Yet the fact is that, when we devote ourselves to pursuing pleasure, it ceases to be a delight. Our appetites become jaded, and require even more stimulation. On the other hand, when we devote our lives in loving obedience to God, and to serving one another, we find that pleasures which eluded us when we made them our priority, now come unbidden into our lives to surprise us. To seek pleasure is to seek disillusionment, and to seek God is to find pleasures for evermore.

AUGUST 19TH

"Among the smooth stones of the stream is your portion; they, they, are your lot! Even to them you have poured a drink offering, you have offered a grain offering. Should I receive comfort in these?" Isaiah 57:6.

For me, Isaiah is the writer of writers regarding the use of contrasts, and here is a classic. What is the portion of the idol worshipper? Smooth stones! People go down into streams, choose smooth stones, and then worship them. "They, they, are your lot," says God. Imagine stones in the place of the living God! What a contrast! Drink and grain offerings are being offered to stones, and God asks if He should receive any comfort in these offerings? He receives no comfort whatsoever, and the whole absurdity of what these people are doing brings God's wrath on their heads.

"If a son shall ask bread of any of you that is a father, will he give him a stone?" asked the Lord Jesus. Our souls cry out for spiritual bread, for we cannot live by earthly bread alone. Seneca, in his *Letter from Exile* to his Mother, Helvia, wrote: "Gaius Caesar, whom, as it seems to me, Nature produced merely to show how far supreme vice, when combined with supreme power, could go, dined one day at a cost of ten million sesterces; and though everybody used their ingenuity to help him, yet he could hardly discover how to spend the tribute-money from three provinces on one dinner! . . . He, therefore, who keeps himself within the bounds of nature will not feel poverty; but he who exceeds the bounds of nature will be pursued by poverty, even though he had unbounded wealth." Think of it: even if you did have the tribute-money of three provinces to spend on one meal, you can only eat one meal at a time; and even that will not satisfy the needs of your soul. Only the Lord, the Bread from Heaven, can do that.

"On a lofty and high mountain you have set your bed; even there you went up to offer sacrifice. Also behind the doors and their posts you have set up your remembrance; for you have uncovered yourself to those other than Me, and have gone up to them; you have enlarged your bed and made a covenant with them; you have loved their bed, where you saw their nudity." Isaiah 57:7-8.

These are sickening verses. They expose pre-exilic Israel, being influenced and moulded by the society around them, and losing their distinctive moral stance in the world. Let us always remember that differences make a difference. God's teaching regarding family life is summed up succinctly in two sentences: "Therefore a man shall leave his father and mother and be joined to his wife, and they shall become one flesh. And they were both naked, the man and his wife and were not ashamed" (Genesis 2:24, 25). The Israelites had blatantly disobeyed this foundational statement on marriage, as the basis for family life.

God's blueprint for marriage and family life is, without question, the best. First, there is severance – the cord with parents needs to be broken. It does not mean abandoning parents; but it does mean breaking those tight, emotionally-dependent strings, to allow the marriage to breathe and grow. Parents need to truly release their children into marriage. Second, there is permanence. It means absolute commitment. The command is to 'leave,' and 'be joined to'. Each couple needs to view the commitment as irrevocable. Third, there is unity. The two become as one. When severance, permanence and unity are in place, the delight of intimacy can be enjoyed. If any one of these three is broken, intimacy is seriously affected.

Today's text exposes Israel for practising sexual immorality in the name of worship; and obviously not the worship of Jehovah. Prostitution in the name of religion was common practice among pagans, and Israel was influenced by what was going on. The meaning of these verses seems to be that, while they had the 'mezuzah' posted on their doors, behind them they were deeply involved in immorality.

What is the 'mezuzah'? This was the practice of putting Scripture on the door posts of their houses, displaying the command, "Hear, O Israel: the Lord our God, the Lord is one! You shall love the Lord your God with all your heart, with all your soul, and with all your strength . . . You shall write them on the door posts of your house and on your gates" (Deuteronomy 6:4, 5, 9). Jews would touch their doors as a token of obedience. The hypocrisy of pre-exilic Israel was obvious.

Let us be careful, in our day and generation, that we do not profess one thing and practise another. God detests hypocrisy. Paul wrote, 'Do not be conformed to this world, but be transformed by the renewing of your mind, that you may prove what is that good and acceptable and perfect will of God' (Romans 12:2).

"You went to the king with ointment, and increased your perfumes; you sent your messengers far off, and even descended to Sheol. You are wearied in the length of your

way; yet you did not say, 'there is no hope.' You have found the life of your hand; therefore you were not grieved." Isaiah 57:9-10.

Let these verses of scripture search our lives. Their accuracy is pungent. The background is that Judah, under King Ahaz, got disastrously involved with Tiglath-Pileser, the king of Assyria. Ahaz asked Tiglath-Pileser to come and save him from Syria and Israel, who had risen up against him. In our recent readings we learned about the worship of fertility cults: Ahaz 'burned incense on the high places, on the hills, and under every green tree' (2 Kings 16:4). God's people also sent ambassadors to Egypt, '. . . to strengthen themselves in the strength of Pharaoh, and to trust in the shadow of Egypt' (Isaiah 30:2). These alliances were a disaster, and in vain.

God's people had said that they were making a covenant with death (Isaiah 28:14,15), but they were becoming aware that it was not working to their advantage. They were wearied with it all, but they still did not face up to the fact that it was a waste of time and energy, and would end up in a hopeless cul-de-sac. So they found the strength to try one more time. The evidence was staring them in the face, but they did not want to take it to heart. The grief of it should have led them to repentance, and to acknowledge that the Lord's way is the best.

When God's test came against their alliance, it would not survive: "Your covenant with death will be annulled, and your agreement with Sheol will not stand", said the Lord, "when the overflowing scourge passes through, then you will be trampled down by it. As often as it goes out it will take you; for morning by morning it will pass over and by day and by night; it will be a terror just to understand the report" (Isaiah 28:18-19).

Are you in an alliance that is wrong? Are you associated with something that does not adhere to the Word of God; but which gives you a stronger position socially or financially? You know that, spiritually speaking, it is an alliance with death, and will bring you great grief. These people did find 'a quickening of their strength' (RV), and continued to bolster these wrong alliances. Perhaps you have found a new lease of life to go on with this thing that is burdening and wearying you? Face it this very day, for the hopeless thing that it is, and don't let it drag you down any longer. Break the alliance; be done with it. You have the Lord; He is enough. You don't need to increase your gifts of 'perfume'(v.9). The Lord is your shield, and your exceeding great reward (Genesis 15:1). Selah.

AUGUST 22ND

"And of whom have you been afraid, or feared, that you have lied and not remembered Me, nor taken it to your heart? Is it not because I have held My peace from of old that you do not fear Me? I will declare your righteousness and your works, for they will not profit you." Isaiah 57:11-12.

The people of God had feared their enemies to such an extent that they had been untruthful: they said they were trusting in the Lord, but they were actually trusting in their unholy alliances. They feared people more than they feared God, and God was very angry with them because they had forgotten Him. They had compromised their faith and stubbornly gone down the wrong way, forgetting all the resources and blessings that were available through faith in God.

God raised a very important question with His people: "Is it not because I have held My peace from of old that you do not fear Me?" Just because God did not intervene in judgment, they hardened their hearts. It is like the taunt of the ungodly, who 'set their mouth against the heavens . . . and they say, "how does God know? And is there knowledge in the Most High?" (Psalm 73:9-11). They think that God is passive because they are not wiped out in immediate judgment. In exile, Israel had begun to think like the ungodly, using the excuse of an un-intervening God, to sin, but all this wrong-headed thinking will be exposed. Although Israel think they are righteous, and that their works will stand in the time of judgment, they are in for a shock. They will discover there is no profit whatsoever in what they have done. When God says there is no profit in something, then it would be wise to listen to Him.

What, then, does God consider to be profitable? 'In all labour there is profit, but idol chatter leads only to poverty' (Proverbs 14:23). I went to school with a chap called John McCammon. He became a very successful dentist, and one day he and a colleague discovered that there was a way of removing a needle from a syringe without handling it. They patented their discovery and it became successful world-wide. Lives will be saved as a result. Duane Pearsall was testing a device that controls static electricity, when he noticed that the smoke from a technician's cigarette caused a reaction in the meter. He was annoyed that he had to have a new meter installed, but later he realised that the meter's reaction to smoke might prove valuable. He invented the first American-made smoke detector alarm system!

Golden opportunities in life are frequently right under our noses, while we idle away our time with chatter. Don't be lazy, get into the habit of looking for them. That's wisdom. In fact, if we only realised it, infinity is right under our noses.

AUGUST 23RD

"When you cry out, let your collection of idols deliver you. But the wind will carry them all away, a breath will take them. But he who puts his trust in Me shall possess the land, and shall inherit My holy mountain." Isaiah 57:13.

We have seen the tragedy of unbelievers worshipping idols. Now the Lord shows us the tragedy that awaits His own people who worship those idols. When the time of judgment comes and they cry out in alarm, the objects of their trust are so flimsy that the wind will carry them all away, a breath will take them. Is your confidence in the Lord? You have turned away from all earthly idols to put your trust in Him, so you look odd in the eyes of others. They call you eccentric, even old-fashioned. Driven by fear of losing their jobs, accidents, illness, financial disaster, circumstances beyond their control, they turn to earthly idols to save them. Could your confidence in the Lord be misplaced? Will you find yourself disillusioned or disappointed in Him?

I had just finished preaching and sat down, when a young Spaniard got into conversation with me. She was in Britain to study English. Having taught the subject for some time, I was interested to know which English writer impressed her most. Jane Austin, Thomas Hardy, or Charles Dickens, perhaps? "Lord Byron," she said, "because he believed in seizing the moment." He did indeed, but it brought him incalculable sorrow. His hedonism led him to say, 'the worm, the canker, and the grief are mine alone.' Seize the moment, yes; but seize it for God's glory. Put your confidence in Him, live your life for Him, and Lord Byron's grief will never be yours. 'The blessing of the Lord makes one rich and He adds no sorrow with it' (Proverbs 10:22).

Of course, days will come when it will seem that our confidence in the Lord is going to be overwhelmed by events. Jesus said:

"There will be signs in the sun, in the moon, and in the stars; and on the earth distress of nations, with perplexity, the sea and the waves roaring; men's hearts failing them from fear and the expectation of those things which are coming on the earth, for the powers of the heavens will be shaken. Then they will see the Son of Man coming in a cloud with power and great glory. Now when these things begin to happen, look up and lift up your heads, because your redemption draws near" (Luke 21:25-28).

The final part of today's text says, "But he who puts his trust in Me, shall possess the land, and shall inherit My holy mountain." Your confidence in the Lord will not be overwhelmed by events. So, do as Jesus advised: look up, and lift up your head, because your redemption draws near.

24TH AUGUST

And one shall say, "Heap it up! Heap it up! Prepare the way, take the stumbling block out of the way of My people." For thus says the High and Lofty One Who inhabits eternity, whose name is Holy: "I dwell in the high and holy place, with him who has a contrite and humble spirit, to revive the spirit of the humble, and to revive the heart of the contrite ones." Isaiah 57:14-15.

As in Isaiah 40, now comfort is again being given to the faithful amongst God's people. In chapter 40, the call was, "prepare the way of the Lord; make straight in the desert a highway for our God." Now, in chapter 57, the call is, "prepare the way, take the stumbling block out of the way of My people." They were to come home out of exile by a way that had been cleared of all obstacles. But there is even more comprehensive truth here, referring to the wider journey taken by all believers to the final goal of all the people of God.

Having recently made a special video of the life of John Bunyan in Bedford and district in England, I have been powerfully reminded that all believers are pilgrims, travelling through this world to the Celestial City. In John Bunyan's famous hymn, a beautiful phrase says: 'there's no discouragement shall make him once relent his first avowed intent to be a pilgrim.'

The Lord is described as 'the High and Lofty One.' 'He shall be exalted and extolled and made very high' (Isaiah 52:13). Following His resurrection, He has been exalted far above all. He 'inhabits eternity.' This means He has always existed. And now this One, whose name is Holy, wants to share the high and holy place where He dwells with us.

We have seen those who are unfaithful to the Lord trying to shore up their position with the rich and powerful of earth. They carried gifts to the godless, hoping for their protection. They denied the God whom they professed to follow, saying, 'we have made lies our refuge, and under falsehood we have hidden ourselves' (Isaiah 28:15). It will all come to nothing. Yet the richest, most powerful, Father of Eternity, the Creator Himself, says that He dwells 'with him who has a contrite and humble spirit.' In this context, 'contrite' means one who is beaten down and crushed in spirit. Such a person is not among earth's 'high ones.' In the estimation of the world, he or she would be very low.

But such pilgrims will be revived in spirit; they will be able to carry on with verve and enthusiasm. "Take the stumbling block out of the way of My people," says the Lord. Should that stumbling block be Giant Despair or Mr. Worldly Wise Man; should the obstacle be Talkative, Ignorance, Formalist, Hypocrisy, Timorous, Mistrust, or even Apollyon himself, all obstacles will be removed to encourage the pilgrim on his or her journey home. Vanity Fair will be overcome, the Slough of Despond conquered, and, if they have to face it, even the River of Death itself will be crossed in victory. Mount Zion, the Paradise of God, will be reached, and all the pilgrims shall inherit God's Holy Mountain.

AUGUST 25TH

"For I will not contend forever, nor will I always be angry; for the spirit would fail before Me, and the souls which I have made." Isaiah 57:16.

The subject of the anger of God is taboo in most of our Western society. Few mention it at all, but the Bible mentions it constantly. From the banishment of Adam and Eve out of the Garden of Eden, to the great assizes of Revelation chapters 17, 18 and 20, we find that the anger of God is spoken of more times than the love of God. Let us never forget that anger is one of God's attributes. God detests sin, and executes frightful vengeance upon it.

'God is jealous, and the Lord avenges; the Lord avenges and is furious. The Lord will take vengeance on His adversaries, and He reserves wrath for His enemies; the Lord is slow to anger and great in power, and will not at all acquit the wicked . . . who can stand before His indignation? And who can endure the fierceness of His anger? His fury is poured out like fire, and the rocks are thrown down by Him. The Lord is good, a stronghold in the day of trouble; and He knows those who trust in Him. But with an overflowing flood He will make an utter end of its place, and darkness will pursue His enemies' (Nahum 1:2-8).

We must also remember, of course, that in all generations, people do have a choice. They can either choose their own way, or choose to follow the light God gives to lead them to Him.

"And this is the condemnation, that light has come into the world, and men loved darkness rather than light, because their deeds were evil. For everyone practising evil hates the light and does not come to the light, lest his deeds should be exposed. But he who does the truth comes to the light, that his deeds may be clearly seen, that they have been done in God" (John 3:19-21).

It is beautiful to read in today's text that God says, "I will not contend forever, nor will I always be angry." There is One who stands between an angry God and us. He deals with our sin, and through repentance and faith in Him we need no longer fear Hell.

'But God demonstrates His own love toward us, in that while we were still sinners, Christ died for us. Much more then, having now been justified by His blood, we shall be saved from wrath through Him' (Romans 5:8-9).

In chapter 53, Isaiah has portrayed the work of the Perfect Servant at Calvary. Resting in that finished work, 'we have turned to God from idols to serve the living and true God, and to wait for His Son from heaven, whom He raised from the dead, even Jesus who delivers us from the wrath to come' (1 Thessalonians 1:9, 10). Wrath averted! Guilt cancelled! The believer in Jesus is forgiven and accepted as righteous. Go forward this day, Christian, in the joy of it all.

26ᵀᴴ AUGUST

"For I will not contend forever, nor will I always be angry; for the spirit would fail before Me, and the souls which I have made. For the iniquity of his covetousness I was angry and struck him; I hid and was angry, and he went on backsliding in the way of his heart. I have seen his ways, and will heal him; I will also lead him, and restore comforts to him and to his mourners." Isaiah 57:16-18.

Commentators match these verses with the story of Noah's day. 'Then the Lord saw that the wickedness of man was great in the earth, and that every intent of the thoughts of his heart was only evil continually . . . but Noah found grace in the eyes of the Lord' (Genesis 6:5, 8). Man's inherent perverseness, selfishness and greed had once again incurred God's anger. Israel's sins were as gross as those of Noah's day; so she had been brought into exile. The Lord had shown grace to Noah and his family, and after the judgment He promised that He would never utterly destroy humankind again by a flood. Today's verses are proof of that promise, for the unfaithful in Israel certainly deserved similar judgment to Noah's generation.

Yesterday, we saw how the Lord promises healing to the contrite in heart. In today's text, He promises that He will personally lead them and restore comforts to them, and to all who mourn amongst them.

The Lord still carries out this ministry. To all who are contrite in heart towards him, He brings healing. We can all identify with God's definition of Israel:

'. . . the whole heart faints. From the sole of the foot even to the head there is no soundness in it, but wounds and bruises and putrefying sores; they have not been closed or bound up, or soothed with ointment' (Isaiah 1:5, 6).

God can heal all that sin has inflicted upon us, healing of mind, soul, spirit, and body. Binding up broken hearts is a work requiring a touch that particularly belongs to God. When the Children of Israel came to Marah, and could not drink the bitter waters, God made the waters sweet, declaring, "I am the Lord who heals you" (Exodus 15: 26). He still does.

"I create the fruit of the lips: peace, peace to him who is far off and to him who is near,"
says the Lord, "and I will heal him." Isaiah 57:19.

Wherever they are, God promises to bring peace to those who are contrite in heart. Notice the double mention of the word 'peace,' meaning 'perfect peace.' It has the same meaning as Isaiah 26:3: 'You will keep him in perfect peace, whose mind is stayed on You.' With their repentance and contrition, the mourners will find perfect peace, and songs of worship and praise will flow in appreciation. "I create the fruit of the lips," God declares. This is one of His great ministries.

Sometimes I find myself in difficult situations, and simply do not know what to say. In my heart I cry to the Lord for the right word, and He guides me to it. 'A word fitly spoken is like apples of gold in settings of silver' (Proverbs 25:11). The language of praise that the Lord gives to the contrite in heart is a very precious thing.

The celebrated photographer, Lord Snowdon, was down by Brighton Pier one day, when he noticed a little man paddling in the sea. "Every day Mr. Philips moved almost imperceptibly," says Snowdon, "in and out with the tide, leaving his shoes at the high water mark. I suddenly realised he was a deaf mute, and talked to him in the sign-language which I had learned at school, because one wasn't allowed to talk after lights-out. He said he lived in a bed-sit in Hove, and that no one had spoken to him for 20 years." Lord Snowdon took a photograph of the man on the beach – it is entitled 'Mr. Philips 1966.' It haunts me, every time I see it.

Yet there is a disability much worse than impaired hearing or speech, and the difficulties in communication that accompany it. Every day God came to the Garden of Eden and talked with Adam. It is something God loves to do. As originally made, human beings were intended to hold conversation with God, but when Adam sinned he did not want to talk with God any more. Silence reigned. Man now wanted to be God; Satan had convinced him that God was a killjoy. Across the centuries millions have believed his lie. Would you believe it: there are people who haven't spoken to God in 20 years or more, and some haven't spoken to Him at all. It is Satan's desire to turn this earth into a silent planet, as far as communication with God is concerned.

Has God left the situation like that? Certainly not! He sent the Lord Jesus into the world, and all kinds of people began to talk to Him with deep enthusiasm; including people who would never have entered a place of worship. 'No one ever spoke the way this Man does,' they said. They could not believe that God was like this! He loved them, He cared for their children, He had not come to condemn them but to save them. He was breaking into their prison of silence. He was stronger than the strong one, who had held so many lives in his grip for such a long time. Satan, the father of lies, had misrepresented God, and millions were in spiritual captivity. The living Saviour had broken through Satan's defences, and was talking to the prisoners! Through His death and resurrection, He has led captivity captive.

If anyone repents towards God and puts faith in the Lord Jesus, that person becomes a Christian. Life, with its talents and gifts, can be used in Christ's service to bring blessing to any community anywhere on earth. Across the last 2000 years, Christ has brought peace and forgiveness of sins to multitudes. He has loosened silent tongues, brought 'beauty instead of ashes, and a garment of praise instead of a spirit of despair.' If you have been given the wonderful garment of praise, don't you think it would be a dreadful thing if you didn't put it on?

AUGUST 28TH

But the wicked are like the troubled sea, when it cannot rest, whose waters cast up mire and dirt. "There is no peace," says my God, "for the wicked." Isaiah 57:20-21.

Isaiah gives us another of his graphic contrasts. While the contrite in heart know perfect peace, the wicked experience the very opposite. They are like the troubled sea: they are not at rest with themselves, they are not at rest with others, and they certainly are not at rest with God. As the troubled sea crashes on to the shoreline casting up mire and mud, so the wicked cast up the results of their corrupt and sinful lives. Society is strewn with the flotsam and jetsam. The fruit of their lips is not praise, but blasphemy and filth.

There is a verse of Scripture that puzzles me: 'Now I saw a new heaven and a new earth, for the first heaven and the first earth had passed away. Also, there was no more sea' (Revelation 21:1). Why will there be no more sea in the new heaven and the new earth? An incident in my life shed great light on the subject.

I was preaching in the fishing town of Buckie in Scotland. One afternoon one of the local Ministers took me to see his Church at Findochty, a village close at hand. There, on a steep hill above the harbour, stood the Church. "Observe the men walking on the leeward side of the Church," he said. So I watched as several men paced across from the Church wall to the edge of the hill and back. "They are retired seamen," he said, "and they are walking the length of their boat. Notice that they walk sideways, for you cannot walk straight in a fishing boat when it is at sea. They are restless, after a life at sea." I watched as another man joined them, and he too immediately began the restless, sideways walking – up and down, up and down!

Next morning the thought suddenly occurred to me that there was a connection between what those men were doing, and the text in Revelation, 'there shall be no more sea.' Today's verse is the connection. The sea is restless, its waves at the shore never stop crashing. This is the image used by Isaiah to epitomise the stance of the impenitent. "There is no peace," says my God, "for the wicked." There will be perfect peace in heaven, so there will be no more sea.

When I rose to speak at the morning service, I decided to mention my thinking on the non-existence of the sea in the new heaven and the new earth. Afterwards a lady approached me. Her father had spent a lifetime as a fisherman. "Men walking up and down beside the Church?" she said; "you want to see my father when he has his friends in for the evening, as he paces up and down the front room!" So, men of Findochty, thank you for your insight. May the perfect rest of the just be yours forever.

"Cry aloud, spare not; lift up your voice like a trumpet; tell My people their transgression, and the house of Jacob their sins. Yet they seek Me daily, and delight to know My ways, as a nation that did righteousness, and did not forsake the ordinance of their God. They ask of Me the ordinances of justice; they take delight in approaching God." Isaiah 58:1-2.

The Lord now commands His prophet to cry with a full throat, to lift up his voice like a trumpet, to declare their rebellion to the unfaithful in Israel, and their sins to the house of Jacob. What God really detests about His people's behaviour is their self-righteousness. From the outward appearance, they look like a people who conformed to the ways and ordinances of God. They enjoyed approaching God in their external religion. The sad fact was, they were hollow: there was no substance to it at all. In their hearts they were not contrite, nor was there true communion and fellowship with the Lord.

Some scholars see the background to this, as a great company of Jews being called on the Day of Atonement. The people are fasting in preparation for cleansing from sin. Isaiah stands up right in the middle of the solemn service, and, with a voice like a trumpet-blast, he startles them. He then gives them God's opinion of their behaviour. It was totally unexpected; they never imagined that God would condemn them.

A word to waken us up is always good for us, even if it comes in the most unexpected circumstances. Such was the word given in 1978 by Alexander Solzhenitsyn as a Harvard commencement speech. These speeches are usually innocuous. But this one created a huge stir in the media, and started a debate that shook the cultural and intellectual circles in America. It was entitled, *A world split apart*. Solzhenitsyn maintained that the world had become dangerously split, culturally, economically, and philosophically. He said that it was wrong for Westerners to assume that all global cultures were lining up to follow in the West's path. He claimed that the Bible's wisdom was true: a kingdom divided against itself cannot stand. He warned that in Western Culture an unhealthy reliance was put upon the legal process for solving social problems, and coping with injustice. He declared that freedom in the United States had deteriorated into hedonistic self-indulgence, which left society defenceless against evils like pornography and crime. He criticised the media for its invasion of privacy and its refusal to acknowledge errors. He proposed that the West had become spiritually exhausted, and could not provide a legitimate model for Russia to follow, once the Communist rule had gone. He said that the ideas that came to the fore at the Renaissance were the primary reason for the West's current weakness: that men and women are independent of God, responsible to no one but themselves. He warned that materialism, and a widespread abandonment of the belief that we are subordinate to God, meant that we are approaching a major crisis. Only a return to Christian spirituality would produce a way out of the crisis, and there was no other way out but upward.

The New York Times called Solzhenitsyn 'dangerous.' *The Washington Post* said he didn't understand Western society. One famous American commentator said Solzhenitsyn's speech sounded like the wanderings of a mind split apart. Yet the speech was prophetic and powerfully relevant. It still is today, even after September 11th 2001.

Our text today highlights the power of a prophetic voice. Maybe in some speech, newspaper, radio interview, some public place this month, you'll get a chance to sound a prophetic voice, based on God's word. Give it full throat! There is no telling what it might do.

30ᵀᴴ AUGUST

'Why have we fasted,' they say, 'and You have not seen? Why have we afflicted our souls, and You take no notice?' *"In fact, in the day of your fast you find pleasure, and exploit all your labourers. Indeed you fast for strife and debate, and to strike with the fist of wickedness. You will not fast as you do this day, to make your voice heard on high."* Isaiah 58:3-4.

This is anything but a pleasant scene. Here are people who outwardly fast to the glory of God, but inwardly their motivation is to get something from God for themselves. We are not told exactly what was going on; but while they fasted they were exploiting their employees. Perhaps, while they had their days of fasting, their employees had to do double work, and were being driven too hard.

We also discover that those who were fasting were extremely irritable and bad tempered, with the whole thing ending in fist-fights. Quarrelling, physical and verbal violence, and exploitation, under a cloak of pious self-righteousness, was not the right basis for prayer. This behaviour did not enable their voice to be 'heard on high.'

I want to pick up on the motivation for their prayer life, which was to get something from God for themselves. Jesus told a very perceptive parable about this kind of behaviour (Matthew 20:1-16). Peter had just seen the rich young ruler walk away from commitment to Christ. "See, we have left all and followed You," he said. "Therefore what shall we have?" As part of His reply, Jesus told the parable of a landowner who went out early in the morning to hire labourers to work in his vineyard, and again at the third, sixth, ninth, and eleventh hour of the day. When the end of the day came, he paid the eleventh-hour workers the same as those he had hired in the early morning. The early-morning workers complained, saying, "These last men have worked only one hour, and you made them equal to us who have borne the burden and heat of the day."

All kinds of explanations have been offered as to the meaning of this parable; but the heart of its teaching lies in the answer of the owner of the vineyard: 'But he answered one of them and said, "Friend, I am doing you no wrong. Did you not agree with me for a denarius? Take what is yours and go your way. I wish to give this last man the same as to you. Is it not lawful for me to do what I wish with my own things?"

What did he mean? He meant that the early-morning workers had agreed to a denarius for their day's work. To all the other workers, the owner had said, "whatever is right I will give you." They had no contract, and were looking to the owner to give what was appropriate. Christ was exposing the wrong spirit in Peter. He wanted a contract, but God's service is not based on a contract. We must not say, 'Lord, if you give me such and such, then I will serve you.' We serve Him for His glory, and He gives what is right. In fact, He gives more than any contract could ever offer. If you serve Him with the right spirit, you will find you are not limited to any contract. We serve a God, 'who is able to do exceedingly abundantly above all that we ask or think' (Ephesians 3:20). No contract could match His generosity. Selah.

AUGUST 31ST

"Is it a fast that I have chosen, a day for a man to afflict his soul? Is it to bow down his head like a bulrush, and to spread out sackcloth and ashes? Would you call this a fast, and an acceptable day to the Lord? Is this not the fast that I have chosen: to loose the bonds of wickedness, to undo the heavy burdens, to let the oppressed go free, and that you break every yoke?" Isaiah 58:5-6.

God now describes the kind of fast-days that please Him. Is it a day in which people hypocritically go through the pain of denial, humbling themselves meaninglessly, like the nodding of a reed in the wind, parading around in sackcloth and ashes, without true repentance? Is this the kind of fast-day that God likes? Is it acceptable to the Lord?

Just as the Sabbath was a celebration of freedom from slavery, fast-days were also about liberty. While fasting, there was nothing to stop them spending their time breaking bonds of injustice, lifting burdens from people's lives, relieving oppression, breaking totally unnecessary yokes. Wouldn't you like to meet people like that at any time, not just on fast-days?

Jesus sets this kind of ministry in a beautiful context. "Moreover,' he said, "when you fast, do not be like the hypocrites, with a sad countenance. For they disfigure their faces that they may appear to men to be fasting. Assuredly, I say to you, they have their reward. But you, when you fast, anoint your head and wash your face, so that you do not appear to men to be fasting, but to your Father who is in the secret place; and your Father who sees in secret will reward you openly" (Matthew 6:16-18). The person who is fasting should do it in a way that no one would ever know.

I know no better example of this than Esther. The story is familiar. An evil man had risen in Persia, bringing about a holocaust for its Jewish inhabitants. Esther is challenged by Mordecai to do something about it. Taking her life in her hands, she decides to go in before the king to attempt to bring about the salvation of her people. She sends a fascinating message to Mordecai: "Go, gather all the Jews who are present in Shushan, and fast for me; neither eat nor drink for three days, night or day. My maids and I will fast likewise. And so I will go to the king, which is against the law; and if I perish, I perish!"

When she got there, she invited the king and the evil plotter, Haman, to a banquet. How would Esther have had time to prepare such a banquet? Even when you don't have to do the nitty-gritty of laying out everything yourself, such banquets take time to prepare. So, when did she prepare it? It must have been during the three days that she was fasting, but to look at her you would never have known that she was fasting. The result of her actions was that huge numbers of her people were freed from oppression and injustice. This is still commemorated in the Jewish festival, Purim, celebrated on the 14th and 15th days of the month Adar (February-March). Why not be an Esther for someone today?

September

This photograph shows a linen warp at the back of a weaving loom. This is part of the progression of converting yarn into fabric. In the Bible, God describes His love of Jerusalem as that of finding her 'thrown out into the open field,' naked on the day she was born; but caring for her and clothing her in 'fine linen' and making her 'exceedingly beautiful.'

"Is it not to share your bread with the hungry, and that you bring to your house the poor who are cast out; when you see the naked, that you cover him, and not hide yourself from your own flesh? Then your light shall break forth like the morning, your healing shall spring forth speedily, and your righteousness shall go before you; the glory of the Lord shall be your rear guard. Then you shall call, and the Lord will answer; you shall cry, and He will say, 'Here I am.'" Isaiah 58:7-9a.

Here Isaiah gives God's people some guidelines for activities in their fast-days. He suggests that they share their bread with the hungry, open their homes to the homeless, clothe those who are shivering and unclad, and make sure that, while they are busy ministering to others, they do not neglect those in their own homes.

The resulting spiritual blessings of such activity are far reaching. First, lives will have a fresh beginning: it will be like a new dawn. Isn't that what you would like in your life? If we are living self-centred lives, they will get more and more depressing. Open up your life to helping others, and you will be amazed at what will happen. My publisher, Dr. Samuel Lowry, sometimes points out that so many people live their lives as if the world owes them something. That is a miserable way of life. Reach out to others in need, and the light of what you do will rise as the dawn of a new day.

The second consequence of a ministry to others is healing. The Hebrew word used in our text is of 'new flesh growing over an old wound' (Alec Motyer, *Isaiah*, IVP, p.362). Have you ever been wounded by all kinds of things in your life? Have people said terrible things about you? Have they been ruthless, say, in seeking to draw your business customers away? Have people lied to you? Maybe you have been a hypocrite yourself, and have been wounded by the inconsistency of your own life? Repent of it, reach out to people in need, and your wounds will heal. Don't let those who have hurt you hold you back from ministering to those who need you.

The third outcome of a ministry to others will be 'security with righteousness as a protective advance guard, and glory as a rear guard' (Motyer, IVP, p.362). Isaiah's superb images are at work once more. We have read of obedience to the Lord resulting in righteousness, like the powerful waves of mid-ocean. Now, righteousness, or doing that which is right with the Lord, is described as being like the advance guard of a great army, clearing the way for a coming victory, getting rid of oppression and evil. The glory of the Lord, or the personal presence of the Lord, will protect from behind. What a lifestyle! And what's more, your prayers will be answered promptly.

"If you take away the yoke from your midst, the pointing of the finger, and speaking wickedness . . ." Isaiah 58:9b.

A life of ministry to others and a commitment to doing away with oppression in our society is highly commendable. However, there is something we must make sure to exterminate. It is the habit of pointing the finger at others, with malicious or evil intent. The only other occurrence of this phrase comes in Proverbs 6:

'A worthless person, a wicked man, walks with a perverse mouth; he winks with his eyes, he shuffles his feet, he points with his fingers; perversity is in his heart; he devises evil continually, he sows discord. Therefore, his calamity shall come suddenly; suddenly he shall be broken without remedy.' Proverbs 6: 12-15.

Could there be a greater antithesis to what God would have us to be, as described in Isaiah chapter 58, than the person of Proverbs 6? Instead of extending his soul to the hungry, and seeking to satisfy the afflicted soul, he is out to devise unbelief; to sow discord instead of righteousness and love. This man makes his eyes, his feet and his fingers instruments of unrighteousness (see Romans 6:13-19). He is a pest to society, whereas the righteous are a blessing. Wouldn't it be a shame if, in the midst of pouring out our lives in a ministry to others, we spoil it by picking up one of this man's horrible traits, and demean people by pointing the finger at them? It is so easy to do. By slipping in a little story about someone, that 'brings them down a peg or two,' we can hint that we are superior.

I sometimes smile at the story told of the little man in the grey coat. It is only a story, but it is a very good parable. The local church had invited a guest preacher, and he was standing at the door shaking hands with his congregation as they were leaving. A little man in a grey coat came along, and said, "You used notes, and they weren't worth reading." He then went out the front door, entered the building again by a back door, and joined the queue of people waiting to shake hands with the preacher. This time he said, "You are a liberal, and we are not having you back again." He repeated the process quite a few times, throwing in all kinds of critical comments. As the preacher was leaving, he said to a church officer, "I have had a good time today, but could I ask a question: who is the little man in the grey coat?" "Oh! Don't worry about him;" replied the officer, "he only repeats what he hears other people saying." The finger-pointers were busy that day. Don't be one of them this Sunday.

SEPTEMBER 3RD

"If you extend your soul to the hungry and satisfy the afflicted soul, then your light shall dawn in the darkness, and your darkness shall be as the noonday. The Lord will guide you continually, and satisfy your soul in drought, and strengthen your bones; you shall be like a watered garden, and like a spring of water, whose waters do not fail." Isaiah 58: 10-11.

W onderful blessings are promised to those who care for others. Even the godly have rough times, but the Lord will always be their guide. Unfailingly, He will show them which way to turn, and which road to take. Just as night becomes noonday, God will send light into the dark circumstances of their lives, so impossible circumstances become the opportunity for the display of God's power and glory.

As the scorching, unrelenting sun, and deadly drought creeps forward across the unprotected land, so the godly face bleak periods in their lives; but the Lord will give strength to face such frightening times. In those bleak days they will experience refreshment, as a well-watered garden experiences the touch of a caring gardener with his hose or watering can. The Lord will be like a spring, whose waters never fail.

Let me take the phrase, 'you will be as a well watered garden,' and make a New Testament application. I sometimes think about Apollos. He was a Jew who came from Alexandria in Egypt. Somehow or other, he had travelled to Israel and had heard John the Baptist preach. Moved by what he heard, he had repented of sin and was baptised by John. Apollos taught the Jewish faith from the Scriptures, and one day he arrived at Ephesus. Paul's two friends, Aquila and Priscilla, heard him, and they saw clearly that there were gaps in his spiritual knowledge. So they invited him to their home and explained to him the way of God more accurately. Now, fully equipped, this gifted man began to exercise an incredible ministry amongst the emerging churches.

For the Christians, the early days of the New Testament church were harsh. The unrelenting sun of persecution scorched down upon a very vulnerable people. They were exposed to Jewish religious persecution, and often to Roman contempt. Idolaters did not take kindly to the Christians' claim of only one true God. Into these burgeoning churches came Apollos. Without any trace of jealousy, Paul called him 'the watering can' of the New Testament church: 'I planted, Apollos watered, but God gave the increase. So then neither he who plants is anything, nor he who waters, but God who gives the increase. Now he who plants and he who waters are one, and each one will receive his own reward according to his own labour. For we are God's fellow workers, you are God's field, you are God's building' (1 Corinthians 3:6-9).

Isaiah is saying that the Lord is our source of refreshment, vitality and strength in bleak times; and, drawing on that strength, we too can be a refreshment and blessing to others. Apollos was 'eloquent,' 'mighty in the Scriptures,' 'fervent in spirit' (Acts 18:24, 25). I have met people who were eloquent, but not mighty in the Scriptures. I have met people who were mighty in the Scriptures, but they were not eloquent. I have met people who were eloquent, mighty in the Scriptures, but not fervent. To meet somebody who is all three, now there is refreshment indeed!

SEPTEMBER 4TH

"Those from among you shall build the old waste places; you shall raise up the foundations of many generations; and you shall be called the Repairer of the Breach, the Restorer of Streets to Dwell In." Isaiah 58: 12.

The operative word in the passage of Scripture we have been studying is the word 'if.' 'If' God's people do away with the yoke of oppression, pointing the finger, and malicious talk; and 'if' they spend themselves on behalf of the hungry and satisfy the needs of the oppressed, then the blessings will flow. Now Isaiah speaks of the practical outcome of this blessing. If they do what God asks: rebuild the ancient ruins and raise up age-old foundations, they will get a new name – 'Repairer of Broken Walls, Restorer of Streets with Dwellings.'

At the risk of repeating myself, I want to mention again that in the past few days I have been in the beautiful county of Bedfordshire in England. I have been involved in the presentation of a video on the life of John Bunyan, and we have been filming at the local scenes that inspired his classic work *The Pilgrim's Progress*. We filmed the famous wicket gate in the North door of Elstow Parish Church, and the High Cross at Stevington. Then we went down the hill to the site reputed to be the inspiration for the sepulchre into which Christian's burdens rolled, never to be seen again. It is an ancient well. We filmed the superb stain glass windows at the 'Bunyan Meeting,' a present day church where Bunyan was once Pastor. The windows depict scenes from *The Pilgrims Progress*. I even had the privilege of interviewing a lady who once lived in Bunyan's house.

Of all the scenes that inspired me (and there were many), I think the Rectory at St. Mary's Parish Church in Bedford was the most moving, because of what happened there in the life of John Bunyan. In those days a Pastor called John Gifford occupied the house. As Bunyan came to faith, he went through a very troubled time, and he had many questions to ask. Imagine a humble tinker, coming to John Gifford in that Rectory to pour out deep questions about his soul and salvation. Gifford spent hours listening to Bunyan, explaining the scriptures, and patiently leading him to that moment when he finally put all his trust in Jesus Christ.

In *The Pilgrim's Progress*, Gifford's Rectory became the House of the Interpreter, where Christian learned many spiritual lessons about the Christian faith. It was there he met Patience and Passion, saw the man in the iron cage, witnessed the fire into which oil was poured on one side and water on the other. It was there he saw the figure with a book in his hand, and his eyes lifted heavenward. Today *The Pilgrim's Progress* is outsold only by the Bible. Millions upon millions of people have been spiritually blessed by it. Yet a huge debt is owed to the kindly and patient John Gifford, who has become known immortally as 'The Interpreter.' So, teachers, get to your work. In their shattered land, the godly Israelites would become known as 'Repairers of Broken Walls, Restorers of Streets for Dwelling.' Tell me, what name will you be known by?

SEPTEMBER 5TH

"If you turn away your foot from the Sabbath, from doing your pleasure on My holy day, and call the Sabbath a delight, the holy day of the Lord honourable, and shall honour Him, not doing your own ways, nor finding your own pleasure, nor speaking your own words . . ." Isaiah 58: 13.

The Lord is now calling Israel to the true and proper keeping of the Sabbath, just as He had called them to true and proper fasting. And, just as they had been hypocritical on their fast days, so they were now being hypocritical on Sabbath days. They engaged in living for their own pleasure, pursuing their own ways, and engaging in any business as if it were their own. There was no rest in this kind of activity on any day, never to speak of the

Sabbath. God said, "Stop bringing meaningless offerings! Your incense is detestable to me. New Moons, Sabbaths and convocations – I cannot bear your evil assemblies. Your New Moon festivals and your appointed feasts my soul hates. They have become a burden to me; I am weary of bearing them" (Isaiah 1:13, 14, NIV).

One particular thing that the Lord abhorred was His people's talk on the Sabbath. They were speaking idle words: words of no value, gossip, boasting, mere talk. As Shakespeare put it, 'Words, words, words.'

There is an inspiring Christian in Scotland, of whom I think the world. His name is William McLachlan, and he lives in the town of Airdrie. He once explained to me how that, when flying kites in Scotland, children speak of putting a 'divot to their draigon.' This means that when their kites (draigons) will not fly, they get a piece of grass and soil (a divot) and tie it to the string of their kites. It gives weight to the kite and it will soar.

> Boys, when flying kites,
> Haul in their white-winged birds.
> You cannot do that,
> When you're flying words.

Remember, once a word is spoken, it is gone. You can never recall it; though you might long to do so. Our Lord warned that we will have to give an account for every idle word we have spoken – that is, for every unprofitable word we have uttered. How, then, can we be sure that our words are profitable? How can we ensure that they have weight? Jesus gave the solution. To hypocritical Pharisees, He said:

"Make a tree good and its fruit will be good, or make a tree bad and its fruit will be bad, for a tree is recognised by its fruit. You brood of vipers, how can you who are evil say anything good? For out of the overflow of the heart the mouth speaks. The good man brings good things out of the good stored up in him, and the evil man brings evil things out of the evil stored up in him" (Matthew 12:33, NIV).

So, Christian, live a Spirit-filled life, and the fruit of your lips will have value and influence beyond price.

SEPTEMBER 6TH

"Then you shall delight yourself in the Lord; and I will cause you to ride on the high hills of the earth, and feed you with the heritage of Jacob your father. The mouth of the Lord has spoken." Isaiah 58:14.

The other evening I was staying at the Hind Hotel in Wellingborough, Bedfordshire. As I climbed the stairs to bed in this hotel, where Cromwell and his officers slept on the night before the Battle of Naseby, I noticed a statue of a golden hind on the balcony. On the way home I visited the grounds of Woburn Abbey, and watched the famous herd of deer grazing in the evening sunlight, as the swallows arched home. The young deer raced about, swiftly and nimbly. It was all very memorable. It led me to think of the Scriptures where God promises to give me feet like hinds' feet. Harts are stags, or male deer; hinds are female deer. The fleetness of the hind is referred to by both David and Habakkuk, almost 400 years apart.

'He makes my feet like the feet of the deer (hinds, AV), and sets me on my high places.' Psalm 18:33.

'Though the fig tree may not blossom, nor fruit be on the vines; though the labour of the olive may fail, and the fields yield no food; though the flock may be cut off from the fold, and there be no herd in the stalls – yet I will rejoice in the Lord, I will joy in the God of my salvation. The Lord God is my strength; He will make my feet like deer's feet, and He will make me walk on my high hills.' Habakkuk 3:17-19.

Isaiah, too, writes of joy in the Lord, and of His people being able to ride on the heights of the land. As Habakkuk teaches, no matter how difficult our circumstances the Lord will enable us to rise above them. Sometimes we call it 'higher ground.' I remember so well going to see my friend, David Lennox. A terrorist bomb had scarred his face, and I struggled to comfort him. "If God can bring order out of the chaos of the cross, He can bring order out of the chaos of my face," he said gently. That is what I call being able to walk on the heights of the land, despite adverse circumstances.

Do I write for someone today who feels they will never rise to higher ground? Is your experience like Bunyan's *Slough of Despond*? Then remember there are stepping-stones right across that bog; you will soon reach higher ground, and be as nimble as any hind. In fact, you will reach the Celestial City, and gaze on Him who is exalted far above all.

September 7th

Behold, the Lord's hand is not shortened, that it cannot save; nor His ear heavy, that it cannot hear. But your iniquities have separated you from your God; and your sins have hidden His face from you, so that He will not hear. Isaiah 59:1-2.

How often have you heard the question, "Why would a loving God permit this to happen?" God is blamed for being impotent and indifferent. But it is not God's impotence that makes Israel appear to be out of His reach. It is their iniquities. The sins of God's people have alienated them from God, to the extent that He will not hear them. His arm can still save, His ear can still hear, but their sins have separated them from Him. God is not the problem – they are!

The phrase that grips me in these verses is, 'your sins have hidden His face from you.' In the Old Testament, the word 'face' is used literally, figuratively, and idiomatically. 'My face,' often means nothing more than an idiomatic way of saying, 'I.' To 'spit in someone's face,' is an expression of absolute contempt (see Numbers 12:14). To 'harden the face,' means to harden oneself against any sort of appeal (Proverbs 21:29). To 'fall on one's face,' was a sign of frustration before God (Genesis 17:17). To 'set one's face,' was a sign of determination (Luke 9:51). To 'cover one's face,' was an expression of mourning (2 Samuel

19:4). Here, in Isaiah, we have the averted face of God, which is the equivalent of disapproval or rejection.

Who in the 21st Century has not thrilled to John Rutter's setting of Aaron's Blessing? It is one of the most stirring pieces of music in our civilisation. The words are exquisite:

"The Lord bless you and keep you; the Lord make His face to shine upon you, and be gracious to you; the Lord lift up His countenance upon you and give you peace" (Numbers 6:24-26).

To have the Lord lift up the light of His countenance upon us – that is the greatest blessing we can know. To have His approval is the greatest approval possible.

In Revelation 6:15-16, we read of a day, when

'the kings of the earth, the great men, the rich men, the commanders, the mighty men, every slave and every free man, hid themselves in the caves and in the rocks of the mountains, and said to the mountains and rocks, "Fall on us and hide us from the face of Him who sits on the throne and from the wrath of the Lamb!"'

The contrast between having the Lord's approval, and experiencing His wrath could not be greater. Yet, there is hope for sinners. We might hide, as it were, our faces from the despised and crucified One (Isaiah 53:3); but when we come to Him in repentance and faith, we will know His forgiveness. Then it is our responsibility to add to our faith 'virtue, to virtue knowledge, to knowledge self-control, to self-control perseverance, to perseverance godliness, to godliness brotherly kindness, and to brotherly kindness love. For if these things are yours and abound, you will be neither barren nor unfruitful in the knowledge of our Lord Jesus Christ' (2 Peter 1:5-8).

May we never have to know the experience of Peter on the night of his denial of Christ, when the Lord turned and looked upon him. What words could describe that look?

SEPTEMBER 8TH

For your hands are defiled with blood, and your fingers with iniquity; your lips have spoken lies, your tongue has muttered perversity. Isaiah 59:3.

Isaiah now gets specific. He spells out the sins that have separated God's people from Him, and shows them up for what they really are. Four parts of the human body are identified as proof of widespread corruption. They have been guilty of violence; their *hands* are stained with blood. The Hebrew word means, 'the grip of the hand.' They have had personal involvement in hurting and even killing others. They are a guilty people. Their *fingers* have been involved in constructing altars to false gods (Isaiah 17:8). Their *lips* have been guilty of lying, and their *tongues* are deviant. The deep-rooted infection of sin has ruined their lives and witness. God is not fooled by their outward display of fasting and Sabbath keeping.

I live in a land, sadly famous for its violence, and for most of my life I have been surrounded by it. Recently I listened to a Christian leader called Ajith Fernando tell of his native Sri Lanka, where recently thousands of people have been killed in ethnic fighting. During a particularly violent period in his city of Colombo, he told of bodies floating down the river every day; some of them were people that he knew.

I sometimes wonder if people who murder others ever have any conscience about what they do. Does it ever haunt them that their hands are stained with blood? Just a few days ago I was challenged by the fact that it happens even in the land where I live. I was listening to Bishop Ken Clark preaching. Suddenly he stopped in his sermon, and played a recording of Senator George Mitchell, Chancellor of Queens University, speaking on radio about a Protestant paramilitary who had violently killed a Roman Catholic 'friend.' Before he hanged himself, the paramilitary left a suicide note in which, amongst other things, he said that the day he killed his 'friend' he had lost something that he had never got back again. He was tired now, and decided to put an end to it all.

Is there someone reading these lines, who is tempted to use violence for political ends? Or for personal ends? Let the words of that paramilitary warn you that, if you do violence to anyone, you will lose something that you will not get back again. As Frances Ridley Havergal wrote in her famous hymn, let Christ take your hands, lips, feet, silver and gold, heart and life. He will make something of them. The use of violence, threats and bullying, will lead only to remorse.

SEPTEMBER 9TH

No one calls for justice, nor does any plead for truth. They trust in empty words and speak lies; they conceive evil and bring forth iniquity. Isaiah 59: 4.

This is a very poignant diagnosis of society. The rot that had set in, had begun at the top. There were no moral leaders to take a public stand for justice and truth. There was a legal system, but the people were using it for illegal purposes. The immoral state of Israel was such that it trusted in empty arguments, and used lies as a basis for its actions. Mischief was conceived, and trouble was born. When leaders fail to stand up for what is right, who will do it?

Isaiah's diagnosis is truly relevant to today's world. Take the financial world in Western Society recently, with the WorldCom and Enron scandals: lies and corruption on a multi-billion dollar scale. Just recently I lifted a copy of *The Times*, and read the headline, 'Judge damns foul-mouthed culture of City bullies.' In a 69-page indictment, Mr. Justice McCombe exposed how the Square Mile 'has imported the foul language and obscene culture of block-buster movies with everyday life' (July 30th 2002). After three weeks of evidence, the Judge concluded that, in the world of Stockbrokers and their bosses, 'the use of obscenities was at all times commonplace. It seemed to be language reminiscent of the quick fire exchanges in American office scenes, familiar from the cinema; using language that, years ago, would have been wholly unacceptable, but now is, perhaps regrettably, common place in many places of work, as the machismo image of Hollywood is imported into real life.' "Perhaps regrettable," the Judge says! Why didn't he say, 'wholly unacceptable'? Why didn't he condemn it outright?

Ah, Wilberforce, you should be living at this hour! In 1787 he persuaded King George III to reissue a proclamation for the encouragement of devotion to God and good behaviour. The proclamation called for a return to public worship in churches on Sunday, and for judges, sheriffs and justices to be 'very vigilant and strict in the discovery and punishment of people for excessive swearing and cursing . . . or other dissolute, immoral or disorderly practices.' That summer he travelled far and wide, calling on people all across England to recruit and support his new Proclamation Society, to assist in carrying the King's Proclamation on Good Behaviour into effect.

If you stand before his statue outside his birthplace in Hull, you will read a very moving statement: 'The world owes him the abolition of slavery, and England owes him the reformation of manners.' In Georgian times, the word 'manners' was used for behaviour. How times have changed!

SEPTEMBER 10ᵀᴴ

They hatch vipers' eggs and weave the spider's web; he who eats of their eggs dies, and from that which is crushed a viper breaks out. Their webs will not become garments, nor will they cover themselves with their works; their works are works of iniquity, and the act of violence is in their hands. Isaiah 59: 5-6.

The society in Israel has come to trust in that which is unstable and worthless. People are not trusting in the Lord; so no matter what else they trust in the result will be disaster.

Two metaphors are chosen by Isaiah to describe what has happened. The first is the hatching of basilisk eggs. If you eat the egg you will die, and if you tread on the egg you will disturb the snake, and it will spring out and bite you. Evil is never going to be good for you. The second metaphor shows how valueless and unsatisfying sin actually is. It is like depending on a spider's web to clothe you. These people cannot cover themselves with their weaving of evil. Listen to Bildad's comment: 'whose confidence shall be cut off, and whose trust is a spider's web. He leans on his house, but it does not stand. He holds it fast, but it does not endure' (Job 8:14-15). The clothing that the Lord provides for us is far superior to the clothing of evil.

At times I have pondered the amazing story of Ruth's approach to Boaz. Ruth had a claim on him as a kinsman-redeemer, after the death of her husband. Her mother-in-law, Naomi, told her to go to the threshing floor, uncover Boaz's feet, and lie down. Obviously this was not an inducement to immorality, as the Law of Moses would have brought death to Ruth for such behaviour. It was an indication that she was laying claim to her rights. When she was discovered, Ruth asked Boaz to spread the corner of his garment over her, 'since you are a kinsman-redeemer.' It must have been a sign of redemption. "The Lord bless you my daughter," said Boaz, "I will do all that you ask." The next day he did not rest until she was redeemed and became his wife. Ruth's grandson was King David; and from the seed of her womb down many generations came the Saviour of the World.

I think of the Lord Jesus, my Kinsman-Redeemer, going to Calvary for me, and in repentance and faith I lay claim to His garment of righteousness. It moves me deeply, when I think that the soldiers gambled for His garments, even as He was being crucified. He was stripped, that I might be clothed. Isaiah teaches that all my righteousnesses are like filthy rags (64:6). But Christ has provided for me a garment that will take me to the greatest of all weddings, the Marriage Supper of the Lamb. Clothed in His righteousness alone, I can take my place there.

Then I remember that He cast aside His outer clothing, wrapped a towel around His waist, and washed His disciples' feet. He encouraged them to be kind to each other: "For I have given you an example, that you should do as I have done to you. Most assuredly, I say to you, a servant is not greater than his master; nor is he who is sent greater than he who sent him" (John 13:15, 16). Let's set about working to improve our serve.

SEPTEMBER 11TH

Their feet run to evil, and they make haste to shed innocent blood; their thoughts are thoughts of iniquity; wasting and destruction are in their paths. The way of peace they have not known, and there is no justice in their ways; they have made themselves crooked paths; whoever takes that way shall not know peace. Isaiah 59:7-8.

Here is the litany of a morally bankrupt society. When godly, moral standards break down, moral corruption is contagious: trouble-making is everywhere, disruptive behaviour is common, people rush to sin. Even as I write, on this infamous day, they are swift to shed innocent blood. When people are morally corrupt, their thoughts are evil, and wherever they go they leave a trail of ruin and destruction behind them. They destroy many of the lives they touch.

Thank God, this world is not the final home of the righteous. We wait for the new world. We are passing through to a better place. It is not possible for those who do not allow the Lord to have His way in their lives to enjoy the way of peace. They follow their own paths, to their own hurt. They make crooked paths for themselves, and do not submit to God's judgment as to what is right or wrong. No one walking in such paths will find peace.

If you play in the snow with a group of children, you will find that they love making patterns with their footprints. If one of those children were to ask you, 'How can I make a straight line with my footprints?' what would you say? The secret is to get your eye on an object ahead of you, and walk towards it. And so, in His Word God has set the standard for right living. If we keep that standard as our aim, we shall make straight paths for our feet and we will know peace.

Will God judge those who kill, maim, shed innocent blood, and bring waste and destruction in their paths? If they do not repent before death, they will face the wrath of God in eternal punishment. If God did not judge them, He would have to apologise to Sodom and Gomorrah.

Therefore justice is far from us, nor does righteousness overtake us; we look for light, but there is darkness! for brightness, but we walk in blackness! We grope for the wall like the blind, and we grope as if we had no eyes; we stumble at noonday as at twilight; we are as dead men in desolate places. We all growl like bears, and moan sadly like doves; we look for justice, but there is none; for salvation, but it is far from us. Isaiah 59: 9-11.

What is it at the heart of these sad verses? Barry Webb points out that it is a lament for the absence of justice. Justice here means a life that is conformed to the Lord's decisions. It is a state of affairs that should exist amongst God's people, when they live in obedience to His Word. He also points out that it refers to the right state of affairs that will exist when God has fully established His Kingdom on earth. This final salvation has not yet come, and only God can bring this deliverance.

So, justice in both senses is in today's text. Firstly, it is in the future. Darkness is still in and around God's people. As a blind person, they are groping along a wall but cannot find an exit. Pagan priorities still control them. Secondly, true justice was lacking among God's people themselves. They longed for the coming justice:

'Until the spirit is poured out upon us from on high, and the wilderness becomes a fruitful field, and the fruitful field is counted as a forest. Then justice will dwell in the wilderness, and righteousness remain in the fruitful field. The work of righteousness will be peace, and the effect of righteousness, quietness and assurance forever.' Isaiah 32:15-17.

But the lack of justice made them impatient, like growling, angry bears, and frustrated, like moaning doves. Despite the fact that, in the Book of Isaiah, this is certainly one of the lowest points that the people of God get to, all is not lost. Hope lies in the fact that they now at least care about their state. The prophet has changed his pronouns, from 'they,' to 'we.' The people are now taking the blame for the sin that has separated them from God's righteousness and justice. "Blessed are those who mourn," said the Lord Jesus, "for they shall be comforted . . . Blessed are those who hunger and thirst for righteousness, for they shall be filled" (Matthew 5: 4, 6). If you do care about the spiritual and moral state of your life, and that of your nation, there is hope both for it and for you.

For our transgressions are multiplied before You, and our sins testify against us; for our transgressions are with us, and as for our iniquities, we know them: in transgressing and lying against the Lord, and departing from our God, speaking oppression and revolt, conceiving and uttering from the heart words of falsehood. Isaiah 59:12-13.

We are back in Court! This time Sin is the Prosecutor, and the Lord is the Judge (Motyer, *Isaiah* IVP p.367). All of us have sat in this Court, and realised that the case against us is watertight. Whether we are Jews like these people, or Gentiles, we have all missed the mark.

'For there is no partiality with God, for as many have sinned without the law will also perish without law, and as many have sinned in the law will be judged by the law. . . . For there is no difference; for all have surely sinned and come short of the glory of God' (Romans 2:11-12; 3:22-23).

As we sit in the Court, the Prosecutor stacks up the evidence against us. We have constantly transgressed and wilfully rebelled against God. God knows our specific sins, and they testify against us. Our transgressions are something we are constantly aware of; and we must acknowledge our iniquities. The Judge has been offended, for we have deliberately sinned against the Lord. We have turned our backs on God, and conceived falsehood in our hearts that has surfaced on our lips.

It all starts in the heart. The very first captivity we read about in the Book of Judges is an eight-year captivity to the king of the very country from which Abraham had been called to start the Hebrew nation! The problem started when the Children of Israel married those who did not love the Lord. Satan had used those whom their hearts loved to lead Israel away; and it was by the heart the Lord brought them back.

The restoration came through a Judge called Othniel. He fell in love with Achsah, Caleb's daughter, and eventually married her. Achsah was the right woman for Othniel, and their union led the nation to blessing. Eventually the Lord delivered Cushan-Rishathaim, King of Mesopotamia, into Othniel's hand, and the land had rest for forty years

'My son, give me your heart, and let your eyes observe my ways' (Proverbs 23:26). God does not ask for pompous ceremony or a magnificent building. He does not ask for your home, your money, your ambitions, or even your hands, feet, or tongue. He asks for the motivating principle behind all that we are and do. He says, 'give Me your heart.' Everything hangs on this point. Give God your heart, and incalculable blessing will be yours. Withhold it, and incalculable ruin is certain. When your heart is truly the Lord's, lies and falsehood will disappear from your lips.

SEPTEMBER 14TH

Justice is turned back, and righteousness stands afar off; for truth is fallen in the street, and equity cannot enter. So truth fails, and he who departs from evil makes himself a prey. Then the Lord saw it, and it displeased Him that there was no justice. He saw that there was no man, and wondered that there was no intercessor; therefore His own arm brought salvation for Him; and His own righteousness, it sustained Him. Isaiah 59:14-16.

Since the beginning of Isaiah chapter 56, the Lord has been looking at the standing of His people. He has presented His ideal for them, and they have confessed how abysmally they have failed. Now we have a summary of the situation, and the Lord's reaction to it all.

First, justice – that is, a life conformed to the Lord's decisions – has been driven back. Any society which does that, is on the slide. Second, righteousness is sidelined. Third, truth has fallen in the street – it has stumbled and tripped over. Fourth, there is no room for fair-play. In public and private life, truth is missing. What is more, 'he who departs from evil makes himself a prey.' Not to participate in wrong, makes a person stand out and become the object of persecution. I wonder if there could just be someone reading this piece, who is in such a situation. You have stood up for justice, righteousness, truth and equity, at huge cost to yourself. In fact, you may be linked to a group who have experienced it together. Let me share an encouraging story with you. The full details are found in the book, *Lest Innocent Blood be Shed*, by Philip Hallie (Harper Collins Publishers Inc.).

An extraordinary thing occurred during the days of the Second World War. It was in Le Chambon, a small town of 3,000 people, located in German-occupied Southern France. A group of devout French Huguenots, encouraged by their indomitable Pastor, Andre Trocmé, and his wife Magda, took a stand against injustice, unrighteousness, and lies. They presented a letter to the Minister for Youth in Vichy, telling him that, if the Jews in their town received an order to let themselves be deported, or even examined, the Huguenots would encourage them to disobey orders, and then do their best to try to hide them. They based their action on the truths of the Christian gospel. The Minister turned pale and told them that these matters were not his affair, so they must speak to the Prefect. Prefect Bach was very angry, and told them that he had already received orders regarding Jews in their area. European Jews were being regrouped in Poland, where they would have houses and land. He then threatened the Pastor with deportation, but he and the Chambonnais were committed to sheltering the Jews and stood by their decision. Andre Trocmé was eventually arrested. Madame Trocmé courageously invited the very policemen who detained him to dinner!

A Jewish girl who had been rescued by the Chambonnais wrote these moving words:

"If today we are not bitter, like most survivors, it can only be due to the fact that we met people like the people of Le Chambon, who showed us simply that life can be different, that there are people who care, that people can live together and even risk their own lives for their fellow-man."

Those brave people saved more than 5,000 Jewish children, who would have been sent to the death camps. These children have risen up to call the people of Le Chambon 'blessed'.

Our text says that in such times, 'he who departs from evil makes himself a prey.' I think Pastor Trocmé and his people felt it was eternally worth it. If you and your friends are paying the price for standing up for justice, truth, and righteousness, you too will find that it is a price well worth paying.

SEPTEMBER 15TH

He saw that there was no man, and wondered that there was no intercessor; therefore His own arm brought salvation for Him; and His own righteousness, it sustained Him.
Isaiah 59:16.

N ow we read the Lord's reaction to the state of affairs amongst His people. As He surveyed the scene, He saw that there was no justice; and there was not a single person to correct the situation. What particularly astonished and appalled Him was that there was no intercessor. As God looks around your community, I wonder what He sees?

Is justice turned back, righteousness distanced, and truth fallen in the street? Are the people who depart from evil being persecuted? Is there no intercessor? "I sought for a man among them," said God "who would make a wall, and stand in the gap before Me on behalf of the land, that I should not destroy it; but I found no one" (Ezekiel 22:30). Could you be that intercessor?

Let me share another inspiring story. In 1815 Daniel O'Connell (he of O'Connell Street, Dublin, Ireland) shot and killed a man in a duel. The widow and mother of two children, 18 year-old Jane D'Esterre, fled in distress to the little town of Ecclefechan on the Scottish-English Border. Going down one day to a local river, Jane contemplated suicide. Suddenly she looked up, and there was a ploughboy, about her own age, beginning his work in the field across the river. He set about his work with such skill and meticulous attention to detail, that Jane became absorbed in watching him as with pride he turned his furrows. He was well known for whistling Christian hymns at his work. On the edge of death, Jane was jolted into life. "Why should I descend into self-pity?" she mused. Her two little children were entirely dependent upon her. If the ploughman was dedicated with such relish to his responsibility, she should return to Dublin and her responsibilities. Chastened, yet inspired, Jane returned to Ireland. Some weeks later, she came to faith in the Lord Jesus Christ.

After fourteen years, Jane married Captain John Guinness, the youngest son of Arthur Guinness, the famous Dublin brewer. She decided to pray consistently for her family, down through a dozen generations. That means she prayed for her children, her grandchildren, her great-grandchildren, her great-great-grandchildren, etc. If you trace Jane's line through that illustrious Guinness family, you will find the most outstanding succession of missionaries, Christian workers, pastors, ministers and Christian leaders.

One of them is my good friend, Dr. Os Guinness, whose mother was a missionary surgeon in China, and his father was the last doctor to the last Emperor. As I watch Os, making an impact for Christ on leaders across the world through his wonderful work with The Trinity Forum, I am reminded that he is Jane D'Esterre's great-great grandson! All work done for the glory of God is significant; but I often wonder, could the whistling ploughboy of Ecclefechan in that field so long ago ever have realised just how significant his would turn out to be?

SEPTEMBER 16TH

He saw that there was no man, and wondered that there was no intercessor; therefore His own arm brought salvation for Him; and His own righteousness, it sustained Him. For He put on righteousness as a breastplate, and a helmet of salvation on His head; He put on the garments of vengeance for clothing, and was clad with zeal as a cloak. According to their deeds, accordingly He will repay, fury to His adversaries, recompense to His enemies; the coastlands He will fully repay. Isaiah 59:16-18.

All of this corruption required action, and without the Lord's intervention His people could not be saved. Since there was no one to co-operate with God, He would bring about the salvation of His people Himself. God's work of salvation lies here in the future; but it is given in the past tense, because 'it expresses what the Lord has determined upon' (Motyer, *Isaiah*, IVP, p.368). Once again, this is the wonderful theme of His mighty arm: His personal strength in action to save the situation. He is the All-sufficient Lord: within Himself He has all that is needed for every situation. He puts on righteousness as a breastplate, and a helmet of salvation on His head. He puts on vengeance, or vindication, and zeal, like garments of clothing. He will never allow His character to be violated. The gates of hell will not prevail against His people. The Lord will have the ultimate victory.

"Isaiah's vision reaches near-apocalyptic proportions. It is too bold, too absolute, to be exhausted by any historical moment, short of the final one, which will bring history itself to an end" (Gary Webb, *The Message of Isaiah*, IVP, p.229). The coastlands referred to here, embrace the furthest nations of the Gentiles (W. E. Vine, *Expository Commentary on Isaiah*, Nelson, p.172). The day will come when the nations of the Gentiles will be federated against the Lord and against His Christ. They will be led by the Antichrist, the man of sin:

'. . . the man of sin is revealed, the son of perdition . . . who opposes and exalts himself above all that is called God . . . whom the Lord will consume with the breath of His mouth and destroy with the brightness of His coming.' 2 Thessalonians 2:3-8.

The Lord will show fury to His adversaries, and His enemies will receive what is their exact due.

Let us be inspired again by the fact that the Lord personally intervenes in world affairs. He does not stand by, and let history roll on in a random way – not even your own personal history. Let us heed the instructions in the Psalm about the Messiah's triumph and kingdom:

'Serve the Lord with fear, and rejoice with trembling. Kiss the Son, lest He be angry, and you perish in the way, when His wrath is kindled but a little. Blessed are all those who put their trust in Him.' Psalm 2:11, 12.

SEPTEMBER 17TH

So shall they fear the name of the Lord from the west, and His glory from the rising of the sun; when the enemy comes in like a flood, the Spirit of the Lord will lift up a standard against him. Isaiah 59:19.

The coming, final rebellion against the Lord, is described as being 'like a flood.' They will seem to be unstoppable, overwhelming all opposition. But then the Spirit of the Lord will intervene, and lift a banner against the enemy. All the forces of the Lord will rally to His banner, and there will be a great, world-wide victory. The Name of the Lord shall be feared from the West, and reverenced from the rising of the sun in the East:

'The wolf also shall dwell with the lamb . . . and a little child shall lead them . . . for the earth shall be full of the knowledge of the Lord as the waters cover the sea . . . In that day there shall be a Root of Jesse, who shall stand as a banner to the people; for the Gentiles shall seek Him, and His resting place shall be glorious.' Isaiah 11: 6, 9, 10.

Today's text has a wonderful application to our personal lives as well. Again and again history shows that, when the Lord's enemies would seem to be on the verge of completely crushing His truth and light, the Lord puts on His armour. The Spirit of God raises His banner, or standard, and the mighty Arm of the Lord brings victory. The Spirit of God has used all kinds of people to raise His standard. In the evil days before the Flood, He used Noah. Later we have people like Abraham and Joseph, Moses and Joshua, and, of course, the Judges. From little Samuel, listening to the Lord speaking at Shiloh, and Jotham on Mount Gerizim, to Paul at Mars Hill – the Scriptures inspire us with true stories of people who let the Spirit of God use them. Outside of the Scriptures, of course, there numerous stories of people who turned the flood of evil by the Spirit's power. One of my favourites is Jim Vaus.

After flying from Boston to New York in a little plane, I was privileged to visit one of the most fascinating characters I have ever met. Jim Vaus was a 'wire-tapper.' For example, he would intercept the racing results as they were transmitted from race meetings to betting shops. Before he released the results, he would place money on the winning horses, and make a huge personal profit. This man of crime went to hear Dr. Billy Graham preach the gospel in a large tent in Los Angeles. He repented of his sins, and trusted Christ as his Saviour. As a declaration of his new-found faith, he got one mile of telephone cable that he had stolen from the Bell Telephone Company, and gave it back to them! He dedicated himself to serving the Lord, and by the time I met him in his office he had become a living legend of the power of Christ to change lives. He was deeply into reaching young people for Christ in Harlem, where there had been a lot of gang warfare. His work was intensely practical. God had mightily used him to raise up a standard in His Name, to drive back a floodtide of violence.

So, today, try to remember that Christ's touch has not lost its ancient power. Where you live, He can use you to turn the tide of godlessness and evil.

SEPTEMBER 18TH

"The Redeemer will come to Zion, and to those who turn from transgression in Jacob," says the Lord. "As for Me," says the Lord, "this is My covenant with them: My Spirit who is upon you, and My words which I have put in your mouth, shall not depart from your mouth, nor from the mouth of your descendants, nor from the mouth of your descendants' descendants," says the Lord, "from this time and forevermore." Isaiah 59:20-21.

Again, the awesome introduction of the coming Redeemer surfaces in Isaiah's Prophecy. One day He will return to Zion to effect a final salvation. The Perfect Servant will rectify all the injustice, falsehood, unrighteousness and lack of equity in the world, and bring about the restoration of all things. His promised redemption is both to those 'in Jacob,' and to all those Gentiles who have turned from their transgressions.

Notice that He is a covenant-keeping Redeemer. For all those who love the Lord, this searching passage of Isaiah comes to an end in great encouragement. There are three personal pronouns: 'My covenant,' 'My Spirit,' and 'My words.' First, He is bound by a covenant relationship with us. Second, He dwells with us by His Spirit. Third, He assures us that His word will remain in the mouth of His people forever. No opposition, no matter how strong or violent, can ultimately suppress God's Word – not even opposition arising from within the community of God's people. Those who outwardly confess to believe His word, but deny its power, will not stop its effectiveness. Since the recent fall of Communism, which was long opposed to the Scriptures, the resurgence of hunger for God's word is wonderful to see. Over the past ten years some German Christians have been offering a free John's Gospel in the Russian Newspapers. They have got millions of replies. Isaiah promises that in every age there will be those who, upheld by His Spirit, will speak God's Word.

I think of a Chinese girl I once interviewed for her story. Born and raised in China, she entered a University and began to study English. An overseas lecturer arrived, and showed videos of famous novels to her class. This Chinese girl, who took the English name of Jess, noticed that the lecturer fast-forwarded parts of the videos that were questionable. Then Jess was disgusted when a friend of hers returned a clock that the lecturer had given her as a prize for winning a debate. This behaviour was a 'no-no' in Chinese society – the clock turned out to be broken, and in China one doesn't return broken gifts. How would the lecturer react? She quietly took it back and said she would have it fixed. Jess could contain herself no longer. She approached the lecturer and asked why she was so different? "If there are any characteristics in me that are different," the lecturer replied, "it's Jesus in me." "Who is Jesus?" asked Jess. Eventually Jess was converted, through reading a verse from the Letter to the Hebrews in the Bible. She became the Personal Assistant to the President of the largest pharmaceutical company in China. (That's a lot of pills!) Then she gave up her highly-paid post, and worked in an Orphanage for no salary whatsoever. By the time I came across her, she was studying for a degree at an English University, preparing to return to China to serve the Lord.

The presence of God's Spirit in a Christian lecturer, and the power of God's Word, were used to reach Jess. God's promise through Isaiah still stands, and who can tell what could be achieved through your witness today?

SEPTEMBER 19TH

Arise, shine; for your light has come! And the glory of the Lord is risen upon you.
Isaiah 60:1.

Now we come to Isaiah's superb vision of the New Creation. In my view, this is not the rebuilt city of Jerusalem after the exile. It is the kingdom of God, the Church of Christ, come down to earth. This is a vision of the eternal state, the New Jerusalem, as John also saw it in Revelation 21:22-27. (For further references in Isaiah to the coming glory of this eternal state, read the beautiful texts in 2:2-4; 4:2-6; 25:6-10a; 26:1-6; 35:1-10.)

The contrast between today's verse and Isaiah 59:10 could not be greater; when God's people were groping 'for the wall like the blind,' and 'stumbling at noon day as at twilight.' As we await the coming eternal state, there are very practical truths for us in these texts. To all who have experienced the Light of the World in their hearts and lives, the call is to enjoy its benefits. We are to rise up and shine. The coming New Jerusalem will have no need of the sun or moon in it, for the Lord will be its light, dispelling all darkness. In our present world of darkness, that same Saviour gives light to all who trust Him. Many people who have become Christians have said that it was like a light being turned on in their minds.

Be glad, Christian, that you have been 'delivered from the power of darkness and conveyed into the Kingdom of the Son of His love' (Colossians 1:13).

'For it is the God who commanded light to shine out of darkness, who has shone in our hearts to give the light of the knowledge of the glory of God in the face of Jesus Christ.' 2 Corinthians 4:6.

'But you are a chosen generation, a royal priesthood, a holy nation, His own special people, that you may proclaim the praises of Him who called you out of darkness into His marvellous light; who once were not a people but are now the people of God, who had not obtained mercy but now have obtained mercy.' 1 Peter 2:9.

As His light has shined upon you, now you must shine for Him. So, reject negative thinking, self-absorption, narrow, blinkered living, and enjoy the light you now have. The Light Giver has come! Get out this week and share your light with others. It will do you no harm at all to hum that little tune now and again, 'This little light of mine, I'm going to let it shine.'

SEPTEMBER 20TH

You shall also be a crown of glory in the hand of the Lord, and a royal diadem in the hand of your God. Isaiah 62:3.

It is significant that the penultimate plague in Egypt was darkness. 'Then the Lord said to Moses, "Stretch out your hand toward heaven, that there may be darkness over the land of Egypt, darkness which may even be felt"' (Exodus 10:21). When the darkness fell the people could not see one another, and no one rose from his place for three days. But all the time the Children of Israel had light in their dwellings.

Again and again Pharaoh had had his opportunity to repent, but he refused. To constantly refuse God's light is a very dangerous thing. One day, spiritual darkness will fall permanently on those who do not obey the gospel of our Lord Jesus Christ. At the time when whole nations will receive the light of God's truth and submit to God and to His Christ, those who refuse it will perish (Isaiah 60:12).

Not many kings in our modern world bow in submission to the King of Kings. However, I inadvertently did come across the story of one. I was chatting one day to the then Chief Constable of the Isle of Man, a delightful Christian called Robin Oak. He told me of a man he had heard speak at a Christian service, called 'Milky Williams.' He was called Milky, because, prior to his Police career, he had been a milkman. He became one of the Policemen who protected the British Royal Family.

One day Milky was on duty in the grounds of Buckingham Palace when he met King George VI out walking. The King was actually three weeks from death, and very ill. His breathing was difficult, but he spoke to Milky about 'going home.' Going home? Was his home not all around him?

But the king was referring to heaven.
A more permanent place
Than any home among an earthly race.
Through the King's witness, Milky was converted,
And often was found to have asserted
That King George VI led him to Christ,
The King of all Kings, with whom he made a tryst.

SEPTEMBER 21ST

"Lift up your eyes all around, and see: they all gather together, they come to you; your sons shall come from afar, and your daughters shall be nursed at your side." Isaiah 60:4.

The worldwide drawing power of the Lord's glory is awesome. The whole family of true faith will be drawn to the New Jerusalem. Israel's wayward, but repentant, sons and daughters will be restored to the Lord; and those to whom the Saviour referred as 'other sheep I have who are not of this fold,' will come into His eternal fold.

When Jesus was on earth, Caiaphas, the High Priest made an amazing prophecy: '. . . that Jesus would die for the nation, and not for that nation only, but also that He would gather together in one the children of God who were scattered abroad' (John 11: 51-52). In today's verse Isaiah also prophesies about this amazing gathering of the people of true faith. He asks us to lift up our eyes and see this vast pilgrimage of people: some who have come from a great distance, and even some who are infirm, arriving in the New Jerusalem. What is it that draws such a disparate group? It is the glory of the Lord. Isn't it always the glory of the Lord that inspires true pilgrims?

The gentle martyr, Stephen, boldly began his great defence of the gospel before the Jewish Court with the words, "Brethren and fathers, listen: the God of Glory appeared to our father Abraham when he was in Mesopotamia, before He dwelt in Haran, and said to him, 'Get out of your country and from your relatives, and come to a land that I will show you' (Acts 7: 2, 3).

What was it that kept Abraham going, through all those long and often extremely difficult years of pilgrimage? 'The God of Glory' had called him. As Stephen stood before the Council, facing their accusations, the Bible tells us that his face was 'as the face of an angel.' At the end of his address, in which he outlined how God had led the people, from Abraham, until 'the coming of the Just One, of whom you have become the betrayers and murderers,' they gnashed at him with their teeth. 'But he . . . gazed into heaven and saw the glory of God, and Jesus standing at the right hand of God.'

When they are asked to pass through times of testing, what keeps modern day Christians going, on their pilgrimage to the New Jerusalem? Let Peter give us the answer.

'Beloved, do not think it strange concerning the fiery trial which is to try you, as though some strange thing happened to you: but rejoice to the extent that you partake of Christ's

248

sufferings, that when His glory is revealed, you may also be glad with exceeding joy.' 1 Peter 4:12-13.

So, as we continue on our pilgrimage to the coming revelation of God's glory, let's make sure that we 'walk worthy of God who calls you into His own kingdom and glory' (1 Thessalonians 1:12).

SEPTEMBER 22ND

Then you shall see and become radiant, and your heart shall swell with joy; because the abundance of the sea shall be turned to you, the wealth of the Gentiles shall come to you. Isaiah 60:5.

This is a welcome little expression: 'Then you shall see and become radiant, and your heart shall swell with joy.' Isaiah prophesies of multitudes coming to the New Jerusalem by the sea. He speaks of the nations of earth that have amassed wealth, now bringing that wealth into the service of the Kingdom of God. It is little wonder that Israel will be radiant. Paul once asked, 'Does this blessedness then come upon the circumcised only, or upon the uncircumcised also?' (Romans 4:9). He further speaks of Abraham, being 'the father of all those who believe.' Gentiles who have exercised faith in Christ also have righteousness attributed to them (Romans 4:11). Now both Jew and Gentile are united in Christ.

'For He Himself is our peace, who has made both one, and has broken down the middle wall of separation . . . so as to create in Himself one new man from the two, thus making peace, and that He might reconcile them both to God in one body through the cross, thereby putting to death the enmity.' Ephesians 2:14-16

Then faces shall surely be 'radiant,' and 'hearts shall swell with joy.' The Revised Version translates it, 'Then thou shalt see and be lightened, and thine heart shall tremble and be enlarged . . .'

In the interim, can there be such joy and radiance? I think so. The biographer, Meryle Secrest, tells a story about the eminent English art historian and TV writer, Kenneth Clark. Whilst writing a book, he had 'a moment of divine inspiration.' Clark was working in his hotel room in Aldeburgh, and had just finished a passage on Rubens. He realised that he was shaking, so he took a walk along the seafront to calm himself. She surmises that it was, perhaps, the examination of Rubens' superb work, that had produced in Clark a sudden, vivid awareness of the mysterious origins of creation. It raised the quandary, if you accept the idea of inspiration, then you have to believe in a source.

My daughter Kerrie, who is a gifted graphic designer, told me over dinner last night that she hopes to visit the Van Gogh Museum in Amsterdam this Christmas. She was ecstatic at the prospect, for Van Gogh is her favourite artist. When inspired creativity brings such joy, what will it be like when the glory of the Creator is revealed? Words fail me here. In the meantime, we can worship with a swelling heart and a radiant face. Maybe Tozer was right, when he suggested that we suspend all our church services and activities for a time, and simply meet to worship.

SEPTEMBER 23RD

The multitude of camels shall cover your land, the dromedaries of Midian and Ephah; all those from Sheba shall come; they shall bring gold and incense, and they shall proclaim the praises of the Lord. All the flocks of Kedar shall be gathered together to you, the rams of Nebaioth shall minister to you; they shall ascend with acceptance on My altar, and I will glorify the house of My glory. Isaiah 60: 6-7

A s Isaiah foresees the coming glories of the Kingdom of God, in today's texts his theological poetry depicts a rich scene. He writes of streams of camel caravans covering the land. Young camels will come from Midian, Israel's former enemy; as well as from Ephah in the East. They will come from Sheba in Arabia, bringing gold and incense; but now they honour a greater than Solomon. Sheep and rams will be driven from Kedar and Nebaioth in the North East, to provide animals for religious sacrifice. All these people are coming from afar to be where the Lord is amongst His people. They want to proclaim the praises of the Lord.

Let's look at the transformed Midian, now praising the Lord. Have you ever come across a spiritual nomad? You know the type; they want spiritual food, but they are not prepared to go to the bother of getting it for themselves. They go around churches, raiding them, and taking what they can get for nothing. They cause arguments and division; and then they are away, leaving a wilderness of trouble behind them. They have no notion of settling, they are nomads.

In a physical sense, the Midianites were just like that. They came up to the land flowing with milk and honey, and took, as it were, the milk and honey away. They didn't plough, nor did they sow seed by the sweat of their brow. They simply waited for the Israelites to have all that done, and then they came up like locusts at harvest-time, stripped the crops, and left no sustenance for Israel. This went on for years, until God chose Gideon to bring a stop to it. Now the Midianites have changed. Instead of coming to take things away from Israel, they are bringing caravans loaded with gifts. What's more, the praises of the Lord are on their lips.

Isn't it interesting that, when the Saviour healed the blind beggar Bartimaeus, he no longer lived by saying 'give me, give me, give me.' The Scripture says, 'he followed Jesus on the road.' A life of taking from others turned to a life of serving the Lord. The 'New Creation' Midianites are truly a prime example of this.

SEPTEMBER 24TH

"Who are these who fly like a cloud, and like doves to their roosts? Surely the coastlands shall wait for Me; and the ships of Tarshish will come first, to bring your sons from afar, their silver and their gold with them, to the name of the Lord your God, and to the Holy One of Israel, because He has glorified you." Isaiah 60:8-9.

250

T he concept of 'waiting for the Lord,' is not one with which the nations of this world are familiar. It means to put all hope in Him, to confidently trust Him. It is to look to Him for guidance and direction, and when it is given, to obey it. Nations and empires are not famous for such behaviour. They rise in power on the strength of their weapons, and fall again, just as surely as time passes. They trust in human power and skill, and no nation more so than the Romans. Reflect on this statement by Edward Gibbon from *History of the Decline and Fall of the Roman Empire, VIII*:

'The hill of the Capital on which we sit was formerly the head of the Roman Empire, the citadel of the earth, the terror of kings; illustrated by the footsteps of so many triumphs, enriched with the spoils of so many nations. This spectacle of the world, how it is fallen! How changed! How defaced! The path of victory is obliterated by vines and the benches of the Senators are concealed by a dunghill.'

'Everything disintegrates in the hands of men,' said Rousseau. Consider, then, Isaiah's beautiful image of far-flung nations, eagerly rushing to be in the immediate presence of the Lord. They have put their hope and confidence in the Lord, and it is not misplaced.

'For unto us a Child is born, unto us a Son is given; and the government will be upon His shoulder. And His name will be called Wonderful, Counsellor, Mighty God, Everlasting Father, Prince of Peace. Of the increase of His government and peace there will be no end, upon the throne of David and over His kingdom, to order it and establish it with judgement and justice from that time forward, even forever. The zeal of the Lord of hosts will perform this.' Isaiah 9:6-7.

Wait for Him now, in His day of rejection, and you will be recompensed when you see Him in His day of glory. Use what talents the Lord has given you to work for Him, and in that Eternal State you will serve Him in an even wider capacity.

SEPTEMBER 25TH

"The sons of foreigners shall build up your walls, and their kings shall minister to you; for in My wrath I struck you, but in My favour I have had mercy on you. Therefore your gates shall be open continually; they shall not be shut day or night, that men may bring to you the wealth of the Gentiles, and their kings in procession. For the nation and kingdom which will not serve you shall perish, and those nations shall be utterly ruined." Isaiah 60:10-12.

A gain we are given a glimpse of the heart of God, as this beautiful poem continues to portray the coming glories of the Kingdom of God. A truly international scene opens up before us. The gates of Zion are open day and night, as people of all nations enter into the service of the King of Kings. It is not an exercise of self-indulgence but of committed service. Revelation 22:3 says, 'His servants shall serve Him.' There is work to be done. No one is suspicious of foreigners, an amazing reconciliation has come about: 'the scores of foreigners shall build up your walls and their kings shall minister to you.' This is not an exclusively Jewish state; Israel's Gentile oppressors have now bowed to the Messiah.

"In my wrath I struck you, but in my favour I have had mercy on you." The heart of God is revealed as the force behind this place of eternal security, where they will neither study nor practise war any more. If we would truly know God, then we must acknowledge that there are two sides to His character. There is His wrath, and there is His grace and kindness. In a famous text, Paul describes the two aspects of God's character:

'Therefore consider the goodness and severity of God: on those who fell, severity; but toward you, goodness, if you continue in His goodness. Otherwise you also will be cut off.' Romans 11:22.

The goodness of God declares His moral perfection. '"Please, show me Your glory," said Moses. 'Then He said, "I will make all my goodness pass before you, and I will proclaim the name of the Lord before you. I will be gracious to whom I will be gracious, and I will have compassion on whom I will have compassion'" (Exodus 33:18, 19). All of us have known the goodness of God.

"Those who do not respond to God's goodness by repentance and faith and trust and submission to His will, cannot wonder or complain if sooner or later the tokens of His goodness are withdrawn, the opportunity of benefiting from them ends, and retribution supervenes" (J. I. Packer, *Knowing God*, Hodder & Stoughton, 1973, p.183).

On repentance and faith, as the result of Christ's death, wrath is replaced by love and mercy. Nations who refuse the goodness of God, which is meant to lead them to repentance, will know His wrath (Romans 2:1-10). They will be ruined and cut off. So let us not take God's favour and goodness for granted, but let them lead us to repentance and faith. Then we shall be among those servants who shall serve in the Eternal Kingdom.

SEPTEMBER 26TH

"The glory of Lebanon shall come to you, the cypress, the pine, and the box tree together, to beautify the place of My sanctuary; and I will make the place of My feet glorious. Also the sons of those who afflicted you shall come bowing to you, and all those who despised you shall fall prostrate at the soles of your feet; and they shall call you The City of the Lord, Zion of the Holy One of Israel." Isaiah 60:13-14.

Just recently I visited Woburn Abbey in Bedfordshire for the first time. As the baby deer darted about, and the sun was setting, I walked with a friend into a courtyard. In it stood the most beautiful Cedar of Lebanon that I have ever seen. It is several hundred years old it, and it has been carefully maintained. While the Abbey is magnificent, the Cedar is breathtaking. The place is worth a visit, if for the Cedar alone!

The Cedar of Lebanon is a magnificent evergreen, often 120 feet high and 40 feet in girth. The wood of the cedar does not easily decay, and along with the hard woods of cypress and box, it has become another symbol of reconciliation in the new creation. David McKenna points out that, in Isaiah 40:16, the hard woods of Lebanon are used for idols. Now these hard woods enjoy a great reversal. They have become the symbol of the exodus from Babylon under the sustaining hand of God, as the people took their journey home. They had been an object of worship in themselves; now they are used to beautify the place of God's presence. W. E. Vine informs us that what is referred to here is not timber for the Sanctuary of God, but for 'the place,' that is, the vicinity (*Expository Commentary on Isaiah*, <u>Nelson</u>, p.175). These magnificent trees shall be planted in the vicinity where the transcendent Creator's feet will touch the earth.

The very natural creation that groans 'will at last be delivered from the bondage of corruption into the glorious liberty of the children of God' (Romans 8:20-22). Not only is the natural creation now to be used for the glory of God, but converted people acknowledge the true worth and place of the Holy One of Israel. Those who had opposed God's people now join with them in service to His glory. In a world of division, war, hatred, envy, selfishness and evil, the promise of this prophecy could not be more exhilarating. Our response is: "Even so, come, Lord Jesus!"

SEPTEMBER 27TH

"Whereas you have been forsaken and hated, so that no one went through you, I will make you an eternal excellence, a joy of many generations. You shall drink the milk of the Gentiles, and milk the breast of kings; you shall know that I, the Lord, am your Saviour and your Redeemer, the Mighty One of Jacob." Isaiah 60:15-16.

Mark well what God can do. Jerusalem was so despised, that people from other nations wouldn't even pass through it. She was forsaken, hated, and avoided. But in a coming day, the New Jerusalem will be a place of eternal excellence. Hampered as we are by our consistent failures and flaws, who does not long for excellence in what we do? Even when we do achieve high standards, something comes along to drag those high standards down. God will make Zion a place of unending excellence. Nothing that defiles shall ever enter into it (Revelation 21:27).

The coming City of the Lord will be changed from being a place to which people were hostile, to a place that will be 'a joy of many generations.' I live in a city that is famous to the ends of the earth for its hostilities. What would a lot of us not give, to see Belfast become a city of joy? Just last night, at our church prayer meeting in the city, one of our members told how he had intended to go to Jerusalem last month to study at the University. The place where he would have been eating became the tragic target of a suicide bomber.

God promises to make Jerusalem a City of Joy. Once ignored and unvisited, it will become a place into which nations and their Royalty will pour vital energy, just as a mother gives her milk to a child. It is a far cry from the horrors of the Nazi persecution of Jewish people, which, in the darkest midnight of the 20th century, did not blink at wiping out millions of European Jewry. The ruthless, diabolical destruction by the Nazis of Jewish life in Europe, was long preceded in history by the expulsion of Jews out of almost every European country, including England. Even in Tsarist Russia, they were confined to a special region known as 'The Pale.' Prejudice against Jews continues, even into our modern day. The transformation in the New Jerusalem, only made possible by God's power, will be recognised world-wide.

Notice the four names of God given in today's text: 'Lord,' 'Saviour,' 'Redeemer,' and 'Mighty One of Jacob.' No one else can do what our God can do. That same Lord, Saviour, Redeemer, and Mighty One is at work in your life, Christian. Even if you, too, may be forsaken, hated, and avoided, He will bring you to that place of eternal joy. Be assured of it.

"Instead of bronze I will bring gold, instead of iron I will bring silver, instead of wood, bronze, and instead of stones, iron. I will also make your officers peace, and your magistrates righteousness. Violence shall no longer be heard in your land, neither wasting nor destruction within your borders; but you shall call your walls Salvation, and your gates Praise." Isaiah 60:17-18.

Here is an upgrade to surpass all upgrades! The city is transformed in every respect. Gold replaces bronze, silver replaces iron, bronze replaces wood, iron replaces stone. The Hebrew word used here shows that peace and government are 'the exact definition of each other' (Motyer, *Isaiah*, IVP, p.374): 'I will make your officers peace, and your magistrates righteousness.' Speed the day, we cry! The daily diet of TV News will be redundant. There will be no more governments to criticise, no more law cases to dismay us.

There will be no opposition to righteousness and peace in the New Kingdom. Violence will not occur any more, mindless vandalism with its waste and destruction will cease. Imagine the walls of a city being called 'Salvation,' and the gates, 'Praise'! These are not idealistic names, they are real. Salvation has come, and praise will flow as a response.

In the in-between times, as we await the glories of the coming Kingdom, we must constantly remind ourselves that we are to be a counter-culture on earth. When Paul wrote to the church at Philippi, he spoke of them as being people, whose 'citizenship is in heaven, from which we also eagerly wait for the Saviour, the Lord Jesus Christ' (Philippians 3:20). Philippi was a colony of Rome – Rome in miniature. The Emperor Augustus gave to it the coveted possession of the *ius Italicum.* This was the privilege, 'by which the whole legal position of the colonists, in respect of ownership, transfer of land, payment of taxes, local administration and law, became the same as if they were on Italian soil' (K. Lake and H. J. Cadbury, *The Beginnings of Christianity,4,* ed. F. J. Oakes and K. Lake, MacMillan, 1933, p.190).

Paul is showing the Philippians that they are 'a colony of heaven' (as Moffat puts it). Citizens of Philippi were citizens of Rome, where their Emperor lived. Whilst being on earth, as Christians they were actually citizens of heaven, where their Lord lives. After 48BC a common title for the Roman Emperor was 'the universal saviour of mankind.' The Philippian Christians were waiting for the appearance of their Lord, the Saviour of mankind.

As the coming New Jerusalem will be marked by praise, in response to the salvation wrought by the Lord Jesus, may we in today's church be a 'colony' of what is coming, and let praise mark us at every turn. We should constantly wear the garment of praise. William Seeker said, 'a drop of praise is an unsuitable acknowledgement for an ocean of mercy.'

"The sun shall no longer be your light by day, nor for brightness shall the moon give light to you; but the Lord will be to you an everlasting light, and your God your glory. Your sun shall no longer go down, nor shall your moon withdraw itself; for the Lord will be your everlasting light. . ." Isaiah 60:19-20.

I shall never forget him, the kindly sheep farmer. He collected me at the airport, and headed for the multi-storey car park with my baggage. I settled into my seat in his pick-up truck, belted up, and discovered I had a very confused driver on my hands. He was completely disorientated. Eventually (I repeat, eventually!) we got out of the car park; and as soon as he saw the sun he took off. He worked out its position in the sky, and immediately used its guidance to head for home. The sun ruled the sheep farmer's day in a very special way, and I was glad of it.

In modern life, our days are very much ruled by the sun. The sun is a star that is about 150,000 km from the earth. Its light and heat make life on earth possible, coming from nuclear reactions, which take place inside the sun. It is about 1,390,000 km in diameter – about 109 times the diameter of the earth. The moon, which is a satellite of the earth, has no light of its own, and shines only because it reflects the light of the sun. As it turns on its axis, only once in every journey round the earth, each part of the moon's surface has about two weeks of darkness first, and then about two weeks of sunlight. We can see only that part which is turned towards the earth. We speak of the moon 'waxing,' which means that it grows larger as more of its lighted surface can be seen; then it wanes, or grows smaller, until it becomes a thin C-shaped crescent. The rise and fall of the moon affects the tides of the sea.

In the New Creation, life will not be governed by the sun and moon, but by the presence of the Lord. The glory of the Lord will be the source of everlasting light. It will not go down, as the sun goes down, or wane, like the moon. The brightness of uncreated light, radiating from the presence of God, will be like nothing else. I like to think that the people of God in the Eternal State will reflect that light in their appearance. Says Paul, '. . . the Lord Jesus Christ . . will transform our lowly body that it may be conformed to His glorious body' (Philippians 3:21).

As we presently live in a world of evil and darkness, the promise of eternal light is comfort beyond description. As Chrysostom said, 'If one man should suffer all the sorrows of all the saints in the world, yet they are not worth one hour's glory in heaven.'

SEPTEMBER 30TH

". . and the days of your mourning shall be ended.' Isaiah 60:20b.

As I write about the promises of Isaiah 60, I feel like a little boy at the seaside trying to get the ocean into his bucket. We have read that the Eternal State is a place of eternal light, and, because of eternal security, the gates are always open. We have read of eternal beauty, and of eternal excellence, and have discovered that government and peace are eternally synonymous. Yet, somehow, the promise of today's text is the promise of all promises. We read that mourning shall be ended forever.

For days now, as I have been writing on these matters, the horrific story has been unfolding in the village of Soham in Cambridgeshire, England, of the abduction and murder of the two ten-year old children, Holly Wells and Jessica Chapman. Millions have been deeply shocked by the magnitude of evil in this story; and now they are in mourning over the deaths of these two precious young girls. Anyone who has known the death of a loved one knows what grief is like; and the truth is that in this life you never get over the loss. You just have to get used to living without them. There is numbness and lethargy with grief; there is anger at what has happened. Eventually, there is acceptance that the loved one has gone; but the mourning continues, that they are no longer here to share our joys.

When we think of the recent slaughters in Rwanda and the Balkans, the killing fields of Cambodia, the horrors of the Gulag; the millions upon millions of lives lost in the First and Second World Wars – all these wars still lay ahead at the time of Isaiah. Despite his knowledge of Israel's coming exile, with courage he looked away to the Eternal State, and declared that their days of mourning would end.

In the Book of Revelation we read, 'and God shall wipe away every tear from their eyes; there shall be no more death, nor sorrow, nor crying. There shall be no more pain, for the former things have passed away' (21:4). And to think that this is an eternal state! I love the story of C. S. Lewis in Oxford, when he was taking his leave of a friend who was returning to the United States. Lewis crossed the street, but suddenly he stopped on the opposite footpath and shouted to his friend over the busy traffic, "Christians never have to say Goodbye!" We glory in the truth that, though death may be the king of terrors, Jesus is the King of Kings.

October

This photograph shows the detail from a damask loom, where the warped yarn is being lifted to the surface of the fabric by the harness to produce design. In the Scriptures we read of Aholiab, who was a 'designer, a weaver of blue, purple and scarlet thread, and of fine linen.'

"Also your people shall all be righteous; they shall inherit the land forever, the branch of My planting, the work of My hands, that I may be glorified. A little one shall become a thousand, and a small one a strong nation. I, the Lord, will hasten it in its time."
Isaiah 60: 21-22.

To all the lovely promises of Isaiah chapter 60, five more are now added. In the eternal state we are told that righteousness will reign in the hearts of the people. There will be eternal moral excellence. The people will also be able to claim their rightful inheritance of the land promised to them. One day, the Lord said to King David,

"Moreover I will appoint a place for My people Israel, and will plant them, that they may dwell in a place of their own and move no more; nor shall the sons of wickedness oppress them any more, as previously . . . and your house and your kingdom shall be established forever before you. Your throne shall be established forever." 2 Samuel 7:10, 16.

Sin had caused God's people to forfeit their birthright of the inheritance of land (see Deuteronomy 28: 58-68). Now it is restored on the basis of faith and an imputed righteousness. The promise is also given, that the branch of God's own planting will be restored. In Hebrew, this is a 'green shoot,' or 'sprout.' In the English text, the word is 'branch.' In 11:1, Isaiah also refers to Christ as 'a Branch,' so God's people are being made like their Messiah. He planted them: they are the work of His hands. He is glorified in them: they will display His splendour. The full-grown flower will have a beauty that earth has not yet known.

As this exquisite chapter comes to an end, God's promises, "A little one shall become a thousand, and a small one a strong nation." It all started with Abraham's active faith on that starry night long ago, when he believed God's promise of children as numerous as the stars of the sky. Beginning with Isaac, that number has continued to grow until, in the book of Revelation, we read of an incalculable number:

"After these things I looked," said John, "and behold a great multitude which no one could number, of all nations, tribes, peoples, and tongues, standing before the throne and before the Lamb . . . and crying with a loud voice, saying, 'Salvation belongs to our God who sits on the throne, and to the Lamb!'" Revelation 7:9, 10.

The final promise given in today's text is that, when the time for the fulfilment of all these promises comes, the Lord will hasten it. As we wait for that time, the New Testament issues an intense challenge as to our lifestyle. May we truly take it to heart:

'But the day of the Lord will come as a thief in the night, in which the heavens will pass away with a great noise, and the elements will melt with fervent heat; both the earth and the works that are in it will be burned up. Therefore, since all these things will be dissolved, what manner of persons ought you to be in holy conduct and godliness, looking for and hastening the coming of the day of God, because of which the heavens will be dissolved, being on fire, and the elements will melt with fervent heat? Nevertheless we, according to His promise, look for new heavens and a new earth in which righteousness dwells.' 2 Peter 3:10-13.

OCTOBER 2ND

"The Spirit of the Lord God is upon Me . . ." Isaiah 61:1.

Isaiah's fifth Servant Song arrives quietly with no introduction, but with worldwide implications. The authority behind the Song is the person of the Servant-Messiah, for He is the speaker. Here is prophesied, in heart-warming detail, the Saviour's ministry of comfort to our heart-broken world. It is one of the great foundations upon which we affirm that the Scriptures are the unerring Word of God, for Christ read from this song in the synagogue at Nazareth, and said, "Today this Scripture is fulfilled in your hearing" (Luke 4:16-21). The accurate fulfilment of biblical prophecy proves God's Word to be true. He has gloriously fulfilled every expectation that this Song raises, and He continues to do so.

Christ's ministry is, first and foremost, an anointed one. In connection with His incarnation, Isaiah says, 'the Spirit of the Lord shall rest upon Him' (11:2). Mary, His mother, must have found the words of the angel quite awesome: "The Holy Spirit will come upon you, and the power of the Highest will overshadow you; therefore, also, that Holy One who is to be born will be called the Son of God" (Luke 1:35). In 42:1, Isaiah is referring to the baptism of Jesus at the beginning of His public ministry, when the Spirit descended upon Him in bodily form like a dove, accompanied by a voice from heaven saying, "You are my beloved Son; in You I am well pleased" (Luke 3:22).

If you and I would have a ministry of comfort to others, then we too need the Holy Spirit's power. Remember, the Holy Spirit is Christ's gift to you (Acts 2:33). The Holy Spirit is God, and possesses all the characteristics that are His hallmarks. He is Holy – pure (1 Corinthians 6:19). He is eternal – He always was, and always will be (Hebrews 9:14). He is omnipotent – He is all-powerful (Luke 1:35-75). He is omnipresent – He exists everywhere (Psalm 139:7). He is omniscient – He knows everything (1 Corinthians 2:10-11).

As you reach out to others in your ministry, remember that the Holy Spirit is active in your life. For your encouragement, let me remind you what He does. He convicts (John 16:8-10). He guides into all truth (John 16:13). He explains about Jesus (John 15:26), and God (1 Corinthians 2:12). He empowers (Acts 1:8). He indwells (Romans 8:9; 1 Corinthians 12:13). He leads (Psalm 143:10; Acts 13:2; 15:28). He helps in our prayer life (Romans 8:26-27; Ephesians 6:18). Above all, He glorifies the Lord Jesus Christ (John 16:14). Yield to Him today, and your ministry will flourish.

OCTOBER 3RD

". . . because the Lord has anointed Me to preach good tidings to the poor; He has sent Me to heal the brokenhearted, to proclaim liberty to the captives, and the opening of the prison to those who are bound." Isaiah 61:1.

The gospel is good news for all people. It reaches out to the poor: all across the world there are millions who are disadvantaged because of their circumstances. Given half an opportunity, they soon prove that there is no such thing as an ordinary person. The gospel reaches them exactly where they are. Paul asked Philemon to receive back Onesimus his runaway slave. He was newly converted, so he was to be received, "no longer as a slave but more than a slave – a beloved brother, especially to me but how much more to you, both in the flesh and in the Lord. If then you count me as a partner, receive him as you would me' (Philemon 1:16-17). The gospel sets the standard for the protection of the downtrodden. The words of James thunder against any discrimination towards the poor in the church.

'Listen, my beloved brethren: has God not chosen the poor of this world to be rich in faith and heirs of the kingdom which He promised to those who love Him? But you have dishonoured the poor man. Do not the rich oppress you and drag you into the courts? Do they not blaspheme that noble name by which you are called?' James 2:5-7.

And what of the brokenhearted? Christ 'heals' the broken hearted – the word is the same as a comforting bandage. "Where do broken hearts go?" sang Whitney Houston. It's a good question. God knows, the world is full of brokenhearted people. You'll find them in every city and town, village and hamlet. Tell them of Christ's gospel. It has power to bind up broken hearts, like no therapy on earth.

In Leviticus we read that the blasting of the ram's horn trumpet introduced the year of Jubilee, which proclaimed liberty throughout Israel (see Leviticus 25:9,10). In a Jubilee, or the 50th year, liberty was proclaimed to all Israelites who were in servitude to any of their fellow citizens, and a return of family possessions to those who had been compelled to sell them because of poverty. The Jubilee was to be a year of rest for the land. Theologians reckon that today's text is an allusion to the year of Jubilee, in which debts were cancelled, slaves were set free, and the poor received their land back again. It is through the gospel that those held in captivity to every kind of sin are set free: the devil's hold upon them is broken. So, go with the gospel key today, and use it to set the prisoners free.

OCTOBER 4TH

"To proclaim the acceptable year of the Lord, and the day of vengeance of our God; to comfort all who mourn." Isaiah 61:2.

Notice here the contrast between 'year' and 'day.' 'Year' means, literally, 'the year of the Lord's good pleasure.' It does not mean a year of a particular date, but a particular season – the season that we are currently enjoying. It is the season of the proclamation of the grace of God, through the gospel of the Lord Jesus Christ, which will last until His Second Coming.

Now, all that Christ achieved at Calvary is available to those who repent and believe. What a great contrast to the 'day' that will come at the end of this time. It will not be prolonged, but it will be swift. It is 'the day of vengeance of our God.' The Scriptures teach that vengeance is not ours: "Vengeance is Mine," says the Lord (Deuteronomy 32:35). When the Lord puts on the 'garments of vengeance for clothing' (Isaiah 59:57), people will get their due deserts. The former practice of Judges, 'donning the black cap,' to pass the death sentence, will be pale in its terror, compared to the wrath of God. If you have not received the Lord Jesus as your Saviour, do not delay to do so this very day, while it is still the season of the Lord's favour.

When our Lord read from this passage in the synagogue at Nazareth, He stopped with the phrase 'to proclaim the acceptable year of the Lord.' He closed the book, gave it to the attendant, and sat down. Why did He stop there? It was because He was proclaiming the great era of grace, and not the swift era of vengeance. When John the Baptist came preaching about Christ, he warned, "His winnowing fan is in His hand, and He will thoroughly clean out His threshing floor, and gather the wheat into His barn; but the chaff He will burn with unquenchable fire" (Luke 3:17). What John warned of was true, but it was not yet the time. John was beheaded: no fire took away the chaff, called Herod, who had organised his execution. History tells us that when Herod was buried, it was in a golden coffin. The godly John was buried in indescribable ignominy. Why did God not have Herod's head cut off? For that matter, why not the head of every terrorist or tyrant? It is because 'the day of vengeance of our God' has not yet come. If God cut the head off everyone who has broken His law, we would all be headless. This is the time of His favour; but the day of vengeance is coming.

OCTOBER 5TH

"To console those who mourn in Zion, to give them beauty for ashes, the oil of joy for mourning, the garment of praise for the spirit of heaviness; that they may be called trees of righteousness, the planting of the Lord, that He may be glorified." Isaiah 61:3.

We are now given further details about the matchless ministry of the Servant-Messiah. He is the Great Transformer. As an illustration of today's text, David McKenna asks us to imagine a woman heading for a funeral, when she receives a message that an error has been made. The announcement of the death should have been an invitation to a wedding. Her dress and attitude would be completely transformed. The ashes would be washed from her face and her head. She would put on a crown of beauty, a headdress, or a garland of flowers, perfumed body oil would express the joy she is experiencing, and a beautiful dress would replace the sackcloth and ashes.

When the Lord Jesus enters people's lives, He is able to bring consolation to those who mourn. "I am the Resurrection and the Life," He told the grieving Martha. Those who believe in Him, and are alive at His return, will never die; and those who believe in Him, and die before His return, shall live (John 11:25, 26). Every person who has trusted Christ as Saviour has experienced His power to replace ashes with beauty. The idolater 'feeds on ashes' (Isaiah 44:20). When we turn from all the idols of earth to worship our Lord Jesus, a beauty comes into our lives.

'The fruit of the Spirit is love, joy, peace, patience, kindness, goodness, faithfulness, gentleness and self-control.' Galatians 5:22, 23.

God has begun the process of conforming us to the image of His Son – and He is beautiful Joy replaces mourning, and praise replaces the spirit of heaviness. It happens in millions of lives every day. Instead of being like chaff, we become 'trees of righteousness,' and 'the planting of the Lord.'

OCTOBER 6TH

And they shall rebuild the old ruins, they shall raise up the former desolations, and they shall repair the ruined cities, the desolations of many generations. Strangers shall stand and feed your flocks, and the sons of the foreigner shall be your plowmen and your vinedressers. But you shall be named the priests of the Lord, they shall call you the servants of our God. You shall eat the riches of the Gentiles, and in their glory you shall boast. Isaiah 61:4-6.

I s there someone reading today's text, and there has been a breakdown in your family over many generations? Somebody did something very wrong a long time ago, and the rancorous repercussions continue to this day. Is there some Christian worker, and the work of God once flourished in your area, and you are desperately trying to rebuild something for His glory? Do you live in a city like mine, which has suffered civil strife for hundreds of years – even last night? Do you wonder if you will ever see a better day? Isaiah now gives two great definitions of God's people. They are called, 'the priests of the Lord,' and 'the servants of our God.' Their work is to rebuild the old ruins, and repair the ruined cities by raising up new ones out of the wreckage of the old. Those whose lives have been changed by the Great Transformer, now become priests and servants of God. All believers are part of a Kingdom of priests, whose ministry it is to bring the Word of God to men and women and lead them to Christ (Exodus 19: 6; 1 Peter 2:4-9; Revelation 20: 6).

In a spiritual sense, believers can be used to repair 'the desolations of many generations.' All of this will come to a glorious conclusion in the eternal state. The work of priests and servants continues now in a very real way, but it is by no means easy.

I often think of Elisha's servant, Gehazi. His master wanted to reward a Shunammite woman for her kindness, and when he asked what should be done for her Gehazi was able to point out that she had no son and her husband was old. Elisha prophesied that within a year she would have a son. Gehazi's service began very well indeed, but it is not easy to take second place all the time. When the child died and Gehazi was not used to bring about a miracle, it must have been very disappointing for him. It was through Elisha that the child was brought back to life. When the sons of the prophets were hungry in a famine, Gehazi was told to make stew for them; but the stew turned out to be inedible. Elisha then called for some flour, and the stew turned out fine. Being a failed cook must not have been easy in front of all those important people. Eventually, when Elisha refused to take anything from the healed Naaman, Gehazi went after him, lied to him, and took the money and clothes for himself. As a punishment, the leprosy of Naaman passed to Gehazi. If God treated all of His servants like this, when through discouragement they reach out for something for themselves, we would all be lepers. Gehazi's punishment was given as a warning beacon to future generations. Servanthood is not easy, but its rewards are incalculable. Don't spoil your service by selfishness.

OCTOBER 7TH

Instead of your shame you shall have double honour, and instead of confusion they shall rejoice in their portion. Therefore in their land they shall possess double; everlasting joy shall be theirs. "For I, the Lord, love justice; I hate robbery for burnt offering; I will direct their work in truth, and will make with them an everlasting covenant. Their descendants shall be known among the Gentiles, and their offspring among the people. All who see them shall acknowledge them, that they are the posterity whom the Lord has blessed." Isaiah 61:7-9.

The people who had received 'double for all' their sins, are now told that they will receive 'double honour.' Instead of confusion, disgrace and disappointment, the people of God can rejoice in what the Lord has apportioned them. He has doubled their possession of land, and given them the incomparable gift of everlasting joy.

Are we Gentiles to be left out? No! Writing about Israel, Paul says:

'I say, then, have they stumbled that they should fall? Certainly not! But through their fall, to provoke them to jealousy, salvation has come to the Gentiles. Now if their fall is riches for the world, and their failure riches for the Gentiles, how much more their fullness! . . . For if their being cast away is the reconciling of the world, what will their acceptance be but life from the dead? . . . and if the root is holy, so are the branches. And if some of the branches were broken off, and you, being a wild olive tree, were grafted in among them, and with them became a partaker of the root and fatness of the olive tree, do not boast against the branches. But if you do boast, remember that you do not support the root, but the root supports you.' Romans 11:11-18.

The work of grace that reaches undeserving Jews and Gentiles is not based on some flimsy, cheap foundation. The very highest standards of justice have been met. The Perfect Servant has laid down His life so that both Jew and Gentile might be reconciled to God. The teaching of Ephesians is hugely relevant here.

'. . . you were without Christ, being aliens from the commonwealth of Israel and strangers from the covenants of promise, having no hope and without God in the world. But now in Christ Jesus you who once were far off have been brought near by the blood of Christ. For He Himself is our peace, who has made both one, and has broken down the middle wall of separation, having abolished in His flesh the enmity, that is, the law of commandments contained in ordinances, so as to create in Himself one new man from the two, thus making peace.' Ephesians 2:12-15.

It was the Hebrew people who first believed and trusted in the Messiah; and then the Gentiles did the same through the preaching of the gospel. 'We have been sealed with the Holy Spirit of promise, who is the guarantee of our inheritance until the redemption of the purchased possession, to the praise of His glory' (Ephesians 1:13-14).

I will greatly rejoice in the Lord, my soul shall be joyful in my God; for He has clothed me with the garments of salvation, He has covered me with the robe of righteousness, as a bridegroom decks himself with ornaments, and as a bride adorns herself with her jewels. For as the earth brings forth its bud, as the garden causes the things that are sown in it to spring forth, so the Lord God will cause righteousness and praise to spring forth before all the nations. Isaiah 61:10-11.

Some see the speaker here as the Messiah, others as the Redeemed. They may be right, but along with Barry Webb I simply like to think that it is Isaiah himself (*The Message of Isaiah*, IVP, p237). Writing of all these stupendous themes, I think Isaiah can contain himself no longer, and bursts into praise of the God who is about to fulfil all the promises of His everlasting covenant. The man is singing for the very joy of it all.

Next time your church meets, or even now as you read these words, may you be caught up in these two peerless themes: to 'greatly rejoice in the Lord,' and to 'be joyful in your God.' He has clothed you with the 'garments of salvation,' and all fear and guilt have gone. You're saved! He has covered you with 'the robe of righteousness,' and you are right with God. At a Western wedding the bridegroom puts on his special suit, or 'tails' and striped trousers, a buttonhole-flower, special shirt and silk tie; the bride adorns herself in a tiara, or diamond earrings and bracelets. It is their special day, and they dress appropriately! As a bridegroom and his bride are specially dressed, Isaiah tells us that God has so clothed His people in garments of salvation and righteousness. They are not our garments – a Gracious Hand has given them to us.

Then Isaiah mixes his metaphors again. For his next image he turns to the garden. 'The Lord will cause righteousness and praise to spring forth before all nations.' But it all began like a small seed in the earth, and generated and grew into full bloom.

Think of Isaiah's own experience. In the year that King Uzziah died, Isaiah saw the Lord, 'sitting on a throne, high and lifted up' (Isaiah ch. 6). Above the throne there stood seraphim – the word means 'burning ones.' They are celestial beings. Isaiah saw them as having faces, feet, hands, and voices of men. They stood upright. Their description is fascinating: 'Each one had six wings: with two he covered his face, with two he covered his feet, and with two he flew. And one cried to another, and said: "Holy, Holy, Holy is the Lord of Hosts; the whole world is full of His glory!"'

As these beings worshipped and adored God, Isaiah was overcome by a sense of awe and reverence in the presence of the King, the Lord of hosts. He suddenly became aware of how sinful he was, and how unclean were his words and the words of those around him. One of the seraphim touched his lips with a live coal, and said, ". . . Your iniquity is taken away, and your sin purged." Isaiah was given the righteousness of God, and called to further service. He exulted in it, and praised God's name. In today's text, he is thrilled by the fact that righteousness and praise shall spring up across the earth, just as a garden blooms and grows. In the meantime let us listen as the Lord says, "Whom shall I send, and who will go for us?" Like Isaiah, let us answer, "Here am I! Send me."

For Zion's sake I will not hold My peace, and for Jerusalem's sake I will not rest, until her righteousness goes forth as brightness, and her salvation as a lamp that burns.
Isaiah 62:1.

T he Lord Jesus promises to be in constant prayer for those He is going to save, and it takes our minds to the stunning words of Hebrews 7:25: 'Therefore He is also able to save to the uttermost those who come to God through Him, since He always lives to make intercession for them.' Our Lord does not behave impassively with those He saves. He will not hold His peace on their behalf, and His prayers will be answered. From small seeds, righteousness has become a beautiful garden; and now 'brightness' and 'salvation as a lamp that burns,' are promised. While in this chapter we read about Zion the City, the real glory of Zion will be its people. 'The chapter as a whole is much more about God's delight in His people than about bricks and mortar. City, land, walls, people, glory, are all aspects of one dazzling reality: God with His people and they with Him forever' (Gary Webb, *The Message of Isaiah*, IVP, p.238).

While the Lord promises intercessory prayer for His people, He also promises that He 'will not rest' until their blessing is assured. This takes us back again to Naomi in the Book of Ruth, and her famous words, "Sit still, my daughter, until you know how the matter will turn out; for the man will not rest until he has concluded the matter this day" (Ruth 3:18). Ruth had just returned home, after placing her rightful claim to redemption at the feet of Boaz, and I reckon she was suffering from a very modern complaint – nerves! Was it all too good to be true? Would Boaz really redeem her? Ruth must obviously have been restless, for Naomi had to tell her to sit still. Perhaps doubt was also at the root of Ruth's restlessness. Naomi encourages her to rest in the integrity of the word of Boaz. While Ruth worried, Boaz was in the city, busily dealing with the problems, one by one.

So it is with our Heavenly Boaz. The Lord neither slumbers nor sleeps. The promise in today's text is that He will not rest until all His promises are fulfilled. Away with doubting, then! Through the victory of Calvary, we have a Holy Spirit to guide us, a salvation that saves, and a Christ to redeem us. We do not understand it all; and we were never expected to fully understand it. Yet we realise that the deepest needs of our hearts have been met. We are like little children who need a Father; we are sinners who need a Saviour; we are troubled and need the Spirit, the Comforter. If the Lord will not cease to pray for us, nor rest until His promises are fulfilled, what have we to fear? Sit still.

The Gentiles shall see your righteousness, and all kings your glory. You shall be called by a new name, which the mouth of the Lord will name. You shall also be a crown of glory in the hand of the Lord, and a royal diadem in the hand of your God. Isaiah 62:2-3.

The transformation of God's people is here explained in sublime figurative language. Their sins had hidden God's face from them, their hands were stained with blood, their fingers were defiled with iniquity, their lips had spoken lies, and their tongue had muttered perversity. Now they are to be given a new name. The name is mentioned in Jeremiah 33:16: 'In those days Judah will be saved, and Jerusalem will dwell safely. And this is the name by which she will be called: The Lord our Righteousness.' From a Christian perspective, we remind ourselves of 1 Corinthians 1: 30-31, 'But of Him you are in Christ Jesus, who became for us wisdom from God – and righteousness and sanctification and redemption – that, as it is written, "He who glories, let him glory in the Lord"'

As they display the righteousness of God before a watching world, two metaphors are used to describe the people of God. The first is a crown, or coronet, of glory in the hand of the Lord. The Hebrew here for 'hand,' is the palm, or the open hand, in which the coronet is held out for display. The second metaphor is that of a royal diadem in the hand of the Lord. In Scripture this is used to describe the mitre, or turban, of the High Priest. Both images show the joy and delight that the Lord receives as the result of His redemptive work: His people are truly as a crown and mitre in His hands.

We sometimes forget the God-ward side of redemption's work. Think of the statement the Lord made to the Church at Laodicea. "Behold, I stand at the door and knock. If anyone hears my voice and opens the door, I will come into him and dine with him, and he with Me" (Revelation 3:20). Notice there are two aspects to this spiritual feast. Those who respond to the invitation will dine with Christ – that I can understand; for I have often done it. The stupendous surprise is – He dines with me! There is something in my worship that feeds God. Think about that the next time He comes to dine with you. It would be a sad thing if you had nothing for Him.

OCTOBER 11TH

You shall no longer be termed Forsaken, nor shall your land any more be termed Desolate; but you shall be called Hephzibah, and your land Beulah; for the Lord delights in you, and your land shall be married. For as a young man marries a virgin, so shall your sons marry you; and as the bridegroom rejoices over the bride, so shall your God rejoice over you. Isaiah 62:4-5.

The many images that the Lord uses for His people in the book of Isaiah are quite something: from smouldering flax to lambs; from mounting eagles to coronets and mitres; from captives to widows. Now there comes another beautiful image. It is of a woman who has lived a lonely, desolate life; now love has come, and she can hardly believe it. She is absolutely overcome with delight in the love of her husband, and he wonders how he ever lived without her.

God's people were forsaken; their land was desolate, and ruined by those who hated them. Then the Lord came, and His love for them was beyond all other loves – so great that He laid down His life for them. Now they are called 'Hephzibah,' meaning 'my delight;'

and their land is called 'Beulah,' meaning 'married.' The sons of Israel have 'married' their Mother-city, and God rejoices over His people as a Bridegroom rejoices over his Bride.

I confess that at times I forget the love that God has for me. I have failed Him so often, constantly falling short of what is best, and I feel that He just puts up with me, or He 'tholls' me, as we say in Ulster. Seldom do I see myself as His 'delight.' Yet it is so. Do I love Him? I certainly do. Has He won my heart? Like no other. Then, let these beautiful verses grip my heart and life. I am no longer termed 'Forsaken': there is no way God has cut me off. He came after me, like the lost sheep, and brought me home on His shoulders to His fold. Since Christ has entered my life there is no way it can be termed 'Desolate.' I am now part of His bride – the Church that is joined to Him in a spiritual union. 'You also', writes Paul, 'have become dead to the law through the body of Christ, that you may be married to another – to Him who was raised from the dead, that we should bear fruit to God' (Romans 7:4).

As you raise your family, run your business, work in the hospital, teach in the school, go to that factory or office, or serve in that café or restaurant, just remember God 'delights' in you and rejoices over you, everyday.

OCTOBER 12TH

I have set watchmen on your walls, O Jerusalem; they shall never hold their peace day or night. You who make mention of the Lord, do not keep silent, and give Him no rest till He establishes and till He makes Jerusalem a praise in the earth. Isaiah 62:6-7.

Intercessors are likened by the Lord to watchmen on the walls of Jerusalem. The thought behind these verses is akin to the position of the 'remembrancer' in the king's court. He recorded all that was happening, took the minutes of meetings, and noted down all that the king had promised his subjects. Later he would remind the king of what had been said and promised, and held him accountable. So the watchmen act like 'remembrancers,' constantly reminding God in their prayers of His promises; and in particular holding Him to the promise, that He would 'make Jerusalem a praise in the earth.'

This is not a narrow promise, to make only Jerusalem great. It is saying that, 'in saving His people, the Lord has also saved a world-wide people' (Alec Motyer, *Isaiah*, IVP, p.382). "Ho! Everyone who thirsts, come to the waters; and you who have no money, come, buy and eat. Yes, come, buy wine and milk without money and without price" (Isaiah 55:1). The Lord will not rest until He has accomplished His promise; and all who pray for the peace of Jerusalem should not rest either. They should pray on until they see the earth praising Jerusalem, rather than hating and opposing her.

Jesus told a parable of the widow who persistently came to the unjust judge, asking for justice from her adversary. The judge did not fear God nor regard men. Eventually, though, he helped her, simply to get rid of her (Luke 18:1-8). Jesus did not liken God to the unjust judge, of course. He was teaching that, if a godless, hard, unresponsive man would sometimes do good (albeit from a bad motive), how much more will God do right by those who 'cry out day and night to Him, though he bears long with them?' The parable says that He will speedily avenge His own. Of course, this is in terms of God's time. 'With the Lord one day is as a thousand years, and a thousand years as one day' (2 Peter 3:8). As Isaiah has already told us, the Lord will act speedily when it is the correct time. God's delays in answering our prayers immediately are for very good reasons, known particularly to Him.

What is happening to me now may well be in answer to the prayers of people centuries ago. What will happen in the future may be in answer to my prayers now. Here is the power of prayer. The Lord will neither be offended nor grow weary of your intercession. Don't neglect it.

OCTOBER 13TH

The Lord has sworn by His right hand and by the arm of His strength: "Surely I will no longer give your grain as food for your enemies; and the sons of the foreigner shall not drink your new wine, for which you have laboured. But those who have gathered it shall eat it, and praise the Lord; those who have brought it together shall drink it in My holy courts." Isaiah 62:8-9.

The Lord swears by His right hand, and by the arm of His strength. 'For when God made a promise to Abraham, because He could swear by no one greater, He swore by Himself, saying, "Surely blessing I will bless you, and multiplying I will multiply you"' (Hebrews 6:13-14). In chapter 40 we saw how awesome that hand is, and we learned that His arm is not shortened that it cannot save. Away back in Moses' time, the Lord made a promise to Israel:

"Now it shall come to pass, if you diligently obey the voice of the Lord your God, to observe carefully all His commandments which I command you today, that the Lord your God will set you high above all nations of the earth." Deuteronomy 28:1.

He also promised that if they did not obey His voice and His commandments:

"A nation whom you have not known shall eat the fruit of your land and the produce of your labour, and you shall be only oppressed and crushed continually." Deuteronomy 28:32.

In reality, the history of Israel has constantly been the latter. Whether it was the Midianites, or the Romans, or whoever, other nations have constantly sought to oppress Israel and rule her. In today's text, what is God swearing to? He promises that the day will come when Israel's grain will no longer be given as food to her enemies; her wine will no longer be drunk by the sons of foreigners. Gentile powers will no longer strip the land of the food for which God's people have laboured. Those who have gathered it shall eat it and praise the Lord; and those who have brought it together shall drink it in God's holy courts.

Of course, we don't have to wait until the eternal state to thank and praise God for our food and drink. We can do it now. Millions of people have been touched by Norman Rockwell's famous painting of the woman and the little boy in a railway café, bowing their heads in a grace for their food. In the painting, the expressions of the worldy-wise onlookers depict people 'being stopped in their tracks.' For them, the simplicity and beauty of the sight are a rare occurrence. In 1 Timothy 4:5 Paul teaches, "For every creature of God is good, and nothing is to be refused if it is received with thanksgiving; for it is sanctified by the word of God and prayer." That includes the food we eat. At our meal times, let praise be lifted to the God who spreads our table.

OCTOBER 14TH

Go through, go through the gates! Prepare the way for the people; build up, build up the highway! Take out the stones, lift up a banner for the peoples! Indeed the Lord has proclaimed to the end of the world: "Say to the daughter of Zion, 'Surely your salvation is coming; behold, His reward is with Him, and His work before Him.'" And they shall call them the Holy People, the Redeemed of the Lord; and you shall be called Sought Out, A City Not Forsaken. Isaiah 62:10-12.

Here comes the proclamation! It goes out to the ends of the earth. The roads are to be resurfaced and every imaginable obstacle is to be removed. From across the world the nations are called to come to Zion. The work of salvation that the Lord set out to do, will be finished to the very last soul. The reward for all His mighty work will be with Him: they will be called, 'The Holy People, The Redeemed of the Lord,' and 'Sought Out, A City not Forsaken.'

The New Testament teaches that our Lord will come: 'To those who eagerly wait for Him He will appear a second time, apart from sin, for salvation' (Hebrews 9:28). Think of it this way. Jesus came back to Bethany to raise Lazarus from the dead. Then He sat down with Mary and Martha, who were obviously still alive; and with Lazarus, who had died in His absence. Then those from Bethany, and others, went in triumph with Christ to Jerusalem, where the people cried, "Blessed is He who comes in the name of the Lord." There were some Pharisees standing by. Do you remember what they said? "Look, the world has gone after Him!" (John 12:19). They did not know how prophetically accurate their statement was. At the Second Coming, Christ will first raise the bodies of those believers who have died while He has been away, and take both them, and those still alive who are in Him, and set them down at the marriage supper of the Lamb (Revelation 19:7). One day, we shall reign with Him in the New Jerusalem.

Consider these beautiful names for God's people. 'The Holy People': there will be nothing to sully their names. No longer will they serve Him with a sinning heart. 'The Redeemed of the Lord': the perfect work of bringing back God's people has been accomplished, and Satan's work will be finally wiped out. 'Sought Out': from every tongue, and people, and nation, the Saviour has sought and found people. In a vision, John saw the city that was once detested and forsaken:

'Then I, John, saw the holy city, New Jerusalem, coming down out of heaven from God, prepared as a bride adorned for her husband. And I heard a loud voice from heaven saying, "Behold the tabernacle of God is with men, and He will dwell with them, and they shall be His people. God Himself will be with them and be their God."' Revelation 21:2, 3.

Who is this who comes from Edom, with dyed garments from Bozrah, this One who is glorious in His apparel, travelling in the greatness of His strength? – "I who speak in righteousness, mighty to save." Why is Your apparel red, and Your garments like one who treads in the winepress? "I have trodden the winepress alone, and from the peoples no one was with Me. For I have trodden them in My anger, and trampled them in My fury; their blood is sprinkled upon My garments, and I have stained all My robes.
Isaiah 63:1-3.

Not all will submit to the Lordship of Christ. There are those who have always opposed our King, and sorely persecuted those who have stood for Him. One of those ancient enemies was the Edomites. The ancestors of Esau never lost their hatred for the sons of Jacob. Their behaviour and its deserved punishment are summed up in Amos 1:11:

'Thus says the Lord: "For three transgressions of Edom, and for four, I will not turn away its punishment, because he pursued his brother with the sword, and cast off all pity; his anger tore perpetually, and he kept his wrath forever."'

From a foreign land God's people expressed a longing for Zion, and spoke of sitting down by the rivers of Babylon, and hanging their harps upon willows. In the midst of their anguish they prayed, 'Remember, O Lord, against the sons of Edom the day of Jerusalem, who said, "Raze it, raze it, to its very foundation!"' (Psalm 137:7). God will answer their prayers: "For My sword shall be bathed in heaven; indeed it shall come down on Edom, and on the people of My curse, for judgment" (Isaiah 34: 5). Edom is 'the final eschatological enemy' (Alec Motyer, *Isaiah*, IVP, p.384).

The watchmen see an unrecognised figure approaching: "Who is this who comes from Edom?" they ask. His garments are vivid, and He is striding forward with confidence. As he comes near they see that the vivid colour of His garments is, in fact, a stain, as if He had been treading grapes. It transpires that this lone avenger is the Lord, coming from the defeat of His enemies. He had trodden a winepress of wrath – the stain is blood. W. E. Vine links this passage with Psalm 29, which poetically describes the overthrow of the Lord's enemies. He teaches that the overthrow begins in Lebanon (vv.5-6), and sweeps down to the wilderness of Kadesh (v.8), the centre of which is Bozrah. He states that the distance from Sirion in Lebanon, to Bozrah in Edom, is 200 miles, or 1600 furlongs – which is exactly the distance mentioned in Revelation 14:20, a passage that is the parallel of Isaiah 63! (W. E. Vine, *Expository Commentary on Isaiah*, Nelson, p.183).

Whatever eschatological view is taken of this passage, the message is clear. The other side to God's love and mercy is His overwhelming wrath and righteous vengeance. Again we can clearly see why in Nazareth the Lord shut the book at the words, 'to proclaim the acceptable year of the Lord.' The very next line says, 'and the day of the vengeance of our God.' Thank God that Calvary stands between the two.

"For the day of vengeance is in My heart, and the year of My redeemed has come. I looked, but there was no one to help, and I wondered that there was no one to uphold; therefore My own arm brought salvation for Me; and My own fury, it sustained Me. I have trodden down the peoples in My anger, made them drunk in My fury, and brought down their strength to the earth." Isaiah 63:4-6.

Why does the Lord trample out the vintage? (Bozrah, the capital city of Edom, means 'vintage'). He now gives the explanation. The long predicted day of vengeance has come, and the Redeemer is about to bring His wrath and vengeance upon the enemies of His people. The Lord undertook Calvary alone, when He bore God's wrath on behalf of our sin. Now all who have refused His invitation to come, take His yoke upon them, and learn from Him, will face God's vengeance. It is not as though they were not warned; God's word is full of warnings. So it is their choice. God's vengeance is not sinful, but judicial; it is not cruel spite, but righteous requital. In Adam's case, he chose to hide from the Lord, and keep clear of the Lord's presence. He was allowed to have his choice, and a flaming sword barred his return to the garden. If nations wish to do without God, then they need not complain if He lets them have their choice. If they constantly kill and persecute His people (more people were slain for their faith in Christ in the 20th Century than in any other), those nations or peoples need not complain if He avenges that innocent blood. It is not as if they do not have a chance to repent.

Notice the perfectly balanced nature of the Lord. His love and His wrath are not contradictory: one would be inadequate without the other. He is committed to both the day of vengeance, (which, according to Romans 9:28, is short) and to the year of His Redeemed. A solemn warning comes through in these awesome texts: those who persecute God's people, persecute Him. The unrepentant perpetrators will be held to account.

I will mention the lovingkindnesses of the Lord and the praises of the Lord, according to all that the Lord has bestowed on us, and the great goodness toward the house of Israel, which He has bestowed on them according to His mercies, according to the multitude of His lovingkindnesses. Isaiah 63:7.

In this closing section of the Book of Isaiah, we have been hearing about intercession. The watchmen were to intercede with God day and night, until all His promises were fulfilled (Isaiah 62:6). The Lord's remembrancers were to give themselves to the task of reminding the Lord of all His promises. This is something He longs for us to do.

Now we see a superb example of intercessory prayer (Isaiah 62:1– 64:12). I take it that the speaker of this prayer is Isaiah himself. Others think that it is one of the watchmen.

Either way, it certainly brings before us all the dynamics of intercessory prayer. All through the Bible and history, people have stood between heaven and earth as intercessors. "I sought for one who would . . . stand in the gap before Me on behalf of the land . . ." (Ezekiel 22:30). You can be such a one.

Today's verse is a very helpful guide to interceding in prayer. How does the prayer begin? It begins by telling God about God. How can we successfully intercede with a God whom we do not know? When you know what God loves and what He hates, what He desires and what His overall aims are, then you can intercede intelligently for your own life and circumstances, and for others. When you know, for example, that He opposes the marriage of a believer to an unbeliever, you can pray intelligently in such a circumstance. When you know that He will not share His glory with another, it will steer you away from self-centred praying.

Don't listen to anyone who criticises prayers that tell God about God, saying, 'What's the point of telling God what He already knows?' The point is that it is not for God's benefit, but for ours. So Isaiah begins by speaking to God of His lovingkindnesses. This is the Lord's pledged love for His people, demonstrated in the things He has done. Not only has He been good to us, He has been abundantly good to us. His gracious acts of love and favour are beyond calculation. Just think about them, before you intercede with God about something today.

'Because your lovingkindness is better than life, my lips shall praise You. Thus I will bless You while I live; I will lift up my hands in Your name. My soul shall be satisfied as with marrow and fatness, and my mouth shall praise You with joyful lips.' Psalm 63:3-5.

October 18TH

For He said, "Surely they are My people, children who will not lie." So He became their Saviour. In all their affliction He was afflicted, and the Angel of His Presence saved them; in His love and in His pity He redeemed them; and He bore them and carried them all the days of old. Isaiah 63:8-9.

Isaiah reflects on what God did for His people in the first Exodus, when He had committed Himself to them. He completely identified with them: their affliction became His affliction. In Judges 10:16 we actually read a very thought-provoking sentence regarding God's empathy: 'His soul could no longer endure the misery of Israel.'

If empathy were not enough for them, God also saved them by 'the Angel of His Presence,' or 'the Angel of the Lord.' This is a mysterious phrase; and one that I approach nervously. Over many years I have wondered what it means. It is clear that the Angel who appeared to Hagar in Genesis 16:7-14 was, in fact, the Lord. The two names are distinct, yet they refer to the same person. Another example is given in Genesis 22:11, 12, when the Angel of the Lord told Abraham not to sacrifice Isaac, saying, ". . . since you have not withheld your son, your only son, from Me." In Exodus 3, it was 'the Angel of the Lord,' who appeared to Moses in the burning bush; and it was the Lord, who called to him from the bush. Some think that it is the Lord's appearance in angelic or human form, foreshadowing His coming in the flesh. Others think it is the Lord's presence among His people in the person of His angel – 'who speaks as the Lord and is yet distinct from Him, in whom the Holy God 'accommodates Himself to live among sinners' (Alec Motyer, *Isaiah*, IVP p.387). One thing is certain: 'the Angel of His Presence' saved His people, again and again.

God's love and pity for His redeemed people are beautifully portrayed in the famous Song of Moses:

'He found him in a desert land and in the wasteland, a howling wilderness; He encircled him, He instructed him. He kept him as the apple of His eye. As an eagle stirs up its nest, hovers over its young, spreading out its wings, taking them up, carrying them on its wings, so the Lord alone led him, and there was no foreign God with him' (Deuteronomy 32:10-12).

Surely the remembrance of all these past blessings to God's people should embolden us, as intercessors, to seek them anew.

OCTOBER 19TH

But they rebelled and grieved His Holy Spirit; so He turned Himself against them as an enemy, and He fought against them. Isaiah 63:10.

Intercessors need to know the nature of the living God with whom they are interceding. Isaiah the intercessor now speaks of the way that Israel rebelled against the lovingkindness and favour of God. He particularly emphasises the effect of their rebellion on the Person of the Holy Spirit. Isaiah obviously understood the personal nature of God the Holy Spirit. He says that Israel's rebellion grieved the Holy Spirit, and their behaviour turned God from being their friend into their enemy.

Paul warns against grieving the Holy Spirit: 'And do not grieve the Holy Spirit of God, by whom you were sealed for the day of redemption' (Ephesians 4:30). Marcus Barth once said that the God in Ephesians is not 'an unmoved mover.' The Holy Spirit indwells believers, and He is the guarantee of the redemption of their bodies in a coming day. Paul and Isaiah both agree that it is possible to grieve and hurt that very same Spirit. In Greek, to grieve, means, 'to cause sorrow, pain or distress.'

How is it possible to do such a thing? Paul outlines unacceptable Christian behaviour: lying, sinful anger, stealing, corrupt communication, fornication, covetousness, filthiness, drunkenness, loveless marriages, people-pleasing, bitterness, malice, wasting opportunities, dishonouring parents, unbalanced parenting, and a wrong attitude to everyday work. All of these things bring sorrow, pain and distress to the Holy Spirit. Rebellion against God's ways grieves the Holy Spirit.

If it is possible to grieve the Holy Spirit, the other side of Paul's serious directive is that it is also possible to bring Him pleasure. He empowers us to put on the new self and the saving life of Christ. Then our lives can produce the fruit of the Spirit. Let me list a few examples:

a kindly word, a neighbourly act, a helpful letter or email. A positive attitude, a turning of the other cheek, an hour of our time to make a child's heart glad. A smile instead of a frown. A giving-up of our comfortable seat. Patience when the check-out machine is broken down, a tolerant reaction when the computer crashes; to walk away, when staying would mean disaster, or vice-versa. Such actions make life sweeter for others. The amazing fact is that they also bring immense pleasure to God the Holy Spirit. Do you enjoy bringing pleasure to other people? Remember that the Holy Spirit is a Person, who feels pain, and enjoys pleasure.

OCTOBER 20TH

Then he remembered the days of old, Moses and his people, saying: "Where is He who brought them up out of the sea with the shepherd of His flock? Where is He who put His Holy Spirit within them, who led them by the right hand of Moses, with His glorious arm, dividing the water before them to make for Himself an everlasting name?"
Isaiah 63:11-12.

As Isaiah is in intercession, he casts his memory back across the history of God's dealings with His people. Suddenly he recalls that God did the very same thing. In the midst of Israel's serious rebellion, and His legitimate punishment of their sin, He remembered how He had to bear His people in grace for a very long time. What thinking! What is God's view of His own action?

First He asks, "Where is He who brought them up out of the sea?" He is no different now than He was then. It is Israel who have missed out. God had to carry out His promise, that if they did not obey He would scatter them. Why, oh why, are God's people like this so consistently? When they could know untold blessing in their lives, all through history they have thwarted that blessing by rebellion, and flirting with other gods. Even in the 21st century they are so stubborn, and will not stop leaning on their own understanding. Why do they not lean on the Lord, and do what He asks them to do? God meditates on the days when He led them by Moses, the man He had chosen for the work, 'the shepherd of His flock.'

Again the theme of the arm of the Lord is presented. Behind the guiding hand of Moses was the glorious (or, literally, 'beautiful') arm of the Lord. He personally intervened at the Red Sea and in Jordan, when the waters were divided for His people to pass over as on dry land. That arm is still strong to save: it can still clear the way for you, if you will go forward in His will.

God muses on the motivation for all His gracious kindness to His people. He did it, He says, 'to make for Himself an everlasting Name.' He still leads us 'in the paths of righteousness for His name's sake' (Psalm 23:3). If He does not lead you, then His reputation is at stake; just as surely as it would have been if He had failed to bring the Children of Israel to the land of promise. Sadly, the first generation perished because they did not trust Him. Out of all of that generation, only Joshua and Caleb were allowed into the Promised Land. If your trust is in Him, He will lead you and bring you through. His reputation, now and always, will remain intact. His is an everlasting Name.

OCTOBER 21ˢᵗ

"Who led them through the deep, as a horse in the wilderness, that they might not stumble?" As a beast goes down into the valley, and the Spirit of the Lord causes him to rest, so You lead Your people, to make Yourself a glorious name. Isaiah 63:13-14.

A s Isaiah the intercessor comes to the end of his review of the lovingkindnesses of the mighty God, what particular aspect of His character does he select? It is His unchanging nature. He concludes that the God who guided and led His people in the past, still leads and guides them, to make Himself 'a glorious name.' Indeed, of all the comfort we receive from the teaching of Isaiah, there is none greater than the truth of the immutability of God. David is in absolute accord with Isaiah on this:

'Blessed be the Lord God of Israel from everlasting to everlasting! Amen and Amen.' Psalm 41:13.

We all face problems in our lives. In these verses Isaiah uses beautiful imagery to depict the unerring, unchanging guidance of our immutable God. Let us draw comfort from it.

The first image is in relation to the way the Lord led His people across the Red Sea.

'Then Moses stretched out his hand over the sea; and the Lord caused the sea to go back by a strong east wind all that night, and made the sea into dry land, and the waters were divided. So the children of Israel went into the midst of the sea on dry ground, and the waters were a wall to them on their right hand and on their left.' Exodus 14:21-22.

Isaiah says that the Lord led them through the deep, as a horse in the wilderness. In the open country of the wilderness, a horse is sure-footed and there are no barriers to impede its progress. So the Lord led His people across the abyss of the Red Sea, with massive walls of water banked up on either side of them. I suspect that, among the two million or so people who crossed the Red Sea with Moses, many a little child, or older person, never mind the middle-aged, looked up in trepidation at those huge walls of water. What if they collapsed? What if God changed His mind? But that was impossible. They were as sure-footed as a horse in open country. But the Egyptians, attempting to do so, were drowned. How did those Israelites keep going, despite the formidable sight on either side of them? The Bible says they did it 'by faith' (Hebrews 11:29). Faith still removes mountains; and the God of the Red Sea can still lead you sure-footedly through all your problems.

The second image is of cattle being led into a beautiful valley of pasture. The One who leads them knows where He is taking them. He has been there ahead of them; and now leads them to the luscious grass they need. Isaiah says that the Spirit of the Lord guides even animals to pasture and rest. If He can do that, the implication is that He can do the same for you and me. God will make a way for you, and lead you to rest. He is famous for such guidance. Trust Him.

OCTOBER 22ᴺᴰ

Look down from heaven, and see from Your habitation, holy and glorious. Where are Your zeal and Your strength, the yearning of Your heart and Your mercies toward me? Are they restrained? Doubtless You are our Father, though Abraham was ignorant of us, and Israel does not acknowledge us. You, O Lord, are our Father; our Redeemer from Everlasting is Your name. Isaiah 63:15.

K nowing the character of God, and having reviewed the long history of His lovingkindness towards His people, Isaiah now turns his attention from retrospection, to the best perspective of all: a view of the Sovereign God, high and lifted up in His heaven. His habitation is 'holy and glorious.' We remember that Isaiah began his ministry with a vision of the Lord, 'high and lifted up.' When you are interceding with God, a realisation that He is still on the throne is a very good perspective to hold. Notice that Isaiah addresses God as 'Father.' The subject of the Fatherhood of God does not arise very often in the Old Testament, but Abraham takes a huge public stand for it. He pulled out of Ur, where he was opposed to the worship of goddesses. Nowhere in Scripture is it taught that God may be addressed as 'He/She,' or 'She.' God is our Father, and Jesus taught us to address Him as such in prayer. Christians identify with the words of Paul in Romans 8:15:

'For you did not receive the spirit of bondage again to fear, but you received the Spirit of adoption by whom we cry out, "Abba, Father"'

'Abba' is the Aramaic word for 'Father.' It is in the spirit of the special bond between a child and its father that Isaiah brings his requests, couched with questions. He asks if his heavenly Father's zeal, strength, love and mercy are restrained towards him. Is Isaiah doubting God? Certainly not. It is Isaiah's way of asking God to display the zeal, strength, love, and mercy he knows He has, in Israel's circumstances. He knows these blessings have been restrained because of Israel's sin; and now he wants them to be released.

Isaiah has no doubts as to who God is, and what He can do: "Doubtless you are our Father, though Abraham was ignorant of us, and Israel does not acknowledge us." There are two views of what he means here. One is that Israel as a nation is so far away from God that Abraham and Jacob (Israel's original name) would no longer recognise her. Another view, the one which I take, is that Abraham and Jacob are dead, but the God of Abraham and Jacob is still the Living God. He is still a Father who cares; 'our Redeemer from Everlasting' is His name. It is a very contemporary prayer for all intercessors. May God's zeal, strength, love and mercy be evident in your own circumstances, as you intercede for your nation at this hour.

OCTOBER 23RD

O Lord, why have You made us stray from Your ways, and hardened our heart from Your fear? Return for Your servants' sake, the tribes of Your inheritance. Isaiah 63:17.

I saiah is in no way blaming God for the sins of His people. Just as he recognised that God's hand was restrained in His zeal, strength, love and mercy because of Israel's sin, he realises that God must allow them to learn sin's consequences. As with Pharaoh, they had reached a point in hardening their hearts against God so often, that God now did the hardening. Today's text makes us think of Hebrews 6:4-6.

276

'For it is impossible for those who were once enlightened, and have tasted the heavenly gift, and have become partakers of the Holy Spirit, and have tasted the good word of God and the powers of the age to come, if they fall away, to renew them again to repentance, since they crucify again for themselves the Son of God, and put Him to an open shame.'

The point is that God does not say it is impossible to forgive their sins. What He says is that it is impossible to get them to change their minds after this. Why? Because the only thing that could possibly bring them to repentance is the Holy Spirit's power. 'Once they have felt that and have deliberately rejected it, there is no other power in God's universe that could possibly reach them. The Holy Spirit, after all, is God. Reject Him finally and knowingly, and there is nothing else that could save them . . . God Himself has no power greater than that of the Holy Spirit by which to renew them to repentance' (David Gooding, *An Unshakeable Kingdom*, IVP, p.149-150). Isaiah is interceding for his people, and for himself. He comes in repentance, not rejecting the Holy Spirit, to ask the Lord to return in blessing to His people.

The story is told of the Christian farmer, who was living far from the Lord. He was always withdrawn in his attitude to other people. One freezing, snow-bound, winter's evening on his farm, he heard the 'tap, tap, tap' of some little sparrows on his kitchen window. They were trying to get into the heat and warmth. He decided that he would try to get them into his barn. So, crossing the yard in the snow, he opened the barn doors, put on the lights, threw down some straw, and laid a trail of crackers across the snow to entice them in. It was all to no avail; he just frightened them. He even tried to get behind them and 'shoo' them in, but it didn't work. Later in his kitchen he thought, 'the only way I could possibly get those sparrows to follow me into that barn would be to become a sparrow myself.' Just then, the awesome thought flooded his mind: 'That's just what God did. He became one of us, to save us.' But if we harden our hearts to Him, then there is no other salvation.

OCTOBER 24TH

Your holy people have possessed it but a little while; our adversaries have trodden down Your sanctuary. We have become like those of old, over whom You never ruled, those who were never called by Your name. Isaiah 63:18-19.

It is a salutary lesson to consider just how far God's people can stray. Today's text takes us back to the haunting Song of Moses at the end of his life. 'For the Lord's portion is His people; Jacob is the place of His inheritance. He found him in a desert land and in the wasteland, a howling wilderness; He encircled him, He instructed him, He kept him as the apple of His eye . . . He made him ride in the heights of the earth.' Deuteronomy 32:9-10, 13.

The Lord had brought His people to a promised land. But, says Isaiah 'Your holy people have possessed it but a little while'. Imagine the people who are known as 'the Lord's portion,' now carrying descriptions like, 'You did not rule them,' and 'Your name was not given them.'

Somehow, though, there is reality here. The intercessor, Isaiah, is facing the truth about how far God's people have gone in their backsliding. He is admitting that the situation is so bad that there is now no discernable difference between God's people and those over whom God had never ruled. At least, he is not ignoring the problem. He is facing it, and that is where the hope lies. He knew they needed help; and he knew where to look for it.

As we read today's text, let us ask ourselves a searching question: 'If we were up in Court under the accusation of being a Christian, would there be enough evidence to convict us?' What does the surrounding society see in us that makes them discern that we are different? We are called to be different. In rejecting his stereotype as a Sixties icon, Bob Dylan said, "I am glad I'm not me." At least the man was honest! Christian, let the real you emerge, and be what you are! Do not despise the fact that following the Lord Jesus makes you stand out as conspicuously as a city set on a hill. Glory in the difference.

Let the beauty of Jesus be seen in your every move. In the way you handle lust – make a covenant with your eyes, just like Job did (Job 31:1). In the way you handle greed – be content with such things as you have. In the way you handle anger – don't let the sun go down on your wrath. In the way you do your work – do everything as to the Lord. In the way you handle pride – let nothing be done through selfish ambition or deceit, but in lowliness of mind let each esteem others better than him or herself. Remember, it's the differences that make a difference.

OCTOBER 25TH

Oh, that You would rend the heavens! That You would come down! That the mountains might shake at Your presence – as fire burns brushwood, as fire causes water to boil – to make Your name known to Your adversaries, that the nations may tremble at Your presence! When You did awesome things for which we did not look, You came down, the mountains shook at Your presence. Isaiah 64:1-3.

The prayer of Isaiah moves now from intercession, to a bold cry that God should intervene in Israel's present circumstances on the basis of His previous displays of strength. His presence and power were so powerful at Mount Sinai, that it made the mountain quake.

'Then it came to pass on the third day, in the morning, that there were thunderings and lightnings, and a thick cloud on the mountain; and the sound of the trumpet was very loud, so that all the people who were in the camp trembled. And Moses brought the people out of the camp to meet with God, and they stood at the foot of the mountain. Now Mount Sinai was completely in smoke, because the Lord descended upon it in fire. Its smoke ascended like the smoke of a furnace, and the whole mountain quaked greatly. And when the blast of the trumpet sounded long and became louder and louder, Moses spoke, and God answered him by voice.' Exodus 19:16-19.

The other evening, after a day's writing, I was walking at sunset in a beautiful park near my home. It was given to our city as a gift by Sir Thomas and Lady Dixon. I saw a Christian that I know, Mr. Marshall Milne, sitting on one of the benches in the rose garden, quietly reading. I greeted him and sat down for a chat. He was reading from a little pocket Bible! I told him that I was writing about Isaiah, and that at times I had found myself almost trembling, lest I got the wrong meaning. I was learning so much about the awesomeness of God. He told me that, just the previous evening, he had been thinking of people in Scripture who 'trembled'.

Moses trembled in the presence of God at the burning bush: '. . . and Moses hid his face, for he was afraid to look upon God' (Exodus 3: 6). Paul trembled as he went down the Damascus road: 'suddenly a light shone around him from heaven . . . he fell to the ground, and heard a voice . . . so he, trembling and astonished, said, "Lord, what do You want me to do?"' (Acts 9:3-6). Felix, the Roman Procurator, trembled when Paul reasoned with him about righteousness, self-control and the judgment to come. He answered, "Go away for now; when I have a convenient time I will call for you" (Acts 24:25). Felix was a favourite of the Emperors, Claudius and Nero. Tacitus said of Felix: 'He revelled in cruelty and lust, and wielded the power of a king with the mind of a slave.' Yet he trembled when He heard God's Word. May we do the same.

Isaiah calls on God to manifest His power in such a way that the very nations will tremble at His presence. Now that's what I call bold praying! Does it make your church prayer meeting appear inhibited?

OCTOBER 26TH

For since the beginning of the world men have not heard nor perceived by the ear, nor has the eye seen any God besides You, who acts for the one who waits for Him. You meet him who rejoices and does righteousness, who remembers You in Your ways . . . Isaiah 64:4-5a.

Since time began people have worshipped millions of gods. But nobody has ever imagined, heard, or seen a God to compare with the Lord. What is it about Him that is unique? Many things mark Him out; but Isaiah identifies in particular the principles upon which He acts for people.

Firstly, He 'acts for the one who waits for Him.' To wait for the Lord, is to have absolute faith in what He has promised. It is to believe that He cannot, and will not, fail. Even when God seems to withdraw, or when His way is currently unknown, faith holds fast to His promises. This is exemplified in people like Noah, as he prepared for the coming flood; Abraham, leaving Ur; Jacob, blessing Joseph's sons, when he was dying; Moses, on leaving Egypt; Joshua at Jericho; and David before Goliath. I know you may face huge odds today – more than I have ever known – but remember that simple faith in the Living God invokes His action on your behalf.

Secondly, God acts on behalf of people who gladly do what is right. What more haunting example, than Abigail? Her husband, Nabal, was a fool, and she knew it. Nabal had not treated David right; and now David and 400 of his men are determined to murder him. Abigail rides out to meet them, and bows her face to the ground. She has an abundance of food for his men loaded on donkeys. She pleads with David to disregard Nabal, and not avenge himself by shedding blood. She reminds him of his famous victory over Goliath: '. . . the lives of your enemies He shall sling out, as from the pocket of a sling!' When God has fulfilled His promise and set him on Israel's throne, David will not have to grieve over unrighteous actions. He says, "Go up in peace to your house. See, I have heeded your voice and respected your person." Subsequently, the Lord dealt with Nabal. May Abigail's influence increase!

Thirdly, God acts for people who keep in mind the way He works. Remember principles one and two, and then watch God act on your behalf.

OCTOBER 27TH

You are indeed angry, for we have sinned – in these ways we continue; and we need to be saved. But we are all like an unclean thing, and all our righteousnesses are like filthy rags; we all fade as a leaf, and our iniquities, like the wind, have taken us away. And there is no one who calls on Your name, who stirs himself up to take hold of You; for You have hidden Your face from us, and have consumed us because of our iniquities.
Isaiah 64:5b-7.

The Lord constantly acts on behalf of those who exercise faith in Him, who delight in doing what is right, and remember Him in His ways. But, just as constantly, the people have sinned; and indeed continue to do so. It raises the question: 'Shall we be saved?' (RV). Is there any hope for them? Isaiah acknowledges the apostate condition of God's people. Their best efforts, tainted by sin, were as a filthy garment. Decay had set in: they were like a faded leaf. The inherent destructiveness of sin had come, like the wind, and swept them away.

Isaiah laments before God on the lack of devotion amongst His people. There is no one who calls on the name of the Lord, nor stirs himself up to take hold of God. What an indictment! Again it makes me think of one who did call on the Lord's name, and stirred herself to take hold of God. 'So Hannah arose after they had finished eating and drinking in Shiloh . . . and prayed to the Lord and wept in anguish' (1 Samuel 9, 10). The great annual religious festivals at Shiloh did little for Hannah. Gatherings for worship do not always turn out to be splendid. The reality was that Israel was far from God, and the evil priests had made the people to sin. At Shiloh there was an outward form of godliness, but they denied the power of it. Eli, the High Priest, thought Hannah was drunk. One translation puts Eli's stinging words as, "How long will you go on, you drunken creature? Away with you; go and sleep off your drunkenness." But Hannah was not deterred, and continued to believe that God would answer her prayer. Her baby was born. Samuel grew up to become a prophet and a judge in Israel. He anointed David king, from whose line centuries later came the Saviour of the world – Immanuel, 'God with us.'

The Lord will not hide His face from any prodigal who in repentance comes home; nor from even the weakest believer upon his or her knees.

But now, O Lord, You are our Father; we are the clay, and You our potter; and all we are the work of Your hand. Do not be furious, O Lord, nor remember iniquity forever; indeed, please look – we all are Your people! Isaiah 64:8-9.

On the basis of His lovingkindnesses and past interventions, Isaiah has interceded with God on behalf of Israel. He acknowledges that both he and they have miserably failed to obey His word. Now he pleads from another point of view: God is their Creator. Would a potter want to deny the pot that he had made? Would he say that it had just appeared? A potter cannot ultimately disown his own work. God was their heavenly Father, so they have a special relationship with Him. Isaiah pleaded with God that He would not permanently show His anger to Israel, nor remember their iniquity forever.

This is an amazing intercessory prayer; and I want to emphasise again that Christians in the 21st century can learn a huge amount from it. Where are the clichés with which we are now so familiar in modern day praying? It would seem too bold for modern day public prayer. When did you hear last someone pray, 'Since You made us, Lord, please look at our circumstances'? Here is an intercessor who believes he is in as close a relationship with God, as clay is with the potter. If the clay is broken or marred, it can be refashioned or remade. The staggering implication is that Isaiah is looking at the possibility of the Lord remaking the nation. Can God remake a nation? Of course He can. What is more, He will even remake the earth into a new earth.

Yield, then, to the Potter's hand in repentance and humility, and let Him remake your life and ministry. You may have disastrously failed; but the One who made you in the first place can remake you. He can still take you up as a very useful vessel in His hand. Saul of Tarsus, the bigoted and cruel Israelite, was truly a broken vessel when the Lord regenerated him. Ananias was hesitant about seeing him, but God said: 'Go, for he is a chosen vessel of Mine to bear My name before Gentiles, kings, and the children of Israel' (Acts 9:15). Who knows where you will bear His name before this week is out?

Your holy cities are a wilderness, Zion is a wilderness, Jerusalem a desolation. Our holy and beautiful temple, where our fathers praised You, is burned up with fire; and all our pleasant things are laid waste. Will You restrain Yourself because of these things, O Lord? Will You hold Your peace, and afflict us very severely? Isaiah 64:10-12.

I saiah's final pleas in this prayer look to the coming days, when his prophecy will be fulfilled. He knows what is coming: the holy cities, including Jerusalem itself, will become a wilderness. The temple, where God dwelt and generations praised His name, will be burned up with fire. Everything that God's people treasured will be laid waste. It must have been grim for Isaiah to have to carry such a prophetic vision in his mind and heart. What occupies Isaiah's mind is: what will happen after the prophecies have been fulfilled? Will the Lord hold Himself back? Will He keep silent and punish His people beyond measure? Will He react at all to the repentance of His people?

The Lord's response will be the subject of the last two chapters from the pen of Isaiah. His matchless contribution fittingly stands as leader of the seventeen prophetic books in the Bible. As we come to the end of his intercession, we see Isaiah throw himself and his people upon the mercy of the Lord. He knows that God is merciful, and He will not abandon His children. Isaiah does not expect to be denied or disappointed.

From a Christian perspective, as we look at Bible prophecies regarding future events, we, too, are comforted in the absolute assurance of the mercy of God to all who repent and believe His word. As we see earthquakes, floods, catastrophic disasters of one kind or another, wars and rumours of wars across the earth, we know that we can find shelter in the Lord Jesus. He is our 'rock in a weary land.' Isaiah was tested on all that he had taught, and we will be tested too. There is still mercy with the Lord. When the storms come, He will hold us. The hand that reached out and saved the sinning and erring Peter more than once, will reach out and save us. The final chapters of Isaiah show how awesome and far reaching that salvation will be.

OCTOBER 30TH

"I was sought by those who did not ask for Me; I was found by those who did not seek Me. I said, 'Here I am, here I am,' to a nation that was not called by My name." Isaiah 65:1.

T he response from the Lord to Isaiah's intercession makes my heart leap; for the simple and profound reason that He mentions a Gentile like me! Paul, the great apostle to the Gentiles quotes Isaiah 65:1, to confirm that Gentiles are included in God's great plan of mercy and grace.

But I say, did Israel not know? First Moses says: "I will provoke you to jealousy by those who are not a nation, I will move you to anger by a foolish nation." But Isaiah is very bold and says: "I was found by those who did not seek Me; I was made manifest to those who did not ask for Me." Romans 10:19-20.

The import of this truth that Isaiah and Paul are teaching is that God was reaching down to me, even before I thought of reaching up to Him! Throughout history, millions of Gentiles have found that God was seeking them. In the most amazing circumstances, as they were searching in other places for the answers to life's meaning, and trying to find satisfaction in sources far from God, they discovered that they were being searched out. Suddenly God says, "Here I Am, here I Am." (Don't you love the double affirmation?)

Magdalen College is one of the loveliest colleges in Oxford. Situated just outside the old city walls on the banks of the River Cherwell, it has some of the most hauntingly beautiful buildings of Oxford. To the north is the deer park, and to the east is a great meadow around which runs Addison's Walk, just under a mile long.

It was the evening of September 19th, 1931. An Ulsterman called C. S. Lewis, a Fellow and tutor at Magdalen, had just had some guests to dinner at the college. They were strolling along Addison's Walk, talking about myths. One of the guests, Professor J. R. R. Tolkien, was the Rawlinson Professor of Anglo-Saxon. He shared with Lewis a deep love of mythology, particularly the mythology of Scandinavia. C. S. Lewis had long been an atheist, but in recent times he had discovered that God was searching for him. He stated that he had no more been searching for God, than a mouse would search for a cat!

Now Lewis was a theist – he believed in the creation of the universe by one God – but he was not yet a Christian. As they walked together, Tolkien maintained that myths preserved something of God's truth, although often in a distorted form. Lewis could not see the relevance of concepts in Christian truth, similar to those found in pagan mythologies. For instance, the ideas of sacrifice, the shedding of blood, communion, and redemption. Tolkien maintained that the difference between the Christian story and other stories was that it came from a God who was real; and from a God whose dying could transform those who believed in Him. Tolkien talked with Lewis until three o'clock in the morning and then went home. Hugo Dyson, another friend and academic, continued to talk with Lewis, who was now striding up and down the arcades of New Buildings. Dyson emphasised that everyone who believes in Christ receives peace and forgiveness of sins. Three days later, while sitting in the sidecar of his brother's motorcycle en route to Whipsnade Zoo, C. S. Lewis was converted to Jesus Christ. To his dying day, he would maintain the truth in today's text. That truth still stands. God is often found by those who did not seek Him; and He says, "I am here, I am here," to those who did not even care. Lewis was one of them.

OCTOBER 31ST

"I have stretched out My hands all day long to a rebellious people, who walk in a way that is not good, according to their own thoughts; a people who provoke Me to anger continually to My face; who sacrifice in gardens, and burn incense on altars of brick; who sit among the graves, and spend the night in the tombs; who eat swine's flesh, and the broth of abominable things is in their vessels." Isaiah 65:2-4.

We have discovered many contrasts through Isaiah's profusion of imagery. Today's text presents a contrast that could not be more dramatic. Here the Lord responds to the intercessions of Isaiah, telling things from His perspective. He says that, in fact, day after day He has stretched out His hands to a rebellious people. In Romans 10:21 Paul tells us that this rebellious people was Israel. Of what greater contrast could we read, than the Living God holding out His hands to bless people, who invariably turn their backs on Him? What greater irony could there be than the Creator wanting to guide His people into a way of true prosperity, while they insist on walking in a way that is not good?

God describes their lifestyle and attitude as, according to their own thoughts; and, continually provoking Him to His face. Let's just review where their own thoughts have led them. Mainly into idolatry. They no longer come to God's temple to offer sacrifices to the Lord in the prescribed way; but now they sacrifice in gardens to other gods. In Gideon's day, God asked him to go and chop down the altar of Baal and the wooden image beside it that his father had. Baal was the fertility god of the land: owning and controlling it, with the increase of crops, fruits and cattle. Farmers were completely dependent on Baal, and offered sacrifices to him in their gardens. In complete defiance to God's express word, they used bricks to build altars to Baal (Exodus 20:25). The Israelites had also got involved in spiritism, for they sat among graves to get messages from the dead. They spent nights in crypts, eating forbidden food and broth of abominable things.

God's ways are best: they always have been, and they always will be. They are healthy and wholesome for family and national life. The Ten Commandments were intended to put backbone into any nation. These people, to whom they were originally given, had disobeyed them.

As we look across the world today, these verses are particularly applicable to our day and generation. The rise of the occult in Western civilisation is massive. The Lord and His Word are being despised; millions live 'according to their own thoughts.' What should we do?

'Therefore strengthen the hands which hang down, and the feeble knees, and make straight paths for your feet.' Hebrews 12:12-13.

Let's heed God's Word, and turn to His outstretched hands. We will not be sorry.

November

Here we have the cards of a Jacquard loom which is controlling the lifting of the harness cords. The Jacquard card is commonly accepted to be the earliest form of the digital computer. Joseph Marie Jacquard of Lyons in France invented the loom that bears his name. One skilled weaver could successfully operate it. In the Book of Isaiah the prophet berates the women of Israel for being 'haughty' while wearing 'fine linen'!

". . . who say, 'Keep to yourself, do not come near me, for I am holier than you!' These are smoke in My nostrils, a fire that burns all the day." Isaiah 65:5.

If you were to approach these idolaters with the truth of God and His word, how would they react? If you were to point out that there is a better way through life than sacrificing to a fertility god in your garden, or sitting among graves at night trying to get in touch with the dead, or eating some witch's brew – would they say, 'Maybe you have a point there'? I'm afraid not! More likely, they would say, 'Keep to yourself, do not come near me, for I am holier than you.'

Here is a phrase which has become part of the English language. Wherever people exercise an exclusive attitude in the area of spirituality, we talk about them as being 'holier-than-thou.' Perhaps, though, this text indicates that they think they are holier than the Lord Himself. They know better than God; but their pride is like smoke in His nostrils, from a fire that burns all day. All day long God has stretched out His hand to these people, but they profoundly aggravate Him, drawing out His righteous, justified retribution.

Even in the Christian church it is a sad fact that believers can come very close to idolatry. Paul had to warn against those who said, "I am of Paul," while others said, "I am of Apollos." He asked them, 'Was Paul crucified for you? Or were you baptised in the name of Paul?' (1 Corinthians 1:12-13). The 'I-am-of-Paul,' and the 'I-am-of-Apollos,' contentions seem very much like the 'I-am-holier-than-you' syndrome.

In these days, when New Age teaching is saying that we are all gods, let us heed the Lord's warning to the prince of Tyre:

"Because your heart is lifted up, and you say, 'I am a god, I sit in the seat of gods, in the midst of the seas,' yet you are a man, and not a god, though you set your heart as the heart of a god . . . I will bring strangers against you . . . and defile your splendour." Ezekiel 28:2, 7.

Our hearts are very easily deceived, and there is no end to the pride with which they can be tempted. The wisest man on the earth once said:

'Walk prudently when you go to the house of God; and draw near to hear rather than to give the sacrifice of fools, for they do not know that they do evil. Do not be rash with your mouth, and let not your heart utter anything hastily before God. For God is in heaven and you on earth; therefore let your words be few.' Ecclesiastes 5:1-2.

Anything you and I have that is worthwhile, we were given. Let us never – by thought, word, or even inflection – show a holier-than-you attitude to anyone, anywhere, ever.

"Behold, it is written before Me: I will not keep silence, but will repay – even repay into their bosom – your iniquities and the iniquities of your fathers together," says the Lord, "who have burned incense on the mountains and blasphemed Me on the hills; therefore I will measure their former work into their bosom." Isaiah 65:6-7.

God has made a note of what His rebellious people have done, and He will bring retribution on the unrepentant. There is salvation for the repentant; but there is judgment for those who refuse His outstretched hands – both in past and succeeding generations. God will not ignore such blasphemy. He finds the smell of their incense obnoxious. Judgment will be measured out exactly as they have sinned.

Alec Motyer carefully points out that coming generations are not pre-doomed in Scripture by the sins of the past. He lays emphasis on the fact that, 'failure to break with the past involves the entail of the past' (*Isaiah*, IVP, p.395). Jesus said

"Woe to you! For you build the tombs of the prophets, and your fathers killed them. In fact, you bear witness that you approve the deeds of your fathers; for they indeed killed them, and you built their tombs. Therefore the wisdom of God also said, 'I will send them prophets and apostles, and some of them they will kill and persecute,' that the blood of all the prophets which was shed from the foundation of the world may be required of this generation, from the blood of Abel to the blood of Zechariah who perished between the altar and the temple. Yes I say to you, it shall be required of this generation." Luke 11:47-51.

It was because the succeeding generation approved of what their fathers had done, that they brought the judgment of God on their heads. If they had only stepped out of the cycle and repented, they would have known His blessing.

The words of Ezekiel are a powerful commentary on today's texts.

"If, however, he begets a son who sees all the sins which his father has done, and considers but does not do likewise; who has not eaten on the mountains, nor lifted his eyes to the idols of the house of Israel, nor defiled his neighbour's wife; has not oppressed anyone, nor withheld a pledge, nor robbed by violence, but has given his bread to the hungry and covered the naked with clothing; who has withdrawn his hand from the poor and not received usury or increase, but has executed My judgments and walked in My statutes – he shall not die for the iniquity of his father; he shall surely live!" Ezekiel 18:14-18.

Is there someone reading these lines, and you long to break out of your family's long, sinful history, or their current behaviour? If you turn away from it, you will not be held responsible for what they have done. The evil Saul had a son called Jonathan, who strengthened David's hand in God. Be a Jonathan to a David today, despite any sinful practice in your family for which you are not responsible.

NOVEMBER 3ᴿᴰ

Thus says the Lord: "As the new wine is found in the cluster, and one says, 'Do not destroy it, for a blessing is in it,' so will I do for My servants' sake, that I may not destroy them all." Isaiah 65:8.

One view of this powerful image in today's text is that there are sweet and sour grapes in God's vineyard. The remnant of God's people who have been faithful to the Lord are likened to the sweet grapes, and those who have been unfaithful are likened to the sour grapes. For the sake of His faithful servants, God will not destroy the entire nation of Israel.

The word used here for 'new wine' is 'juice.' According to F. S. Fitzsimmons (*Wine*, NBD, p.1242), this wine is made from the first drippings of the juice, before the press is trodden. It has been suggested that this word 'found,' suggests that 'the grapes were oozing as they were picked; and this is specially prized' (Alec Motyer, *Isaiah*, IVP, p.396). Hence the phrase: 'for a blessing is in it.' Whatever view is taken, it is clear that God has found something special in His people. Isaiah is using another beautiful image for those who love and follow the Lord. I pray that as the Lord of the vineyard comes to pick His grapes, He will find in my life a sweetness and a blessing for His glory. God forbid that I should be a fruitless tendril in His vineyard. What is the secret in being that sweet grape, or that ripe juice?

"I am the true vine, and My Father is the vinedresser. Every branch in Me that does not bear fruit He takes away; and every branch that bears fruit He prunes, that it may bear more fruit." John 15:1-2.

The vine is certainly a fruit tree; but it cannot stand upright like other fruit trees. Its branches are very pliant, and it requires a skilful hand to guide them along the trestles. God achieves His purposes through His people; and if there are to be good, fruit-producing branches, then we must yield ourselves to the loving hand of the Vinedresser. We may sincerely desire to grow in a certain way, but our purposes and sense of direction could be far removed from what the Vinedresser wants. He may twist us, fasten and nail us in a certain place, much against our will; but what is the result? The result is luscious grapes. Just as Christ, the True Vine, yielded to His Father's will, to the blessing of the world; so too, if we yield to the Vinedresser, we will be a blessing, beyond our expectations.

NOVEMBER 4TH

"I will bring forth descendants from Jacob, and from Judah an heir of My mountains; My elect shall inherit it, and My servants shall dwell there. Sharon shall be a fold of flocks, and the Valley of Achor a place for herds to lie down, for My people who have sought Me." Isaiah 65: 9-10.

In today's text we have God's commitment to His faithfulness: Israel will possess His mountains and dwell there. The trust of the Psalmist was not unfounded: 'Behold, the eye of the Lord is on those who fear Him, on those who hope in His mercy, to deliver their soul from death, and to keep them alive in famine' (Psalm 33:18-19); 'And now, Lord, what do I wait for? My hope is in You' (Psalm 39:7).

The beautiful certainty of this hope is seen in what God promises for two places in particular: Sharon, and the Valley of Achor. Sharon has always been famous for its flowers (Song of Solomon 2:1). It stretches along the coastal region from Joppa to Carmel. It is a place of rich pasture (Isaiah 35:2). But in Isaiah 33:9 we read that Sharon had become like a wilderness. The valley of Achor had long been associated with the sin of Achan, who 'took of the accursed things' (Joshua 7:1). The name means, 'the valley of trouble,' and it was named after him. Now we read that Sharon, once a wilderness, will become again a place where sheep will safely graze on rich pasture: it shall be 'a fold of flocks.' The valley of Achor, once renowned for its association with disobedience and sin, will be 'a place for herds to lie down.' Why all this transformation? It is because the faithful amongst God's people have sought Him; so the new earth they longed for will surely come, and they will be gathered into it.

They wanted to be in the presence of the Lord, to enjoy Him forever. The new earth would be of no use to them if the Lord were not present, would it? In my youth I went to hear Dr. Martyn Lloyd-Jones speak on False Ecumenism. It was an unforgettable experience. Addressing a crowd of about 3,000, he asked, "Is Christ not enough for you any more?" He also pointed out that if you unite dead churches, you will only have death. So let those who truly seek the Lord unite; and let their desire for His presence and His glory be what unites them.

November 5th

"But you are those who forsake the Lord, who forget My holy mountain, who prepare a table for Gad, and who furnish a drink offering for Meni. Therefore I will number you for the sword, and you shall all bow down to the slaughter; because, when I called, you did not answer; when I spoke, you did not hear, but did evil before My eyes, and chose that in which I do not delight." Isaiah 65:11-12.

The faithful among God's people are shown in contrast with the apostate. The faithful sought God in His temple, and on His holy mountain at Jerusalem. On the mountains, the apostates burned their incense to false gods; and on the hills, they blasphemed God. Two gods are highlighted in particular. Sadly, they are still very much with us today. The first is Gad. He was a Caananite god, and his name means 'Fortune.' Gad was worshipped as the god who decided on a person's prosperity. Feasts would be held in honour of Gad, and the custom was that his image would be placed on cushions. People may not spread out cushions to honour Fortune today; but millions certainly give their lives, and sell their very souls, to him. The truth is that he delivers emptiness and incalculable disillusionment; but people still see him as the fountainhead of happiness. He never satisfies, because people who grasp what he has to offer always want more.

The second god is Meni. His name means 'Destiny.' Apostate Hebrews would fill up mixed wine drink-offerings for him. Meni was worshipped as the god who decided, or foreordained, a person's 'fate;' or the course of events they would have to pass through. In these days there are millions who turn to the occult to find out their destiny. It is an area of great temptation; for who would not be interested in finding out what is ahead of us?

God had called these people. He had a destiny for them that was incalculably fulfilling, but they ignored His call. God spoke to them, promising everlasting satisfaction, but they refused to hear, brushing Him off. They deliberately chose what God hated; and the ultimate destiny of their choice was death.

Let your fortune and destiny lie in doing those things that delight God. You will find that your fortune is made, and your destiny is secure.

Therefore thus says the Lord God: "Behold, My servants shall eat, but you shall be hungry; behold, My servants shall drink, but you shall be thirsty; behold, My servants shall rejoice, but you shall be ashamed." Isaiah 65:13.

This text is full of great contrasts, and I do not think it is wrong to spiritualise it. In any generation, if you compare the life and lifestyles of those who love and follow the Lord with those who don't, you will find them to be very different in what they deliver. Let us take, for example, a Christian perspective.

'Then Jesus said to them, "Most assuredly, I say to you, unless you eat the flesh of the Son of Man and drink His blood, you have no life in you. Whoever eats My flesh and drinks My blood has eternal life, and I will raise him up at the last day."' John 6:53-54.

These words are not speaking about the Lord's Supper. To take that view would mean that a vast number of people who have been converted, but who have never broken bread or drunk wine in remembrance of the Lord Jesus, would not be the possessors of eternal life. Apart from that, I honestly do not believe that these words are teaching that, when taken in remembrance of His death, bread and wine become the literal body and blood of Christ. If they were, it would mean that when He was holding the bread, and said, "This is my body," Christ would have been referring to two bodies, wouldn't He?

These words are an analogy, telling us that just as we have to ingest food, and let it become part of us, if we want to maintain life; so Christ in us is the hope of glory. That's why, after Christ had fed the 5,000, the disciples were told to gather up all the fragments that were left. It represented Him as the Living Bread. If that Living Bread is within you, it will never be lost. And with all my heart I believe, neither will any true believer. "He who eats this bread," said Christ, "will live forever" (John 6:58). He will raise up all believers at the last day: in such assurance we can face not only the terror of death, but we can face the fury of life.

Christ's disciples found the saying about eating Christ's flesh and drinking His blood hard to understand, and offensive. Instead of softening His statement to accommodate them, though, Christ strengthened it, by pointing out that He had not just come to lead a good life. He had come into this world in order to bring us on our journey to the next one. He is the means to maintain us on that journey: we feed upon Him as we go. Praise His Name that He refused to take back the statement He made. If others are offended by it, why should we be? As Isaiah points out, the alternative is hunger and thirst. In fact, in spiritual terms, the alternative is an eternal famine and an eternal thirst. Selah.

290

'Behold, My servants shall sing for joy of heart, but you shall cry for sorrow of heart, and wail for grief of spirit." Isaiah 65:14.

Y ou don't have to look around our world long to know that there is not much joy about. You only have to watch the evening News to realise that locally and internationally the world is filled with misery. When was the last time you heard an infectious laugh? In these tough times, should the issues that we all have to face eclipse every expression of joy?

Let's go back to Paul's joyful letter to the Philippians:

'I thank my God upon every remembrance of you, always in every prayer of mine making request for you all with joy . . . For to me, to live is Christ, and to die is gain . . . I am hard pressed between the two, having a desire to depart and be with Christ, which is far better. Nevertheless to remain in the flesh is more needful for you. And being confident of this, I know that I shall remain and continue with you all for your progress and joy of faith, that your rejoicing for me may be more abundant in Jesus Christ by my coming to you again . . . Therefore if there is any consolation in Christ, if any comfort of love, if any fellowship of the Spirit, if any affection and mercy, fulfil my joy by being like-minded, having the same love, being of one accord, of one mind.' Philippians 1:3, 4, 19, 22-26; 2:1, 2.

When comparing being with Christ in heaven to staying on earth in His service, Paul considered one as a gain and the other as a joy. How did he encourage the Christians to work together in harmony? He said that by doing so it would make his joy complete: he was joyful, but they could make him even more joyful! Paul wanted to send a friend called Epaphroditus to see the Philippian Christians; and he asked them to 'receive him with all joy' (Philippians 2:25-30). He expected friendship to be joyful. Again and again, Paul called on the Philippians to 'rejoice in the Lord!' In fact, as he was concluding his letter, he wrote, 'Rejoice in the Lord always. Again I will say, rejoice!'; and when the Christians showed concern for him, it caused him to rejoice in the Lord 'greatly!' (Philippians 4: 4, 10). And all this from a man in prison for the Lord's sake!

The disappointment of an unfulfilled life is the ultimate regret of those who do not follow the Lord. Isaiah says they shall be 'ashamed', 'cry for sorrow of heart,' and 'wail for grief of spirit.' Contrast this, with God's servants rejoicing and singing 'for joy of heart.' There is no competition.

"You shall leave your name as a curse to My chosen; for the Lord God will slay you, and call His servants by another name; so that he who blesses himself in the earth shall bless himself in the God of truth; and he who swears in the earth shall swear by the God of truth; because the former troubles are forgotten, and because they are hidden from My eyes." Isaiah 65:15-16.

The clear demarcation between the apostates and the faithful among God's people will be seen in their names. One will leave a name that would become a curse, and the other will be known by a new name, which is not given. It is linked with a new day, a day when former troubles are forgotten and hidden from God's eyes. Anyone who prays for a blessing on the land will use the name, 'the God of truth,' meaning, literally, 'the God of the Amen.' Whoever takes an oath in the land will also use the name, 'the God of the Amen.' This beautiful name of God denotes the God who fulfils His word, and will carry out His covenant-promises to His people. Paul explains this concept by saying, 'For all the promises of God in Him are Yes, and in Him Amen, to the glory of God through us' (2 Corinthians 1:20). John was told to write to the angel of the church of the Laodiceans, and say, 'These things says the Amen, the Faithful and True Witness' (Revelation 3:14).

When God makes a promise, He adds His Amen to that promise. Paul distinctly teaches that God adds His Amen to all His promises. When God said to Abraham, 'I will make your descendants multiply as the stars in the heaven; I will give to your descendants all these lands; and in your seed all the nations of the earth shall be blessed' (Genesis 26:3, 4), He added His Amen to it. His Amen affirmed His promises away back in Noah's time. When God made His promise regarding the birth of Christ to Mary through the Angel Gabriel, He told her to call her Son, Jesus. He said, "He will be great, and will be called the Son of the Highest; and the Lord God will give Him the throne of His Father David." This too caused His Amen, as it did when the promise was made through Isaiah, that a Child would be born, and a Son given (Isaiah 9:6-7).

Whatever your circumstances, even though they might not all be good, the Lord has promised that 'all things work together for good to those who love God, to those who are the called according to His purpose' (Romans 8:28). When it is all over, you will see what God has been doing. When it started, He said a special Amen; and you'll say a special Amen at the end.

NOVEMBER 9ᵀᴴ

"For behold, I create new heavens and a new earth; and the former shall not be remembered or come to mind." Isaiah 65:17.

Imagine something new that is so wonderful, that you cannot remember the old! That will be the reality in the coming new creation. All God's creatorial powers of the old creation will be brought to bear upon the new. The beauty of the old heavens and earth, with the stars and planets, mountains and oceans, flowers and forests, will be surpassed. All the old pain and sorrow, divisions and hurt, wars and trouble, will be gone: 'the former shall not be remembered or come to mind.' Even the political structures of Governments will no longer exist; the power structures of earthly leadership, with all their envy, jealousy and in-fighting, will go.

Recent newspaper articles and TV programmes were looking back, one year later, on the September 11ᵗʰ 2001 attacks on New York and Washington. We can all remember where we were when it happened. As mentioned before, it was on that day I agreed with my Publisher o write this book on Comfort, from Isaiah. Virtually every day since I have been engaged in writing it. In the face of the huge questions that have arisen as a result of the outrage, do I regret taking on the project? I gently and honestly can say, 'certainly not.'

In the *Guardian* Newspaper (4.11.02), I read how a church Pastor called Alvin Durant said, "We were all hugging and crying at Ground Zero, but for the most part we went back to our segregated neighbourhoods. And that's got to tell you something. All that togetherness didn't last – and I knew it wouldn't. I said it wouldn't. I told people in my sermons, 'a bigot's a bigot, and some day soon it's all going to be the way it was.'" A Columbia University English Professor was quoted as saying, "The amazing thing, talking to my students, is not how much September 11th matters to them, but how little; but then the City is so much bigger than almost anything, that life just goes on." It is true that September 11th 2001 did not bring a utopia of unity, and a cessation of grief, sorrow and trouble in the United States, or in any other nation; yet I am glad that the Professor did say that New York was 'so much bigger than *almost* anything.' Our studies in Isaiah have shown us that God is bigger than, not almost anything, but absolutely everything. He is so big that, when He replaces the old order of creation, even a vast city like New York will not appear big any more – it will be forgotten!

The Bible teaches that the Lord Jesus will bring about the restoration of all things. This world, with the evident inability of its people to live together in peace, its inherent bias towards violence, sin and evil, will not be completely transformed until the Lord transforms it. Meanwhile His gospel goes out to the ends of the earth; and to all who believe it, a new transforming power enters their life. Bigots do not remain bigots, if they trust and truly follow the Lord Jesus. The Apostle Paul, who was one of the most famous former bigots, said: "For I am not ashamed of the gospel of Christ, for it is the power of God to salvation for everyone who believes" (Romans 1:16).

Despite the terrors of September 11th and its aftermath, I can say with Paul:

"I am persuaded that neither death nor life, nor angels nor principalities nor powers, nor things present nor things to come, nor height nor depth, nor any other created thing, shall be able to separate us from the love of God which is in Christ Jesus our Lord." Romans 8:38-39.

How about you?

November 10th

"I will rejoice in Jerusalem, and joy in My people; the voice of weeping shall no longer be heard in her, nor the voice of crying." Isaiah 65:19.

The poem contained in Isaiah 65:17-25 encapsulates, perhaps more than any other passage in Scripture, the coming bliss of the eternal state. God calls on us to 'be glad and rejoice forever' in what He is about to create. The coming new city of Jerusalem describes metaphorically God's perfect work of creating a place of safety and security. It is a great comfort to read, 'the voice of weeping shall no longer be heard in her, nor the voice of crying.'

Dr. M. R. de Haan once calculated that, if all the tears shed in the world could be barrelled and poured into a canal, such a waterway would stretch from New York to San Francisco. He maintained it would make a river where barges could float. Few would doubt him; and yet Christians need to be balanced in their thinking regarding weeping. We look forward to the day when the causes of all weeping and crying will be removed, but we do not want to be Stoics. A lady approached me one day, with a comment that haunts me even now as I write about it. She told me that her husband had died, and her Christian friends had said to her, "You let the Lord down by crying so much." I wish I could talk to her friends; for with friends like that she could do with a change.

The world often follows the doctrine of Stoicism, and I want to categorically state that Christian teaching denies it at every turn. Exponents of Stoicism, from Cicero to the present day, have taught that nothing is within man's power except imagination, desire and emotion. By cultivating a detachment from the world, and mastery over his reactions to outside intrusion, the Stoic can achieve freedom and happiness. In its early days it rigorously excluded pity, denied pardon, and suppressed general feelings. Sin was simply an error of judgment, rectified by a change of opinion. Whatever his position in life, if even a slave, the Stoic could be inwardly free. It also ruled out obedience to a personal God.

Christian truth presents a very different story. It is about a Christ who stands by the grave of a friend and weeps; who stands over a city and weeps; and who goes to a garden and prays with strong crying and tears. He commands that His followers rejoice with those who rejoice, and weep with those who weep. It does not countenance Stoicism. God created human beings with a capacity to weep. Indeed, it is one of the most important characteristics in a human being. Research shows that people who do not allow themselves to weep are probably storing up emotional troubles for the future. Weeping is natural in the expression of grief, and we must let people weep. Scripture records that Joseph wept on seven different occasions. It is not a sign of weakness; it is the sign of a heart that is moved by pain or distress. Won't it be bliss to be in a place where neither pain nor distress will ever be present?

November 11th

"No more shall an infant from there live but a few days, nor an old man who has not fulfilled his days; for the child shall die one hundred years old, but the sinner being one hundred years old shall be accursed." Isaiah 65:20.

In the future state, one who is one hundred years old will be a youth; and the elderly will not be robbed of fulfilment either. Longevity will return, and the power of death will be unknown. What does the phrase mean, 'but the sinner being one hundred years old shall be accursed'? Alec Motyer states, "We are again dealing with metaphor: even if, *per impossible,* a sinner were to escape detection for a century, the curse would still search him out and destroy him. In reality, just as death will have no more power, so sin will have no more place" (*Isaiah,* IVP, p.399).

'He will swallow up death forever, and the Lord God will wipe away tears from all faces; the rebuke of His people He will take away from all the earth; for the Lord has spoken. And it will be said in that day: "Behold, this is our God; we have waited for Him, and He will save us. This is the Lord; we have waited for Him; we will be glad and rejoice in His salvation."' Isaiah 25:8-9.

In the meantime, if the Lord has not come, we all face the possibility of death. How do we anticipate it? My view is influenced by an incident at dinner one evening in a friend's house, when a guest leaned over to me and asked, "Did you hear what the man said to the lamplighter?" (The questioner, the godly Mr. Tom Pinkerton, had been a lamplighter for many years in the Stranmillis area of Belfast. Every evening at twilight he would light at least 60 lamps; then one hour before dawn he would get up and put them all out again. He told me that children would play on his ladder, and as he passed by their homes, folk would talk to him of their lives and their troubles.) "The man asked the lamplighter," continued Tom, "if he was scared of the dark." "No," replied the lamplighter, "because when one light is out, I keep my eye on the next one; and when that one is out, I keep my eye on the next one; and by the time the last one is out – it is dawn!"

So it is that the Saviour of the World lights lamps of guidance through life's labyrinthine ways. Through His Word, through circumstances, through the peace He gives which passes all understanding, He has guided millions from a destiny of blackness of darkness to the dawn of an eternal day. If death is 'the valley of the shadow,' then there must be a light there. You cannot have a shadow without a light. That light is Christ. When a believer approaches death, they will find it is like a shadow. A shadow does not harm anyone. If a foe comes to attack, but only his shadow touches you, then you are safe. Death is but the valley of the shadow we travel through, in order to reach the glory that lies on the other side, where death is unknown. Trust in the 'divine Lamplighter,' and you will find His guidance unerring, His love infinite, and your destiny secure.

NOVEMBER 12TH

"They shall build houses and inhabit them; they shall plant vineyards and eat their fruit." Isaiah 65:21.

Recently I watched an interesting building project, right across the road from my own front door. New neighbours moved in. They had the house they bought bulldozed, and laid the foundations for another. Access would have been impossible, so any major ground excavation had to be done before the building started. Fascinated, we watched as ponds, and even a river, were created. Fifty tonnes of glazier deposit, known as Mourne Mountain granite, were dropped on the site. Then the building began on the house. The water in the new garden is pumped from the bottom pond through a series of buried pipes, at the rate of 40,000 gallons per hour, returning to the pond through a waterfall. The garden-planting consists of azalea, taxus, juniper and bamboo, hedera and wisteria, amongst others.

It was all designed by the TV gardener, Colin Donaldson. It is just beautiful: a piece of the Mourne Mountains in South Belfast. Then the neighbours moved in to inhabit their beautiful new home; and when they go on holiday they give us the key!

There are few greater joys than inhabiting your own home, whether it is a mansion, a cottage, a city flat, or a country farmhouse. To shut your own door, sleep in your own bed, eat at your own table, sit in your favourite chair – these are among life's greatest pleasures. Imagine, then, what it would be like to build a house, and not to live in it! To plant a garden and not be able to enjoy it!

God warned Israel through Moses: ". . . you shall build a house, but you shall not dwell in it; you shall plant a vineyard, but shall not gather its grapes . . . A nation whom you have not known shall eat the fruit of your land and the produce of your labour" (Deuteronomy 28:30-33). The warning was not without foundation; the day came when their enemies came and inhabited their land and homes.

The promise given by Isaiah for the future state is that there will be no more confiscation and displacement. No enemy will ever again attack and drive them out of their habitations. They will enjoy to the full the work of their hands. Like a tree that has grown for centuries from deep, well-nourished roots, in the place where it was first planted, so God's people will prosper forever. We shall go to that place of 'many mansions' (John 14:2), and will never suffer eviction or confiscation of any kind. So you see, I was not wrong in saying this little poem in Isaiah is one of the best descriptions of the future state ever written, was I?

November 13ᵀᴴ

They shall not labour in vain, nor bring forth children for trouble; for they shall be the descendants of the blessed of the Lord, and their offspring with them. Isaiah 65:23.

L et's recap on what Isaiah has been saying in this poem. The future state will be so wonderful that the past will be forgotten. It will be filled with joy; and weeping and crying will be unknown. Death will be removed; confiscation of houses and land will cease forever. All enemies will be subjugated: the causes of grief will be gone. Now Isaiah refers to the cause of one of life's greatest griefs: tragedy in the life of one's child.

Just a few weeks ago I was counselling a friend whose child was faced with the possibility of death. As fathers, we both agreed that, if possible, we would die in place of our children, in order that they could live on. It brought to mind Grant, an outstanding teenage lad, whose early death still stirs up deep sadness in the hearts of all who knew him. He showed a particular interest in a message I had given on the subject of Heaven, in which I quoted from a wide-ranging number of Christians. Among them was Dr. Martyn Lloyd Jones, the outstanding Bible expositor. His daughter, Lady Elizabeth Catherwood, had been praying by his bedside, asking God to spare her dying father to God's people for a little while longer. He was in great weakness, but reached for a pen, wrote a statement on a piece of paper, and handed it to Lady Catherwood. It read, 'Don't hinder me from the glory!'

When the day of Grant's funeral came, I spoke at his graveside in a howling storm. After prayer, and having committed his body to the earth, we stood by the open grave. His father quietly turned to me, and said, "Only the Lord could bring him out of that." I went away through that storm, comforted in the knowledge that not only could He, but God would bring Grant's body 'out of that.'

Years later I stood in a graveyard, where a pregnant woman and two of her relatives were being laid to rest. They had been killed in a terrorist outrage. It was horrendous; probably one of the greatest tragedies I have ever witnessed. Suddenly, Alan, the young mother's grieving husband, saw me, and said, "We do not sorrow as those who have no hope." I had gone to the funeral to comfort him, and he ended up comforting me! In the face of the death of his loved ones, including his unborn child, he found comfort that stayed his heart and mind in the promise of a land where we will never experience tragedy again. In the new earth, the eternal blessing is assured of both parents and children.

NOVEMBER 14TH

"It shall come to pass that before they call, I will answer; and while they are still speaking, I will hear. The wolf and the lamb shall feed together, the lion shall eat straw like the ox, and dust shall be the serpent's food. They shall not hurt nor destroy in all My holy mountain," says the Lord. Isaiah 65:24-25.

Here is the final undoing of Satan and all his works. In the new earth, fellowship with God will be unbroken and undisturbed. The perfect harmony between the redeemed and the will of God will be such that, before they call, He will answer; and while they are still speaking, He will hear. I have always longed to serve God with an unsinning heart, haven't you? I am aware that my prayers have very mixed motivations. 'If I regard iniquity in my heart, the Lord will not hear,' said David (Psalm 66:18). In that coming day we will never again experience iniquity hindering our close fellowship with God.

Not only is there the perfect harmony of fellowship in the eternal state, but also perfect harmony in creation. Paradise is regained; the law of the jungle is reversed. Nature, which is red in tooth and claw, will be reformed. The wolf and the lamb will feed together. The lion will no longer have to kill to eat; its very nature will be changed, for it will eat straw like the ox. But the curse on Satan and sin will remain. The promise to the serpent stays the same: "You shall eat dust all the days of your life" (Genesis 3:14). The Lord will bring these changes about in His new creation by His own word and power. It has nothing to do with Evolution.

It is a breathtaking vision. There will be no more war in the New Jerusalem: people will not hurt nor destroy in all God's Holy Mountain. In our world, with its killing and violence, the comfort of this promise could not be greater. Only last evening I watched an interesting TV documentary on the 'Ice Man,' found high in the Alps. His frozen body was carbon-dated at over 5,000 years old – long before Isaiah's time. The scientists examining his body tried to find the cause of death. After several years of research, a specialist noticed something very tiny on an x-ray. They believed it was an arrowhead, and a corresponding wound was discovered on his shoulder. It appears the 'Ice Man' was shot with a bow and arrow, and had escaped to a high altitude. As I watched it, I thought of how long violence has permeated humanity. Now we no longer threaten each other with bows and arrows, but with nuclear bombs, and weapons of mass destruction. With knowledge of genetics in the wrong hands, the very issues of life could be destroyed. Praise God, the Lord will intervene, and be victorious. He has promised a new world for all who trust Him. Are you on His side?

NOVEMBER 15TH

Thus says the Lord: "Heaven is My throne, and earth is My footstool. Where is the house that you will build Me? And where is the place of My rest? For all those things My hand has made, and all those things exist," says the Lord. "But on this one will I look: on him who is poor and of a contrite spirit, and who trembles at My word." Isaiah 66:1-2.

God was not against the temple. When His people returned from captivity, the rebuilding of the temple was a top priority, and with the encouragement of the prophets, Haggai and Zechariah, the work was eventually completed. As we learned from Isaiah 44:28, it was God who chose King Cyrus to start the whole process. At the dedication of the first temple, however, Solomon pointed out that no house on earth can truly contain God: "Behold, heaven and the heaven of heavens cannot contain You. How much less this temple which I have built!" (1 Kings 8:27). Heaven is God's throne, and earth is His footstool.

What, then, is the final chapter of Isaiah about? I think Barry Webb sums it up succinctly, when he says that God was 'not against the temple, but against ecclesiasticism, that ugly distortion of true religion which inevitably reasserts itself where there is no recognition of the greatness of God or heartfelt contrition before Him' (*The Message of Isaiah*, IVP, p.247).

If I could paraphrase the heart of today's texts, it seems to me God is saying, 'Since heaven is my throne and earth is my footstool, I do not actually need a house erected by man. What I am primarily looking for is a humble and contrite person, who trembles at My Word.' It is not that God did not condescend to live in His temple at Jerusalem. He did! He has a greater priority: to live in the life of someone who loves and obeys Him.

All these wonderful Scriptures, about the Lord preparing a place for us in heaven, are extremely comforting. It lifts your day to know that a place is being prepared for you. But what about in the meantime? Christ does not wait until we get to heaven before He introduces us to the Father. He proposes to bring us to the Father now, already in this life. How? – By the Father and Son making their home in our hearts here on earth, through the Spirit. Mark well what Jesus said:

"If anyone loves Me, he will keep My word; and My Father will love him, and We will come to him and make Our home with him." John 14:23.

What pleases God much more than a great building, is for His home to be in the life of a humble and contrite person, who is reverently responsive and obedient to His Word.

298

"He who kills a bull is as if he slays a man; he who sacrifices a lamb, as if he breaks a dog's neck; he who offers a grain offering, as if he offers swine's blood; he who burns incense, as if he blesses an idol. Just as they have chosen their own ways, and their soul delights in their abominations, so will I choose their delusions, and bring their fears on them; because, when I called, no one answered, when I spoke they did not hear; but they did evil before My eyes, and chose that in which I do not delight." Isaiah 66:3-4.

Those who tremble at God's word, are now contrasted with those who choose their own ways. Not being anchored in God's word, these Old Testament people introduce things into their worship that are an abomination to the Lord. The words, 'as if,' repeated in the text, can be left out. We then have Scriptural and unscriptural actions set out side by side. The killing of a bull in sacrifice, is in line with God's Law; the killing of a man is not. Sacrificing a lamb is scriptural; strangling a dog is not. Offering a grain offering is Scriptural; putting pig's blood on the altar is not. Burning incense is Scriptural; blessing an idol is not. These apostates delight in what they do: their hearts are in it. They have made a deliberate choice to go their own way.

Just as these people made a choice, so God makes His. They acted the way they did in order to protect themselves from all kinds of fears and terrors. So God allows those fears and terrors to come, as a punishment upon them. Notice again the great theme of choice in Isaiah. God called; but they chose not to answer. God spoke; but they chose not to listen. Now the very things they dreaded would come upon them, and their false religion would afford no protection whatsoever.

I was talking with a lady recently, and speaking of another person she said, "She is good at making bad decisions!" I trust I will not be good at making bad choices. Right through to the very last chapter of Isaiah, two very distinct groups of people emerge. Those who believe that 'He is God, and there is none else.' They turn to the Lord and are saved. Then there are those who do not trust in the Lord. One way leads to life; the other to destruction. One brings joy and fulfilment, peace and security; the other brings misery, disillusionment, fear and terror. One ends up in heaven; the other in Hell. The situation has been clear since chapter 1:

"Come now let us reason together," says the Lord, "though your sins are like scarlet, they shall be as white as snow; though they are red like crimson, they shall be as wool. If you are willing and obedient, you shall eat the good of the land; but if you refuse and rebel, you shall be devoured by the sword." Isaiah 1:18-20.

Whatever you do today, choose deliberately to let God's Word and ways guide your choice. You will not be sorry: not now, not ever.

NOVEMBER 17TH

Hear the word of the Lord, you who tremble at His word: "Your brethren who hated you, who cast you out for My name's sake, said, 'Let the Lord be glorified, that we may see your joy.' But they shall be ashamed." The sound of noise from the city! A voice from the temple! The voice of the Lord, who fully repays His enemies! Isaiah 66:5-6.

Now the taunts rise against those who tremble at the Word of God. Notice how much store God sets by someone who truly reverences what He has to say. It certainly marks them out; it also brings them into ridicule. These apostates have substituted pagan superstition and all sorts of nonsense for the law of God, as laid down for life and worship. They see themselves as being far superior to those who cling to the Scriptures. They think they know better! They regard having any hope in Jehovah as a deception. A literal translation of their sarcastic taunt is, 'Let Jehovah glorify Himself, that we may see your joy.' People sometimes say, 'If he's so clever, why isn't he rich?' It is like saying, 'If God is all you say He is, why aren't you happy?'

I wonder has someone been taunting you because of your faith in God and His Word? The Psalmist was deeply depressed: 'My tears have been my food day and night," and people taunted him with the question: 'Where is your God?' (Psalm 42:3). His plans had been frustrated, leading him to depression; but the taunt of the scoffer added to his despair. The scoffers had their physical gods that they set up in their temples or homes. Here was the Psalmist, who happened to be far from Jerusalem, claiming that the Living God was invisible. The scoffers mocked him, implying that his God certainly seemed to be as inactive as He was invisible. Otherwise, why his tears? The Psalmist was sensitive to their ridicule. The sharp pain of their scoffing was like a mortal wound in his body. He writes, 'As with the breaking of my bones, my enemies reproach me, while they say to me all day long, "Where is your God?"' (Psalm 42:10). Their taunts are very similar to the taunt in today's text.

I wonder if the taunts of the 'superior-minded' has got you to the point of doubting your salvation? At 45 years of age, Charlotte Elliott, the hymn writer, was suffering from ill health. She got so depressed that she began to question the reality of her spiritual life. Down in Brighton one day, overwhelmed with doubts, fears and spiritual depression, she felt she must fight out this battle once and for all. Getting pen and paper, she began to examine the truths that were the foundation of her faith. She thought of God's love for her, of Christ's death at Calvary on her behalf, and of the promises of God in the Bible. A poem emerged which contained these wonderful words:

> Just as I am, though tossed about
> With many a conflict, many a doubt,
> Fightings within and fears without,
> O, Lamb of God, I come.
>
> Just as I am, Thou wilt receive;
> Wilt welcome, pardon, cleanse, relieve.
> To Thee, whose promise I believe,
> O, Lamb of God, I come.

Millions have been touched and blessed by Charlotte's poem, that has become one of the most famous hymns in history.

So, ignore the scoffers. Today's text says, 'But they shall be ashamed.' Their trust is in nonsense; your trust is in the Lord, and those who trust Him shall never be put to shame. The Lord will deal with His enemies: the city will be stirred by His action, and His voice will be heard in the temple. Remember: because you trembled at God's Word, you will never be caused to blush.

NOVEMBER 18TH

"Before she was in labour, she gave birth; before her pain came, she delivered a male child. Who has heard such a thing? Who has seen such things? Shall the earth be made to give birth in one day? Or shall a nation be born at once? For as soon as Zion was in labour, she gave birth to her children. Shall I bring to the time of birth, and not cause delivery?" says the Lord. "Shall I who cause delivery shut up the womb?" says your God. Isaiah 66:7-9.

Much discussion surrounds this prophecy. Is it speaking of the sudden deliverance of God's people from Babylon? They were out of it, almost before they knew it. Is it the image of setting up the Christian church in the world, with the astonishing, immediate success of the gospel? It owed a great debt to the mother who gave it birth, namely Israel. Both scenarios certainly had results.

The New Bible Commentary is very helpful in its section on Isaiah's final chapter (Davidson, Stibbs, Kewan, IVF, 1953, p.607). "This chapter is in the nature of an epilogue, summarising and carrying out the principles of the rule of Jehovah as they apply to all ages to come." Commenting on today's verses, Alec Motyer says, "Everything comes down to what the Lord is. First, He is faithful to the end: He does not advance His purposes (bring to the moment of truth), only to abandon them. Secondly, He is sovereign: what He initiates He completes – (lit.) 'Do I beget and then close (the womb)?'" (*Isaiah*, IVP, p.402).

God's principles of action are unchanging. When He begins a work, He completes it; no matter whether Sennacherib, Herod, Nero, Stalin, Mao tse Tung, or whoever, stands in His way. Often He seems to be slow in bringing about His purposes; but suddenly they are born, in a day they are accomplished.

Whatever else you do in your life, do not 'marry' the spirit of this age. If you do, you will soon be a 'widower,' or a 'widow.' These apostate Jews we have been reading about were certainly moulded by the age they lived in; but the day came when they were left ashamed and lost. The power that brought about the exodus from Babylon, the birth of the Christian church, and the eternal state itself, is the same power that now works in every Christian's life.

'Now to Him who is able to do exceeding abundantly above all that we ask or think, according to the power that works in us, to Him be glory in the church by Christ Jesus to all generations, forever and ever. Amen.' Ephesians 3:20-21.

The power that raised up Jesus from the dead, is the very same power at work in you. The power that brought Jew and Gentile together, to form the church and make them one, is at work in you. You don't need to manipulate your life, or grovel to men and women of influence. There is a power at work in your life, as limitless as the love that makes it available. Don't listen to the scoffers. Lean on the promises of God, and go on for Him. Remember God's powerful questions: "Shall I bring to the time of birth, and not cause delivery? . . . Shall I who cause delivery shut up the womb?"

NOVEMBER 19TH

"Rejoice with Jerusalem, and be glad with her, all you who love her; rejoice for joy with her, all you who mourn for her; that you may feed and be satisfied with the consolation of her bosom, that you may drink deeply and be delighted with the abundance of her glory." Isaiah 66:10-11.

In the New Testament, Paul teaches that Gentiles were deprived of five elements: they had no relationship to Christ; no part in God's purposes; they were excluded from the covenants made with Abraham and David; they were without hope; they lived without God (Ephesians 2:12). Now, because of the Messiah's work, those who were once far off, can believe and be brought near by the blood of Christ.

'For He Himself is our peace, who has made both one, and has broken down the middle wall of separation, having abolished in His flesh the enmity, that is, the law of commandments contained in ordinances, so as to create in Himself one new man from the two, thus making peace.' Ephesians 2:14, 15.

Yet, despite all being one in the church, Gentiles must always respect the mother who gave us birth. She did not come from us, but we from her. When our ancestors were running around worshipping gods of wood and stone, the faithful amongst the Hebrew people were testifying to the glory of the living God. Today's verses are exhorting us to rejoice with Jerusalem, and be glad with her. Yes, we mourn for her sins, and are pained by her trials; but we are glad of all the good she has stood for. The day is coming on the new earth, when the full glory of the New Jerusalem will be enjoyed. We will then 'drink deeply and be delighted with the abundance of her glory.'

'You have come to Mount Zion and to the city of the living God, the heavenly Jerusalem, to an innumerable company of angels, to the general assembly and church of the firstborn who are registered in heaven, to God the Judge of all, to the spirits of just men made perfect, to Jesus the Mediator of the new covenant, and to the blood of sprinkling that speaks better things than that of Abel.' Hebrews 12:22-24.

NOVEMBER 20TH

For thus says the Lord: "Behold, I will extend peace to her like a river, and the glory of the Gentiles like a flowing stream. Then you shall feed; on her sides shall you be carried, and be dandled on her knees. As one whom his mother comforts, so I will comfort you; and you shall be comforted in Jerusalem." Isaiah 66:12-13.

The 18th century historian, Sir John Fortescue, writing about the aftermath of fighting in Europe, wrote these haunting lines:
'Far as the eye could reach over the whitened plain, were scattered gun-timbers, wagons full of baggage, of stones, of sick men, sutlers' carts and private carriages. Beside them lay the horses, dead; around them scores and hundreds of soldiers, dead; here a straggler who had staggered on to the bivouac and dropped to sleep in the arms of the frost; there a group of British and Germans around an empty rum-cask; here forty English Guardsmen huddled together around a plundered wagon; there a pack-horse with a woman lying alongside it, and a baby swathed in rags, peeping out of the pack with its mother's milk turned to ice upon its lips – one and all stark-frozen-dead.' *History of the British Army*, Volume IV, Part 1, pp.320-1.

Think of how many have perished in all the battles in the history of the world. The final tally of lives slaughtered by war hardly bears thinking about, and we still live in a world of war and rumours of war. The promise in today's text is mind-bending: of coming international peace in an city long associated with war. From the destruction of Jerusalem by Nebuchadnezzar, through the razing of the city by the Romans, to present day terror within its walls, God's people have prayed for the peace of Jerusalem (Psalm 122:6). Now God says that the city will be like a mother to the Gentile nations flowing into her: she will 'feed them, carry them on her sides, and dandle them on her knees.' Each nation, with its own particular characteristics and individuality, will be brought to its full glory and maturity.

Once the enemy came in like a floodtide. In a future day, mature nations will come to the city in peace. God says, "I will extend peace to her like a river, and the glory of the Gentiles like a flowing stream." I love all Isaiah's images, but this one 'takes the biscuit'! Isn't it just incredibly beautiful to think of nations being carried by Israel, like a mother carries her child on her side, and enjoying the same delight as a child being bounced on its mothers knees?

Who of us have not been comforted by our mother? So the Lord will comfort us in the New Jerusalem. God is our Heavenly Father, but He also has all the virtues of a mother.

NOVEMBER 21ST

When you see this, your heart shall rejoice, and your bones shall flourish like grass; the hand of the Lord shall be known to His servants, and His indignation to His enemies. Isaiah 66:14.

There is a great problem with human living. When life is going well and our world is flourishing, we can suddenly find it all threatened. An enemy rises up to wreck it. Maybe the enemy is driven by jealousy – someone wanting what we have; or by some prejudice against us. I have found jealousy to be as cruel as the grave; and prejudice the greatest enemy of truth. Are you a successful academic, but someone in these categories is threatening your flourishing teaching career? Are you a successful businessperson, and a cruel rival is threatening all your hard work and dedication? Perhaps you are a public person, and your career is being threatened by the scorn of poisoned tongues? Or are you a quiet, steady individual, who wants to live in peace, for the blessing of others, but turmoil has erupted in your circumstances? Someone always threatens our joys and successes.

Here we read of a superb promise. In a coming day your heart will rejoice; when you see what God is doing in the New Jerusalem, your joy will be full. And the wonderful thing is that no enemy whatsoever will threaten your joy, or disturb your peace. 'Your bones shall flourish like grass:' you will never be stressed out again through the action of an enemy. They will not be able to hurt you or harm you in any way. God will judge all the enemies of truth, goodness, and true success: "The day of vengeance is in My heart, and the year of My redeemed has come" (Isaiah 63:4).

Since we started our studies in chapter 40, do you remember the references to the Lord's hand? It was in the hollow of His hand that the waters of the world were measured; and the heavens between his finger and thumb (v.12). In chapter 41 He promised to 'open rivers in desolate heights, and fountains in the midst of the valleys; I will make the wilderness a pool of water, and the dry land, springs of water.' This was all done so that 'they may see and know, and consider and understand together, that the hand of the Lord had done this' (41:20). Just as the Perfect Servant is as a polished arrow, you are in His quiver in the shadow of God's hand for use just as He needs you (Isaiah 49:2). In your life, His hand has not been shortened, that it cannot save (59:1). Now we are promised that in the eternal state, 'the hand of the Lord shall be known to His servants' (66:14). Your enemies will never touch you again, and you will flourish eternally under the loving hand of God. There will be nothing, no nothing, to mar your bliss.

NOVEMBER 22ND

For behold, the Lord will come with fire and with His chariots, like a whirlwind, to render His anger with fury, and His rebuke with flames of fire. For by fire and by His sword the Lord will judge all flesh; and the slain of the Lord shall be many. Isaiah 66:15-16.

God detests sin. He does not treat it lightly, and He will take frightful vengeance upon it. We must always remember that sin is absolutely heinous to God. Keeping His attitude to sin constantly before us will create a true fear of God in our souls.

'. . . let us have grace, by which we may serve God acceptably with reverence and godly fear. For our God is a consuming fire.' Hebrews 12:28-29.

In today's text we learn that the Lord will come against sinners with fire, which speaks of His holiness. The whirlwind speaks of His sweeping judgment, which leaves nothing behind. His sword speaks of the application of His judgement against each individual (Alec Motyer, *Isaiah*, IVP, p.404). The image of a chariot speaks of pursuit. There is no escape from the judgment of God for those who have refused His grace and love.

Chariots are mentioned often in the Bible. It was a two-wheeled vehicle, drawn by two horses. Joseph rode in Pharaoh's second chariot. Pharaoh and his army pursued the children of Israel in chariots. Solomon built establishments to house his chariots, and imported many from Egypt. Nahum vividly describes the Assyrian chariot: 'The chariots come with flaming torches in the day of his preparation, and the spears are brandished. The chariots rage in the streets, they jostle one another in the broad roads; they seem like torches, they run like lightening' (Nahum 2:3-4).

'The chariots of God are twenty thousand, even thousands of thousands; the Lord is among them as in Sinai, in the Holy Place. You have ascended on high, You have led captivity captive; You have received gifts among men, even from the rebellious, that the Lord might dwell there. Blessed be the Lord, who daily loads us with benefits, the God of our salvation! Selah.' Psalm 68:17-19.

David's words in this Psalm are quoted by Paul in Ephesians 4: 8, to describe the resurrection of Christ. He is saying how Christ defeated Satan by His power – the stronger overcoming the strong; and now He has divided His spoils. Habakkuk writes of God's chariots of salvation (Habakkuk 3:8). The imagery of God having chariots is to emphasise His power. God's power will pursue impenitent sinners in judgment, just as His love pursues repentant sinners in love. He has a great purpose to fulfil.

Think of it like this. Here is, say, a gifted writer, and she writes of the transient things of time and sense. Then she is converted and starts writing for Christ. Now her writing can have eternal influence. Here is a gifted musician, but he uses his gift in the service of himself. Then he hears the gospel, trusts the Saviour – and what happens? His gift, once held by the strong, is now employed by the stronger. It can be used to God's glory for untold blessing among his generation. In His risen power, Christ is constantly dividing the spoils of His victory. To each Christian is given a charisma – a grace/gift. Are you using yours for His glory, or for your own?

NOVEMBER 23RD

"Those who sanctify themselves and purify themselves, to go to the gardens after an idol in the midst, eating swine's flesh and the abomination and the mouse, shall be consumed together," says the Lord. Isaiah 66:17.

We have been here before with Isaiah. Fearlessly, he has pointed out the absurdity of idol worship. We have sat in God's court, and watched Him give the idols of earth their opportunity to do something. But He proved that they were absolutely powerless to do anything. "Indeed you are nothing, and your work is nothing; he who chooses you is an abomination . . . Indeed they are all worthless; their works are nothing; their moulded images are wind and confusion" (Isaiah 41:24, 29).

These people know the truth about the Living God who stands all day long holding out His hands to them; and they deliberately turn their backs on Him, and go to gardens and worship idols. Then they eat a disgusting meal of pigs and mice, probably an initiation ritual. Have you ever read the frightening passage in Ezekiel, where the prophet is taken by the Lord to see what is going on?

'So He brought me to the door of the court; and when I looked, there was a hole in the wall. Then He said to me, "Son of man, dig into the wall;" and when I dug into the wall, there was a door. And He said to me, "Go in, and see the wicked abominations which they are doing there." So I went in and saw, and there – every sort of creeping thing, abominable beasts, and all the idols of the house of Israel, portrayed all around on the walls. And there stood before them seventy men of the elders of the house of Israel, and in their midst stood Jaazaniah the son of Shaphan. Each man had a censer in his hand, and a thick cloud of incense went up. Then He said to me, "Son of man, have you seen what the elders of the house of Israel do in the dark, every man in the room of his idols? For they say, 'The Lord does not see us, the Lord has forsaken the land.'" Ezekiel 8:7-12.

Earlier in this last chapter of Isaiah, we read of nations that would come to Jerusalem, to 'drink deeply and be delighted with the abundance of her glory' (v.11). God said He shall 'extend peace to her like a river . . . then you shall feed . . .' Compare this spiritual feast with the disgusting feast at the altars of false gods. Let us be careful how we feed our spiritual appetite, for Satan has all kinds of abominable things ready to serve; and you won't have to go to the idols' gardens to get it. Just switch on your television, sit for a night in most local cinemas, or lift the nearest novel, and before very long the most abominable things will be dished up. Give me the Living Bread, any day.

NOVEMBER 24TH

"For I know their works and their thoughts. It shall be that I will gather all nations and tongues; and they shall come and see My glory." Isaiah 66:18.

We now come to the last paragraph of the Book of Isaiah. Some see the coming gathering of all nations and tongues as a post-Pentecost event; others see it as what happened at Pentecost itself, when the gospel was let loose to the nations of the world. I incline towards Barry Webb's exposition, that today's text is a summary of the entire programme for the evangelisation of the world (*The Message of Isaiah*, IVP, p.251). God reacts to mankind in grace, to provide a way where repentant sinners of all nations can come to see His glory. The whole point of Christian mission is that God will be glorified, and people will come to know who He really is. The wrath and grace of God are two of His great attributes. The chariots of wrath and the chariots of salvation are His. Whether the event in today's verse came at Pentecost, or is still in the future, the ultimate purpose of God's dealings with us is that we should not perish, but that we should be saved and see His glory.

The glory of the Lord is both physical and spiritual. We read that, when the angel of the Lord appeared to the shepherds outside Bethlehem, 'the glory of the Lord shone around them, and they were greatly afraid' (Luke 2:9). In John 17:22, the Lord Jesus prayed: "the glory which You gave Me I have given them" (His disciples). When evangelising, please remember that all you do should be aimed at giving glory to God, and bringing people to see and know the glory of God. It is so easy to let other things get in the way. Sadly, even gifts given by God to glorify Him are often glorified for themselves, and God is forgotten. When, for example, you hear of some gift being glorified out of proportion, just slip in the little phrase, 'Wasn't God good to have given him/her that gift?'

When you have been blessed of God in some area of your life, be sure to give Him the glory.

NOVEMBER 25TH

"I will set a sign among them; and those among them who escape I will send to the nations: to Tarshish and Pul and Lud, who draw the bow, and Tubal and Javan, to the coastlands afar off who have not heard My fame nor seen My glory. And they shall declare My glory among the Gentiles. Isaiah 66:19.

Although Isaiah does not tell us what the sign is that God will set among His people, some commentators agree that it can surely be nothing other than the cross of Christ. In the context that does seem clear. Like Isaiah, those who first preached the message of the cross were those who had escaped the judgment of God by being faithful to His word. It was to such – His own disciples – that Jesus committed the spread of the gospel (Matthew 28:18-20); and upon them first came the Holy Spirit's power, to be witnesses to Christ 'in Jerusalem, Judea, and Samaria, and to the end of the earth' (Acts 1:8). Notice that Peter saw himself as having been liberated, when he exhorted the Jews at Pentecost: "Be saved from this perverse generation" (Acts 2:40).

The gospel goes out to Tarshish in Spain, southward to Libya, and to Lydia, famous for its archers; to Tubal in the far north (perhaps Turkey); and to Javan in Greece. The islands represent the far corners of the earth. In all of these places there are people who have not heard of the Lord's fame, nor seen His glory. The gospel declares many things; but at its heart it spreads the Lords fame and shows forth His glory.

Over the last few days, my wife and I have been at a famous riverside in Scotland, for the 25th anniversary of a church. The River Dee was flowing, with its peaty-brown colour still reflecting the azure blue of the sky. At the Bridge of Feugh we watched salmon leaping with awesome tenacity and strength against the torrents of water. We sipped coffee by the banks of the river, and watched the heron and buzzards, and falling leaves, and were glad to be alive. Over the week-end, the Deeside Christian Fellowship Church celebrated what God had done amongst them in a unique and wonderful way, despite formidable hurdles. Now one of the largest churches in Aberdeenshire, we have been thrilled at the way God has touched His people. Somehow, as I write today's meditation on Isaiah 66:19, I want to dedicate it to all the Christians in that Fellowship. It has been a privilege to be associated with them all this time. The fame and glory of God has certainly blazed out from them:

Isaiah's promise stretched even to Royal Deeside! Let's keep God's fame and glory at the heart of all that we do.

"Then they shall bring all your brethren for an offering to the Lord out of all nations, on horses and in chariots and in litters, on mules and on camels, to My holy mountain Jerusalem," says the Lord, "as the children of Israel bring an offering in a clean vessel into the house of the Lord." Isaiah 66:20.

The climax of Isaiah's great Prophecy is here. Drawn from all the nations of earth, Jew and Gentile converts to Christ are now covenant brothers. Those who have been influential in winning them, bring them as an offering (Hebrew, 'gift') to the Lord. As a grain offering was given to the Lord, so these soul-winners bring their harvest to Him. It is the greatest in-gathering of souls in history. The mention of horses, chariots, litters, mules, and camels on the transportation list is 'impressionistic' (Alec Motyer, *Isaiah*, IVP, p.406). All manner and means of transportation will bring God's people from every corner of the earth to the place where God dwells. I remember standing on a street in Jerusalem, and a mounted rider who had come to the city from the wilderness manoeuvred his horse around in front of me.

A vast harvest of souls will be cleansed from sin through the Messiah's mighty death and resurrection, and presented to the Lord, 'as the children of Israel bring an offering in a clean vessel into the house of the Lord.' Are you a soul winner? How can you ever say you are evangelical, without being evangelistic? It is impossible! Bev Shea used to stir multitudes of Christians with the haunting words of a hymn, which came in the form of some questions:

> Must I go and empty handed?
> Must I meet my Saviour so?
> Not one soul with which to greet Him –
> Must I empty handed go?

Let's go back again to the church at Laodicea, who were 'lukewarm, and neither cold nor hot.' They were watered down with worldliness, and their spiritual temperature was falling. Amongst other things, the Lord told them that they were blind; and He commanded them to anoint their eyes with eye salve that they may see (Revelation 3:18). There was a School of Medicine as part of a temple complex in Laodicea. They followed the teaching of Hierapolis, and had a famous eye medicine which was produced in tablet form. This had to be crushed and broken down into ointment before being applied to the eyes. The Lord is saying 'I will give you My eye salve.'

All around us there are those in need of the gospel. Ask the Lord to give you His eye salve, so that you will see them. He will clear your vision. Then as you respond, He will help you win them; and on that great harvest day you will bring them as a gift to Him. 'Lord, open our eyes to the lost,' is today's prayer.

"And I will also take some of them for priests and Levites," says the Lord. Isaiah 66:21.

T he Lord promised that Israel would be to Him a kingdom of priests (Exodus 19:6). This promise is repeated in Isaiah 61:6. Only some were priests and Levites, but through their ministry Israel became God's priestly people. At the beginning of the church age, the Word of God was ministered through Jews – like Paul, Peter, and Apollos. Paul writes, 'that I might be a minister of Jesus Christ to the Gentiles, ministering the grace of God, that the offering of the Gentiles might be acceptable, sanctified by the Holy Spirit' (Romans 15:16). Eventually the leadership moved to non-Jews as well; for instance, Titus (Galatians 2:3). So the church is constituted of 'fellow heirs' (Ephesians 3:6), and 'kings and priests' (Revelation 1:6). All members of the church of Jesus Christ are priests.

To help us in our evangelistic witness, let's learn a practical lesson from this truth of the priesthood of all believers. When the burnt offering had been consumed by the fire on the altar, the priest was commanded to 'carry the ashes outside the camp to a clean place. And the fire on the altar shall be kept burning on it; it shall not be put out. And the priest shall burn wood on it every morning, and lay the burnt offering in order on it . . .' (Leviticus 6:10-12). Every day fresh wood must be brought to the fire for the burnt offering. The embers of yesterday's ashes were not to be used.

We too are presenting a sacrifice. It is the story of the sacrifice of Christ to a lost world. If we would be effective, we need to keep the evangelistic fire burning in our hearts. How? By putting on fresh wood every day, and not the embers of yesterday's ashes. When they feed the fire of their souls with the Scriptures, some people get stuck in favourite areas. They are always drawing from John's Gospel, or Ephesians, or the Psalms, and you never hear them mention any other sections of Scripture. Then the fire begins to burn low. They need to get into the other vast tracks of Scripture, and put fresh wood on their fire. I sincerely trust that this study of Isaiah has helped you to do just that. If it helps your fire to burn with a fresh blaze again, I would consider this year's work to have been more than worthwhile.

"For as the new heavens and the new earth which I will make shall remain before Me," says the Lord . . . Isaiah 66:22a.

I confess that sometimes a rather chilling thought enters my head. What if, in the new creation, there was another Fall? What if Satan were to tempt those who are on the new earth, and corrupt it all? Is there a promise that this will never happen? Yes, there is; and we have it in today's text. The earth and heavens, as we know them, will pass away.

'But the day of the Lord will come as a thief in the night, in which the heavens will pass away with a great noise, and the elements will melt with fervent heat; both the earth and the works that are in it will be burned up.' 2 Peter 3:10.

The Lord is in the process of making a new heaven and a new earth that will remain before Him. The Lord puts His name to this promise, so it will be impossible for peace and stability to ever be disturbed. Satan will never touch the new creation. The execution of the sentence on the devil is stated in Scripture in a very few words. 'The devil, who deceived them, was cast into the lake of fire and brimstone where the beast and the false prophet are. And they will be tormented day and night forever and ever' (Revelation 20:10). Satan was defeated at Calvary (Colossians 2:15); but for some reason known only to God the sentence had not yet been executed. In the prisons of the United States, men sometimes live on Death Row for years after they have been sentenced to death. So, how are we to have victory over Satan?

In his book *Satan, No Myth* (Lakeland, 1974) J. Oswald Saunders tells a story from the life of Dr. Donald G. Barnhouse. As a young Christian, Dr. Barnhouse found it a struggle. He had told other people, 'Resist the devil and he will flee from you.' But he kept telling God that, instead of the devil fleeing from him, it seemed as though he fled at him. He turned to James 4:7, and put his finger on the promise; but no relief came. Finally, he felt God saying to him, 'read the whole verse.' He saw that he had been quoting only half the verse. When he read it all, his perspective was quite different. 'Therefore submit to God. Resist the devil and he will flee from you.' If we fail to submit to God, then we will not see the devil fleeing from us.

"So shall your descendants and your name remain. And it shall come to pass that from one New Moon to another, and from one Sabbath to another, all flesh shall come to worship before Me," says the Lord. Isaiah 66:22b-23.

Not only will the new creation be permanent; God's people will be permanent too. No more will corruption mar the Feasts of the Lord. The Feasts that once brought God such pain, will now bring Him eternal joy. At the beginning of his book, Isaiah brought the word of the Lord to his people:

"Bring no more futile sacrifices; incense is an abomination to Me. The New Moons, the Sabbaths, and the calling of assemblies – I cannot endure iniquity and the sacred meeting. Your New Moons and your appointed feasts My soul hates; they are a trouble to Me, I am weary of bearing them." Isaiah 1:13, 14.

Now Isaiah's vision goes to the eternal state, where 'each month as it comes and each week as it comes is met by joyful dedication of life's programme to the Lord' (Alec Motyer, *Isaiah*, IVP, p.407).

I once asked Professor David Gooding if he thought time would stop in Heaven. He replied, "No one knows exactly what time is; but the idea, that in eternity there is no past and no future, is manifestly false. There was a period in eternity when the Second Person of the Trinity was not yet human; and eternity looked forward to the Incarnation." I certainly feel that Isaiah's use of the phrases, 'New Moon,' and 'one Sabbath to another,' is hinting at very special periods in the future eternal state.

What will our worship be like? Please do not think I am being trite, but let me quote David Gooding again. In an interview for *The Belfast Telegraph* (October 22nd, 1999), I referred to Lady Thatcher speaking, tongue-in-cheek, of 'twanging a harp' in Heaven, and I asked him, "What do you really think people will be doing in Heaven?' He answered:

"The phrase, 'twanging a harp,' is a deliberate caricature. In actual fact, Lady Thatcher herself would probably be prepared to buy an expensive ticket to hear an earthly harp played by an expert. Certainly, music is one of the highest expressions of the human spirit; its composers and performers are highly acclaimed. If the Redeemed in Heaven did nothing but worship God in music, no higher or nobler activity could be imagined.

But there is more than one kind of music. All the activities of the Redeemed will be under the baton of the Great Conductor. The whole, vast, co-ordinated activity will together express the variegated wisdom and love of God; and its unimpeded, uncompromised, goal will be the glory of God. It will fill the Universe with rapturous music – a welcome relief from the strident voices of self-seeking party politics, the ugly voices of international discord, the jarring jangling of family break-ups, the insane cacophonies of genocide, and the dirge of death."

NOVEMBER 30TH

"And they shall go forth and look upon the corpses of the men who have transgressed against Me. For their worm does not die, and their fire is not quenched. They shall be an abhorrence to all flesh." Isaiah 66:24.

I can understand why Jewish congregations find the last verse of Isaiah so negative, that they bring it to a close with the final, beautiful, positive affirmation of 66:23: '"All flesh shall come to worship before Me," says the Lord.' Some scholars even argue that the last verse is tacked on to the text of this great Prophecy. No so! We must not cut it out. The gospel divides saint and sinner, true worshipers and idolaters, those who submit to God and those who rebel. The Lord Jesus quoted this text three times in Mark 9:43-48. It is showing what Hell will be like for the one who has turned away from God's grace. The sinner's conscience will continue to work in Hell. It will gnaw eternally. As we learned from Isaiah 48:22, "There is no peace," says the Lord, "for the wicked." Here is the reality of eternal punishment. Gehenna was the public rubbish dump that took even the bodies of animals and criminals. It was situated south west of Jerusalem in the valley of Hinnom, where the worms did not stop eating and fires did not stop burning. Jesus used 'Gehenna' eleven times to describe Hell, and let us remember that a thing being symbolised is greater than the symbol.

So it is that Isaiah finishes his awesome Prophecy with a prophecy. Just as the people in Jerusalem were aware of Gehenna, the Redeemed in the New Jerusalem will be aware of the ultimate destination of the lost. They will be aware of death – the wages of sin – and will loathe it. They will also be joyfully aware of eternal life – the gift of God that has come through Jesus Christ our Lord. The distance between verses 23 and 24 of Isaiah 66 could not be greater. It is Heaven and Hell:

'And besides all this, between us and you there is a great gulf fixed, so that those who want to pass from here to you cannot, nor can those from there pass to us' (Luke 16:26).

Thank God that at the heart of Isaiah's message there is a Messiah, who was wounded for our transgressions, bruised for our iniquities, and by His stripes we are healed. The glorious, unmistakable fact remains: the greatest barrier to Hell is the Cross of Calvary. To pass by it is to face eternal peril.

$\mathcal{D}$ecember

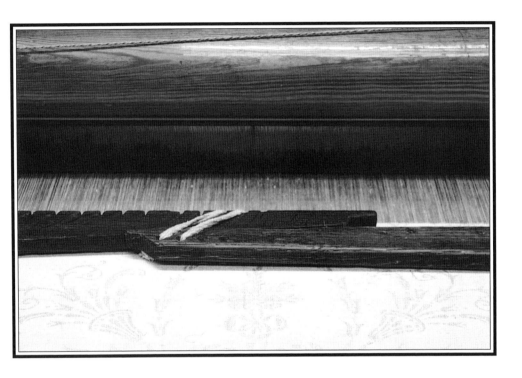

This photograph shows the point of creation of damask linen, which is made from natural, undyed yarn. The design effect is entirely due to the lustre of the yarn. In the Book of Revelation we read of the marriage supper of the Lamb, where it is granted to His wife to be 'arrayed in fine linen, clean and bright, for the fine linen is the righteous acts of the saints.'

DECEMBER 1ST

Hear, O heavens, and give ear, O earth! For the Lord has spoken: "I have nourished and brought up children, and they have rebelled against Me; the ox knows its owner and the donkey its master's crib; but Israel does not know, My people do not consider."
Isaiah 1:2-3.

For the final days of our year of Devotional Readings, I want to concentrate on some texts from the first 39 chapters of Isaiah. I set out to cover chapters 40-66; and did so in eleven months. Now I want to move into some of the other glories and challenges in Isaiah's Prophecy. In today's text, God is mocking His people for failing to do what animals perform by instinct! Scripture often does this. In the Book of Proverbs, for instance, the lazy person is thus advised:

'Go to the ant, you sluggard! Consider her ways and be wise, which, having no captain, overseer or ruler, provides her supplies in summer, and gathers her food in the harvest. How long will you slumber, O sluggard? When will you rise from your sleep? A little sleep, a little slumber, a little folding of the hands to sleep – so shall your poverty come on you like a prowler, and your need like an armed man.' Proverbs 6:6-11.

By instinct the little ant gets ready for the future, by being busy in the present. But the lazy person, knowing full well the consequences, decides to sleep; and so in the future will experience poverty. Jeremiah reminds us,

"Even the stork in the heavens knows her appointed times; and the turtledove, the swift, and the swallow observe the time of their coming. But my people do not know the judgment of the Lord." Jeremiah 8:7.

My uncle, on the family farm in County Down, tells me that he got frustrated by the swallows building in his barn. So, one year, while they were away he closed up the barn doors. When those little swallows returned to Ulster from South Africa, they swooped on him in anger when he crossed the farmyard! God is saying that the swallow, the swift, and the turtledove come back; but His people do not repent and return. When they refuse to do so, they are contradicting the very purpose for which they were created.

In the first few verses of Isaiah's Prophecy, the awesome, living God calls on the heavens and earth to hear what He has to say. He laments that He has brought up children, who don't stop to think about Him, or consider His ways. From the day Abraham set out from Ur, to the day Solomon reigned in Jerusalem, they knew His comfort and blessing. But now they have rebelled against Him. My mother used to tell me about a farmer, whose animals one day nuzzled him in recognition. Today's text came into his mind, and it led him to repentance and faith in Jesus Christ. Selah.

DECEMBER 2ND

"Come now, and let us reason together," says the Lord, "though your sins are like scarlet, they shall be as white as snow; though they are red like crimson, they shall be as wool."
Isaiah 1:18.

W e learned yesterday that the Lord abhors the fact that He has given us minds, which we fail to use to follow His will and ways. So now, God calls us to reason with Him. Our relationship with Him is not all emotion – our minds matter. God calls us to love Him, not only with all our heart and strength but also with our entire mind. Not to use our mind is a sin.

Here God calls us to reason with Him, as in a Court that has firmly established our guilt. In vivid language, God describes our sinful condition:

'The whole head is sick, and the whole heart faints. From the sole of the foot even to the head, there is no soundness in it, but wounds and bruises and putrefying sores; they have not been closed nor bound up, or soothed with ointment.' Isaiah 1:5-6.

God's justice condemns us outright, so we must think about it. Does this verse describe you? Are your sins as scarlet, and red like crimson? These are vivid sins: there is no escaping their presence. Now God asks you to bring your mind to bear upon the problem. He is arguing that there is only one answer to the guilt of our sin and rebellion against Him, and that is His free grace. What other answer is there? If He does not intervene and forgive us, we will unquestionably perish.

What hope is there for us? The incredible message of Isaiah is that we can be pardoned through the death of the Lord Jesus. I trust that this wonderful fact has been made unmistakeably clear over this year of Readings. By repentance toward God and faith in Jesus Christ, we can be given a new nature. Our sins can be washed as white as wool, and as pure as driven snow.

Let me repeat that all this is reasonable. He is not afraid to use the words 'know,' 'consider,' 'reason.' When we come to the New Testament, in order to prove His authenticity the Lord Jesus performed seven great miracles. Our faith is not based on speculation: it is based on evidence. You can rest your mind, heart, and soul, upon Christ's once-and-for-all, mighty, finished work at Calvary, and be sure of eternal peace with God.

DECEMBER 3RD

He shall judge between the nations, and rebuke many people; they shall beat their swords into plowshares, and their spears into pruning hooks; nation shall not lift up sword against nation, neither shall they learn war anymore. O house of Jacob, come and let us walk in the light of the Lord. Isaiah 2:4-5.

I always remember my first visit to the United Nations building in New York. Outside, I found the sculpture of a man beating a sword into a ploughshare, and underneath it the words from Micah chapter 4. It is reckoned by expositors that Micah was quoting from Isaiah, rather than vice-versa. Isaiah's vision in today's text was a direct revelation from God.

Isaiah sees away beyond his present circumstances to what he calls 'the latter days,' or the culmination of days. The Lord will be reigning, and the nations walking in His ways. They will love and obey the Word of the Lord. The Lord will settle all disputes and judge all issues. It is a compelling vision, and the memorable imagery has obviously gripped people throughout history, right down to the present day. In a world bristling with weaponry (and now moved from swords to nuclear bombs and inter-continental ballistic missiles), it is achingly beautiful to think of a prophet, around 800 years before Christ, writing of swords being beaten into the blade of a plough, and spears into pruning hooks – an agricultural tool used in the cultivation of the vine, with a sharp knife-like end for pruning.

Where in the world has war not left its scar, or the threat of it not caused inordinate spending on defence weapons? When politics fails, war and violence inevitably erupt. The century that has just passed was the most murderous in all human history. During the 20th century, more than two hundred million human-beings were killed by fellow human-beings. The promise of a day, when 'nation shall not lift up sword against nation, neither shall they learn war any more,' is (to quote the sub-title of this book), *the incomparable comfort of Isaiah.*

As we muse on Isaiah's famous imagery, we must ask the question: Will goodness only come on the earth when the Lord reigns? Isaiah gives the answer. He calls on his contemporaries to live now in the light of the coming rule of God: 'O house of Jacob, come and let us walk in the light of the Lord.' Even in the 21st Century, there is no reason why God's people cannot live with integrity in a world of evil. The darker the night gets, the brighter the light shines. The storm extinguishes a small fire, but a large fire is enhanced by it. Strong faith gets even stronger when it is under threat.

DECEMBER 4TH

Now let me sing to my Well-beloved a song of my Beloved regarding His vineyard: My Well-beloved has a vineyard on a very fruitful hill. He dug it up and cleared out its stones, and planted it with the choicest vine. He built a tower in its midst, and also made a winepress in it; so He expected it to bring forth good grapes, but it brought forth wild grapes. "And now, O inhabitants of Jerusalem and men of Judah, judge, please, between Me and My vineyard. What more could have been done to My vineyard that I have not done in it? Why then, when I expected it to bring forth good grapes, did it bring forth wild grapes? Isaiah 5:1-4.

This is a powerful metaphor of what God has done for His people. It is drawn from the world of viticulture. A vineyard-owner chose good soil on a fruitful hill, he carefully cleared away the weeds and stones, and planted the very best vines. He built a watchtower and a winepress, and looked forward to a generous yield of luscious grapes. But all he got for his hard work was bad fruit – literally 'stink-fruit.' Although God had done everything possible to help her, Israel did not fulfil what God required of her. He looked for a good crop, but it did not come.

In the New Testament Luke tells us how the Lord Jesus took Isaiah's vineyard metaphor, and turned it into a parable (Luke 20:9-18). In the parable, God was the Owner, the people were the vineyard, and the religious leaders were responsible for cultivating it to the Owner's satisfaction. At harvest time the Owner sent servants to collect fruit, but they were beaten and sent away empty-handed. Eventually, the Owner sent His Son, the heir, but they murdered Him, to keep the inheritance. So the Owner destroyed those vinedressers and gave the vineyard to others.

A certain famous and very wealthy young man sat in the kitchen of a godly couple, and complained. He was a believer; but his life lacked direction, and he was unhappy. The lady of the house, whom I know, suddenly looked him in the eye and said some very brave words: 'To whom much is given, much is expected.' Eventually her husband took him to see the poverty in India, and it completely turned his life around. He has since done immense good for the poor in the world.

The challenge in our lives is: are we going to give the Owner His rights to our faith, love, obedience and service; or are we going to live for ourselves? At the end of this year, when the Owner comes looking for some luscious grapes, is He going to find (putting it bluntly) 'stink-fruit'? Whatever I take for myself will end up as a place of death. Judas found this to be true: his betrayal money was used to buy a cemetery.

December 5th

In the year that King Uzziah died, I saw the Lord sitting on a throne, high and lifted up, and the train of His robe filled the temple. Isaiah 6:1.

It must have been a sad year for Isaiah. It was the year that Judah's King, Uzziah died. Uzziah had become king at 16 years of age, and reigned for 52 years in Jerusalem. He began well, and did what was right in the sight of the Lord. 'As long as he sought the Lord, God made him prosper' (2 Chronicles 26:5). Sadly, when he became successful, 'his heart was lifted up, to his destruction, for he transgressed against the Lord his God by entering the temple of the Lord to burn incense on the altar of incense.' This was a task given by the Lord only to the consecrated priests, the sons of Aaron. When challenged, Uzziah became furious, and God struck him with leprosy. He was a leper until the day of his death, and 'dwelt in an isolated house.' Isaiah must have known a lot about King Uzziah, because he wrote his biography. 'The rest of the acts of Uzziah, from first to last, the prophet Isaiah the son of Amoz wrote' (2 Chronicles 26:22). Now that his long, bittersweet reign had come to an end, I have no doubt that Isaiah felt it deeply.

It was in that year that Isaiah was given a vision of another King. The contrast between the two could not have been greater. Uzziah died as a leper for violating God's holiness; now the prophet is given a view of that holiness. Two seraphim cry, 'Holy, holy, holy is the Lord of hosts;' and Isaiah feels his own unworthiness. On confession of his sin, he is cleansed and restored to further service. When God asks, "Whom shall I send, and who will go for Us?" Isaiah responded immediately, "Here am I! Send me."

Let's be honest, the vision of the Lord which Isaiah saw in the year of Uzziah's death, did not so much comfort him as it challenged him not to repeat the sins of Uzziah and the people. To all who serve God, the challenge remains: in trying to lead people to a Holy God, we must live holy lives ourselves.

"Ask a sign for yourself from the Lord your God; ask it either in the depth or in the height above." But Ahaz said, "I will not ask, nor will I test the Lord!" Then he said, "Hear now, O house of David! Is it a small thing for you to weary men, but will you weary my God also?" Isaiah 7:11-13.

D espite the fact that Uzziah's successor, King Ahaz, broke out in open defiance of God, God showed him mercy. God told Isaiah to take his son and go and meet Ahaz. He was to tell him that a confederacy, which had combined to invade Judah and attack Jerusalem, would be overthrown. He was to warn him, "If you will not believe, surely you shall not be established." This emphasises the importance of faith in the promises of God, even in the face of seemingly insurmountable problems.

When God makes a promise, do you really believe Him? Do you exercise a daily faith in that promise? The Lord challenges Ahaz: "Ask a sign for yourself from the Lord your God; ask it either in the depth or in the height above." God is being flexible, so that He can strengthen Ahaz's faith. But he replies, "I will not ask, nor will I test the Lord!" He is quoting Scripture (see Deuteronomy 6:16). It is a sin to test, or 'tempt,' the Lord. He appears to be pious, but at heart he has no intention of joining the ranks of God's faithful, and throwing himself on the promises of God. Ahaz has decided to turn to Assyria for help, not to the Lord. By refusing to ask for a sign in these circumstances, Ahaz was showing gross unbelief. What is the sin in testing or tempting God? It is 'refusing to trust Him and His past faithfulness unless He proves Himself trustworthy all over again' (Alec Motyer, *Isaiah*, IVP, p.77).

I love the story of how Gideon asked God for a sign.

"'I shall put a fleece of wool on the threshing floor; if there is dew on the fleece only, and it is dry on all the ground, then I shall know that You will save Israel by my hand, as You have said"... When he rose early the next morning and squeezed the fleece together, he wrung the dew out of the fleece, a bowlful of water.' Judges 6:37, 38.

The next night he asked God to reverse the process, and in the morning it was just as he had asked. In Hebrew thinking, dew represents unity (see Psalm 133:1-3). Gideon wanted to see if he could control the unity of his army by prayer. God was delighted to show him by these signs that he could. God's responds to faith, but disbelief wearies Him. Are you wearying God today?

"Therefore the Lord Himself will give you a sign: Behold, the virgin shall conceive and bear a Son, and shall call His name Immanuel. Curds and honey He shall eat, that He may know to refuse the evil and choose the good." Isaiah 7:14, 15.

A s Christmas approaches, across the world millions prepare to remember the birth of the Lord Jesus at Bethlehem. We do not expect to find a prophecy about it in the circumstances of the unbelieving King Ahaz; yet that is exactly where it occurs.

Yesterday, we learned that Ahaz refused to ask for a sign from God. Today, we learn that God chose a sign for him. The House of David had failed to fulfil its responsibilities, and Ahaz epitomised their lack of trust. The God who would move heaven and earth to bring a sign to encourage the faith of Ahaz, now moves heaven and earth to encourage the faith of the whole world. His sign would be the birth of the Saviour. He promises that the heir to David's unbelieving dynasty would be a child called Immanuel, meaning 'God with us.'

Ahaz trusted Assyria, and it led to ruin and desolation. He, and all who followed his way, did not share in the glorious fulfilment of this prophecy; but, by faith, we do. When prophesying of Mary, Isaiah very carefully chooses the Hebrew word *almah*, which denotes one who is mature and ready for marriage. Here we have the doctrine of the Incarnation, which teaches that the Eternal Son of God became human, without in any way diminishing His divine nature. He had a supernatural conception and a natural birth. When we come to the New Testament, we find today's text from Isaiah cited by Matthew as he writes about the Virgin Birth of Christ (Matthew 1:23). Matthew endorses the virgin birth interpretation of Isaiah's statement; and, with all my heart, so do I.

This gift is wrapped in prophecy, history and mystery. The prophecy is in today's text, and in Micah 5:2. God moved in history to bring about the birth of the Saviour at Bethlehem. The Romans made the roads along which Mary travelled from Nazareth. The Emperor Augustus declared a census, and because Joseph was from the family of David, they had to go to Bethlehem. There he was registered, with Mary, 'his betrothed wife, who was with child' (Luke 2:4-5). And the whole story is wrapped in mystery:

'And without controversy great is the mystery of godliness: God was manifested in the flesh, justified in the Spirit, seen by angels, preached among the Gentiles, believed on in the world, received up in glory.' 1 Timothy 3:16.

'Thanks be to God for His indescribable gift.' 2 Corinthians 9:15.

DECEMBER 8TH

". . . and shall call His name Immanuel." Isaiah 7:14b.

While musing on the far-reaching implications of this verse, these words came to me. May they help you to truly worship the Lord this Christmas:

Prophecy said it in words clear and strong,
History revealed it in a census throng,
Angels sang it in celestial song:
Immanuel, God with us!

Wise Men knew by an Eastern Star,
Shepherds rushed in through a door ajar,
In a manger He lay, who came from afar:
Immanuel, God with us!

The mystery of Godliness, manifest in flesh;
The glory of Heaven, without a crèche.
A baby's cry from lips that unfurled space:
Immanuel, God with us!

Wonderful! Counsellor! The Mighty God!
The Everlasting Father! Spread it abroad –
It's the best news the world ever heard:
Immanuel, God with us!

Trust Him as Saviour, own Him as Lord.
One day He'll beat a plough from a sword.
He will rule a new earth, and be forever adored:
Immanuel, God with us!

DECEMBER 9TH

"Curds and honey He shall eat, that He may know to refuse the evil and choose the good." Isaiah 7:15.

Ah, this man Isaiah has got to me! When I read a prophecy like this, my heart trembles, and my very soul stirs. How could anyone have known the diet of a child that would be born nearly eight centuries later? The mighty Spirit of God now tells us through Isaiah that the Christ-child will eat butter and honey! His diet was an indication of the poverty of His birth and childhood, and also of a devastated land. Curds, or thickened milk, and honey was the food eaten by desert nomads.

This prophecy is not telling us that it was all He ate; but it is telling us that there were no luxuries in His home. Paul wrote to the Christians in the great city of Corinth, and reminded them of Christ's poverty:

'For you know the grace of our Lord Jesus Christ, that though He was rich, yet for your sakes He became poor, that you through His poverty might become rich.' 2 Corinthians 8:9.

How could I ever capture in words the deep meaning of the contrast between 'He was rich,' and 'He became poor'?

The letter to the Hebrews says that God has appointed His Son to be 'heir of all things, through whom also He made the worlds' (Hebrews 1:2). We hear people speak with bated breath about heirs to a fortune. Christ is not merely heir to a fortune; He has been appointed heir of everything! See Him in Nazareth, where provisions are restricted because of poverty. The heir to everything stoops down, to live with only the bare essentials, that we might become children of God. 'And if children, then heirs – heirs of God and joint heirs with Christ' (Romans 8:17). Human greed grasps all it can get; but Christ – who did not consider equality with God a thing to be grasped –

'. . . made Himself of no reputation, taking the form of a bondservant, and coming in the likeness of men. And being found in appearance as a man, He humbled Himself and became obedient to the point of death, even the death of the cross.' Philippians 2:6-8.

We do not know many details about the childhood of the Lord Jesus; but from today's Reading we learn that, when He made choices, He knew to refuse evil and choose good. Now that He is your Saviour, He can help you to do the same. As you pass through your day, choose that which is good.

DECEMBER 10TH

There shall come a Rod from the stem of Jesse, and a Branch shall grow out of his roots.
Isaiah 11:1.

There are many images that come to our minds as we approach Christmas. We think of a star and a manger, shepherds and angels, or even frankincense and myrrh. But I have never seen a Christmas card that depicts the birth of Christ as a young shoot growing out of a tree stump, or a sapling budding from its roots. This is one of the images that Isaiah gives of the coming of the Messiah.

From the time of Ahaz, the Davidic monarchy was in serious decline. By the Fall of Jerusalem in 586 BC, the monarchy had been well and truly felled. Yet a stump remained, inside of which was vital life. God promised David that his dynasty would be established forever; but few continued to believe it when the Roman powers eventually subjugated Israel. All promises of future glory seemed to be almost extinguished.

Isaiah likens the humble origins of the Messiah to a young shoot coming out of a tree stump. Eventually the shoot would take the place of the stump, and a glorious tree would emerge. From 'a root out of dry ground,' there would grow up 'a tender plant' (Isaiah 53:2).

The Wise Men came to Herod looking for the King, whose star they had followed from the East. The Chief Priests and Scribes told this puppet king that the Scriptures foretold that the Messiah would be born in Bethlehem. The Wise Men continued on their journey to Bethlehem, where 'they saw the young Child with Mary His mother, and fell down and worshipped Him.' Directed by God, they went home without telling Herod. In his great anger, Herod destroyed every little boy in Bethlehem that was less than two years of age. But the 'sapling' that he sought, had escaped. Herod's own death soon followed. What a vulnerable 'sapling' Christ was; but the promises of God have all come true. How we love to sit under His expansive shade, and His fruit is sweet to our taste.

DECEMBER 11TH

The wolf also shall dwell with the lamb, the leopard shall lie down with the young goat, the calf and the young lion and the fatling together; and a little child shall lead them.
Isaiah 11:6.

The future rule of the Messiah is represented here. Because of Christ's presence, Creation shall no longer be marked by the Fall. The predator and its prey are no longer at enmity: the wolf shall live with the lamb, the leopard and the young goat shall lie down together; the calf shall eat with the young lion; and a little child shall look after them all. In the future, children will be just as important as they are in the present.

It was F. W. Boreham, who first drew my attention to four kinds of children. First, 'the child that used to be.' The parents once had a little child, but through illness or tragedy their child has died. Wonderful dreams were bound up in that child; but now it has gone, and the heartbroken parents are left with the memories. I have talked with such parents, and life is not easy for them. Then there is 'the child that is.' The parents' schedules and entire lifestyles are turned upside down. Millions know all about this, and I am certain that many reading these lines have not had a full night's sleep for a long time, because of 'the child that is'! You long to have a quiet night, uninterrupted by spelling reviews, car-runs to various extra-curricular activities, or colds and flu. Not to mention the famous phrase, "Dad, can I . . .?" Be patient because one day, when they have left your care, you will long to have all that noise and activity back again.

When raising my children I wrote a little poem, entitled 'To make a child's heart glad.' It may help you at this stage in your busy life:

It's not hard to make a child's heart glad.
A little thing will please, will ease
A tear-filled afternoon –
A walk, a ride across the park,
A lollipop, a wine gum, red,
A 'Let's pretend,' will soon
Make a child's heart glad

Father, busy in your office plush,
Rushing so much: you cannot touch
Your child's heart that way.
O, it may buy him food or toys,
But you must give him time –
Your time – if you would truly say
"I've made my child's heart glad."

Mother, you daily make the mould
In those first, swift, important years,
Edged by fears of how he'll fare:
Make yours the encouraging word,
And hold his love, though he rebels.
Always care, always care!
And you'll make your child's heart glad.

Then, when he's left his parents' care,
Leaving the nest and the rest
To make his own –
When you are old, and childhood's gone
Far from his grasp and reach,
He'll say of you in truth,
"They made my childhood glad!"

Then, there is 'the child that never was.' Childless couples have to live with the sadness of never knowing what parenthood is like. They hold very precious dreams of 'the child that never was.' Let all who have children always hold sympathy in their hearts for childless couples; and talk of their children with care, lest they make their loneliness deeper. Interestingly, it is often the most gifted couples working in church youth work who are childless. They turn their grief into service.

Finally, there is 'the child who is yet to be.' Live in such a way that you will be able say to your child, "Follow in your father's footsteps," or "Do as your mother does." Among the saddest lines I ever read were those written by a famous writer to his child, telling her to do everything her parents didn't do, and she would be perfectly safe. You may be awaiting the birth of your child. No better advice could be given than the following text. Make a covenant to always keep it before you:

'Bring up your children in the training and admonition of the Lord.' Ephesians 6:4.

December 12th

And in that day you will say: "O Lord, I will praise You; though You were angry with me, Your anger is turned away, and You comfort me. Behold, God is my salvation, I will trust and not be afraid; 'For Yah, the Lord, is my strength and song; He also has become my salvation.'" Therefore with joy you will draw water from the wells of salvation. Isaiah 12:1-3.

The media interests me. In our world, it is the main communicator of news and politics. Politics is the art of government, and there are few areas of our lives not affected by the Government. A lot of people say they are not interested in politics, until suddenly they need their Member of Parliament! I am told that TV companies are constantly trying to make politics more accessible, and more interesting to the viewer. I read recently of a TV company who had been commissioned to find new ways of reporting politics. The company came up with the idea that a reporter would travel around Britain speaking to 'ordinary people.' Was the prospective reporter interested in the job? He certainly was. Then he was informed that it would make good television if he were to interview the 'ordinary person' from horseback. He pulled out of the deal, on the grounds that he could not ride a horse! Would a gimmick like this really make politics more interesting? Of course not. Politics was never meant to be fun; it is a serious business. People want to know what a Government is up to with their tax, health, and education; not whether the one asking the questions is on horseback or whatever!

Sometimes those who communicate the gospel use gimmicks to draw attention to it; but the gimmicks only get in the way. There is no area of our lives that the gospel does not touch. We do not need to prove that its message is relevant – it is relevant. What we need to do is to listen to Isaiah's beautiful hymn of praise, from which I have quoted in today's Reading. Isaiah has experienced forgiveness and salvation, and he is looking forward to the day when all who have been saved down through the centuries will praise God in the New Jerusalem. They have all known the removal of God's anger, and the experience of His incomparable comfort. Together, they say, 'Behold, God is my salvation, I will trust and not be afraid.' It is like a well that will never go dry. With joy they constantly draw from it, for the source of their salvation is God Himself.

This is the message our world needs. Don't let gimmicks get in the way of it. You can apply many a method to get it across, as long as it is the message itself that comes across. To make a point, Jesus talked to a wealthy young man who was possessed by possessions. Stephen outlined the history of Israel to preach the gospel. To help those who spread the news, Aquila and Priscilla used their tent-making. All pointed to the Eternal Resource. In this very different post-September 11th world, let us do the same.

DECEMBER 13TH

Because you have forgotten the God of your salvation, and have not been mindful of the Rock of your stronghold, therefore you will plant pleasant plants and set out foreign seedlings; in the day you will make your plant to grow, and in the morning you will make your seed to flourish; but the harvest will be a heap of ruins in the day of grief and desperate sorrow. Isaiah 17:10-11.

I saiah gives five oracles, or divine prophecies, regarding the nations in his day. Over the next few days I want to draw from each of them, to illustrate practical lessons for our lives.

The first concerns Syria, with its capital, Damascus. God was displeased when Ephraim (Israel, the Northern Kingdom) joined with Syria to stand against the threat of Assyria. Note what it is that God holds against His people. They did not fix their eyes upon Him, but forgot the God of their salvation. Yesterday we learned that God is our constant resource, to whom we can turn at any time. When something powerful threatens our faith, we must fix our eyes on God; not on the power of evil. Instead of looking up, Israel looked to an earthly power. Instead of trusting in the changeless Rock of Ages as their stronghold, they tried to shelter under a changing, transient earthly nation. At the time it seemed convenient and realistic to link up with Syria, but it led to disaster.

At the heart of Israel's weakness was her idolatry. She had lost faith in the living God and placed it in the gods of earth. In today's verses, apparently a Canaanite worship ritual is being described. Finest plants and imported vines ('slips of an alien god' RSV) are generated at an artificially fast pace at a shrine to a false god, probably in order to induce fertility. The plants soon shrivel and die. False cults promise so much, but in the end bring a harvest, here graphically described as 'a heap of ruins in the day of grief and desperate sorrow.'

Just last evening I visited a dying lady in hospital. I read to her of comfort from the book of Isaiah, and prayed. Later her daughter told me of her own spiritual pilgrimage. She had been converted as a teenager; but, because of God's seeming inertia regarding people who are suffering in the world, she had turned away from closely following the Lord. God had lovingly drawn her back into His way; and last evening we prayed together, leaning on the comfort of God. In the face of difficult circumstances, it is so easy to get our focus off the Lord and, like Israel, look for shelter elsewhere. Are you tempted to do that today? Please, please, heed the warning of today's reading. All other shelters will end up as a 'heap of ruins;' but the Rock of Ages is unshakeable and eternal.

DECEMBER 14TH

All inhabitants of the world and dwellers on the earth: when he lifts up a banner on the mountains, you see it; and when he blows a trumpet, you hear it. For so the Lord said to me, "I will take My rest, and I will look from My dwelling place like clear heat in sunshine, like a cloud of dew in the heat of harvest." For before the harvest, when the bud is perfect and the sour grape is ripening in the flower, He will both cut off the sprigs with pruning hooks and take away and cut down the branches. Isaiah 18:3-5.

This is an oracle against an alliance between God's people and Ethiopia. The Biblical Ethiopia, or Cush, was a region that included modern Ethiopia, Sudan and Somaliland. In 715 BC, the Ethiopian, Pianchia, gained control of Egypt. A twenty-fifth dynasty was founded, comprising of Ethiopian rulers, lasting until 663 BC. This dynasty sent diplomats out across the world to form an anti-Assyrian alliance, which God's people were asked to join. Isaiah intervenes in this diplomacy, with a word from the Lord.

As Pianchia seeks world diplomacy, Isaiah spells out how the Lord feels about it all. It is a powerful image. God tells Isaiah to let the whole world know that He is quietly watching world affairs. He rests, as diplomats go hurrying on their way to set up their alliances. He is waiting for His moment; and when it comes it will be seen as a banner raised on the mountain, or when a trumpet is clearly sounded. He is not only waiting, but He is watching: "I will look from My dwelling place like clear heat in sunshine, like a cloud of dew in the heat of harvest." God's hand is behind history, moving it to a precise point – just as He sends the heat of the sun and the cool of the dew to mature the a crop for harvest.

The Lord says He will intervene, just when this anti-Assyrian alliance seems to be successful. He will put His sickle into the whole affair, as into a harvest almost ready for gathering. God is not against all alliances between nations, but He is telling His people and the whole world, 'Don't think you can run the world, and leave me out of the equation.' The

Ethiopians, 'a people tall and smooth of skin' (Isaiah 18:7), will bring their homage 'to the place of the name of the Lord of hosts, to Mount Zion.'

As I write, an alliance is being set up against Saddam Hussein and his weapons of mass destruction. As diplomats jet daily across the earth, I find these verses very comforting. As worldly regimes rise and fall, praise God His purposes will work out in the end. So trust Him and be patient, Christian: you are on the victory side.

DECEMBER 15ᵀᴴ

Moreover those who work in fine flax and those who weave fine fabric will be ashamed; and its foundations will be broken. All who make wages will be troubled of soul. Surely the princes of Zoan are fools; Pharaoh's wise counsellors give foolish counsel. How do you say to Pharaoh, "I am the son of the wise, the son of ancient kings?" Where are they? Where are your wise men? Let them tell you now, and let them know what the Lord of hosts has purposed against Egypt. The princes of Zoan have become fools; the princes of Noph are deceived; they have also deluded Egypt, those who are the mainstay of its tribes. Isaiah 19:9-13.

This oracle against Egypt highlights its three major weaknesses. Isaiah is warning God's people not to make an alliance with that which ultimately is going to fail. The first weakness was its religion. The Lord looked down upon their idols, and knew that they would totter in His presence, and have no power to strengthen the hearts of the Egyptians. When the spirit of the nation failed, and they were given into the hand of a cruel master and a fierce king, they consulted 'the idols and the charmers, the mediums and the sorcerers' (Isaiah 19:3).

The second weakness was its total dependence on the River Nile. If it failed, there would be complete economic collapse. Any nation, not only Egypt, would always do well to heed the words of God to Israel: "And you shall remember the Lord your God, for it is He who gives you power to get wealth . . ." (Deuteronomy 8:18). Not only does Isaiah mention the fishing industry in Egypt, but also, interestingly, the linen industry. 'Moreover those who work in fine flax and those who weave fine fabric will be ashamed; and its foundations will be broken. All who make wages will be troubled of soul' (Isaiah 19:9, 10). We know that tomb paintings show scenes of the Egyptians harvesting, sewing, and wearing fine linen clothing. Even gifted and industrious people must remember that putting the Lord first is more important than having a booming economy. Economies can collapse overnight.

The third weakness is Egypt's self-confidence in its great enlightenment and wisdom. Pharaoh's counsellors claimed to be descended from a long line of wise kings in Egypt. They believed that their wisdom was handed down to them, and that they really knew what was happening in the world. Zoan had become the effective capital of Egypt at the time of the twenty-first dynasty; but God calls the princes of Zoan 'fools', and says that their counsellors give senseless advice. The Princes of Noph, or Memphis, are deceived and are misleading the people of Egypt. In all of their deliberations, they fail to discern the hand of he living God in their circumstances. Let us heed these warnings, and determine, by the grace of God, never to align ourselves with such blunders.

No poet caught the weakness of ancient Egypt better than Shelley, in his great sonnet:

> I met a traveller from an antique land,
> Who said, 'Two vast and trunkless legs of stone
> Stand in the desert. Near them on the sand,
> Half sunk, a shattered visage lies, whose frown
> And wrinkled lip and sneer of cold command
> Tell that the sculpture well those persons read,
> Which yet survive, stamped on these lifeless things,
> The hand that mocked them and the heart that fed;
> And on the pedestal these words appear:
> 'My name is Osymandias, King of kings,
> Look on my works, ye mighty and despair!
> Nothing beside remains. Round the decay
> Of that colossal wreck, boundless and bare,
> The lone and level sands stretch far away.'

DECEMBER 16TH

And the Lord will strike Egypt, He will strike and heal it; they will return to the Lord, and He will be entreated by them and heal them. In that day there will be a highway from Egypt to Assyria, and the Assyrian will come into Egypt and the Egyptian into Assyria, and the Egyptians will serve with the Assyrians. In that day Israel will be one of three with Egypt and Assyria – a blessing in the midst of the land, whom the Lord of hosts shall bless, saying, "Blessed is Egypt My people, and Assyria the work of My hands, and Israel My inheritance." Isaiah 19:22-25.

This is a beautiful prophecy, especially in these modern days of conflict in the Middle East. Isaiah's vision stretches forward to a day when the Lord's purposes will be fully realised. Egypt will come to know and acknowledge the Lord. They will worship Jehovah, look to Him in prayer, and He will heal them. God has loving purposes for that nation which once ignored Him, trusting rather in their own wisdom.

Was there ever a book that had such highs and lows as Isaiah? Now we learn that Assyria, Egypt's archrival and one-time deadly enemy of Israel, will also worship the Lord. There will be open borders and a highway all the way from Egypt to Assyria, originally the land between the Upper Tigris and Euphrates rivers with its capital at Nineveh. What an incredible turnaround! These nations will know the blessing of the Lord. The alliance between Israel, Egypt and Assyria will be the start of world peace. This is a fulfilment of Isaiah's vision right at the beginning of his book:

'Now it shall come to pass in the latter days that the mountain of the Lord's house shall be established on the top of the mountains, and shall be exalted above the hills; and all nation shall flow to it. Many people shall come and say, "Come, and let us go up to the mountain of the Lord, to the house of the God of Jacob; He will teach us His ways, and we shall walk in His paths." For out of Zion shall go forth the law, and the word of the Lord from Jerusalem.' Isaiah 2:2, 3.

When we think of all the suffering, hurt, heartache and sorrow brought to the world by nations bent on conquest, it is comforting to read of a day when they will unite to serve the Lord. So, Christian, in light of the eventual triumph of God's kingdom on earth over every regime, religion, power-structure, over every fad or fashion, over every philosophy or school of thought, continue serving the Lord. The kingdom to which you belong will outlast and triumph over them all. The way of the Cross is the highway to international and eternal triumph.

DECEMBER 17TH

Therefore my loins are filled with pain; pangs have taken hold of me, like the pangs of a woman in labour. I was distressed when I heard it; I was dismayed when I saw it. . . . "Babylon is fallen, is fallen! And all the carved images of her gods He has broken to the ground." Isaiah 21:3, 9.

Isaiah now returns to his present circumstances, with a very different message. This time he tells us how he felt when he learned of the fall of Babylon. In Isaiah 21: 5 we read that Hezekiah seems to have greeted the possible alliance with Babylon with a banquet, at which there was a call for an anointing of shields as for a holy war! Isaiah had to declare a very unpopular prophecy in the face of the rejoicing. He is told to appoint a watchman and to let him declare what he sees (Isaiah 21: 6). The watchman's vision is encapsulated in the words, "Babylon is fallen, is fallen! And all the carved images of the gods He has broken to the ground." Isaiah declared the watchmen's vision loud and clear.

Then, in Isaiah 39, we are told that Hezekiah received ambassadors from Babylon because Judah was looking to Babylon as a possible ally against Assyria. They arrived with a present from the king of Babylon, for he had heard that Hezekiah had been sick and had recovered.

'Hezekiah was pleased with them and showed them the house of his treasures – the silver and gold, the spices and precious ointment and all his armoury – all that was found among his treasures. There was nothing in his house or in all his dominion that Hezekiah did not show them.' Isaiah 39:2.

This incident reminds me of a character in the life of David. His name was Abner, the son of Saul's uncle and captain of Saul's army. Joab, David's captain, was deeply suspicious of Abner. Even though he knew Joab's attitude very well, one day Abner came too close, and Joab knifed him to death. David had a besetting sin, but he also had a superb gift: through his poetry he was able to turn the drab into a jewel. As the experiences of life rolled over his head, time after time David lifted his pen and wrote about them. The death of Abner is a perfect example. People wept as they gathered for Abner's funeral. Stirred by his sudden death, David wrote a lament and sang it at his funeral:

"Should Abner die as fool dies? Your hands were not bound nor your feet put into fetters; as a man falls before wicked men, so you fell." 2 Samuel 3:33, 34.

He was saying that Abner need not have died. He was a free man, yet he walked straight into a trap with his eyes wide open.

Did not Hezekiah also behave unwisely? After his illness the Lord had given him fifteen extra years of life. Flattered by the attention he was being shown by the Assyrian ambassadors, Hezekiah displayed Judah's wealth to them. Later, under Sennacherib, Assyria compelled Judah to pay heavy tribute. To be able to pay the tribute, Hezekiah had even to strip gold-plating off the doors and pillars of the temple. 'So Hezekiah gave him all the silver that was found in the house of the Lord and in the treasuries of the king's house' (2 Kings 18:15). Hezekiah was a good man and did many great things; but in the matter of the ambassadors from Babylon, God was testing him (2 Chronicles 32: 31). It would seem that he failed the test.

The message comes down to us even today: be careful with whom you associate yourself. And watch also who you show your treasures to – whatever those treasures might be; for one day they might come and take them all away from you. Israel ended up as exiles in Babylon for 70 years. Selah.

DECEMBER 18TH

He removed the protection of Judah. You looked in that day to the armour of the House of the Forest; you also saw the damage to the city of David, that it was great; and you gathered together the waters of the lower pool. You numbered the houses of Jerusalem, and the houses you broke down to fortify the wall. You also made a reservoir between the two walls for the water of the old pool. But you did not look to its Maker, nor did you have respect for Him who fashioned it long ago. Isaiah 22:8-11.

This oracle, or divine proclamation, is against Jerusalem. The Lord had called His people to repentance, but they thought it was time to have a party. 'In that day the Lord God of hosts called for weeping and for mourning . . . but instead, joy and gladness, slaying oxen and killing sheep, eating meat and drinking wine: "Let us eat and drink, for tomorrow we die!"' Isaiah 22:12-13.

There was shouting and cheering in the streets, and the city was full of noisy celebration. It is little wonder God had to ask, "What ails you?" (Isaiah 22:1). A calamity was coming; but the people of Jerusalem tried to protect themselves, instead of looking to Him 'who fashioned it long ago.'

First, they trusted in their armaments: they looked 'to the armour of the House of the Forest.' They were not the first to do that, nor the last either. How often have we seen modern monarchs, dictators, presidents, and politicians reviewing troops who control the most sophisticated armaments in history? Why do they do it? It is to show off the strength of their nation's power. The strategy of many nations has been to use the power of their armaments as a deterrent. If I have bigger and better weapons than you, chances are you will not use your weapons against me! It is easy to trust in armaments for protection.

Then they trusted in their fortifications: they repaired the weak places in the city wall "You numbered the houses of Jerusalem, and the houses you broke down to fortify the wall,' said God. Today the demand is not for strong, walled cities, but for 'Star Wars' fortifications in the skies, in order to deter inter-continental missiles. For example, Jerusalem now has to consider missiles coming at her from as far away as Baghdad.

The people also used their water-supply as a means of defence. If a city's water is cut off, the people are vulnerable and will soon be overcome. The source of Jerusalem's water supply was the Gihon Spring, which was linked to the city by an aqueduct, known as Shiloah (see Isaiah 7:3). It was Hezekiah who brilliantly decided to make a tunnel from the Gihon Spring to the city (see 2 Kings 20:20; 2 Chronicles 32:2-4). Many visitors to Jerusalem today still visit Hezekiah's tunnel. The reservoir between the two walls referred to in today's texts is almost certainly Hezekiah's tunnel. The people trusted in this ingenious passageway to save them in a siege.

This story could not be more relevant to our day and generation. We must not fully trust in armaments, armies, brilliant technological fortifications, warning systems, security systems, or nuclear bunkers. We should look to the living God who made this earth, and who has numbered the very hairs of our head. It seems to me we would save ourselves endless trouble if we would only talk to the Lord first about our problems. Notice the challenging words in today's reading:

"But you did not look to its Maker, nor did you have respect for Him who fashioned it long ago."

DECEMBER 19TH

Who has taken this counsel against Tyre, the crowning city, whose merchants are princes, whose traders are the honourable of the earth? The Lord of hosts has purposed it, to bring to dishonour the pride of all glory, to bring into contempt all the honourable of the earth. Isaiah 23:8-9.

The last in the series of oracles against particular nations in the book of Isaiah is against the City of Tyre. This great city is synonymous with commercial power and wealth. A Phoenician port south of Sidon, it was defended by rocky promontories that effectively hampered invasion. Cedar forests provided material for the famous Phoenician galleys. One of their most famous exports was Tyrian purple cloth, the dye derived from various shellfish, primarily the murex. To find the precious shellfish Tyrians travelled far and wide. They also traded in metals, which included copper from Cyprus, silver from Spain, and tin from Cornwall. Tyrians explored the coast of Africa and eventually circumnavigated the continent.

Isaiah now prophesies the fall of Tyre. In chapter 23 he speaks of how the news of its fall would reverberate across the Mediterranean world. A silence falls on Sidon, and the news is conveyed with grief to Cyprus. 'When the report reaches Egypt, they also will be in agony at the report of Tyre,' says Isaiah. The Egyptians were large exporters of wheat, and the collapse of Tyre had a huge impact on the wheat trade. Tyrian refugees bring the news of Tyre's fall to the far-flung Phoenician colony of Tarshish in Spain. Like a Barings Bank collapse, or a Wall Street crash, affects modern day economies, the whole Mediterranean area is impacted by the fall of Tyre.

What does God have against Tyre? Is He against good business, or international trading success? Does God oppose business flair? Categorically not! Hiram, a former King of Tyre, was a good friend of King David; and he built David a house with cedar trees. Solomon also traded with Hiram in cedar and fur, and together they built a Navy and supplied it with sailors from the Red Sea. They made expeditions to Ophir and brought back gold (1 Kings 9:28). 'He had merchant ships at sea with the fleet of Hiram. Once every three years they came, bringing 'gold, silver, ivory, apes, and monkeys' (1 Kings 10:22). What, then, is it that God has against Tyre? It was her downright, godless pride. Wealth does not always lead to pride, but often it does. The commercial 'princes' of Tyre considered the living God irrelevant; but they found out that He was exceedingly relevant. Like the rich fool of Luke 12, they discovered there was more to life and eternity than money.

Isaiah is warning God's people not to make an alliance with Godless, crass materialism. May God help us all to keep in mind the truth of the epitaph found on a tombstone:

> What I spent, is gone.
> What I kept, is lost.
> But what I gave will be mine forever.

DECEMBER 20TH

The people who walked in darkness have seen a great light; those who dwelt in the land of the shadow of death, upon them a light has shined. Isaiah 9:2.

As Christmas approaches, let us look at Isaiah's glorious vision of redemption and salvation in chapter 9. For many days now, using this Daily Devotional, we have studied Isaiah's fearless denunciation of the sins and failures of Israel; and latterly, of other nations. His Book is not a sentimental review of past and future events: it is a realistic presentation of the fact that this world is disastrously marked by sin and the Fall. Yet there are few books that could bring greater comfort; and the greatest comfort he brings is the presentation of the Messiah.

At this lovely time of year, millions of people listen to Handel's Messiah. It was first performed on 13th April 1742 in the City of Dublin, Ireland, to an audience of seven hundred. The selection of Scriptural texts for the musical masterpiece was chosen by Charles Jennens, a friend of Handel. Jennens, a Leicestershire Squire, expressed the kernel of his compilation in some words from the Epistles, which he supplied to form a prefix to the word-book of the Oratorio, as follows:

'And without controversy great is the mystery of godliness: God was manifested in the flesh, justified by the Spirit, seen of angels, preached among the Gentiles, believed on in the world, received up in glory.' 1 Timothy 3: 16;

'In whom are hid all the treasurers of wisdom and knowledge.' Colossians 2:3.

Jennens drew widely from the Scriptures in choosing his texts, and Isaiah figures prominently. Today's text is one of them. Handel's amazing master-craftsmanship set the words to unforgettable music.

The immediate context of this beautiful promise of the birth of the Messiah, is that the northern lands of Zebulun and Naphtali were the first part of the Promised Land to fall to Assyria in 733 BC. But the doom changes to delight; the darkness becomes light. In 'Galilee of the Gentiles' (meaning, a good number of Gentiles lived there), the Messiah is to be born (Isaiah 9:1). Isaiah calls it 'the land of the shadow of death': a place where sorrow, trouble and tragedy cast a long shadow. It is there that a light will appear. In dire circumstances, the faithful are waiting and hoping in God (Isaiah 8:17), because of His promise of the coming Messiah. The hope is so sure, that the narrative is in the past tense, as though it had already happened: 'The people who walked . . . have seen . . . dwelt in the land . . . a light has shined.'

As we celebrate Christmas this year in a world still filled with tragedy, suffering, war, famine, destruction and sin, we too hope and wait. We wait for the Second Coming of the Messiah, who will bring about the restoration of all things. Just as surely as Isaiah's prophecy of the first coming of Christ was fulfilled, so this present darkness will give way to eternal light.

DECEMBER 21ST

You have multiplied the nation and increased its joy; they rejoice before You according to the joy of harvest, as men rejoice when they divide the spoil. For You have broken the yoke of his burden and the staff of his shoulder, the rod of his oppressor, as in the day of Midian. For every warrior's sandal from the noisy battle, and garments rolled in blood, will be used for burning and fuel of fire. Isaiah 9:3-5.

The coming Messiah will bring about something no earthly ruler could ever accomplish. God created the nation of Israel, expanding its population and its joy. In the first Exodus, God shattered the yoke of the Egyptians, and broke the staff and rod with which the Israelites were beaten. In Gideon's day, He gave an unknown farmer the honour of defeating the Midianites in His name. Now He is going to use an unknown carpenter from Nazareth, to bring about redemption through the Cross, and then a New Heaven and a New Earth. Again, the imagery of Isaiah soars under the inspiration of the Holy Spirit. In a coming day, the Messiah will oversee the burning of all military equipment: 'for every warrior's sandal from the noisy battle and garments rolled in blood will be used for burning and fuel of fire.'

When the Messiah was born in Bethlehem, there was no room for Him in the places of power. Herod ruled within a dozen miles of Bethlehem, and plotted to have Him killed. He was not known in the palace of the Emperor Augustus. He was not counted among the great philosophers of the time. The One who will oversee the end of all earthly power struggles and initiate a new creation of eternal peace, had no place amongst the leaders of earth.

As we worship the Saviour at this Christmas time, let us consider the words of Charles Haddon Spurgeon (*No Room for Christ in the Inn,* <u>Metropolitan Tabernacle Pulpit</u>, 1968, p.702):

'Alas! my brethren, seldom is there room for Christ in palaces! How could the kings of earth receive the Lord? He is the Prince of Peace, and they delight in war! He breaks their bows and cuts their spears asunder; he burneth their war-chariots in the fire. How could kings accept the humble Saviour? They love grandeur and pomp, and He is all simplicity and meekness. He is a carpenter's son and the fisherman's companion. How can princes find room for the newborn monarch? Why, He teaches us to do to others, as we would have them do to us, and this is a thing which kings would find very hard to reconcile with the knavish tricks of politics and the grasping designs of ambition. O great ones of earth, I am but a little astonished that amid your glories, and pleasures, and wars, and counsels, ye forget the Anointed, and cast out the Lord of All.'

DECEMBER 22ᴺᴰ

For unto us a Child is born, unto us a Son is given. Isaiah 9:6.

I remember hearing Steven Spielberg saying that his film, E.T., was 'a cry to the stars for a friend.' He thought he would create an alien character that would come from outer space and love us instead of fighting us. In the film, his creation was discovered in a back yard. I remember thinking, reverently speaking, that he was 2,000 years too late. The One who never had a beginning – who 'was with God, and who 'was God' – was found lying in a manger at Bethlehem. He had most certainly come to love us, and not to harm us.

It is amazing how many heresies have plagued the church of Jesus Christ, concerning the truth from this beautiful prophecy of Isaiah. One of the earliest heresies was Docetism, which was the belief that Jesus had never been a man at all, but only seemed to be; He was really God in a human guise. This argument has recurred over and over again, and has never ceased to trouble the church. Then in the second and third centuries came the Modalists, who understood the Godhead and the distinctions within it as no more than three 'modes' of the divine unity. After this there was the Arian heresy, which included in a single formula a Father who was fully God, a Son who had the status of a leading creature, and a Spirit who was inferior to the Son. Then came the Nestorians, who conceded the humanity and the deity of Christ; but said that He was two personalities.

In more recent times we have had the Kenosis Theory, which teaches that at the Incarnation we have One who was originally God, but for the period of His earthly life He temporarily renounced His deity, only to resume it at His ascension.

What we believe about the Incarnation is very important; for it deeply affects our view of Christ. The essential doctrine of the Incarnation is that God Himself, in the Person of His Son, became truly man, sin apart, without ceasing to be God. The Son born to us is God, the Holy Spirit is God, and the Father is God. They are distinct from each other. The titles are not names of the same Person, appearing in different places (see the 'I' of John 12:28; John 17: 4; Acts 13: 2). God is the undivided three, and the mysterious one. As for the little one of Bethlehem, we love to sing, 'Tears and smiles like us He knew . . .' But He always was the *Lord* Jesus. Come, let us adore Him.

DECEMBER 23RD

And the government will be upon His shoulder. Isaiah 9:6.

R ecently, in reading Robert McCullough's superbly written biography of John Adams the 2nd United States President, I received the best insight I have ever had of what it must be like to 'shoulder' a government. It is no easy task to guide a country amidst deeply contentious party political divisions. The 'mud-slinging' is frightful; the needs of the population, endless.

It also reminds me of the story of the British politician who entered the House of Commons. Sitting down beside a fellow MP, he looked across the House, and said, 'It is good to get a close look at the enemy.' His colleague replied, 'You will not be here long until you discover that your biggest enemy is not the one in front of you, but the one behind you!' He was emphasising that he would find treachery, even within his own political party.

On a monument in the burial ground at Plymouth for the passengers of the Mayflower, is the following statement:

'Here, under cover of darkness, the fast dwindling company left their dead, levelling the earth above them lest the Indians should know how many were the graves. Reader! History records no nobler venture for faith and freedom than of this Pilgrim band. In weariness and painfulness, in watchings, often in hunger and cold, they laid the foundation of a state wherein every man, through countless ages, should have liberty to worship God in his own way. May their example inspire thee to do thy part in perpetuating and spreading the lofty ideals of our republic throughout the world.'

This is a noble sentiment, and its ideals are high. There is absolutely no reason why people of Biblical faith should not do their very best to encourage justice and good government in any society, nor be actively involved in seeing that these things are brought about. Alexis de Tocqueville replied to Count Arthur de Gobineau, after reading his pessimistic *Essay on Inequality*:

'Yes, I sometimes despair of mankind. Who doesn't? . . . I have always said that it is more difficult to stabilise and maintain liberty in our new democratic societies than in certain aristocratic societies in the past. But I shall never dare to think it impossible. And I pray to God lest He inspire me with the idea that one might as well give up trying.'

The man certainly must not have understood God's Word, for God would never inspire him to give up trying!

After Daniel was shown incredible visions of the future, by the side of the River Tigris, he was told, "Go your way till the end; for you shall rest, and will arise to your inheritance at the end of the days" (Daniel 12:13). Daniel held in his heart and mind those awesome visions of the future; but he had to go back to his everyday work as a government administrator and actively live out the remainder of his long life to the glory of God.

At this Christmas time, again we thrill to the promise that the Baby born at Bethlehem will one day carry upon His shoulder the government of the new creation. It will be stable government, perfect in every way. We hold that vision in our hearts and minds; but in the meantime we seek to hold the truth of the poem found on the tombstone of President John Adams and his wife Abigail, composed by their son, John Quincy Adams:

> From lives thus spent, thy earthly duties learn,
> From fancy's dreams to active virtue turn,
> Let Freedom, Friendship, Faith, thy soul engage,
> And serve, like them, thy country and thy age.

DECEMBER 24TH

And His Name will be called Wonderful, Counsellor, Mighty God . . . Isaiah 9:6.

> What Child is this, who, laid to rest,
> On Mary's lap is sleeping?
> Whom angels greet with anthems sweet,
> While shepherds watch are keeping?

The hymnwriter certainly asked a great question. On this Christmas Eve, Isaiah will answer it perfectly for us. His Name will be called 'Wonderful, Counsellor.' His Name sums up His character. Why is He able to carry the government upon His shoulder? Because He is Wonderful!

'O Lord, You are my God. I will exalt You, I will praise Your name, for You have done wonderful things.' Isaiah 25:1.

He was Wonderful in His birth; He was Wonderful in His earthly life; He was Wonderful in his death; He was Wonderful in His ascension; He was Wonderful in His exaltation; He is Wonderful as our High Priest; He is Wonderful as our Mediator; He is Wonderful as our soon coming Lord; He will be Wonderful as the Ruler of the new creation. Every way we look at Him, we gladly say – He is Wonderful!

'Your counsels of old are faithfulness and truth' (Isaiah 25:1). Anyone who has ever sincerely turned to the Scriptures to determine the revealed mind of God, will freely admit that there is no counsel like it.

> When you are desperate, read Psalm 63:1-3.
> When you are doubting, read 2 Kings 18 and 19.
> When you are bitter, read Romans 14:10-13.
> When you are attacked, read Psalm 54:1-4.
> When you are considering marriage, read Matthew 19:4-6; Ephesians 5:22-25.
> When your faith is weak, read Luke 12:22-32.

When you are far from God, read Psalm 139.
When you are ill, read Psalm 38:3-10.
When you are sleepless, read Proverbs 3:21-26.
When you are tempted to commit suicide, read Psalm 88:1-5, 13 and Isaiah 50:10.
When you are feeling lost, read Luke 11:9, 10.
When you are worried, read Matthew 6:25-34.
When you need guidance, read Romans 12:1-2.
When you need peace, read Isaiah 26:3-4.
When you are lonely, read Genesis 28:15.
When you have lost your job, read Proverbs 16:3, 9.
If you are tempted by sexual immorality, read Proverbs 5:1-21.
If you want to be thankful, especially on a night like this, read Psalm 100.

The Lord truly is a Wonderful Counsellor.

Unhesitatingly, Isaiah tells us that Christ is called none other than 'Mighty God.' God is El, which is the last syllable of Emmanuel. Here we have a further indication of Christ's deity. The baby in the manger is 'God with Us.' As this busy Christmas Eve comes to an end, why not gather your loved ones around you, and before they sleep read to them these seven beautiful lines by the great English poet, John Milton. They express so beautifully what we would want to say on this very special night of the year:

Welcome all wonders in one sight –
Eternity shut in a span,
Summer in winter, day in night,
Heaven in earth, and God in man.
Blest little one,
Whose all embracing birth
Lifts earth to heaven,
Stoops heaven to earth.

25TH DECEMBER

Everlasting Father, Prince of Peace. Isaiah 9:6.

All across the world today, millions of people will celebrate the birth of Christ. As you go through the day, think of these two names that belonged just as much to the Little One of Bethlehem, as they do now to the Lofty One at God's right hand. He is the 'Everlasting Father.' This name means, literally, the Father of Eternity: 'Who inhabits eternity' (Isaiah 57:15). In the word, 'eternity,' we have the endless past and the unending future. Christ lives in eternity; yet He chose to be born in Bethlehem, He worked at a carpenter's shop at Nazareth, ministered to the sick and dying in Galilee, and came to Jerusalem to bring about our redemption at the horrendous Cross of Calvary.

This eternal one is our 'Everlasting Father.'

'As a father pities his children, so the Lord pities those who fear Him. For He knows our frame; He remembers that we are dust.' Psalm 103:13, 14.

The little one who entered our world amidst such poverty, grew to maturity. By His death and resurrection He conquered sin, death and hell. He has all the great characteristics of a perfect father. He is loving, tender and compassionate; but He also disciplines, trains and provides.

'For He will deliver the needy when he cries, the poor also, and him who has no helper. He will spare the poor and needy, and will save the souls of the needy. He will redeem their life from oppression and violence; and precious shall be their blood in His sight.' Psalm 72:12-14.

Luke tells us that, on the night of Christ's birth, an angel appeared to shepherds who were watching over their flocks. He told them of the birth in David's city of a Saviour, who was the Messiah. 'Suddenly there was with the angel a multitude of the heavenly host praising God and saying: "Glory to God in the highest, and on earth peace, goodwill toward men!"' (Luke 2:8-14). Isaiah tells us that His name is 'Prince of Peace': He provides true peace, 'peace to him who is far off and to him who is near' (Isaiah 57:19).

Ultimately, this Prince of Peace will bring eternal peace to His people and to the nations. In the meantime, to all who trust Him, He brings peace with God; and in times of trouble and stress, a peace that passes all understanding.

Many gifts will be given and received today; but He gave us Himself - the greatest gift He could possibly bestow. Take a few minutes to thank God for His unspeakable, indescribable gift!

DECEMBER 26TH

Of the increase of His government and peace there will be no end, upon the throne of David and over His kingdom, to order it and establish it with judgment and justice from that time forward, even forever. The zeal of the Lord of hosts will perform this. Isaiah 9:7.

It was quite a day when the prophet Samuel arrived in Bethlehem and anointed the young shepherd, David, to be king of Israel. Eventually, when David became king, he longed to build a great house for God. But God said 'No' to David's dream, and He sent Nathan to break the news to David. You would be hard pushed to find a direct negative in the whole message. Certainly, it was a message of refusal; but it was surrounded by so many assurances of blessing, that the king was hardly aware of his disappointment. Nathan's words of promise and benediction aroused overwhelming gladness. The final words are awesome: "Your house and your kingdom shall be established forever before you. Your throne shall be established forever" (2 Samuel 7:16).

God gives Isaiah the same prophecy, but in a little more detail. There is to be no limit to the government of Christ, David's greater Son, nor to the peace He brings. All other kingdoms and empires pass away, but there will be no limit of time and space to this one. The Father of

Eternity, the Prince of Peace, will shoulder the burden of its order, establishment, equity and eternality.

As this year draws to a close, let me raise a practical note. Perhaps God has said 'No' to some of your dreams. Maybe He is to be glorified by you staying where you are, rather than moving on as you had envisaged. Or, is it the other way round: God has said 'No' to you staying where you are, and in the coming year you will move on? Remember God's 'No' is infinitely better than man's 'No;' because there is the safety net of His promises to fall into. David may not have built a house for God, but God built a sure house for David. So sure, that it will last forever: limitless in its extension and peace. Every believer has a part in that house.

'Surely goodness and mercy shall follow me all the days of my life; and I will dwell in the house of the Lord forever.' Psalm 23:6.

The zeal, or jealousy, of the Lord of hosts for His people will ensure that this promise is kept. Nothing will stand in His way. Comforting, isn't it?

DECEMBER 27TH

Therefore thus says the Lord God: "Behold, I lay in Zion a stone for a foundation, a tried stone, a precious cornerstone, a sure foundation; whoever believes will not act hastily." Isaiah 28:16.

In the Prophecy of Isaiah we have read some of the greatest promises ever given in history. Now, here is a beautiful encouragement to believe those promises. Scholars have held many discussions about the identity of this stone. Some say it speaks of the Lord Himself: He is a sure foundation, a precious cornerstone. He certainly is a tried and tested cornerstone (literally, 'a stone of proof, or testing'). He has proved Himself more than able to support all those who put their trust in Him. Others say that the stone is David's throne – which we discussed in yesterday's reading. Some say it is the city of Zion itself: the focus of the promises of God. And others that it is referring to the faithful remnant in Israel.

Whichever view you take, this stone bears a message, 'whoever believes will not act hastily,' or 'whoever trusts will never be dismayed.' Often when people are confused and uncertain, they act in haste and have to repent at leisure. They rush into some plan of their own without acknowledging the Lord, and find themselves out of the Lord's will. Has this happened to you, even during the past year?

Let me remind you that the Lord can bring you back into His will. The Bible knows nothing about a second-class believer. Moses acted in haste, and spent 40 years in the wilderness, but God did not treat him as second-class. He brought Moses back into His plans. Abraham acted in haste, and went down into Egypt; but God brought him back to Bethel and to better days. Elijah most certainly acted in haste, when he ran away from Jezebel. He should have been the spiritual leader of the nation; but he was found cowering in a cave at Horeb. God spoke to him in a still, small voice, and revived his faith.

Doing God's will is not like a travel agent's itinerary: if you miss a bus here or a plane there, your whole holiday is ruined. If you have acted hastily, or misread God's will, God does not condemn you to be a failure for the rest of your life. To think that way is downright unbelief. Today's text tells us that those who believe God's Word and trust in it, will be preserved from acting hastily. If we have done wrong, He can restore us.

'For thus says the Lord God, the Holy One of Israel: "In returning and rest, you shall be saved; in quietness and confidence shall be your strength."' Isaiah 30:15.

So don't panic, just trust.

DECEMBER 28TH

Behold, a king will reign in righteousness, and princes will rule with justice. A man will be as a hiding place from the wind, and a cover from the tempest, as rivers of water in a dry place, as the shadow of a great rock in a weary land. Isaiah 32:1-2.

This is one of Isaiah's most famous texts: it is full of hope for the future. In the immediate context, God's people faced adversity from the Assyrians. Isaiah is urging them to consider the glories of a coming kingdom, of which they will form a part. His emphasis is upon the protection that God will afford in those days. No matter what the adversity, here is hope for all believers.

Isaiah writes about the King who is called 'Wonderful, Counsellor, Mighty God, Everlasting Father, Prince of Peace.' He will reign in righteousness, and princes will rule with justice – those who rule with Him will make perfect decisions. 'Do you not know that the saints will judge the world . . . we shall judge angels?' (1 Corinthians 6:2, 3). In that kingdom, protection will be in a Man: 'A man will be as a hiding place . . .' 'For there is one God and one Mediator between God and men, the Man Christ Jesus.' 1 Timothy 2:5.

The King is not only the Messiah: He is a Man. George Cutting wrote a beautiful poem about the Lord Jesus, and gave it the title, *The Man in the Glory* – it is a lovely concept to consider.

Isaiah draws from our everyday life to demonstrate the protection of the Messiah. He will hide us from the wind, and cover from the tempest, or storm. When the wind and storm have passed and the scorching sun beats down on a parched land, He will provide cool, running water. As the shadow of a great rock, He will bring rest to a weary land.

Matthew Henry points out that the hiding place, the covert, and the rock, take the battering of the wind and storm, or scorching heat, to save those who shelter in them. So our Lord Jesus, the Messiah, bore the storm for us, that we might hide in Him.

Today's text can also be translated, 'Each man will be a hiding place . . .': what characterises the Ruler, characterises his administrators also. By the grace of God, let us seek to be a hiding place from the winds of adversity, a cover from the tempest, and as rivers of water in a parched land. And may you cast a long shadow under which many will find rest in a weary land.

The work of righteousness will be peace, and the effect of righteousness, quietness and assurance forever. My people will dwell in a peaceful habitation, in secure dwellings, and in quiet resting places, though hail comes down on the forest, and the city is brought low in humiliation. Blessed are you who sow beside all waters. Isaiah 32:17-20a.

As we look towards the new creation, Isaiah assures us that the effect of the righteous rule of the King will be peace, quietness, and assurance forever. Here is true and everlasting security. It is the Lord's doing; and it will be marvellous in our eyes. Society will be totally harmonious: we will live in a peaceful habitation, in secure dwellings, and in quiet resting places.

Speaking of God's removal of all earthly powers, Isaiah then uses a metaphor of hail coming down in a forest.

'Behold, the Lord, the Lord of hosts, will lop off the bough with terror; those of high stature will be hewn down, and the haughty will be humbled. He will cut down the thickets of the forest with iron, and Lebanon will fall by the Mighty One.' Isaiah 10:33, 34.

Cities being 'brought low in humiliation,' is 'the humiliation of human organisation of the world without God' (Alec Motyer, *Isaiah*, IVP, p.207). The old earth will give place to the wonder of the new, where those who have bowed in repentance and put faith in the Messiah will be truly blessed.

'He will give rain for your seed with which you sow the ground, and bread of the increase of the earth; it will be fat and plentiful. In that day your cattle will feed in large pastures.' Isaiah 30:23ff.

The animals will be free to roam where they choose, and crops will not need protection from marauders. Rivers and streams will flow freely on every mountain and hill.

I like to think there is a word of spiritual comfort here in our present age for all who scatter the seeds of the message of life in Christ; who teach and preach the Word of God; and who seek to live to the glory of God. As I have studied the Prophecy of Isaiah, I have had insights into God and His ways. Now I can share these with others, in gospel witness, personal counselling, and comforting people in stress and trouble. After all, Isaiah sowed his spiritual seed and we have travelled this year feasting on it together. I urge you to sow the seed beside all waters, and you will reap the harvest. In your ministry, school, university, factory, office, at the dinner table, by that bedside, with a fellow-traveller, on that holiday – sow your seed. When you see the eternal harvest, we will rejoice together.

DECEMBER 30TH

The wilderness and the wasteland shall be glad for them, and the desert shall rejoice and blossom as the rose; . . . Strengthen the weak hands, and make firm the feeble knees. Say to those who are fearful-hearted, "Be strong, do not fear! Behold your God will come with vengeance, with the recompense of God; He will come and save you." . . . A highway shall be there, and a road, and it shall be called the Highway of Holiness. . . No lion shall be there, nor shall any ravenous beast go up on it; . . . And the ransomed of the Lord shall return, and come to Zion with singing, with everlasting joy on their heads. They shall obtain joy and gladness, and sorrow and sighing shall flee away. Isaiah 35:1, 3, 4, 8-10.

We have traced the history of the delivery of exiled Israel. This exquisite poem captures the essence of what it was like for the Children of Israel to experience an exodus across the wilderness; but it also points to the great final exodus into a new world and to the New Jerusalem: a glorified environment, where the curse has been removed. Isaiah exploits the promise of it all to urge pilgrims to use our hands in the work of the Lord; and to strengthen weak knees – abandon all thought of quitting. He encourages all who are fearful-hearted to be strong and fearless. God will recompense them. He will come and save His people and deal with their enemies.

Through Calvary's work, what a Highway of Holiness God has prepared for us to walk upon! He paid the ultimate price for us when He laid down His life. No lion or predator will block our way or stop us reaching our final destination. Our Heavenly Boaz will redeem us; we are 'the ransomed of the Lord.' No longer pilgrims, we have reached our journey's end. We will come singing, with everlasting, uninterrupted joy upon our heads!

Like the people of Israel, we Gentiles are exiles too (Ephesians 2:13). As we reach our goal, something wonderful will happen: we shall 'obtain joy and gladness.' We shall be 'overtaken' by joy and gladness. There shall never again be cause for sorrow; not another sigh shall pass our lips. This is what we have been anticipating throughout all the toils and heartaches of our pilgrimage. We will be home! So pilgrim, no matter what you face today, lift up your head and your heart, and cry with me, 'Onward to glory!'

DECEMBER 31ST

Your eyes will see the King in His beauty; they will see the land that is very far off. Isaiah 33:17.

In our year's journey into Isaiah's Prophecy, we have seen the attributes, character, and beauty of the Messiah. He reasons with us, so that we might know how our sins, though red like scarlet, can be as white as snow. He is the great peacemaker, beating swords into ploughshares. He is a green shoot coming out of a stump; and a rock in a weary land. He is the vinedresser; and the Lord sitting on the Throne, high and lifted up.

Isaiah has prophesied of the Messiah coming as the Child of Bethlehem; and even told us about the food He would eat, in the poverty of His upbringing. He described Him as a light shining in the land of the shadow of death, and told us He has the spirit of wisdom and understanding, and that He acts as a banner to the people. We have read his description of Messiah's insight into the weaknesses of nations and cities, and of His powerful oracles against them. Our hearts have trembled as Isaiah unveils Him as the true Judge of all the earth.

Isaiah has written in depth of the Perfect Servant, who does not break bruised reeds or quench the smouldering flax. We have been assured that He never gets discouraged, and He positively will not fail. He opens blind eyes and sets prisoners free, through His work at Calvary. Yet, when He came to accomplish it, He so identified Himself with us that, in terms of looks or impressiveness, 'there was no beauty that we should desire Him.' His indescribable beauty was veiled. When Peter, James and John got a sight of it on the Mount of Transfiguration, Peter did not want to leave! We have read that 'His face was marred more than any man, and His form more than the sons of men.'

In His victory, we have learned that He is the great thirst quencher. He gives comfort to all who mourn, beauty for ashes, the oil of joy for mourning, and the garment of praise for the spirit of heaviness. We have read of His awesome wrath against sinners, and His amazing grace towards the repentant. He blesses all those who wait for Him.

These are some of the things that have filled our hearts and minds. It has been one of the greatest privileges of my life to have studied so much of it with you. On this last day of the year, we focus on Isaiah's promise of what will be the great climax of our earthly pilgrimage. We shall *see* the King in His beauty. When I read Isaiah's promise, that my eyes will see the King in His beauty in that land that is very far off – of all his promises, I find this the best.

Bibliography

F.B. Meyer, *Christ in Isaiah*, Marshall, Morgan and Scott, London, 1952

W.E.Vine, *Expository Commentary on Isaiah*, Thomas Nelson Publishers, Nashville, 1997

Alec Motyer, *Isaiah*, Inter-Varsity Press, Leicester, England, 1999

David McKenna, *Mastering the Old Testament,* Isaiah 40-66,Word Publishing, 1994

Barry Webb, *The Message of Isaiah,* Inter-Varsity Press, Leicester, England, 1996

The Zondervan Bible Dictionary, Marshall, Morgan and Scott, London, 1963

Matthew Henry's Commentary, Broadoak Edition, Marshall, Morgan and Scott, London, 1960

Os Guinness, *Steering Through Chaos*, Nav Press, Colorado Springs, Colorado, 2000 Trinity Forum Series.

Os Guinness, *The Great Experiment*, Nav Press, Colorado Springs, Colorado, 2001, Trinity Forum Series

Os Guinness, *Doing Well and Doing Good*, Nav Press, Colorado Springs, Colorado, 2001, Trinity Forum Series

Os Guinness, *The Journey*, Nav Press, Colorado Springs, Colorado, 2001

Os Guinness, *Entrepreneurs Of Life*, Nav Press, Colorado Springs, Colorado, 2001, Trinity Forum Series.

Grateful thanks is due to Mrs. Dorothy Finn who enthusiastically gave much time and energy helping to type the manuscript of this book.